T0202694

Lecture Notes in Computer Science   14691

Founding Editors

Gerhard Goos
Juris Hartmanis

The series Lecture Notes in Computer Science (LNCS), including its subseries Lecture Notes in Artificial Intelligence (LNAI) and Lecture Notes in Bioinformatics (LNBI), has established itself as a medium for the publication of new developments in computer science and information technology research, teaching, and education.

LNCS enjoys close cooperation with the computer science R & D community, the series counts many renowned academics among its volume editors and paper authors, and collaborates with prestigious societies. Its mission is to serve this international community by providing an invaluable service, mainly focused on the publication of conference and workshop proceedings and postproceedings. LNCS commenced publication in 1973.

Hirohiko Mori · Yumi Asahi

Editors

Human Interface and the Management of Information

Thematic Area, HIMI 2024
Held as Part of the 26th HCI International Conference, HCII 2024
Washington, DC, USA, June 29 – July 4, 2024
Proceedings, Part III

 Springer

Editors
Hirohiko Mori
Tokyo City University
Tokyo, Japan

Yumi Asahi
Tokyo University of Science
Tokyo, Japan

ISSN 0302-9743   ISSN 1611-3349 (electronic)
Lecture Notes in Computer Science
ISBN 978-3-031-60124-8   ISBN 978-3-031-60125-5 (eBook)
https://doi.org/10.1007/978-3-031-60125-5

Foreword

This year we celebrate 40 years since the establishment of the HCI International (HCII) Conference, which has been a hub for presenting groundbreaking research and novel ideas and collaboration for people from all over the world.

The HCII conference was founded in 1984 by Prof. Gavriel Salvendy (Purdue University, USA, Tsinghua University, P.R. China, and University of Central Florida, USA) and the first event of the series, "1st USA-Japan Conference on Human-Computer Interaction", was held in Honolulu, Hawaii, USA, 18–20 August. Since then, HCI International is held jointly with several Thematic Areas and Affiliated Conferences, with each one under the auspices of a distinguished international Program Board and under one management and one registration. Twenty-six HCI International Conferences have been organized so far (every two years until 2013, and annually thereafter).

Over the years, this conference has served as a platform for scholars, researchers, industry experts and students to exchange ideas, connect, and address challenges in the ever-evolving HCI field. Throughout these 40 years, the conference has evolved itself, adapting to new technologies and emerging trends, while staying committed to its core mission of advancing knowledge and driving change.

As we celebrate this milestone anniversary, we reflect on the contributions of its founding members and appreciate the commitment of its current and past Affiliated Conference Program Board Chairs and members. We are also thankful to all past conference attendees who have shaped this community into what it is today.

The 26th International Conference on Human-Computer Interaction, HCI International 2024 (HCII 2024), was held as a 'hybrid' event at the Washington Hilton Hotel, Washington, DC, USA, during 29 June – 4 July 2024. It incorporated the 21 thematic areas and affiliated conferences listed below.

A total of 5108 individuals from academia, research institutes, industry, and government agencies from 85 countries submitted contributions, and 1271 papers and 309 posters were included in the volumes of the proceedings that were published just before the start of the conference, these are listed below. The contributions thoroughly cover the entire field of human-computer interaction, addressing major advances in knowledge and effective use of computers in a variety of application areas. These papers provide academics, researchers, engineers, scientists, practitioners and students with state-of-the-art information on the most recent advances in HCI.

The HCI International (HCII) conference also offers the option of presenting 'Late Breaking Work', and this applies both for papers and posters, with corresponding volumes of proceedings that will be published after the conference. Full papers will be included in the 'HCII 2024 - Late Breaking Papers' volumes of the proceedings to be published in the Springer LNCS series, while 'Poster Extended Abstracts' will be included as short research papers in the 'HCII 2024 - Late Breaking Posters' volumes to be published in the Springer CCIS series.

I would like to thank the Program Board Chairs and the members of the Program Boards of all thematic areas and affiliated conferences for their contribution towards the high scientific quality and overall success of the HCI International 2024 conference. Their manifold support in terms of paper reviewing (single-blind review process, with a minimum of two reviews per submission), session organization and their willingness to act as goodwill ambassadors for the conference is most highly appreciated.

This conference would not have been possible without the continuous and unwavering support and advice of Gavriel Salvendy, founder, General Chair Emeritus, and Scientific Advisor. For his outstanding efforts, I would like to express my sincere appreciation to Abbas Moallem, Communications Chair and Editor of HCI International News.

July 2024   Constantine Stephanidis

HCI International 2024 Thematic Areas
and Affiliated Conferences

- HCI: Human-Computer Interaction Thematic Area
- HIMI: Human Interface and the Management of Information Thematic Area
- EPCE: 21st International Conference on Engineering Psychology and Cognitive Ergonomics
- AC: 18th International Conference on Augmented Cognition
- UAHCI: 18th International Conference on Universal Access in Human-Computer Interaction
- CCD: 16th International Conference on Cross-Cultural Design
- SCSM: 16th International Conference on Social Computing and Social Media
- VAMR: 16th International Conference on Virtual, Augmented and Mixed Reality
- DHM: 15th International Conference on Digital Human Modeling & Applications in Health, Safety, Ergonomics & Risk Management
- DUXU: 13th International Conference on Design, User Experience and Usability
- C&C: 12th International Conference on Culture and Computing
- DAPI: 12th International Conference on Distributed, Ambient and Pervasive Interactions
- HCIBGO: 11th International Conference on HCI in Business, Government and Organizations
- LCT: 11th International Conference on Learning and Collaboration Technologies
- ITAP: 10th International Conference on Human Aspects of IT for the Aged Population
- AIS: 6th International Conference on Adaptive Instructional Systems
- HCI-CPT: 6th International Conference on HCI for Cybersecurity, Privacy and Trust
- HCI-Games: 6th International Conference on HCI in Games
- MobiTAS: 6th International Conference on HCI in Mobility, Transport and Automotive Systems
- AI-HCI: 5th International Conference on Artificial Intelligence in HCI
- MOBILE: 5th International Conference on Human-Centered Design, Operation and Evaluation of Mobile Communications

List of Conference Proceedings Volumes Appearing Before the Conference

1. LNCS 14684, Human-Computer Interaction: Part I, edited by Masaaki Kurosu and Ayako Hashizume
2. LNCS 14685, Human-Computer Interaction: Part II, edited by Masaaki Kurosu and Ayako Hashizume
3. LNCS 14686, Human-Computer Interaction: Part III, edited by Masaaki Kurosu and Ayako Hashizume
4. LNCS 14687, Human-Computer Interaction: Part IV, edited by Masaaki Kurosu and Ayako Hashizume
5. LNCS 14688, Human-Computer Interaction: Part V, edited by Masaaki Kurosu and Ayako Hashizume
6. LNCS 14689, Human Interface and the Management of Information: Part I, edited by Hirohiko Mori and Yumi Asahi
7. LNCS 14690, Human Interface and the Management of Information: Part II, edited by Hirohiko Mori and Yumi Asahi
8. LNCS 14691, Human Interface and the Management of Information: Part III, edited by Hirohiko Mori and Yumi Asahi
9. LNAI 14692, Engineering Psychology and Cognitive Ergonomics: Part I, edited by Don Harris and Wen-Chin Li
10. LNAI 14693, Engineering Psychology and Cognitive Ergonomics: Part II, edited by Don Harris and Wen-Chin Li
11. LNAI 14694, Augmented Cognition, Part I, edited by Dylan D. Schmorrow and Cali M. Fidopiastis
12. LNAI 14695, Augmented Cognition, Part II, edited by Dylan D. Schmorrow and Cali M. Fidopiastis
13. LNCS 14696, Universal Access in Human-Computer Interaction: Part I, edited by Margherita Antona and Constantine Stephanidis
14. LNCS 14697, Universal Access in Human-Computer Interaction: Part II, edited by Margherita Antona and Constantine Stephanidis
15. LNCS 14698, Universal Access in Human-Computer Interaction: Part III, edited by Margherita Antona and Constantine Stephanidis
16. LNCS 14699, Cross-Cultural Design: Part I, edited by Pei-Luen Patrick Rau
17. LNCS 14700, Cross-Cultural Design: Part II, edited by Pei-Luen Patrick Rau
18. LNCS 14701, Cross-Cultural Design: Part III, edited by Pei-Luen Patrick Rau
19. LNCS 14702, Cross-Cultural Design: Part IV, edited by Pei-Luen Patrick Rau
20. LNCS 14703, Social Computing and Social Media: Part I, edited by Adela Coman and Simona Vasilache
21. LNCS 14704, Social Computing and Social Media: Part II, edited by Adela Coman and Simona Vasilache
22. LNCS 14705, Social Computing and Social Media: Part III, edited by Adela Coman and Simona Vasilache

https://2024.hci.international/proceedings

Preface

Human Interface and the Management of Information (HIMI) is a Thematic Area of the International Conference on Human-Computer Interaction (HCII), addressing topics related to information and data design, retrieval, presentation and visualization, management, and evaluation in human computer interaction in a variety of application domains, such as learning, work, decision, collaboration, medical support, and service engineering. This area of research is acquiring rapidly increasing importance towards developing new and more effective types of human interfaces addressing new emerging challenges, and evaluating their effectiveness. The ultimate goal is for information to be provided in such a way as to satisfy human needs and enhance quality of life.

The related topics include, but are not limited to the following:

- *Service Engineering:* Business Integration; Community Computing; E-commerce; E-learning and E-education; Harmonized Work; IoT and Human Behavior; Knowledge Management; Organizational Design and Management; Service Applications; Service Design; Sustainable Design; User Experience Design
- *New HI (Human Interface) and Human QOL (Quality of Life):* Electronics Instrumentation; Evaluating Information; Health Promotion; E-health and Its Application; Human-Centered Organization; Legal Issues in IT; Mobile Networking; Disasters and HCI
- *Information in VR, AR and MR:* Application of VR, AR, and MR in Human Activity; Art with New Technology; Digital Museum; Gesture/Movement Studies; New Haptics and Tactile Interaction; Presentation Information; Multimodal Interaction; Sense of Embodiment (SoE) in VR and HCI
- *AI, Human Performance and Collaboration:* Automatic Driving Vehicles; Collaborative Work; Data Visualization and Big Data; Decision Support Systems; Human AI Collaboration; Human-Robot Interaction; Humanization of Work; Intellectual Property; Intelligent System; Medical Information System and Its Application; Participatory Design

Three volumes of the HCII 2024 proceedings are dedicated to this year's edition of the HIMI Thematic Area. The first focuses on topics related to Information and Multimodality, and Information and Service Design. The second focuses on topics related to Data Visualization, and User Experience Design and Evaluation. Finally, the third focuses on topics related to Information in Learning and Education, Information in Business and eCommerce, and Knowledge Management and Collaborative Work.

The papers in these volumes were accepted for publication after a minimum of two single-blind reviews from the members of the HIMI Program Board or, in some cases, from members of the Program Boards of other affiliated conferences. We would like to thank all of them for their invaluable contribution, support, and efforts.

July 2024

Hirohiko Mori
Yumi Asahi

Human Interface and the Management of Information Thematic Area (HIMI 2024)

Program Board Chairs: **Hirohiko Mori,** *Tokyo City University, Japan* and **Yumi Asahi,** *Tokyo University of Science, Japan*

- Takako Akakura, *Tokyo University of Science, Japan*
- Shin'ichi Fukuzumi, *Riken, Japan*
- Michitaka Hirose, *Tokyo University, Japan*
- Chen Chiung Hsieh, *Tatung University, Taiwan*
- Yen-Yu Kang, *National Kaohsiung Normal University, Taiwan*
- Keiko Kasamatsu, *Tokyo Metropolitan University, Japan*
- Daiji Kobayashi, *Chitose Institute of Science and Technology, Japan*
- Yusuke Kometani, *Kagawa University, Japan*
- Kentaro Kotani, *Kansai University, Japan*
- Masahiro Kuroda, *Okayama University of Science, Japan*
- Yuichi Mori, *Okayama University of Science, Japan*
- Ryosuke Saga, *Osaka Metropolitan University, Japan*
- Katsunori Shimohara, *Doshisha University, Japan*
- Kim-Phuong L. Vu, *California State University, Long Beach, USA*
- Tomio Watanabe, *Okayama Prefectural University, Japan*
- Takehiko Yamaguchi, *Suwa University of Science, Japan*

The full list with the Program Board Chairs and the members of the Program Boards of all thematic areas and affiliated conferences of HCII 2024 is available online at:

http://www.hci.international/board-members-2024.php

HCI International 2025 Conference

The 27th International Conference on Human-Computer Interaction, HCI International 2025, will be held jointly with the affiliated conferences at the Swedish Exhibition & Congress Centre and Gothia Towers Hotel, Gothenburg, Sweden, June 22–27, 2025. It will cover a broad spectrum of themes related to Human-Computer Interaction, including theoretical issues, methods, tools, processes, and case studies in HCI design, as well as novel interaction techniques, interfaces, and applications. The proceedings will be published by Springer. More information will become available on the conference website: https://2025.hci.international/.

General Chair
Prof. Constantine Stephanidis
University of Crete and ICS-FORTH
Heraklion, Crete, Greece
Email: general_chair@2025.hci.international

https://2025.hci.international/

Contents – Part III

Information in Learning and Education

Learning Support System for Relationships Among Forces, Accelerations, Velocities, and Movements in Error-Based Simulation

Nonoka Aikawa[1](✉), Chihiro Hiramoto[2], Takahito Tomoto[3], Tomoya Horiguchi[4], and Tsukasa Hirashima[5]

[1] Graduate School of Engineering, Tokyo Polytechnic University, Atsugi, Kanagawa, Japan
`n.aikawa@st.t-kougei.ac.jp`
[2] Fujisoft Incorporated, Yokohama, Kanagawa, Japan
[3] Faculty of Information and Computer Science, Chiba Institute of Technology, Narashino, Chiba, Japan
[4] Graduate School of Maritime Sciences, Kobe University, Kobe, Hyogo, Japan
[5] Graduate School of Advanced Science and Engineering, Hiroshima University, Higashi-Hiroshima, Hiroshima, Japan
`https://www.takahito.com/members/aikawa/`

Abstract. Error-based Simulation (EBS) simulates "what would happen if the learner's (incorrect) answer were correct." It has been demonstrated that "strange phenomena" by EBS promote learners' reflection and improve achievement in problem solving. However, some learners failed to improve their performance even when learning with EBS. These learners may not have been able to relate the forces they drew to the presented motions. We consider that there is a flow between motion and the force, acceleration, and velocity: 1. the force causes acceleration, 2. the acceleration causes a change in velocity, and 3. the change in velocity is visualized as motion. Therefore, this study proposes a new feedback method for EBS, aiming to enable a correct understanding of the elements involved in motion by learning to relate motion, force, acceleration, and velocity as a series of flows. Experiments were conducted on the developed system, the results suggest that this system improves the achievement of problem solving compared to conventional EBS.

Keywords: Learning support system · Elementary mechanics · Error-based Simulation

1 Introduction

In elementary mechanics, inaccurate understanding of everyday experiences can make it difficult for learners to accept correct scientific knowledge. In conventional classroom learning, learners are sometimes asked to perform experiments aimed at correcting their erroneous understanding. However, in elementary mechanics, there are some errors that cannot be understood through experiments. For example, although a novice learner can understand gravity when

H. Mori and Y. Asahi (Eds.): HCII 2024, LNCS 14691, pp. 3–15, 2024.
https://doi.org/10.1007/978-3-031-60125-5_1

gravitational and vertical reaction forces act on an object resting on the floor, vertical reaction force is more difficult to understand due to the misconception that the floor does not push the object back because "the floor does not generate its own force."

Error-based simulation (EBS) is an effective method for correcting such misconceptions. EBS simulates the "phenomena that would occur if the learner's (incorrect) understanding were correct" based on the learner's answers [2, 4]. In the example of gravitational and vertical reaction forces, if the learner gives an incorrect answer by entering only gravity (Fig. 1(a1)), EBS shows the object falling through the floor, based on action of the gravitational force alone (Fig. 1(a2)). This helps the learner to understand the vertical reaction force. EBS has been shown to promote reflection and improve achievement in problem solving without disrupting learners [3]. However, not all learners improve their performance when learning with EBS.

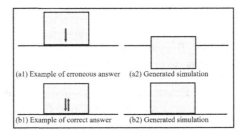

Fig. 1. Example of EBS

Yamada et al. [1] extended EBS by incorporating acceleration and velocity. In their extended EBS approach, learners are asked to draw force, acceleration, and velocity, and the simulated movements based on these drawings are presented. By comparing the movements, learners can understand the relationships among the elements. However, the system does not help learners to understand the series of events, from the application of a force to the occurrence of movement.

Therefore, this study proposes a new feedback method for EBS, with the aim of helping learners to correctly understand the elements involved in generating movement. This method relates the forces, accelerations, and velocities involved in movement as a series of flows. An evaluation experiment was conducted to verify the learning effectiveness of the proposed method.

2   Previous Study

The EBS developed by Hirashima et al. [2, 4] and Horiguchi et al. [5, 6] is designed to help learners solve problems more effectively by making them aware of their errors through simulations of unnatural phenomena that would result from their incorrect answers. In EBS, it is easy for learners to recognize errors in their

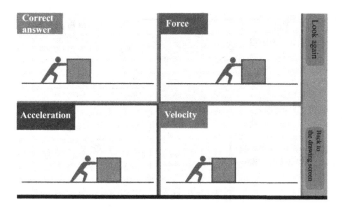

Fig. 2. Screenshot of the EBS system by Yamada et al.

answers to phenomena such as an object moving when it should have been stationary, an object sinking through the floor, and motion in a different direction than what was expected or intended. However, when the direction of motion is correct but the velocity is not, it is more difficult for the learner to notice their error.

Therefore, the EBS developed by Yamada et al. [1] incorporates a method of comparing the simulation results corresponding to the learner's incorrect answers for force, velocity, and acceleration with the correct motion. This is expected to make it easier for learners to understand the difference in velocity between the motion corresponding to their incorrect answers and the correct motion.

As an example, we use the problem of a person pushing a box on a floor that has friction. In the EBS developed by Yamada et al., the motion of the box is given as a phenomenon, and the learner observes the box in constant velocity motion and then inputs the force, acceleration, and velocity of the box using arrows. The system then generates a simulation corresponding to the force, acceleration, and velocity that the learner drew. If the force, acceleration, and velocity entered by the learner are correct, the correct motion will be presented. However, if there are errors, the system generates a simulation of an unnatural phenomenon based on the errors.

The generated simulation is shown in Fig. 2. The motion generated in this case is the motion that corresponds to the force, acceleration, and velocity drawings. The learner can compare these observations with the correct motions in the upper left corner of the screen, which helps the learner to recognize that their answer is incorrect. However, in conventional systems, only the motion is presented to the learner, and most learners can only recognize their errors by comparing with the presented motion.

For example, in the problem of drawing the force, acceleration, and velocity of a box moving at a constant velocity on the floor, many learners drew the correct velocity and the incorrect acceleration and force. Learners who gave incorrect answers subsequently corrected their acceleration answers by comparing the

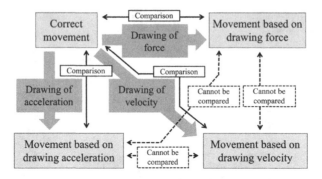

Fig. 3. Learning flow with the conventional EBS

correct motion with the motion corresponding to the acceleration drawing. Similarly, learners compared the correct motion with the motion corresponding to the force drawing and corrected their force answer. In this process, learners did not pay attention to the correct velocity drawing but focused instead on the comparison of the incorrect element and the correct motion.

Thus, although the system of Yamada et al. can help learners to compare incorrect elements with correct motions, it does not promote understanding of the relationships among force, velocity, and acceleration. Therefore, this study aimed to improve upon the system developed by Yamada et al. by helping learners recognize these relationships.

3   Relationships Among Movement, Force, Acceleration, and Velocity

Figure 3 shows a diagram of the learning flow involving comparing movements in the EBS developed by Yamada et al. [1]. Movement is considered to be the result of the following flow involving force, acceleration, and velocity.

1. Force causes acceleration.
2. The presence of acceleration causes a change in velocity.
3. The change in velocity is visualized as movement.

However, in the conventional EBS, when the learner enters the answers for force, acceleration, and velocity, they are all presented on the system as a movement. In this case, the learner will likely only think about what kind of movement the elements they have entered will produce. In other words, it is difficult to make learners think about how the force they enter affects acceleration and how the acceleration they enter affects velocity in the conventional EBS. If learners can be made to think about these relationships, it will lead to thinking such as "It is strange that a force is acting when there is no acceleration," or "It is strange that acceleration exists when the velocity is constant."

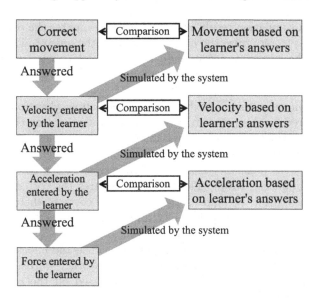

Fig. 4. Learning flow in this study

4 Proposed Method

This study proposes a new solution method and feedback for EBS, aimed at helping learners understand the relationships among force, acceleration, velocity, and motion. Specifically, we design a solution scheme and feedback for learners in three phases: a phase to consider the relationship between motion and velocity, a phase to consider the relationship between velocity and acceleration, and a phase to consider the relationship between acceleration and force.

Figure 4 shows the learning flow in this study. The aim of this study is to help learners understand that "acceleration is generated by a force," "a change in velocity is generated by the presence of acceleration," and "the change in velocity is visualized as movement."

In the first problem, as in the conventional EBS, the correct movement is first presented and the learner is asked to draw the velocity. The result of the drawing is simulated as a movement corresponding to the entered velocity. The correct answer is presented as the same movement as the correct movement, while the incorrect answer is presented as a movement that is different from the correct movement. The learner compares the correct movement with the simulated movement, recognizes the error, and corrects the answer. The goal of this problem is to have the learner understand that changes in velocity are visualized as movement. Once the correct answer is obtained, the learner moves on to the next problem.

In the next problem, the learner is presented with the correct velocity that they drew in the previous problem and is asked to enter the acceleration at that velocity. The system presents the velocity that corresponds to the drawing of the acceleration as a simulation result, and the learner compares the correct velocity with the drawing to recognize the error and correct the answer. The goal of this problem is for the learner to understand the relationship between the presence of acceleration and the change in velocity. Once the correct answer is obtained, the learner moves on to the next problem.

Finally, we move on to the next problem in which acceleration is presented and force is entered. In this problem, too, the correct acceleration that the learner answered in the previous problem is presented, and the learner draws what force is acting on the object when that acceleration is present. When the learner draws the force, the system presents the acceleration corresponding to the drawing of the force as a simulation result. The learner compares the correct acceleration with the one they drew, recognizes the error, and corrects their answer. The goal of this problem is to help learners understand the relationship between acceleration and the force acting on an object.

This method helps learners to consider the cause-and-effect relationships among motion, velocity, acceleration, and force. In other words, the exercises are designed to help learners deduce the cause based on the result, that is, "velocity as the cause of motion," "acceleration as the cause of velocity," and "force as the cause of acceleration." This method helps learners to grasp motion, velocity, acceleration, and force in sequence, thereby promoting understanding of the relationship between each element.

5   System Development

In this study, the system was developed using Android Studio, with reference to the EBS developed by Yamada et al.

Three problems were prepared: 1. a box in linear motion at constant velocity, 2. a box in motion with constant positive acceleration, and 3. a box in motion with constant negative acceleration, all on a frictionless floor.

Figures 5, 6, 7, 8, 9 and 10 show some screenshots of the developed system. In this section, the system is explained using the example of a problem in which a box is in motion with constant positive acceleration on a frictionless floor. First, the system displays a screen showing a box in motion from left to right. After a certain period of time, the system automatically switches to the answer screen shown in Fig. 5.

On this screen, the learner enters the velocity of the box in motion, using arrows. Pressing the "Creating arrows" button in the lower right corner of the screen brings up a screen that allows the user to select the length and direction of the arrow needed for the drawing. After selecting the length and direction of the arrow, the learner presses the "Create" button to create the arrow. The learner can then draw the velocity of the box by moving the created arrow to a point in the center of the box. When they are finished, the learner presses the "Answer" button in the lower left corner of the screen to move to the simulation screen shown in Fig. 6.

In the simulation screen, a box that moves at the correct velocity is presented at the top of the screen, and a box that moves at the velocity corresponding

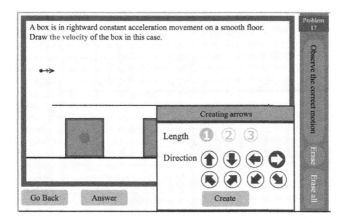

Fig. 5. Answer screen for a problem requiring a velocity to be entered

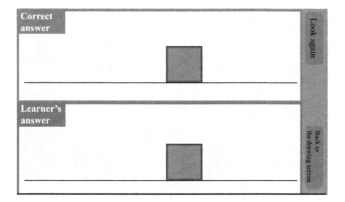

Fig. 6. Simulation screen for a problem requiring a velocity to be entered

to the learner's answer is presented at the bottom of the screen. By comparing the motions on this screen, learners can understand the relationship between the velocity and the motion they drew. If the answer is incorrect, the user can choose to review the simulation of the motion or return to the answer screen, whereas if the answer is correct, the option to proceed to the acceleration phase appears.

Figure 7 shows the answer screen for the acceleration problem. In this screen, a box is shown at the top of the screen, with an arrow representing the velocity that was entered in the previous phase. The learner draws an arrow for acceleration corresponding to the arrow for velocity, as in the previous phase. Figure 8 shows the simulation screen when the user has completed the arrows representing acceleration.

At the top of the simulation screen, a box with an arrow pointing to the correct velocity is presented, and at the bottom, a box with an arrow pointing

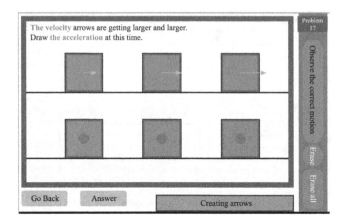

Fig. 7. Answer screen for a problem requiring an acceleration to be entered

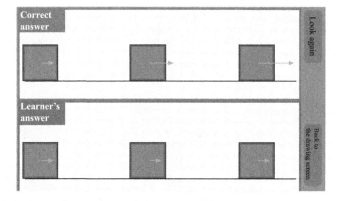

Fig. 8. Simulation screen for a problem requiring an acceleration to be entered (incorrect answer)

to the velocity corresponding to the acceleration that the learner entered is presented. If the learner has answered correctly, the arrow indicating the velocity corresponding to the answer is the same length as the arrow indicating the correct velocity at the top, but if the learner has answered incorrectly, the arrow indicating the velocity is presented at a different length than that at the top. The learner grasps the relationship between the drawn acceleration and velocity by comparing the length of the velocity arrows. If the learner enters the correct acceleration, the system moves on to the force phase.

The phase that requires the learner to enter the force corresponding to the acceleration follows the same sequence as the acceleration phase (Figs. 9 and 10).

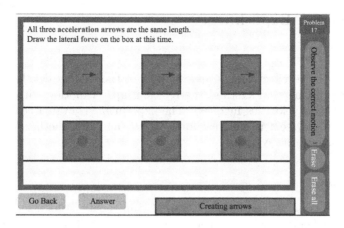

Fig. 9. Answer screen for a problem requiring a force to be entered

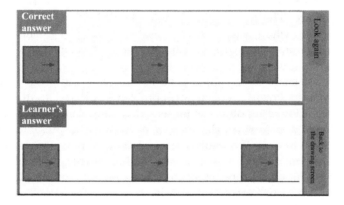

Fig. 10. Simulation screen for a problem requiring a force to be entered

The arrow representing the acceleration corresponding to the learner's drawing of the arrow representing the force may change in terms of direction as well as length. By comparing these acceleration arrows, the learner grasps the relationship between the drawn force and acceleration.

As described above, this system helps the learner to understand velocity from motion, acceleration from velocity, and velocity from acceleration. Furthermore, the system in this study incorporates two additional problems from the conventional EBS—"Solving for acceleration from the presented motion" and "Solving for force from the presented motion"—and adds a new problem, "Solving for force from the presented velocity." These six problems are designed to help learners understand both the problems covered in the previous study as well as the newly added problems in this study.

6   Evaluation Experiment

6.1   Purpose

Here, we verify the effectiveness and validity of the system developed in this study to help learners understand the relationships of motion with the forces, accelerations, and velocities involved. The experiment is evaluated in terms of (1) whether the system is effective for learning, and (2) whether the learners positively evaluate the system.

6.2   Method

The participants in the experiment were 14 university students majoring in science-related fields who had taken a physics course. The experimental procedure consisted of an explanation of the experimental flow, a pre-test (7 min, 30 s), learning involving use of the system (25 min), a post-test (8 min, 30 s), and a questionnaire. The 14 participants were divided into two groups: 7 in the experimental group who learned with the system developed in this study, and 7 in the control group who learned with the system developed in the previous study by Yamada et al.

Evaluation was based on the pre- and post-test results and the questionnaires. The pre-test consisted of 17 problems: two problems in Part 1 to draw the force when the acceleration of an object is presented, six problems in Part 2 to draw the acceleration and force when the velocity of an object is presented, and nine problems in Part 3 to draw the velocity, acceleration, and force when the motion of an object is presented. The post-test consisted of all the problems in the pre-test plus three additional problems in Part 1, two additional problems in Part 2, and three problems in Part 3 as a transfer task, for a total of 25 problems.

6.3   Experimental Results

Test Results. Table 1 shows the test results for the problems that appeared in both the pre- and post-test. The mean correct response rate in the experimental group was 36.1% for the pre-test and 65.5% for the post-test. The mean correct response rate in the control group was 37.0% for the pre-test and 47.9% for the post-test. Analysis of variance (ANOVA) was performed using ANOVA4 in order to test for significant differences in the results. The ANOVA results are shown in Table 2, and the simple main effect test results are shown in Table 3.

In Table 3, A represents the between-subjects factor (experimental and control groups), B represents the within-subjects factor (pre-test and post-test), a1 represents the experimental group, a2 the control group, b1 the pre-test and b2 the post-test.

The ANOVA results showed significant differences between the pre-test and the post-test, indicating that learning effects were achieved through the use of the system. The simple main effect test results showed a significant difference between the pre-test and the post-test of the experimental group, but not

Table 1. Mean percentage of correctly answered problems that appeared in both the pre- and post-tests.

	Experimental group	Control group
Pre-test	36.1%	37.0%
Post-test	65.5%	47.9%
Difference	29.4%	10.9%

Table 2. Analysis of variance results.

Variable factor	$p < .05$
A: Experimental, Control	n.s.
B: Pre-, Post-tests	$p < .05$
AB Interaction	$p < .05$

between those of the control group. These results suggest that the EBS developed in this study is effective in helping learners to understand problems dealing with motion and its related forces, accelerations, and velocities. The mean percentage of correct responses to the transition task of the post-test was 58.9% for the experimental group and 53.6% for the control group. These results suggest that learning with the developed system helps learners to understand the relationships among motion, force, acceleration, and velocity.

Questionnaire Results. Table 4 shows some of the questionnaire results. Items were rated on a 6-point scale (6: Strongly agree, 5: Agree, 4: Somewhat agree, 3: Somewhat disagree, 2: Disagree, 1: Strongly disagree).

These results show that the evaluation of the proposed system was higher than that of the conventional system. This suggests that the proposed method of comparing acceleration, velocity, and force using arrows was well received by the learners. In addition, this system received a high evaluation when asked whether it leads to an understanding of force, acceleration, and velocity. Therefore, we consider that learning with this system is beneficial in terms of grasping the relationships among motion, force, acceleration, and velocity, based on the positive evaluation from the learners and the test results.

Table 3. Simple main effect test results.

Factor	$p < .05$
A (b1: Pre-test)	n.s.
A (b2: Post-test)	n.s.
B (a1: Experimental group)	$p < .05$
B (a2: Control group)	n.s.

Table 4. Questionnaire results (partial).

Item	Exp.	Con.
Do you think simulations based on incorrect drawings can help lead to the correct answer?	5.25	3.67
Do you think the system used in the experiment is helpful for understanding forces?	5.00	3.67
Do you think the system used in the experiment is helpful for understanding acceleration?	5.00	3.00
Do you think the system used in the experiment is helpful for understanding velocity?	5.00	2.67
Do you think it is necessary to relate force, acceleration, and velocity when predicting how an object will move?	5.00	4.33

7 Conclusion

In this paper, we proposed a method for helping learners to grasp the relationships among movement, force, acceleration, and velocity in the dynamics EBS, and conducted evaluation experiments. Previous research on EBS helped learners to understand the relationships between motion and force, motion and acceleration, and motion and force, but it was difficult for them to grasp the relationships among force, acceleration, and velocity. In this study, we proposed a new comparison method to help learners understand the relationship of motion with the forces, accelerations, and velocities involved. In addition, EBS problems were created for learners to use the proposed method, and evaluation experiments were conducted. The test results showed that there was a significant difference between learning using the proposed system and the conventional system, indicating the effectiveness of the proposed system. The results of the questionnaire showed that learners rated the proposed system more highly than the conventional system.

In the future, it will be necessary to investigate whether the understanding the learner gains by using the system is retained over a long period and to confirm the learning effect by increasing the number of problem situations. In addition, we will investigate which errors this method is effective for and which present challenges, by analyzing the content of learners' errors in the pre- and post-tests.

References

1. Atsushi, Y., Tomoya, S., Tomoya, H., Yusuke, H., Tsukasa, H.: Design and development of multi viewpoints error-based simulation and experimental evaluation. The IEICE Trans. Inf. Syst. (Japan. Ed.) **99**(12), 1158–1161 (2016). (in Japanese)
2. Hirashima, T., Horiguchi, T., Kashihara, A., Toyoda, J.: Error-based simulation for error-visualization and its management. Int. J. Artif. Intell. Educ. **9**(1–2), 17–31 (1998)

3. Hirashima, T., Imai, I., Horiguchi, T., Tomoto, T.: Error-based simulation to promote awareness of error in elementary mechanics and its evaluation. In: Proceedings of International Conference on Artificial Intelligence in Education, pp. 409–416 (2009)
4. Hirashima, T., Shinohara, T., Yamada, A., Hayashi, Y., Horiguchi, T.: Effects of error-based simulation as a counterexample for correcting MIF misconception. In: Proceedings of the 18th International Conference on Artificial Intelligence in Education, pp. 90–101 (2017)
5. Tomoya, H., Tsukasa, H.: Simulation-based learning environment for assisting error-correction-management of error-based simulation considering the cause of errors. Trans. Japan. Soc. Artif. Intell. AI **17**(4), 462–472 (2002). (in Japanese)
6. Tomoya, H., Tsukasa, H., Akihiro, K., Jun'ichi, T.: Management of error-based simulation using qualitative reasoning techniques. J. Japan. Soc. Artif. Intell. **12**(2), 285–296 (1997). (in Japanese)

A Study on Forecasting Post-enrollment Grades of Students Using Gradient Boosting Decision Tree

Komei Arasawa[1]([✉]), Shun Matsukawa[1], Nobuyuki Sugio[1], Hirofumi Sanada[1], Madoka Takahara[2], and Shun Hattori[3]

[1] Department of Information and Computer Science, Faculty of Engineering, Hokkaido University of Science, 15-4-1, Maeda 7-jo, Teine-ku, Sapporo-shi 006-8585, Hokkaido, Japan
{arasawa-k,matukawa-s,sugio-n,sanada}@hus.ac.jp
[2] Faculty of Advanced Science and Technology, Ryukoku University, 1-5, Yokotani, Seta Oe-Cho, Otsu-shi 520-2123, Shiga, Japan
takahara@rins.ryukoku.ac.jp
[3] Department of Electronic Systems Engineering, Faculty of Engineering, The University of Shiga Prefecture, 2500, Hassaka-cho, Hikone-shi 522-0057, Shiga, Japan
hattori.s@e.usp.ac.jp

Abstract. The number of dropouts from universities is increasing, and many researchers have claimed that poor academic grade is a major reason that they drop out from the universities. Therefore, there is a need to develop a system that can forecast the post-enrollment grades of the students at an early stage and help the students with poor academic grades. This paper aims to propose a method that forecast whether the rank of Grade Point Average (GPA) after 1 year of a student is in lower in the department based on the machine learning using the feature values, such as his/her study logs on the pre-admission educations of the university, his/her academic grades in high school, and the data on the admission examinations s/he took. In addition, this paper reveals the forecast performance and the explanatory variables that are effective for the task.

Keywords: Educational Technology · Pre-admission Education · Grade Prediction

1 Introduction

1.1 Social Issues on University Dropout

It is one of the serious issues that the number of dropouts from universities is increasing. If the tuition per student at a private university is $6,700 and a student drops out from the university in 1 year, the university loses $26,800 that

S. Matsukawa, N. Sugio, H. Sanada, M. Takahara and S. Hattori—Contributing authors.

H. Mori and Y. Asahi (Eds.): HCII 2024, LNCS 14691, pp. 16–32, 2024.
https://doi.org/10.1007/978-3-031-60125-5_2

it plans to get for the remaining 3 years of 4-year program and the university's management might deteriorate. Hence, the professors of many universities have provided various additional supports for the students with poor academic grades, such as organizing the study-meetings with these students, sharing information related to these students in academic-meetings, and giving supplementary classes for them. However, these activities put a burden on the professors and prevent them from setting aside sufficient time spent on research[1]. Therefore, it is an important to establish a system which can detect the students with poor academic grades early and provide them many focused supports. The system would help to reduce the dropouts from many universities and the burden of the professors and stabilize their managements.

1.2 Forecasting Academic Grades of Students

There are many reasons why students have dropped out form universities. Among them, many studies [1] have shown that the most common reason is their academic grades have been getting worse. Hence, several researchers have developed the systems that forecast Grade Point Average (GPA) of each student to help us detect the students whose academic grades would get worse and support them early [2,3].

In the studies by Nishioka et al. [4] and Matsuo et al. [5], the logs accumulated in LMS (Learning Management System) such as Moodle are utilized to forecast their GPAs of a university course. Specifically, these papers utilize the submission status of the assignments, the score of the short test every lecture, and the number of accesses of the pages of LMS related to the university course. Moreover, there are also studies that discuss the method that takes in new information from LMS every week and updates GPA forecast system [6–8]. However, these methods cannot forecast post-enrollment academic grades of the students before they enroll in the university because they must track the attitudes toward the studies of the students over a period of several weeks.

1.3 Purpose

As previously stated, there is a problem that existing methods cannot forecast the post-enrollment academic grade of each student and detect the students whose academic grades would get worse before he/she enrolls in the university.

It is urgent to solve this problem, because several studies [9] have reported that even if teachers give the students with poor academic grades the supplementary classes after their GPAs of 1st semester are evaluated, it is difficult to recover them. Moreover, it is said that there is a tendency many teachers of universities begin to give students the additional supports after GPAs of them have been gotten worse [10].

Therefore, we need a system that can forecast the post-enrollment grades of the students at the time of pre-admission of them. As a first step for developing

---

[1] https://www8.cao.go.jp/cstp/package/wakate/kenkyu.pdf.

the system, this paper proposes the method that forecasts the post-enrollment grade of each student using GBDT (Gradient Boosting Decision Tree) as a machine learning based on the feature values, such as his/her study logs of the pre-admission educations, his/her academic grades while s/he was in high school, and the information of the admission examinations s/he took. In addition, it aims to build several models that can classify whether the rank of GPA after 1 year of a student is in lower in his/her department and reveal their forecast performances and the features that are effective for forecasting the post-enrollment grades of the students.

2   Related Research

Kondo et al. [11] have proposed the system that analyzes the pre-admission data of a student and forecasts the enrollment status (attending the university or dropping out from the university) after 3 years of each student at a point in time when he/she enrolls in the university.

However, the system cannot detect only 20% of the students whose academic grades would get worse (the recall of the system is 0.222). We guess that the reason is that it utilizes the submission rate of the pre-admission assignments and the attendance rate of the orientations of the students as the pre-admission data for forecasting their post-enrollment grades. These data are not sufficient to forecast the post-enrollment grades of the students because the attendance of the orientation and the submission of the pre-admission assignment are the actions that the students can be done with low academic ability. Hence, because these data do not differentiate among the students, it difficult for the system to judge the post-enrollment grade of each student.

On the other hand, this paper utilizes also 3-month study logs of the students on the pre-admission education using e-learning as the pre-admission data of the students for forecasting their post-enrollment grades. These days have the study times, the frequencies of study, and the scores of the short tests about 5 major subjects, which are considered vary depending on the academic ability and the motivation of a student. Hence, it is expected that these data would be effective for detecting a student whose academic grade would get worse grades after enrolling the university. Moreover, many universities would use this system effectively, because several papers [12] have reported that more and more universities conduct the pre-admission education using e-learning for the students.

3   Method

This section discusses the explanatory variables and the model for forecasting the post-enrollment grades of the students.

Table 1. Explanatory variables for forecasting the post-enrollment grades of the students.

Var.	Outline
1	Sex of student
2	Course where student belonged in high school
3	Career path classification of high school
4	Mean rating value of all subjects in high school
5	Admission examination division
6	Total score of short tests' scores of all units in Basic course
7	Total time spent taking workbooks of all units in Basic course
8	Total number of times taken workbooks of all units in Basic course
9	Total score of short tests' scores of all units in Step up course
10	Total time spent taking workbooks of all units in Step up course
11	Total number of times taken workbooks of all units in Step up course
12	Total time taken for 1st academic tests (min)
13	Total score of 1st academic tests
14	Total time taken for 2nd academic tests (min)
15	Total score of 2nd academic tests
16	Total scores' difference between 1st academic tests and 2nd academic tests

3.1 Explanatory Variables

This paper utilizes 16 explanatory variables. Here, the authors assume the students to be those who enroll in Hokkaido University of Science where the first author belongs. The reminder of this subsection divided these explanatory variables into 4 classes.

3.1.1 Data on Attribute

Var.1 in Table 1 is the data on the attribute of a student of the university. The results of PISA in 2002, 2006, and 2009[2] have reported that female students have higher reading comprehension than male students. On the other hand, they also have reported that male students have higher scores on Math than female students. Hence, the sex of a student might affect also his/her post-enrollment grade. Therefore, this paper utilizes the feature value (male/female) as an explanatory variable for forecasting their post-enrollment grades.

3.1.2 Data on High School

Var.2–4 in Table 1 are the data on the pre-enrollment academic grade of a student and the environment of the high school he/she attended, which are said to affect his/her post-enrollment grade [13].

---

[2] https://www.mext.go.jp/b_menu/toukei/data/pisa/index.htm.

Var.2 is the qualitative variable that is the course where a student belonged in high school, such as General course and Industrial course. Var.3 is the qualitative variable that is the career path classification of the high school, which is the difference of what the post-high school career paths the high school students wish, such as many students try to go to national universities, many students try to go to private universities/vocational schools, and many students try to find a job, and so on. Var.4 is the quantitative variable that is the academic grade of a student in high school. In high schools in Japan, students have rating value (0 or more and less than 5) for each subject. Var.4 is the mean value and between 0 and 5.

3.1.3 Data on Admission Examination

Var.5 in Table 1 is the qualitative variable that is the admission examination division of a student took, such as Comprehensive selection, Recommendation selection, and General selection.

Some papers [14, 15] show there is a relationship between the admission division of each student of a university and his/her post-enrollment grade, while some show there are no relationships [16]. Hence, we cannot conclude the admission divisions of the students do not affect their post-enrollment grades. Therefore, we utilize this difference as an explanatory variable for forecasting their post-enrollment grades.

Here, we want to utilize the score of the admission examination of a student as one of the feature values for this task originally. However, it did not come true in this paper because there is a difference between the content of the examination of each admission division and we cannot enough consider about the method for converting the score of the examination of a student of each admission division into the standardized score.

3.1.4 Data on Pre-admission Education

Var.6–16 in Table 1 are the logs of the pre-admission education the students of the university have been done, which are said to affect their post-enrollment grade [17]. The students who pass the examination of Comprehensive selection/Recommendation selection of Hokkaido University of Science have to take the pre-admission education consisting of 3 steps (Fig. 1).

In the first step, they must take 1st academic tests of 5 subjects (English, Japanese, Society, Mathematics, and Science) and this paper records the total time taken for these tests (Var.12) and the total score of these tests (Var.13) every student. Here, the maximum value of the score of each test is 25. Therefore, the value of Var.13 is between 0 and 125 (25×5 subjects).

In the second step, they must take the online workbooks on 5 subjects for 3 months. This online workbooks have 2 courses, which are Basic course and Step up course and they have a difference on the degree of difficulty of problems. Moreover, both courses have 5 subjects. Each subject has 6 units, and each unit is composed of Short test and Problems related to this unit. Hence, they have to take Short tests and Problems on 30 units (5 subjects × 6 units). And they can take Short test and Problems of a unit repeatedly.

Here, this paper records the total score of Short tests' scores of all units (Var.6/9), the total time spent taking Problems of all units (Var.7/10), and the total number of times taken Problems of all units (Var.8/11). Here, these logs are recorded in both Basic course and Step up course. In addition, the maximum value of Short test of a unit is 100, the value of Var.6/9 is between 0 and 3000 (100 × 30 units).

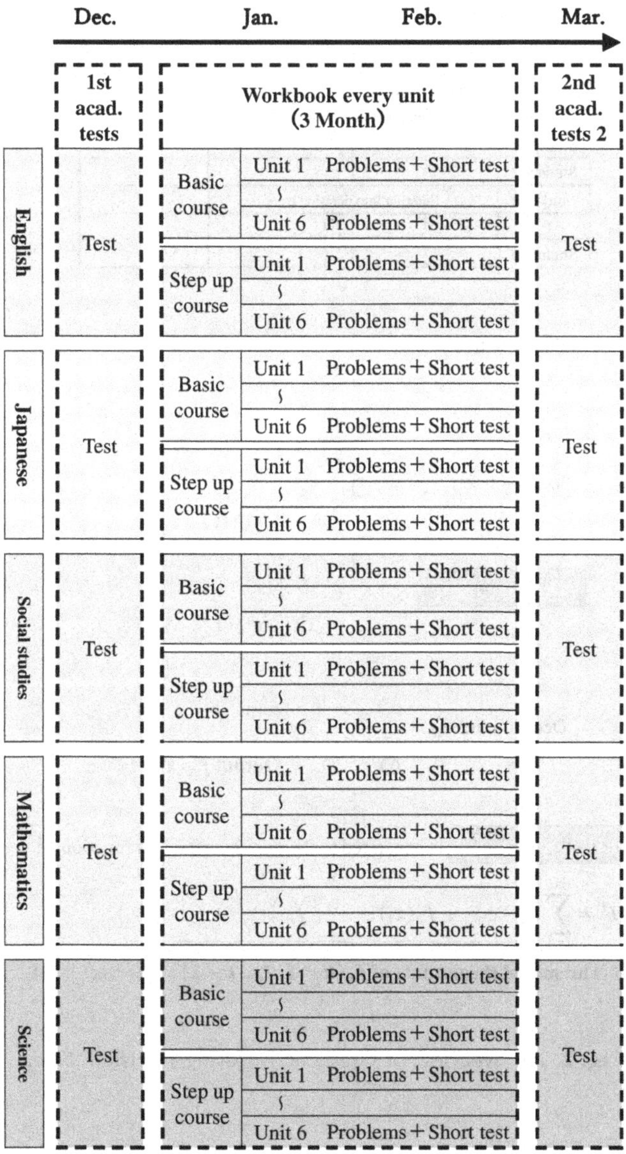

Fig. 1. Pre-admission education in Hokkaido University of Science.

In the third step, they must take 2nd academic tests of 5 subjects. Here, this paper records the total time taken for these tests (Var.14) and the total score of these tests (Var.15) of each student. Here, the value of Var.15 is also between 0 and 125 (25 × 5 subjects). In addition, it records the difference of the total score of the 1st academic tests and the total score of the 2nd academic tests (Var.16).

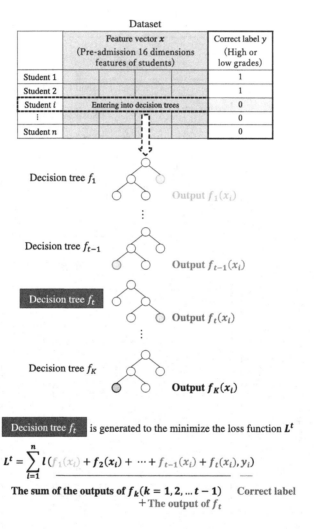

Fig. 2. An overview of Gradient Boosting Decision Tree.

3.2   Method for Forecasting Post-enrollment Grades

This paper utilizes Gradient Boosting Decision Tree (GBDT), which has high performances for many tasks on machine classifications and is able to find out the explanatory variables that have a strong relationship with the objective variable easily. Gradient Boosting Decision Tree combines a decision tree with the one previous decision trees while taking over the information of these trees (Fig. 2).

First, we discuss the flow of forecasting the academic grade when the feature values are inputted in decision trees. This paper supposes the m-dimensional feature vector of i-th student is $\boldsymbol{x}_i$. Moreover, it supposes the objective variable is $y_i = \{0, 1\}$. Then, the rate p_i that shows the rank of GPA after 1 year is in lower in his/her department equals to the value that converts the sum of the output $f_k(x_i)$ of each learner (decision tree) f_k ($k = 1, ..., K$) using Sigmoid function.

$$p_i = \frac{1}{1 + \exp(-\hat{y}_i)}$$

$$\text{where } \hat{y}_i = \sum_{1 \leq k \leq K} f_k(x_i), f_k \in \mathcal{F}$$

Here, when a feature vector $\boldsymbol{x}_i$ falls into a decision tree that has the T leaves, the output $f_k(x_i)$ shows the weight $w_{q(x)}$ of q-th leaf arrived at finally.

$$\mathcal{F} = f(x) = w_{q(x)} \ (q : \mathbb{R}^m \rightarrow T, w \in \mathbb{R}^T)$$

Second, we discuss the optimization of each decision tree. When optimizing a learner f_t, the learners f_k ($k = 1, ..., t-1$) that are before the learner f_t are already optimized. Based on this, the learner f_t is optimized to the minimize the measurement error between the correct label y_i and the value obtained by the output $f_k(x_i)$ and the sum of the outputs of the learners f_k ($k = 1, ..., t-1$).

$$L^t = \sum_{1 \leq i \leq n} l(\hat{y}_i^{(t-1)} + f_t(x_i), y_i)$$

Here, l is the Loss function, which shows Cross-Entropy.

$$l(\hat{y}_i^{(t-1)} + f_t(x_i), y_i) = l(\hat{y}_i^t, y_i)$$
$$= y_i \log p_i + (1 - y_i) \log(1 - p_i)$$

4   Experiment Environment

4.1   Dataset

This paper utilizes the data on the students who enter in Hokkaido University of Science at 2021 as train data, and the data on the students who enter in the university at 2022 as test data. The students in the dataset are the students who passed Comprehensive selection or Recommendation selection, but the rank of GPA of a student in the dataset is the rank in the all students in his/her department (those who passed Comprehensive selection, Recommendation selection, and General selection).

Moreover, the dataset (train data and test data) is divided into 5 faculties in the university (dataset of Faculty of Engineering, dataset of Faculty of Pharmacy, dataset of Faculty of Health Sciences, dataset of Faculty of Future Design, and dataset of All faculties). In addition, the objective variable is 0 (the student whose post-enrollment grade is high) or 1 (the student whose post-enrollment grade is low).

Here, the objective variable has 3 types in this paper, the first is whether the grade after 1 year of each student is in lower $1/2$, the second is whether the grade after 1 year of each student is in lower $1/3$, the third is whether the grade after 1 year of each student is in lower $1/4$. Therefore, we generate the 3 forecast models ($1/2$-forecast model, $1/3$-forecast model. $1/4$-forecast model) every dataset. Table 2 and Table 3 show the number of students we should detect to support additionally.

4.2   Framework of Gradient Boosting Decision Tree

This paper utilizes XGBoost [18] and LightGBM [19] as the frameworks of Gradient Boosting Decision Tree. The hyper parameters of each framework are adjusted using 5-fold cross validation in the range of Table 4.

5   Result

5.1   Forecast Performance

First, we evaluate the overall forecast performance. Table 5 shows the forecast performances of the 3 models for the test data of each dataset. The overall tendency is that the F-measure is high in order of $1/2$-forecast model, $1/3$-forecast model, and $1/4$-forecast model. Because it is common to consider that the more the number of the students with poor grades whom the system should detect increases, the higher the degree of forecast difficulty is, the tendency matches our intuition. The F-measure of $1/2$-forecast model is higher than the others, but it can rough classify only the students into the students with poor academic grades and the others. On the other hand, $1/4$-forecast model tries to detect the few students with poor grades who we should support as a priority, but its precision tends to be lower than the others. We consider that which the model each university selects depends on its purposes.

Table 2. The number of students in the train data of each dataset.

Dataset of All faculties (549 students in the train data)

Lower 1/2	**301 (54.8%)**	**Lower 1/3**	**200 (36.4%)**	**Lower 1/4**	**156 (28.5%)**
Others	248 (45.2%)	Others	349 (63.5%)	Others	392 (71.5%)

Dataset of Faculty of Engineering (231 students in the train data)

Lower 1/2	**134 (57.3%)**	**Lower 1/3**	**83 (35.9%)**	**Lower 1/4**	**66 (28.6%)**
Others	97 (42.0%)	Others	148 (64.1%)	Others	165 (71.4%)

Dataset of Faculty of Pharmacy (65 students in the train data)

Lower 1/2	**32 (49.2%)**	**Lower 1/3**	**25 (38.5%)**	**Lower 1/4**	**19 (29.2%)**
Others	33 (50.1%)	Others	40 (61.5%)	Others	46 (70.1%)

Dataset of Faculty of Health Sciences (169 students in the train data)

Lower 1/2	**88 (52.1%)**	**Lower 1/3**	**60 (35.5%)**	**Lower 1/4**	**46 (27.2%)**
Others	81 (47.9%)	Others	109 (64.5%)	Others	123 (72.8%)

Dataset of Faculty of Future Design (84 students in the train data)

Lower 1/2	**47 (56.0%)**	**Lower 1/3**	**32 (38.1%)**	**Lower 1/4**	**25 (29.8%)**
Others	37 (44.0%)	Others	52 (61.9%)	Others	59 (70.2%)

Table 3. The number of students in the test data of each dataset.

Dataset of All faculties (576 students in the test data)

Lower 1/2	**316 (54.9%)**	**Lower 1/3**	**208 (36.1%)**	**Lower 1/4**	**166 (28.8%)**
Others	260 (45.1%)	Others	368 (63.8%)	Others	410 (71.1%)

Dataset of Faculty of Engineering (214 students in the test data)

Lower 1/2	**129 (60.3%)**	**Lower 1/3**	**92 (43.0%)**	**Lower 1/4**	**71 (33.2%)**
Others	85 (39.7%)	Others	122 (57.0%)	Others	143 (66.8%)

Dataset of Faculty of Pharmacy (103 students in the test data)

Lower 1/2	**51 (49.5%)**	**Lower 1/3**	**32 (31.1%)**	**Lower 1/4**	**25 (24.3%)**
Others	52 (50.5%)	Others	71 (68.9%)	Others	78 (75.7%)

Dataset of Faculty of Health Sciences (172 students in the test data)

Lower 1/2	**89 (51.7%)**	**Lower 1/3**	**55 (32.0%)**	**Lower 1/4**	**46 (26.7%)**
Others	83 (48.3%)	Others	117 (68.0%)	Others	126 (73.3%)

Dataset of Faculty of Future Design (87 students in the test data)

Lower 1/2	**47 (54.0%)**	**Lower 1/3**	**29 (33.3%)**	**Lower 1/4**	**24 (27.6%)**
Others	40 (46.0%)	Others	58 (66.7%)	Others	63 (72.4%)

Table 4. The range of 5-fold cross validation in XGBoost and LightGBM.

Parameter	XGBoost	LightGBM
learning_rate	{0.01, 0.03, 0.1, 0.3}	–
min_child_weight	{2, 4, 6, 8}	–
max_depth	{1, 2, 3, 4}	–
colsample_bytree	{0.2, 0.5, 0.8, 1.0}	{0.4, 0.7, 1.0}
subsample	{0.2, 0.5, 0.8, 1.0}	{0.4, 1.0}
reg_alpha	–	{0.0001, 0.003, 0.1}
reg_lambda	–	{0.0001, 0.1}
num_leaves	–	{2, 3, 4, 6}
subsample_freq	–	{0, 7}
min_child_samples	–	{0, 2, 5, 10}

Table 5. The forecast performances of the 3 forecast models for each dataset.

XGBoost

		Engineering	Pharmacy	Health Sci.	Fut. Design	All faculties
1/2	Recall	0.636	0.529	0.663	0.851	0.652
	Precision	0.796	0.614	0.663	0.714	0.760
	F-measure	0.707	0.568	0.663	0.777	0.702
1/3	Recall	0.500	0.531	0.473	0.448	0.490
	Precision	0.767	0.515	0.520	0.722	0.680
	F-measure	0.605	0.523	0.495	0.553	0.570
1/4	Recall	0.352	0.480	0.435	0.292	0.367
	Precision	0.641	0.545	0.541	0.500	0.565
	F-measure	0.455	0.511	0.482	0.368	0.445

LightGBM

		Engineering	Pharmacy	Health Sci.	Fut. Design	All faculties
1/2	Recall	0.628	0.627	0.652	0.638	0.623
	Precision	0.818	0.552	0.637	0.732	0.767
	F-measure	0.711	0.587	0.644	0.682	**0.688**
1/3	Recall	0.554	0.656	0.509	0.517	0.438
	Precision	0.823	0.438	0.549	0.682	0.650
	F-measure	0.662	0.525	0.528	0.588	**0.523**
1/4	Recall	0.423	0.520	0.413	0.250	0.331
	Precision	0.682	0.481	0.487	0.600	0.585
	F-measure	0.522	0.500	0.447	0.353	**0.423**

In addition, we can find that the recalls of 1/2-forecast model, 1/3-forecast model, and 1/4-forecast model for any dataset (Faculty of Engineering, Faculty of Pharmacy, Faculty of Health Sciences, Faculty of Future Design, and All faculties) are higher than the precisions of them. We discuss the result. If detecting the students with poor grades too much with no confidences, that might lead to the burdens of both of the professors and the students. Hence, in the task that aims to detect the students with poor grades at a point in time when they enroll in the university, the system should not detect the students who do not have problems. Considering this, we can find the result that the precision of our proposed system is high is the result we had expected.

Second, we evaluate the recall and the precision of our proposed method. It was found the system has a large false-negative rate, this is to say, the system has some oversights to detect the students with poor academic grades. Specifically, we can find that the recalls of the forecast models are about from 0.3 to 0.6. Hence, this model cannot detect about from 40% to 70% of the students with poor grades who we want to detect. Because several explanatory variables that would be effective for the task seems to exist still, we aim to discuss these variables in the future works.

On the other hand, it was also found our proposed method has a small false-positive rate, this is to say, this system is less prone to mistake detecting the students with poor academic grades. Specifically, we can find that the precisions of our proposed models are about from 0.6 to 0.7.

From 60% to 70% of the students whom our proposed method detects as the students whose post-enrollment grades would get worse actually became students with poor academic grades after they enroll the university. It is thought the explanatory variables we introduced were not enough as mentioned above but some of them were effective for forecasting the students whose post-enrollment grades get worse.

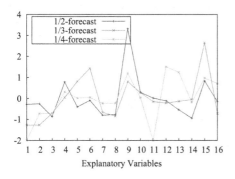 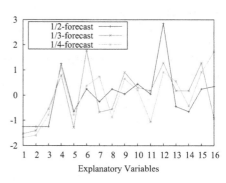

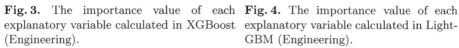

Fig. 3. The importance value of each explanatory variable calculated in XGBoost (Engineering).

Fig. 4. The importance value of each explanatory variable calculated in Light-GBM (Engineering).

28   K. Arasawa et al.

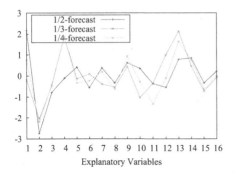
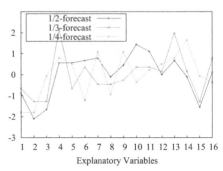

Fig. 5. The importance value of each explanatory variable calculated in XGBoost (Pharmacy).

Fig. 6. The importance value of each explanatory variable calculated in Light-GBM (Pharmacy).

5.2 Explanatory Variables that are Effective for the Task

This subsection discusses which features are effective for forecasting the students whose post-enrollment grades would get worse. From Figs. 3, 4, 5, 6, 7, 8, 9, 10, 11 and 12 show the importance value of each explanatory variable calculated in XGBoost and LightGBM. Here, these importance values are standardized. In addition, Table 6 shows the mean importance value of the explanatory variable calculated in 6 forecast models (3 models by XGBoost and 3 models by LightGBM).

Many forecast models consider that Var.4 (the mean rating value of all subjects in high school) and Var.13 (the total score of 1st academic tests) are important for forecasting the post-enrollment grades of the students at a point in time when they enroll in the university. On the other hand, we find that Var.1 (the sex of the student), Var.2 (the course where the student belonged in high school), and Var.3 (the career path classification of the high school) do not have an importance for the task.

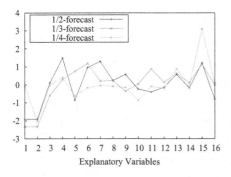
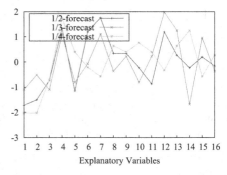

Fig. 7. The importance value of each explanatory variable calculated in XGBoost (Health Sci.).

Fig. 8. The importance value of each explanatory variable calculated in Light-GBM (Health Sci.).

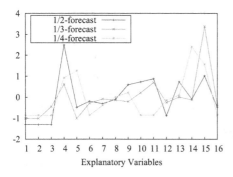

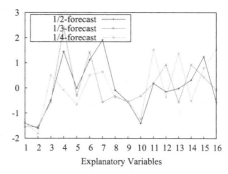

Fig. 9. The importance value of each explanatory variable calculated in XGBoost (Fut. Design).

Fig. 10. The importance value of each explanatory variable calculated in Light-GBM (Fut. Design).

Moreover, we find that the importance values of the explanatory variables of the forecast model vary depending on the dataset (the faculty). The authors have considered that Var.15 (the total score of 2nd academic tests) is important for the task because the variable shows the academic grades of the students just prior to admission. As expected, Var.15 is important in the forecast models for the dataset of Faculty of Health Sciences, the dataset of Faculty of Future Design, and the dataset of All faculties. However, the forecast models for the dataset of Faculty of Engineering and the dataset of Faculty of Pharmacy do not have a importance to Var.15, hence, we aim to analyze the reason in more detail in the future works.

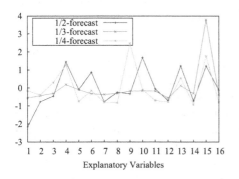

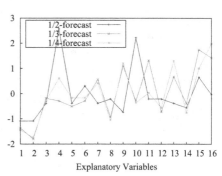

Fig. 11. The importance value of each explanatory variable calculated in XGBoost (All Faculties).

Fig. 12. The importance value of each explanatory variable calculated in Light-GBM (All Faculties).

Table 6. The mean importance values of 6 forecast models.

Var.	Engineering	Pharmacy	Health Sci.	Fut. Design	All faculties
1	−0.103	−0.103	−1.530	−1.250	−1.128
2	−2.022	−2.022	−1.724	−1.356	−1.037
3	−0.782	−0.782	−0.507	−0.522	−0.218
4	1.191	1.191	1.057	1.303	0.966
5	0.056	0.056	−0.385	−0.201	−0.334
6	−0.149	−0.149	0.478	0.285	0.040
7	0.266	0.266	0.625	0.205	−0.225
8	−0.499	−0.499	0.166	−0.161	−0.597
9	0.543	0.543	0.169	−0.165	0.590
10	0.079	0.079	−0.224	−0.475	0.499
11	−0.061	−0.061	0.021	0.437	0.033
12	0.169	0.169	0.439	−0.142	−0.593
13	1.335	1.335	0.709	0.276	0.581
14	0.633	0.633	−0.138	0.487	−0.616
15	−0.763	−0.763	1.004	1.407	1.697
16	0.109	0.109	−0.160	−0.128	0.342

6   Conclusion

The issue that the number of dropouts from universities is increasing gets serious. The main reason is that their academic grades have gotten worse. Hence, we must detect the students whose grades would get worse and give them additional supports early.

This paper has proposed the method that can forecast whether the rank of GPA of a student after 1 year is in lower or not in his/her department based on GBDT (Gradient Boosting Decision Tree). In the evaluation, this paper has aimed to detect the students at Hokkaido University of Science whose academic grades would be in lower $1/N$ ($N = 2, 3, 4$). And it reveals that the mean F-measure of 1/2-forecast model is 0.702, the mean F-measure of 1/3-forecast model is 0.570, and the mean F-measure of 1/4-forecast model is 0.445.

In addition, it has revealed the explanatory variables that are effective for forecasting the students to a university whose academic grades would get worse. Particularly, we find that our proposed forecast models set high importance to the mean rating value of all subjects in high school and the scores the academic tests of 5 subjects that they took when staring the pre-admission education of the university.

In the future works, we plan to conduct interviews to the professors of universities on the performances of our proposed systems because we judge how much the accuracy is needed in the system. Moreover, there is CatBoost [20] as one of the methods of Gradient Boosting Decision Tree. Therefore, we plan to develop a forecast model based on CatBoost and compare its forecast performance to the performances of the methods in this paper.

References

1. Konda, H.: Current status and issues of support measures related to withdrawal from school: from the university practices described in the self-evaluation and inspection report. In: Fukuoka University Annual Review of the Development of Higher Education, vol. 4, pp. 40–49 (2022)
2. Morsy, S., Karypis, G.: Sparse neural attentive knowledge-based models for grade prediction. In: Proceedings of the 12th International Conference on Educational Data Mining, pp. 366–371 (2019)
3. Hu, Q., Rangwala, H.: Reliable deep grade prediction with uncertainty estimation. In: Proceedings of the 9th International Conference on Learning Analytics and Knowledge, pp. 76–85 (2019)
4. Nishioka, K., Mochizuki, H.: Examination of learning log and features analysing grade in the information subject. In: Proceedings of the 84th National Convention of IPSJ, 22H-09 (2022)
5. Matuso, R., Ito, K.: Prediction of score by machine learning in programming class using LMS. In: Proceedings of the 37th JSSST Annual Conference (2020)
6. Shiratori, N., Oishi, T., Tajiri, S., Mori, M., Murota, M.: Clustering of student status in the spring semester of the first year using predicted GPA trends. Trans. Japan. Soc. Inf. Syst. Educ. **39**(4), 440–451 (2022)
7. Kondo, N., Okubo, M., Hatanaka, T.: Early detection of at-risk students using machine learning based on LMS log data. In: Proceedings of the 6th IIAI International Congress on Advanced Applied Informatics, pp. 198–201 (2017)
8. Pongpaichet, S., Jankapor, S., Janchai, S., Tongsanit, T.: Early detection at-risk students using machine learning. In: 2020 International Conference on Information and Communication Technology Convergence, pp. 283–287 (2020)
9. Ookouchi, Y., Yamanaka, A.: Basic scholastic achievement analyzed of the GPA and placement test. For early detection of students with low academic performance in the faculty. Trans. Japan. Soc. Inf. Syst. Educ. **40**(1), 45–55 (2016)
10. Takaoka, A., Nakai, A., Sugiyama, E., Nozue, T., Shimizu, R.: The proposal for multi-faceted student support based on student data base: the collaboration of early detection of at-risk students and student counseling services. Meiji Gakuin Univ. Bull. Psychol. **27**, 81–93 (2017)
11. Kondo, N., Hatabaka, T.: "Modelling of students", learning states using big data of students through the baccalaureate degree program. Trans. Japan. Soc. Inf. Syst. Educ. **33**(2), 94–103 (2016)
12. Ogata, H., Fujimura, N.: Development of the information infrastructure for learning analytics in the university education. IPSJ Trans. Comput. Educ. **3**(2), 1–7 (2017)
13. Taira, T., Okubo, A.: The effect of evaluation in high school and learning consciousness on academic performance in university: from the result of latent growth curve modeling. OCU J. High. Educ. Stud. **16**(1), 16–25 (2018)
14. Iwamura, H.: Types of university entrance examinations and educational performance after admission: case of the department of international studies at Meiji Gakuin University. Meiji Gakuin Rev. Int. Region. Stud. **57**, 1–24 (2020)

15. Akagi, M., Hibino, I., Koeda, T., Hirano, T.: An investigation of the academic achievement in the department of rehabilitation: the difference of the entrance examination category. J. Nagoya Gakuin Univ. Human. Nat. Sci. **47**(2), 73–81 (2011)
16. Uchida, Y.: A study on the relation between the scores of entrance examinations and the academic performance in the department of geography and environmental studies, Faculty of Letters, Kokushikan University. Kokushikan J. Human. **6**, 67–91 (2016)
17. Ito, T., et al.: The Relationship between student performance in a pre-entrance education program and first-semester final grades. OIU J. Int. Stud. **27**(3), 161–174 (2014)
18. Tianqi, C., Carlos, G.: XGBoost: a scalable tree boosting system. arXiv:1603.02754 (2016)
19. Guolin, K., et al.: LightGBM: a highly efficient gradient boosting decision tree. In: Proceedings of the 31st International Conference on Neural Information Processing Systems, pp. 3149–3157 (2017)
20. Liudmila, P., Gleb, G., Aleksandr, V., Anna, V.D., Andrey, G.: CatBoost: unbiased boosting with categorical features. arXiv:1810.11363 (2018)

Understanding Meaningful Arithmetic Operations in Word Problems: A Computational Model and Task Design

Tsukasa Hirashima[(✉)]

Hiroshima University, 1-4-1, Kagami-Yama Higashi-Hiroshima, Hiroshima, Japan
`tsukasa@lel.hiroshima-u.ac.jp`

Abstract. In the context of arithmetic word problems involving multiplication and division relationships between quantities, a typical arithmetic situation leads to two multiplications and four divisions. This paper introduces an educational framework for a meaningful and integrated interpretation of both operations in such situations. It is based on the 'tri-quantitative proposition model', a computational approach representing problems with two existential and one relational propositions. Additionally, this paper describes a problem-posing task designed using this model. Preliminary evaluations with teachers and university students were conducted to assess the task's effectiveness. The results of these evaluations, which are reported here, suggest the usefulness and advanced nature of the proposed framework and task design.

Keywords: Tri-quantity Proposition Model · Arithmetic Word Problems · Problem-Posing

1 Introduction

In mathematics, multiplication and division each have a singular mathematical meaning, with division defined as the inverse of multiplication. However, in arithmetic word problems involving semantic quantities, these operations can assume a variety of meanings. For example, consider a situation with "three apples on one plate and two plates in total, so there are six apples". This leads to multiplication equation $3 \times 2 = 6$. In this context, there are two meaningful divisions: $6 \div 2 = 3$ and $6 \div 3 = 2$, and they are different meanings respectively. The first division ($6 \div 2$) represents "partitive division," signifying a division into two equal parts, while the second division ($6 \div 3$) represents "quotative division," indicating two groups s, each consisting of three apples. Furthermore, in this situation, the quantity '3' can be interpreted as 'apples per plate'. Thus, if we view '3' in this manner, we understand that there exists a fraction 1/3, with the unit being 'apples per plate.' Consequently, this leads to semantic multiplications and divisions involving quantities smaller than one, such as $(1/3) \times 6 = 2$, $2 \div 6 = 1/3$, and $2 \div (1/3) = 6$.

In typical educational settings, these operations of multiplication and division are often taught separately. However, as the previous example demonstrates, these operations

H. Mori and Y. Asahi (Eds.): HCII 2024, LNCS 14691, pp. 33–43, 2024.
https://doi.org/10.1007/978-3-031-60125-5_3

can coexist within the same situation. Therefore, an important educational objective in learning arithmetic word problems that deal with operational relationships between meaningful quantities is to interpret these operations as being closely related within the same context. This paper proposes a framework designed meaningful and integrative explanation for the two types of multiplication and four types of division that can occur in a single arithmetic situation.

In this paper, we first outline tri-quantitative proposition model [1, 2], a computational approach representing problems with two existential and one relational propositions. Then, meaningful and integrated interpretations between basic four operations via the same quantity, and integrated interpretations within an addition-subtraction operations and within multiplication-division operations in the same arithmetic situation are described. Next, we focus on the second integrated that is, intra-scene interpretation of multiplication and division, and discuss in more detail the differences from the common explanations in textbooks and other sources. Furthermore, a learning task and a preliminary experimental evaluation of the integrated interpretation are reported.

2 Tri-quantitative Proposition Model

In the tri-quantitative proposition model, an arithmetic problem solvable by a single operation is assumed to consist of three quantities: two existence quantities and one relational quantity. The existence quantities are independent of the operations, whereas the relational quantity determines the operation to be used. This model can decide the appropriate operation and calculate the answer in a word problem by finding an adequate combination of the three propositions, making it a computational model.

Previous studies in intelligent interactive learning environments, such as MON-SAKUN [3–5] and Triangle Block [6, 7], have utilized the tri-quantitative proposition model as the domain model [8] for arithmetic word problems. These environments are capable of diagnosing learners' responses and providing feedback based on diagnostic results. This representation allows learners, teachers, and the system to share and understand the rationale behind problem-solving. In this sense, the tri-quantitative proposition model serves as a shareable computational model. This paper expands on this concept by exploring the direct learning of the model itself.

3 Meaningful and Integrated Interpretation of the Four Basic Operations

3.1 Inter- and Intra-situation Integrated Interpretation

In this paper, the concept of connecting multiple arithmetic word problems through a shared quantity is defined as "inter-situation integrated interpretation." For example, by utilizing "the number of apples," one can formulate arithmetic situations that incorporate all four fundamental operations: addition, subtraction, multiplication, and division. The inter-situation integrated interpretation is introduced with examples in Sect. 3.2.

Additionally, when a scenario presents a multiplicative or divisive relationship between two propositions of existential quantity, it can be depicted using two expressions for multiplication and four for division. This method provides an integrated interpretation of both multiplication and division within the same context. Similarly, if a scenario exhibits an additive or subtractive relationship between two existential quantity propositions, it can be described with two expressions for addition and four for subtraction. This technique affords an integrated interpretation of addition and subtraction, also within a single context. These methodologies are collectively termed "intra-situation integrated interpretation" in this document. The intra-situation integrated interpretation is explained with examples in Sect. 3.3.

3.2 Inter-situation Integrated Interpretation

Figure 1 illustrates several examples of arithmetic situations centered around the quantity of "eight apples." Based on the tri-quantity proposition model, a situation is composed of three quantity propositions: the rectangle represents the existential quantity and the rounded rectangle symbolizes the relational quantity. This figure delineates nine arithmetic expressions as follows: $8-3 = 5$, $5 + 3 = 8$, $11-3 = 8$, $8 + 3 = 11$, $8-3 = 5$, $8 \times 50 = 400$, $8 \times 2 = 16$, $8 \times 0.5 = 4$, and $8 \div 2 = 4$. In this figure, because distinct six situations are integrated via one relational quantity: "8 apples,", this figure is called inter-situation integrated interpretation.

It's noted that the final two arithmetic expressions are categorized within the same situation. This approach of grouping multiple arithmetic expressions under a single situation will be further discussed as a manifestation of integrative interpretation, particularly within the scope of intra-situation integrated interpretation, in the subsequent subsection.

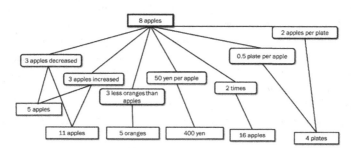

Fig. 1. Integrated Inter-Situation Diagram representing several arithmetic situations involving the same existential quantity proposition (8 apples).

3.3 Intra-situation Integrated Interpretation

Figure 2 demonstrates a situation where a multiplication or division relationship exists between two existential quantities: 8 apples and 4 plates. From this relationship, two relational quantities are derived: "2 apples per plate" and "0.5 plate per apple." Integrating a relational quantity with the two existential quantities yields one multiplication and two distinct divisions. Thus, the situation encapsulates two existential quantities, two relational quantities, two multiplication expressions, and four division expressions. This setup illustrates that when two existential quantities are linked by multiplication or division, the tri-quantity proposition model typically identifies two relational quantities, alongside two multiplication expressions and four division expressions. The division expressions represent quotative and partitive division, respectively, offering an integrated understanding of these concepts within the same situation. This configuration is depicted through a dual triangle diagram, labeled to indicate that (the upper triangle related quantity) is greater than (the lower triangle related quantity).

Furthermore, it is important to note that this integrated interpretation encompasses both multiplication and division with numbers less than 1 within the same situation. Therefore, if learners accept this integrated interpretation, they can logically deduce that multiplying by a number less than 1 reduces the original quantity, whereas dividing by a number less than 1 increases the original quantity.

Figure 3 illustrates the concepts of multiplication and division within the context of 'proportions', using upper and lower triangles to represent these operations. It's a common misconception that units cancel each other out in a manner similar to (pieces/pieces). However, distinguishing between doubling and halving is crucial within this diagram. To do so effectively, one must understand the specific 'pieces' being divided by other 'pieces'. This recognition emphasizes that units do not simply disappear. For instance, comprehending the unit as '(the number of "8 apples") divided by (the number of "4 apples")' is vital. This example parallels the concept of 'quantity per apple', illustrating that quantity—whether doubling or halving in Fig. 3—can be seen as a relational quantity.

When considering the relationship between addition and subtraction involving two existential quantities, we identify two relational quantities: one for addition and another for subtraction. By integrating each relational quantity with the two existential quantities, we can derive one addition expression and two subtraction expressions. Figure 4 illustrates an arithmetic context with 8 apples and 4 oranges. If viewed as a 'combination,' these two existential quantities can be merged with the relational quantity of '12 apples and oranges together' to form the equation $8 + 4 = 12$. Alternatively, viewing this as a 'difference' allows for their combination with the relational quantity ' Four different in number between apples and oranges,' leading to the equation $8 - 4 = 4$. This demonstrates how the same situation can be interpreted differently in 'combining' and 'difference' problems.

Figure 5 is a representation of the "increase" and "decrease" situation. Increasing" and "decreasing" can be regarded as situations in which the quantity of the same object changes over time. Since it is the difference between two different quantities at two different times, it can be regarded as a kind of "comparison. If the less present quantity is before time, it is "increasing", and if it is after time, it is "decreasing". By changing the allocation of time to the same two existential quantities in the right side of Fig. 5, it is possible to graphically represent an increase, a decrease, and the two additions and four subtractions that accompany them, which can be considered a situation integration of addition and subtraction in the situation of increase and decrease.

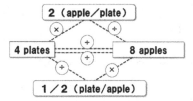

Fig. 2. Dual Triangle Diagram as an Integrated Representation of Multiplication-Division Relationships in a Single Arithmetic Situation of Multiplication

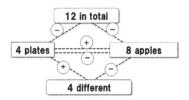

Fig. 3. Dual Triangle Diagram as an Integrated Representation of Multiplication-Division Relationships in a Single Arithmetic Situation Involving Ratios

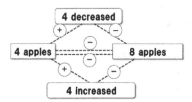

Fig. 4. Dual Triangle Diagram as an Integrated Representation of Addition-Subtraction Relationships in a Single Arithmetic Situation Involving Different/Total

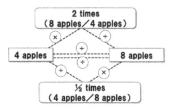

Fig. 5. Dual Triangle Diagram as an Integrated Representation of Addition-Subtraction Relationships in a Single Arithmetic Situation Involving Increase/Decrease

4 Characteristics of Semantic and Integrated Interpretation with the Tri-quantity Proposition Model

4.1 Multiplication and Division as Conversion of Quantity

The tri-quantity proposition model of multiplication and division states that it is the relational quantities that allow transformation by multiplication and division between two existential quantities. The relational quantity has a unit as the division of two existential quantities, and depending on which of the two existential quantities is used as the reference (denominator), there are two relational quantities, and for each combination of a relational quantity and two existential quantities, there are two sets of one-multiplication & two divisions. In the following, we will discuss the differences that arise in the explanation of multiplication and division based on this tri-quantitative proposition model compared to the general explanation and treatment of multiplication and division in a usual textbook of arithmetic.

4.2 Treatment of Partitive Division and Quotative Division

In traditional arithmetic instruction, the same division formula is used to explain two different type of divisions: partitive division and quotative divisions [9, 10]. In this case, the arithmetic situations are different. In contrast, the integrated interpretation described in this paper explains partitive division and quotative division in the same arithmetic situation. In this case, the derived division formulas are different. This difference is discussed.

The conventional method of matching division formulas starts from an equation and explains that there are multiple situations represented by the equation. In other words, the explanation is based on the "making question" approach of deriving a problem or situation from an equation. Although the activity of creating questions and situations from expressions itself is considered to be useful, it is questionable whether it is appropriate for an introductory explanation. If the difference between partitive division and quotative division is to be explained, it would be more natural to show that the two exist in the same situation. From the standpoint of viewing arithmetic problems as "reading the relationship between quantities and quantities," it is clear that agreement of situations is more important than agreement of equations.

The integrative interpretation explains that there are two ways of reading the relationship between quantities, partitive division and quotative division, in the process of reading the relationship between quantities in the same way as when solving. Although the number of operations and the number of results are interchanged in the equation, it is easy to explain that the equation is for the same situation because the same numerical values are used.

4.3 Proper Fraction as the Second Relational Quantity

Figures 2 and 3 illustrate that arithmetic word problems taught in lower grades of elementary school include operations such as multiplication and division with proper fractions (or decimals), which represent quantities less than one. Previous studies have shown that learners typically find it challenging to understand multiplication and division when it involves proper fractions [11, 12]. This difficulty arises because, in these cases, the result of multiplication is smaller and the result of division is larger than the operand. Students often start learning these operations with quantities greater than one, referred to as the 'first relational quantity' (we call a relational quantity less than one "second relation quantity"). Initially, they may believe that multiplication always increases and division decreases a number. While this understanding is acceptable at the beginning, it is crucial to develop a more advanced comprehension as their learning progresses.

The dual triangle diagram reveals that in multiplication involving a relational quantity greater than one, there is also a relational quantity less than one. Therefore, the dual triangle diagram is a promising tool for advanced learning in arithmetic word problems. Additionally, the "tri-quantity proposition model, which forms the foundation of the dual triangle model, is also promising for enhancing learning in arithmetic."

5 Learning Task for Integrated Interpretation

5.1 Integrated Diagram Reconstruction

Figure 1 presents an integrated interpretation of the four basic operations in arithmetic word problems, depict through an existence quantity. We call this representation "integrated diagram". Drawing on this diagram, a reconstruction task has been developed, exemplified in Fig. 6. In this task, each card symbolizes a quantity proposition, and the objective is to construct an arithmetic situation by combining three specific cards. By mandating the use of card (1), all potential situations are unified through the quantity represented on this card.

This task consists of three subtasks: Subtask 1 requires learners to create as many different arithmetic situations as possible by combining three cards. Subtask 2 involves identifying cards that cannot be used within these combinations and then create new cards that enable their use. Subtask 3 encourages learners to discuss their answers collaboratively. The solutions for Subtasks 1 and 2 are illustrated in Fig. 7. In this figure, solid lines indicate the solutions for Subtask 1, while dashed lines represent the solutions for Subtask 2.

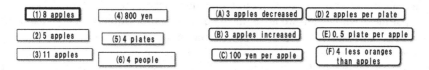

Fig. 6. Reconstruction Task of Integrated Diagram

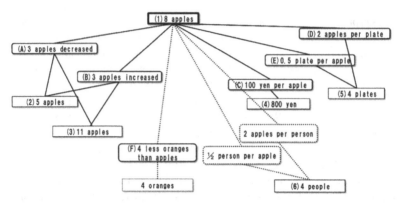

Fig. 7. The solutions of Subtask 1 & 2.

5.2 Pilot Implementation as an Unplugged Task

In this paper, the reconstruction task is presented as an unplugged task. In line with this concept, the author conducted two use experiments with teachers as subjects and three use experiments with college students as subjects. these are described in this subsection.

User Experiment Conducted by Two Groups of Teachers. The first group consisted of two elementary school principals, one elementary school teacher belonging to the board of education, and one middle school vice principal. Group 2 consisted of 13 teachers from the same elementary school. In all cases, the implementation for the teachers was facilitated through discussions. The results suggest that this task requires serious consideration and discussion among the teachers. Consequently, it was agreed that (1) the task was within the scope of arithmetic problems, (2) it represented an advanced but essential learning objective to bridge arithmetic in elementary school with mathematics in junior high school. However, (3) it is not merely an extension of existing content, thus (4) careful consideration should be given to how it integrates with existing content. Based on these discussions, we are now exploring how to incorporate the task into elementary school classes.

User Experiment Conducted by University Student Group 1. The subjects were undergraduate and graduate students in the author's laboratory at an information science department who had heard about the tri-quantity proposition model but had never worked on it as a research topic. The implementation was conducted as shown in Fig. 7, with subjects completing subtask 1 and 2 in 20 min. After 15 min of subtask 3, the students were asked to complete a questionnaire survey using a 5-point scale (5: agree, 4: somewhat agree, 3: undecided, 2: not so much agree, 1: disagree). The results are shown in Table 1. All of the respondents answered that they needed a deeper understanding, and 90% of them said that they learned a lot. All of the participants responded positively to the discussion. Despite the special characteristics of this group of subjects, the results suggest that the task shown in Fig. 7 is worthwhile for university students as well.

User Experiment Conducted by University Student Group 2. The similar task was conducted with students from the third-year at an information-related course at a national

Table 1. Results of Questionnaire for University Student Group 1

	5	4	3	2	1
The task was easy	2	6	2	0	0
It was an assignment that required a deep understanding	6	4	0	0	0
I knew the relationship among arithmetic word problems addressed in the assignment	0	4	1	3	2
It was a study of arithmetic word problems	5	4	1	0	0
I could discuss the answers with others	9	1	0	0	0
Discussing it gave me new insights	7	3	0	0	0

university in Indonesia, and data were collected for 61 students. Subtask 3 was omitted due to its synchronous online mode. The content was translated into English. After a general discussion of knowledge modeling, the students were asked to work on this assignment as a preliminary step to explain the significance of modeling for a task that is considered to be a simple arithmetic problem, and the tri-quantity proposition model was not explained beforehand.

Table 2 summarizes the content and results of the questionnaire, with 80% of the respondents agreeing that the task required in-depth understanding, and nearly 90% felt that they learned a lot. Regarding the validity of the classification of the cards (expressing existential or relational quantities), more than 60% of the respondents agreed with it, while less than 10% disagreed. All the respondents gave some explanation for how the two groups of cards differed. Their answers generally indicated that the classifications were based on the quantities related to existence and relation, suggesting that they understood the intention of the classification.

Table 2. Results of Questionnaire for University Student Group 2

	5	4	3	2	1
The task was easy	12	21	21	4	3
It was an assignment that required a deep understanding	25	24	11	1	0
I knew the relationship among arithmetic word problems addressed in the assignment	4	3	8	15	31
It was a study of arithmetic word problems	35	19	6	1	0
It is appropriate to categorize the cards into (I)–(VI) and (A)–(F)	23	16	20	2	0

User Experiment Conducted by University Student Group 3. The same form as in the implementation 2 was used for the third-year undergraduate students of an information-related course of a national university (in Japan), and data for 81 students were collected. In the implementation 3, (C) in Fig. 7 was replaced with "1/2 times" and

(IV) with "800 yen" in order to include the relational quantity as a ratio express with a proper fraction. All the participants who were able to collect data were able to construct a situation using "proportion" sentences as well as per-quantity sentences. The results of the questionnaire are shown in Table 3, and it can be said that the results were generally the same. The fact that the results did not differ even when the percentage was included suggests that the subjects didn't feel uncomfortable treating per-quantity and percentage as related quantities when considering this issue.

Table 3. Results of Questionnaire for University Student Group 3

	5	4	3	2	1
The task was easy	23	34	16	7	1
It was an assignment that required a deep understanding	46	22	10	1	2
I knew the relationship among arithmetic word problems addressed in the assignment	14	22	19	19	7
It was a study of arithmetic word problems	28	38	9	2	4
It is appropriate to categorize the cards into (I)–(VI) and (A)–(F)	47	22	4	6	2

5.3 Considerations of the Implementation

The reconstruction task depicted in Fig. 7 was well received by both teachers and university students. In particular, almost all participants agreed on its usefulness for discussions. This suggests that: (1) decomposing an arithmetic word problem into three quantity propositions—two existence quantity propositions and one relational quantity proposition—was meaningful and well-received; (2) visualizing and manipulating these components had cognitive validity; and as a result, (3) sharing and discussing these components and their manipulations proved to be meaningful and fruitful.

Based on these results, we plan to continue studying how to effectively utilize the task in educational settings. Furthermore, the fact that the system stimulates discussion indicates tri-quantity proposition model has the potential for realizing a shared, computable representation among learners, teachers, and the system. We refer to this as the "collaborative computational model".

We believe that through the implementation of the university students, we were able to demonstrate its operational feasibility as part of remedial education or reskilling. We believe that this is an important result because it suggests that the integrated interpretation of the four fundamental operations based on the tri-quantitative proposition model and their tasking were provided in a form that was close to the subjects' cognition. The fact that no questions were raised about the separation of existential and relational quantities, and the treatment of "proportion" and "quantity per unit" as relational quantities, suggests the validity of this integrated interpretation.

6 Conclusion

The tri-quantity proposition model is a computable representation that allows us to view the problem as a "quantity" rather than relying on "sentences". By using this model, the composition learning method was established, in which arithmetic sentences are divided into parts by quantity, and questions are composed as a combination of these parts. This paper describes the findings that the quantities as parts in this composition learning are not only computable for the system, but are also computable representations shared by the learners and the teachers. Although originally inspired by knowledge engineering, the creation of a shared computable representation by the learners, teachers and system is one of the goals of knowledge engineering, and this paper may be a successful example of such an approach. Since educational materials are objects with high stability, it is expected that the same approach has great potential for analyzing educational materials.

References

1. Hirashima, T., Yamamoto, S., Hayashi, Y.: Triplet structure model of arithmetical word problems for learning by problem-posing. In: Yamamoto, S. (ed.) HCI 2014. LNCS, vol. 8522, pp. 42–50. Springer, Cham (2014). https://doi.org/10.1007/978-3-319-07863-2_5
2. Hirashima, T., Hayashi, Y.: Educational externalization of thinking task by Kit-Build method. In: Yamamoto, S. (ed.) HIMI 2016. LNCS, vol. 9735, pp. 126–137. Springer, Cham (2016). https://doi.org/10.1007/978-3-319-40397-7_13
3. Hirashima, T., Kurayama, M.: Learning by problem-posing for reverse-thinking problems. AIED **2011**, 123–130 (2011)
4. Supianto, A.A., Hayashi, Y., Hirashima, T.: Visualizations of problem-posing activity sequences toward modeling the thinking process. Res. Pract. Technol. Enhanc. Learn. **11**, 1–23 (2016)
5. Hasanah, N., Hayashi, Y., Hirashima, T.: An analysis of learner outputs in problem posing as sentence-integration in arithmetic word problems. Res. Pract. Technol. Enhanc. Learn. **12**, 1–16 (2017)
6. Hirashima, T., Hayashi, Y., Yamamoto, S., Maeda, K.: Bridging model between problem and solution representations in arithmetic/mathematics word problem. In: Proceedings of ICCE 2015, pp. 9–18 (2015)
7. Hirashima, T., Furukubo, K., Yamamoto, S., Hayashi, Y., Maeda, K.: Practical use of triangle block model for bridging between problem and solution in arithmetic word problems. In: ICCE 2016, pp. 36–45 (2016)
8. Hirashima, T.: Computer-based intelligent support for moderately Ill-structured problems. In: ICSITech 2017, pp. 1–6 (2017)
9. Fischbein, E., Deri, M., Nello, M.S., Marino, M.S.: The role of implicit models in solving verbal problems in multiplication and division. J. Res. Math. Educ. **16**(1), 3–17 (1985)
10. Downton, A.P.: Links between children's understanding of multiplication and solution strategies for division. In: Proceedings of MERGA 2008, pp. 171–178 (2008)
11. Mulligan, J.T., Mitchelmore, M.C.: Young children's intuitive models of multiplication and division. J. Res. Math. Educ. **28**(3), 309–330 (1997)
12. Tirosh, D.: Enhancing prospective teachers' knowledge of children's conceptions: the case of division of fractions. J. Res. Math. Educ. **31**(1), 5–25 (2000)

Effectiveness of Digital Avatars in Student Engagement and Learning

Caryn Hoang, James D. Miles, and Kim-Phuong L. Vu[⊠]

California State University, Long Beach, Long Beach, CA, USA
carynh799@gmail.com, {Jim.Miles,Kim.Vu}@csulb.edu

Abstract. With the recent COVID-19 pandemic, students have reported that online classes not only lack effective teaching practices, but there is also an absence of the collaborative learning aspect that provides students with the ability to have quality interactions with one another and stay engaged (Dumford & Miller, 2018). The purpose of the current study was to assess the efficacy of animated and digital human avatars in comparison to traditional instructors in lecture videos. Data from 58 participants were analyzed. Participants were instructed to watch a total of four 4–7 min instructional videos and answer comprehension questions. The four videos in each condition consisted of two "Easy" Content and two "Hard" Content videos with the respective instructor type in that condition. After viewing a video, participants were asked to rate how much mental effort they devoted to understanding the information presented, and fill out questionnaires about their perceived engagement, trust in the avatar, and perceived usability of the instructional video. The results showed participants scored higher on the quizzes when the video content was hard than when it was easy. Participants also scored higher on the quiz when the video was presented with the human professor than the digital human professor. These results suggest that students may be more engaged, and as a result, showed higher quiz scores with the videos when the topic is more complex or when a human professor was present.

Keywords: Digital avatars · Engagement · Online-learning

1 Introduction

Due to the recent shift to remote learning and online classrooms, a multitude of issues can arise related to the negative impacts associated with eLearning (Bashir et al., 2021). Given that online instruction requires more self-motivation and time management skills, it can negatively impact student performance. Additionally, it can result in social isolation, limited feedback, and disconnection due to the lack of in-person interaction (Quesada-Pallarès et al., 2019). Although online education allows students to build upon their technological skills, develop their own learning styles, and have the flexibility to learn at their own pace, there are also concerns around receiving the same quality of education as in person or face-to-face classes (Palvia et al., 2018). With the recent COVID-19 pandemic, students have reported that online classes not only lack effective teaching practices, but there is also an absence of the collaborative learning aspect that provides students with the ability to have quality interactions with one another and stay engaged (Dumford and Miller, 2018).

Although online classes can affect student engagement and collaborative learning, it can be beneficial for engagement pertaining to quantitative reasoning and performance (Dumford and Miller, 2018). Thus, educational institutions should consider finding ways to increase student engagement when designing online courses content and encourage faculty and staff to find ways to maintain engagement across various course platforms. Supplemental resources may include eLearning gamification, game-based learning, interactive online exercises, animated educational videos, and digital avatars. With today's technology, instructors can implement various supplemental e-learning materials and virtual avatars to their course materials to enhance student engagement, motivation, and performance levels (Hsieh et al., 2019). Even though students like the convenience of online courses, many report having difficulty maintaining attention in asynchronous courses and find the ease of maintaining engagement to be easier in a more structured environment (Jensen, 2011). Therefore, researchers can implement intermittent quizzes into instructional videos with the virtual avatars to reduce mind wandering and increase attention to bring structure and learning to courses in a more consistent manner (Schacter and Szpunar, 2015).

While many gamified learning platforms have been successful in helping students become motivated to learn new concepts, the impact of digital avatars and its effects on student engagement is still obscure (Santos-Guevara and Rincón-Flores, 2021). Instructors are still finding ways to implement new learning methods and adding virtual avatars to their course materials can enhance student engagement (Hsieh et al., 2019). Educators have implemented various forms of technologies to not only create a more valuable and meaningful learning experience for students, but also to promote inclusivity for students who are not able to attend in-person classes. Thus, looking at the role of digital avatars in an online learning space can give us insight on effective ways we can incorporate digital avatars into online learning. Educators should focus on how to implement avatars to various types of learning methods to create a more interactive and engaging learning environment that adopts modern technology (Alblehai, 2021).

1.1 Types of Digital Avatars

There are various types of digital avatars that can be used in online lecture videos such as anime-styled avatars also known as "Vtubers", digital 3D human and animal avatars, as well as low and high-quality avatars. The style and type of each avatar can have varying levels of effectiveness that can impact levels of engagement and learning. Low quality or pixelated avatars that have low anthropomorphism may be ineffective at increasing engagement due to lower avatar identification (Kao and Harrell, 2016). Additionally, participants may not identify with avatars that have a low level of realism and view it as distracting or humorous, leading to less focus and engagement. For example, avatars that resemble animated humans tend to be the most engaging among young adults (Nizam et al., 2022), but how their use impacts learning is still unknown. Thus, researching the differing digital avatar styles in online learning videos can give us insight into effective ways we can incorporate digital avatars into online learning.

1.2 Perception of Digital Avatar Designs

In addition to different avatar styles, the design of the avatar can affect the user's perception of the avatar itself. Research suggests that the more realistic the avatar, the more the user resonates with them and the feeling can be similar to having a sense of identity with the avatar (Kao and Harrell, 2016). Greater avatar identification can lead to higher levels of performance and engagement when users play interactive games with the avatar that they feel more connected to (Kao and Harrell, 2016). Familiarity can also impact the use of avatars in learning where realistic avatar designs may elicit more positive emotional experiences for the user (Kao, 2019). Feelings of familiarity have also been linked to the feeling of presence, which can address issues related to having a lack of connection with asynchronous courses with no live instructor (Schöbel et al., 2019). In other words, familiar avatars may make learning easier for users and increase their engagement. Since performance and engagement have been linked to learning outcomes, considering these avatar types in designing virtual systems may guide future designs of virtual avatars in instructional videos to increase engagement.

On the other hand, digital learning with avatars may also present issues related to cognitive load (Schöbel et al., 2019). Users report having increased cognitive load due to having to adapt to the formatting of the online course material, which includes the lack of instructor interaction and feedback (Costley et al., 2021; Darejeh et al., 2021). Since avatars can provide feedback to users, it is important to consider avatar designs as features and characteristics that resonate with the user can evoke feelings of trust in the avatar, which can result in greater perceived usability of the system and reduce cognitive load (Schöbel et al., 2019). The contexts of avatars in course content material should also be explored to see how different conceptual topics impact engagement and comprehension.

1.3 Implementing Avatars to Instructional Videos

Incorporating avatars into online instruction can facilitate learning and increase student engagement. Further research into the design of avatars in instructional content with varying complexity levels is essential to determining which avatar is the most effective in different types of learning content (Blake and Moseley, 2010). The effects of using avatars in instructional videos of varying content difficulty, such as simple educational topics or more complex, conceptual ones, however, is still unclear. Considering how avatars with high anthropomorphism can provide more positive player experiences through games, the same idea may be applicable to online educational settings where the use of high-fidelity 3D digital human avatars in instructional videos can promote higher engagement among students (Kao and Harrell, 2016). Research on the use of avatars and its effects on learning, engagement, and satisfaction can shed light on how they can impact engagement and student learning outcomes.

Overall, exploring different avatar types and its influence on engagement and performance will introduce best practices for designing and developing the appropriate online learning materials to foster a successful, engaging online learning environment. If certain materials within the lecture course video captures the student's attention, then they will be more focused on those lecture materials, which serves as a form of engagement (Simons and Rensink, 2005). Therefore, digital avatars can play an important role in grabbing students' attention, consequently increasing engagement since they will be more focused. As a result, it is essential to understand the effectiveness of different types of digital avatars that can be implemented into course lecture videos with easy and hard concepts to not only boost engagement, but also ultimately minimize the social isolation and disconnection that exists within the online learning environment.

1.4 Current Study

The purpose of the current study was to assess the efficacy of avatars in comparison to traditional instructors in lecture videos. It was hypothesized that if digital avatar-based teaching is implemented in instructional videos, then students will be more engaged with the content and learning materials compared to traditional human instructor-based teaching. The additional engagement should positively impact learning.

It should be noted that the knowledge and lecture content of the human professor is not being replaced by the digital avatar. Rather, the digital avatar will only replace the professor's physical image. The professor's voice and movements will still be portrayed through the digital avatar, meaning that the professor is still required to teach the course as they normally would in a remote setting. Additionally, it is important to note that these are not AI digital avatars, so they do not replace the professor's knowledge and experience in teaching courses. Instead, the digital avatars will be synced with the professor's facial expressions and movements through the Zoom video function. The differences in student engagement between educator types may be observed by using lecture videos with varying content difficulty (i.e., easy vs. difficult material).

2 Method

2.1 Participants

A total of 58 participants were recruited for this study. Forty (40) participants (female = 14; male = 26) from ages 21 to 61 years ($M = 32.37$, $SD = 7.07$) were recruited from Amazon Mechanical Turk (MTurk), and 18 participants (female = 14; male = 3, non-binary = 1) from ages 18 to 22 years ($M = 19.28$, $SD = 1.32$) were recruited from California State University Long Beach.

2.2 Materials

Instructional Videos. Course lecture videos were recorded from an introductory cognition course taught by a real instructor and were optimized into instructional videos with visual effects using the Camtasia video editing program. Interactive avatars were generated using the Animaze software to portray the instructor in the videos based on their educator type and physical attributes. After creating the avatars, they were then digitally broadcasted to Zoom to record instructor avatars in the instructional videos. Study materials were embedded into Qualtrics along with the consent form, instructional video comprehension questions, short questionnaires, and demographic questions.

Comprehension Questions. Objective engagement was measured through comprehension accuracy scores from the set of questions participants answered after watching an instructional video. Comprehension questions were developed by the researcher based on the material and level of difficulty, where easy content videos consisted of one level of subtopics while hard content videos covered multiple subtopics.

Paas Scale for Mental Effort. Mental effort devoted to understanding content shown in the instructional videos was assessed using the Pass Scale for Mental Effort (Pass, 1992). Following each instructional video, participants indicated how much mental effort they invested to study the information on a 9-point scale from 1 (very, very low mental effort) to 9 (very, very high mental effort).

Trust in Automation Scale. The Trust in Automation Scale is a 12-item questionnaire for measuring trust in automated systems (Jian et al., 1998; Jian et al., 2000). Participants were asked to indicate their impressions of the educator on a 7-point scale ranging from 1 (very inaccurate) to 7 (very accurate).

System Usability Scale (SUS). Perceived usability of the instructional videos was assessed using the 10-item System Usability Scale (SUS) questionnaire (Lewis, 2018). Participants were asked to rate their agreement to statements on a 5-point scale, ranging from 1 (strongly disagree) to 5 (strongly agree).

Learning Activity Engagement. Participants were issued the 7-item Learning Activity Engagement questionnaire where they were asked to choose one or more answers that best explained their intent(s) for performing a particular activity for each respective question (Seo et al., 2021). If the participant never performed in a particular activity, they were asked to skip the question.

2.3 Design

The current study consisted of two parts of an experiment to compare engagement in instructional videos with different levels of content difficulty across educator types. Experiment 1A utilized MTurk participants and employed a 2 (Educator Type: Digital Human Avatar or Human) × 2 (Content Difficulty: Easy or Hard) mixed design. The comparison between the Digital Human Avatar Instructor and the Human Instructor was made to determine whether the avatar instructor impacted participants' engagement compared to the human instructor while viewing instructional videos. Experiment 1B included Introductory Psychology students, recruited via the SONA system, and employed a 2 (Educator Type: Digital Human Avatar or Anime Avatar) × 2 (Content Difficulty: Easy or Hard) mixed design. The comparison between the Digital Human Avatar Instructor and the Anime Avatar Instructor was made to determine whether the features of the avatar impacted participants' engagement while viewing instructional videos.

For both Experiments 1A and 1B, the between-subjects variable was the Educator Type and the within-subjects factor was the Content Difficulty. The educator type was implemented as either a human (real life instructor) or an avatar (digital human avatar or digital anime avatar) in the instructional videos based on the physical characteristics the educator portrays. Again, the digital human avatar portrayed physical characteristics that resemble a real human professor, while a digital anime avatar resembled a 2D-drawn cartoon character. The critical differences between the educator type that can affect the dependent variable includes the design, type, style, and quality of the digital avatar. The content difficulty pertains to the levels of conceptual learning. Content difficulty involves having participants watch two "easy" and two "hard" instructional lecture videos. Easy and hard lectures were dependent on the number of subtopics within the subject. The easy content lectures consisted of one level, while the hard content lectures included multiple subtopics that cascaded deeper into separate subtopics that worked in tandem to explain the main subject. In other words, the hard content lectures require breaking down a concept into smaller parts to understand the overall concept.

The dependent measures were comprehension (objective), which was measured through lecture video quizzes that are administered at the end of each lecture video, and perceived engagement levels (subjective), which was measured by a formative questionnaire after completing all four videos.

2.4 Procedure

Participants were asked to complete an online survey in a single session once they signed up for the study through SONA for Introductory Psychology Students or MTurk. The study was expected to last 45 min to 1 h with most participants spending an average of 1 h and 15 min completing the study. There was a total of three conditions where participants were shown one of three avatars in the instructional videos (i.e., Condition 1: Digital Human Avatar, Condition 2: Anime Avatar, and Condition 3: Human, see Fig. 1, Fig. 2 and Fig. 3). MTurk participants were given either the Digital Human Avatar or the Human Professor (Experiment 1A) while the SONA participants were given either the Digital Human Avatar or the Anime Avatar (Experiment 1B).

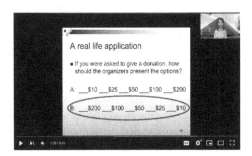 

Fig. 1. Educator Type: Digital Human Avatar (Condition 1)

Participants were instructed to watch instructional videos and answer comprehension questions. Additionally, participants were informed they can pause the video at any time to take notes when needed as if they are watching videos for an online course. In each condition, participants were asked to watch a total of four 4–7 min instructional videos. The four videos in each condition consisted of two "Easy" Content and two "Hard"

Fig. 2. Educator Type: Anime Avatar (Condition 2)

Fig. 3. Educator Type: Human Professor (Condition 3); Picture blurred for privacy.

Content videos with the respective instructor type in that condition. After viewing a video, participants were asked to rate on a scale of 1 to 9 how much mental effort they devoted to understanding the information presented in the previous video, with 1 being very, very low mental effort, and 9 indicating very, very high mental effort. The process repeated until participants watched all four videos.

Following the mental effort scale, participants were asked to complete a short 5-question lecture quiz respective to the video they previously viewed to assess their objective level of comprehension with the content material. Two quality control questions, one at the beginning (after video 2), and one at the end (after video 4) were implemented to ensure that the participants were still paying attention to the survey (e.g., select "Cognition" as the correct answer). Once participants completed all four instructional videos and answered the comprehension questions respective to the condition they were in, they were asked to fill out questionnaires about their perceived engagement, trust in the avatar, perceived usability of the instructional video. Finally, participants completed a Learning Activity Engagement questionnaire and indicated their intent(s) for partaking in a particular activity while watching instructional videos.

3   Results

3.1   Experiment 1A

Comprehension Accuracy. A 2 (Educator Type: Digital Human Avatar or Human) x 2 (Content Difficulty: Easy or Hard) mixed ANOVA revealed a main effect of content difficulty, $F(1, 38) = 4.28$, $p = .045$, $\eta_P^2 = .101$, where participants scored higher on the quiz when the video content was hard ($M = 50.25\%$) than when it was easy ($M = 43.25\%$). There was also a significant main effect of educator type, $F(1, 38) = 4.71$, $p = .036$, $\eta_P^2 = .110$, where participants scored higher on the quiz when the video was presented with the human professor ($M = 52.25\%$) than the digital human professor ($M = 41.25\%$). The interaction between educator type and content difficulty was not significant, $F(1, 38) = .55$, $p = .464$, $\eta_P^2 = .014$. These results suggest that students may be more engaged, and as a result, showed higher quiz scores with the videos when the topic is more complex or when a human professor was present.

Paas Scale for Mental Effort. A 2 (Educator Type: Digital Human Avatar or Human) x 2 (Content Difficulty: Easy or Hard) mixed ANOVA showed a significant main effect of educator type, $F(1, 38) = 5.21$, $p = .028$, $\eta_P^2 = .120$, where participants reported greater mental effort being exerted when the instructional videos featured a human professor ($M = 7.40$) compared to when it featured a digital avatar ($M = 6.66$). No other effects were significant. These findings suggest that participants were devoting more mental effort when a human professor was present.

Trust in Automation Scale. A one-way ANOVA found no significant differences between the digital human (M = 48.95) and the human professor (M = 50.15) in trust in automation, F(1, 38) = .581, p = .451. Results suggest that participants had moderate trust across the two educator types, and participants generally did not view the avatar to be more trustworthy or they did not feel they gained a higher sense of trust with the avatar.

System Usability Scale (SUS). A one-way ANOVA found no significant differences between the digital human (M = 51.13) and human professor (M = 51.00) in perceived usability of the educator type, F(1, 38) = .002, p = .963. Results suggest that participants did not view the avatar to be more usable. Moreover, the SUS scores were low, with the levels typically indicating marginal or poor usability. A possible reason for the lower ratings may be due to the fact that the instructor "box" does not cover the majority of the screen space, but only a small corner of the screen, which made their presence less impactful. Moreover, participants were not interacting with the instructors, which may be a reason for the lower SUS scores.

Learning Activity Engagement. In general, participants reported that they typically use the pause function when watching an instructional video because they need time to reflect on what they just watched (75%, n = 30) or they want to write a note (32.5%, n = 13). Most participants also navigate forward in a video because they want to get the gist of the content before they watch the entire video (65%, n = 26) while some participants typically navigate backwards because it helps them remember the content (75%, n = 30). Participants also changed the playback speed in videos because speeding up saves them time (37.5%, n = 15), they are familiar with the content (35%, n = 14), or because the speaker talks too slowly or too quickly (32.5%, n = 13). Two participants mentioned "other", however, the responses are unclear in explaining their intentions to change the playback speed of videos ("normal speed" and "do not change"). Interestingly, participants report only 'sometimes' pausing videos to take notes (35%, n = 14) or 'never' (30%, n = 12). When asked what features participants would find useful when watching instructional videos, they indicated 'highlighting sections of the video' the most useful (65%, n = 26), followed by 'annotating on the video itself' (40%, n = 16).

3.2 Experiment 1B

Comprehension Accuracy. A 2 (Educator Type: Digital Human Avatar or Anime Avatar) × 2 (Content Difficulty: Easy or Hard) ANOVA showed no significant main effect of content difficulty, $F(1, 16) = .02, p = .905, \eta_P^2 = .001$, and no significant main effect of educator type, $F(1, 16) = .44, p = .518, \eta_P^2 = .027$. In addition, there was no significant interaction of the two variables, $F(1, 16) = .71, p = .411, \eta_P^2 = .043$. Results suggest there are no differences between the two avatar types when it comes to comprehension.

Paas Scale for Mental Effort. A 2 (Educator Type: Digital Human Avatar or Anime Avatar) × 2 (Content Difficulty: Easy or Hard) ANOVA showed no significant main effects of content difficulty, $F(1, 16) = 1.16, p = .30, \eta_P^2 = .068$, or educator type, $F(1, 16) = 2.31, p = .148, \eta_P^2 = .126$. The interaction was not significant either, $F(1, 16) = .81, p = .380, \eta_P^2 = .048$. Results suggest there are no differences between the two avatar types when it comes to mental effort devoted to watching the instructional videos, but the lack of a significant effect may be due to lack of power because of the low sample size.

Trust in Automation Scale. A one-way ANOVA found no significant effects, $F(1, 16) = .20, p = .658$, of trust in automation between the digital human ($M = 60.00$) and the anime avatar ($M = 62.75$). The results may suggest that participants had similar levels of trust for the two types of avatars.

System Usability Scale (SUS). A one-way ANOVA found no significant effects, $F(1, 16) = .25, p = .621$, regarding perceived usability of the avatar types. Participants may have greater perceived usability of the digital human in the instructional videos ($M = 64.25$) than the anime avatar ($M = 59.69$), but this difference was not significant.

Learning Activity Engagement. In general, participants typically pause when watching an instructional video because something else is grabbing their attention or they need a break (50%, $n = 9$) or they want to write a note or need time to reflect on what they just watched (33.3%, $n = 6$). One participant also mentioned that they typically pause videos because it is hard for them to focus after long periods of time. Most participants also navigate forward in a video because they find the content irrelevant, boring or already known to them (50%, $n = 9$). Some participants typically navigate backwards because they zoned out or got distracted (61.1%, $n = 11$). Participants also change the playback speed in videos because the speaker talks too slowly or too quickly (55.6%, $n = 10$) or speed up the playback to save them time (44.4%, $n = 8$). Two participants mentioned "other", however, the responses are unclear in explaining their intentions to change the playback speed of videos ("do not" and "I didn't fast forward"). When asked how often participants pause the videos to take notes, six participants (33.3%) reported only 'sometimes' while others reported 'very often' (27.8%, $n = 5$) or 'rarely' (27.8%, $n = 5$). When asked what features participants would find useful when watching instructional videos, they reported 'annotating on the video itself' (72.2%, n = 13) followed by 'highlighting sections of the video' (66.7%, $n = 12$). One participant reported they would use none of the features.

4 Discussion

Effectiveness of Digital Avatars in Engagement and Comprehension. Although it was anticipated that digital human avatars would be more effective in increasing student engagement, and as a result, better comprehension of the content, the opposite was found. This finding is counter to prior research where digital avatars have found to be more impactful in increasing engagement (Segaran et al., 2021). Use of avatars may only be more favorable among younger high school students compared to college students. Younger students might view the digital human avatar to be more engaging than a traditional professor as the avatar bears similar resemblance to various forms of digital entertainment they are familiar with, such as characters in video games, movies, and educational animated videos. College students also might not find digital avatars effective in increasing engagement because they may find face-to-face interaction more impactful when improving learning outcomes. For instance, being able to see the professor's expressions and emotions can provide a more interpersonal connection between the professor and students, leading to increased engagement (Aldossari and Altalhab, 2022; Gunasekara et al., 2022).

Additionally, the effectiveness of avatars might also vary when it comes to the complexity of the lecture material. Implementing digital avatars in college courses might not be as effective compared to elementary courses since engagement in college courses relies more on the professor's lesson plan and ability to teach the material. As seen from the results, participants reported higher effort and scored higher on the comprehension questions in the hard videos and when they had the human instructor compared to the digital human instructor condition for Experiment 1A. However, the results are still unclear between educator type and content difficulty and whether one avatar would lead to greater engagement in the easy or hard videos.

Even though the use of avatars can positively impact engagement in online learning platforms compared to a human professor, it may only be effective for a short period of time. Digital avatars stray away from the traditional learning setting and implement modern technology that offers a new and exciting way to engage students in online learning. Additionally, the long-term use of digital avatars may lose its novelty to students who enroll in online learning courses often, and levels of engagement may not be as effective or high compared to when they first started. Overall, students who are not engaged will be inattentive and their focus will not be on the lecture material.

Mental Effort. As found in Experiment 1A (MTurk), participants exerted more mental effort in the instructional videos with the human instructor condition compared to the digital human condition. The reason may be due to participants being more attentive, leading them to put more cognitive effort into their mental workspace. In other words, participants might have had the feeling they had to exert more effort into being attentive enough to cognitively process the information (Bruya and Tang, 2018). Although there were no significant effects or interaction found in Experiment 1B (SONA), suggesting that the different types of avatars do not matter, future research should use a larger sample to explore further how different avatars can affect mental effort and attention. This study was limited in the number of participants available for the study.

When participants are paying more attention to the content, they are exerting more effort, therefore, they have more cognitive load in information processing from the effort exerted to be attentive to the lecture material (Kahneman, 1973). Moreover, with the human instructor being presented in a small corner of the screen, it may have played a role in allowing participants to be more attentive to the content and perform better on the comprehension questions (Bai and Vu, 2022). As a result, the human instructor's presence is more impactful and serves an important role in not only helping participants maintain attention, but also increasing participant engagement and learning outcomes. Having an instructor's presence can also improve visual attention in instructional videos that cover easy, conceptual topics, which has led to increased comprehension and learning (Wang and Antonenko, 2017). Additionally, participants may feel that they are being observed and evaluated more effectively from a human instructor, leading them to be more motivated to learn and perform better.

Trust in Automation. In both Experiment 1A and 1B, results suggest that participants had moderate trust across the two educator types. Moreover, participants generally did not view one avatar to be more trustworthy, and they might not have felt a higher sense of trust with the avatar in their respective conditions. Although participants' levels of trust were relatively similar across the anime avatar and digital human avatar condition, the anime avatar condition in particular received slightly more trust. Developers have long strived to create virtual avatars that are more realistic because they are believed to be preferred over less realistic avatars. However, participants may have had less trust in the digital human avatar due to the uncanny valley effect, where characteristics of humanoid figures that closely resemble realistic humans can evoke an eerie feeling and cause uneasiness (Stein and Ohler, 2017).

Even though the digital human avatar portrayed a higher level of realism compared to the anime avatar, there were also subtle imperfections that could have been unsettling. Participants can recognize that the avatar is portraying more human-like characteristics but minor distortions due to glitches and lower quality resolution can negatively impact emotional connectedness. For example, even when the digital human avatar's expressions and movements on screen syncs with the human instructor behind the screen, it may not be completely well calibrated, so oftentimes, the eyes and mouth movements would look out of place and the sense of familiarity with the instructor decreases (Stein and Ohler, 2017). Since familiarity is linked to the feeling of instructor presence and can induce positive emotional experiences, researchers should explore ways to design avatars to not only display a high level of realism in their appearances, but also express realistic emotions to evoke a sense of familiarity and personality to the avatar (Koschate et al., 2016). Given that a more human-like appearance stimulates a sense of familiarity, it still produces a disconcerting feeling if it does not mirror the natural and realistic human emotions and expressions. For instance, making smooth motions and having the avatar's eyes be responsive to various expressions, since the eyes are the most expressive feature that presents a sense of realism (Hsu, 2012). Additionally, implementing these emotionally expressive details to the design of avatars will help reduce the uncanny effect (Tinwell et al., 2013). Although realistic human avatars provide a sense of trust, closeness, and familiarity compared to unrealistic animated 2D avatars, the uncanny valley phenomenon still exists, therefore, it is imperative to design avatars to appear realistic and portray human-like expressive emotions that evoke a sense of connectedness and trust in the avatar (Seymour et al., 2021).

5   Limitations

There are various factors that may have affected participants' comprehension accuracy and engagement levels. Although quality control questions were answered correctly, it does not indicate that participants were fully attentive and watched the entirety of all the instructional videos. In other words, participants might skip through sections in the videos or completely skip the entire video, and provide guesses to the comprehension questions, resulting in their comprehension scores and engagement levels to be not as accurate. The researcher also cannot accurately determine whether participants were fully attentive and engaged since the study does not control for when participants exit the quiz and retake it again at a later time. Time constraints may also prevent participants from maintaining attention and taking their time to accurately answer the comprehension questions, causing them to rush and only answer the first half correctly.

Additionally, given that participants vary in age between Experiment 1A (MTurk participants) and Experiment 1B (SONA participants), so their exposure to the content may differ. Experiment 1A has participants with diverse age groups ranging from 21–61 compared to Experiment 1B whose age group is only from 18–22; this may affect Experiment 1B participants' performance since they may have prior knowledge throughout their educational experiences, which can affect their performance on the comprehension questions. There also might have been some confusion when answering the learning activity engagement questionnaire where a few participants misinterpreted the questions being related to the instructional videos in the study as found in the "Other" response (e.g., normal speed, nothing to change, do not, I didn't fast forward).

Future research should address issues related to participants not watching the videos entirely. Researchers may opt to make the comprehension section more engaging by implementing interactive features that allow for students to answer the comprehension questions by having the questions displayed throughout the video instead of at the end. Gamification features, such as a point system, can also be implemented into comprehension questions to provide instant feedback to students as they watch the instructional videos. Questions can also be made more interactive by adding more visual effects that draw the user's attention to answering the question. For example, when students answer questions correctly, a pop-up check mark can be used as feedback. Instead of quizzes, they may also be approached as knowledge check questions, to reduce stress and anxiety often associated with graded quizzes.

6   Conclusion

The findings from this study provided preliminary data for understanding the impact of avatar-based teaching on engagement in online course lecture videos. If avatar-based teaching leads to better engagement, it would be recommended to use avatars in future online teaching platforms, as well as introduce more asynchronous classes. The present study did not find any advantage of using avatars over a human instructor; however, there were limitations of the present study that prevent firm conclusions at this time. With many instructional modes shifting to online platforms, it is important to consider avatar based teaching and various learning methods to make remote learning and online classrooms more engaging, interactive, and enjoyable. Additionally, significant effects for avatar-based teaching can also encourage the use of modern technology for online instruction to enhance virtual teaching and learning. Although these methods stray away from the traditional learning practices, determining which form of presentation leads to the best engagement will allow educators to recommend best practices in the future design of online teaching or educational games to not only improve learning outcomes, but also ensure that students are receiving a valuable learning experience (Nizam et al., 2022).

References

Alblehai, F.M.: Individual experience and engagement in avatar-mediated environments: the mediating effect of interpersonal attraction. J. Educ. Comput. Res. **60**(4), 986–1007 (2021). https://doi.org/10.1177/07356331211051023

Aldossari, S., Altalhab, S.: Distance learning during COVID-19: EFL students' engagement and motivation from teachers' perspective. English Lang. Teach. **15**(7), 85–109 (2022). https://eric.ed.gov/?id=EJ1352566

Bai, X., Vu, K.P.L.: Online learning: does integrated video lecture help you learn more efficiently?. In: Duffy, V.G., Lehto, M., Yih, Y., Proctor, R.W. (eds.) Human-Automation Interaction. Automation, Collaboration, & E-Services, vol. 10, pp. 531–548. Springer, Cham (2022). https://doi.org/10.1007/978-3-031-10780-1_29

Bashir, A., Bashir, S., Rana, K., Lambert, P., Vernallis, A.: Post-COVID-19 adaptations; The shifts towards online learning, hybrid course delivery and the implications for biosciences courses in the higher education setting. Front. Educ. **6** (2021). https://doi.org/10.3389/feduc.2021.711619

Blake, A.M., Moseley, J.L.: The emerging technology of avatars: some educational considerations. Educ. Technol. 13–20 (2010). https://www.jstor.org/stable/44429772

Bruya, B., Tang, Y.Y.: Is attention really effort? Revisiting Daniel Kahneman's influential 1973 book attention and effort. Front. Psychol. **9**, 1133 (2018). https://doi.org/10.3389/fpsyg.2018.01133

Costley, J., Fanguy, M., Lange, C., Baldwin, M.: The effects of video lecture viewing strategies on cognitive load. J. Comput. High. Educ. **33**, 19–38 (2021). https://doi.org/10.1007/s12528-020-09254-y

Darejeh, A., Marcus, N., Sweller, J.: The effect of narrative-based E-learning systems on novice users' cognitive load while learning software applications. Educ. Technol. Res. Dev. **69**, 2451–2473 (2021). https://doi.org/10.1007/s11423-021-10024-5

Dumford, A.D., Miller, A.L.: Online learning in higher education: exploring advantages and disadvantages for engagement. J. Comput. High. Educ. **30**, 452–465 (2018). https://doi.org/10.1007/s12528-018-9179-z

Gunasekara, A., Turner, K., Fung, C.Y., Stough, C.: Impact of lecturers' emotional intelligence on students' learning and engagement in remote learning spaces: a cross-cultural study. Aust. J. Educ. Technol. **38**(4), 112–126 (2022). https://doi.org/10.14742/ajet.7848

Hsieh, R., Shirai, A., Sato, H.: Effectiveness of facial animated avatar and voice transformer in elearning programming course. In: ACM SIGGRAPH 2019 Posters, 1–2 (2019).https://doi.org/10.1145/3306214.3338540

Hsu, J.: Why uncanny valley human look alikes put us on edge. Sci. Am. (2012). https://www.scientificamerican.com/article/why-uncanny-valley-human-look-alikes-put-us-on-edge/

Jensen, S.A.: In-class versus online video lectures: similar learning outcomes, but a preference for in-class. Teach. Psychol. **38**(4), 298–302 (2011). https://doi.org/10.1177/0098628311421336

Jian, J.-Y., Bisantz, A.M., Drury, C.G.: Foundations for an empirically determined scale of trust in automated systems. Int. J. Cogn. Ergon. **4**(1), 53–71 (2000). https://doi.org/10.1207/s15327566ijce0401_04

Jian, J.-Y., Bisantz, A.M., Drury, C.G., Llinas, J.: Foundations for an empirically determined scale of trust in automated systems. Technical report CMIF198. Air Force Research Laboratory (1998). http://www.dtic.mil/get-tr-doc/pdf?AD=ADA395339

Kahneman, D.: Attention and Effort, vol. 1063, pp. 218–226. Prentice-Hall, Englewood Cliffs (1973)

Kao, D., Harrell, D.F.: Exploring the effects of dynamic avatar on performance and engagement in educational games (2016). https://www.researchgate.net/publication/321994584_Exploring_the_Effects_of_Dynamic_Avatar_on_Performance_and_Engagement_in_Educational_Games

Kao, D.: The effects of anthropomorphic avatars vs. non-anthropomorphic avatars in a jumping game. In: Proceedings of the 14th International Conference on the Foundations of Digital Games, pp. 1–5 (2019). https://doi.org/10.1145/3337722.3341829

Koschate, M., Potter, R., Bremner, P., Levine, M.: Overcoming the uncanny valley: displays of emotions reduce the uncanniness of humanlike robots. In: 2016 11th ACM/IEEE International Conference on Human-Robot Interaction (HRI), pp. 359–366. IEEE (2016). https://doi.org/10.1109/HRI.2016.7451773

Lewis, J.R.: The system usability scale: past, present, and future. Int. J. Hum.-Comput. Interact. **34**(7), 577–590 (2018)

Nizam, M.D., Rudiyansah, N.D., Tuah, M.N., Sani, H.A.Z.: Avatar design types and user engagement in digital educational games during evaluation phase. Int. J. Electr. Comput. Eng. **12**(6), 6449–6460 (2022). https://doi.org/10.11591/ijece.v12i6.pp6449-6460s

Palvia, S., et al.: Online education: worldwide status, challenges, trends, and implications. J. Glob. Inf. Technol. Manag. **21**(4), 233–241 (2018). https://doi.org/10.1080/1097198X.2018.1542262

Pass, F.G.W.C.: Training strategies for attaining transfer of problem-solving skill in statistics: a cognitive load approach. J. Educ. Psychol. **84**(4), 429–434 (1992)

Quesada-Pallarès, C., Sánchez-Martí, A., Ciraso-Calí, A., Pineda-Herrero, P.: Online vs. classroom learning: examining motivational and self-regulated learning strategies among vocational education and training students. Front. Psychol. **10**, 2795 (2019). https://doi.org/10.3389/fpsyg.2019.02795

Santos-Guevara, N.B., Rincón-Flores, E.G.: Avatars and badges, are there differences between genders? In: 2021 IEEE Global Engineering Education Conference, pp. 334–338 (2021). https://doi.org/10.1109/EDUCON46332.2021.9454126

Schacter, D.L., Szpunar, K.K.: Enhancing attention and memory during video-recorded lectures. Scholarsh. Teach. Learn. Psychol. **1**(1), 60 (2015). https://doi.org/10.1037/stl0000011

Schöbel, S., Janson, A., Mishra, A.: A configurational view on avatar design–the role of emotional attachment, satisfaction, and cognitive load in digital learning. In: Fortieth International Conference on Information Systems, Munich (2019). https://doi.org/10.2139/ssrn.3524079

Segaran, K., Mohamad Ali, A.Z., Hoe, T.W.: Does avatar design in educational games promote a positive emotional experience among learners? E-Learn. Digit. Media **18**(5), 422–440 (2021). https://doi.org/10.1177/2042753021994337

Seo, K., Dodson, S., Harandi, N.M., Roberson, N., Fels, S., Roll, I.: Video-based learning activity engagement measure [database record]. Retrieved from PsycTESTS (2021). https://doi.org/10.1037/t81381-000

Seymour, M., Yuan, L. I., Dennis, A., Riemer, K.: Have we crossed the uncanny valley? Understanding affinity, trustworthiness, and preference for realistic digital humans in immersive environments. J. Assoc. Inf. Syst. **22**(3), 9 (2021). https://doi.org/10.17705/1jais.00674

Stein, J.P., Ohler, P.: Venturing into the uncanny valley of mind—the influence of mind attribution on the acceptance of human-like characters in a virtual reality setting. Cognition **160**, 43–50 (2017). https://doi.org/10.1016/j.cognition.2016.12.010

Tinwell, A., Nabi, D.A., Charlton, J.P.: Perception of psychopathy and the uncanny valley in virtual characters. Comput. Hum. Behav. **29**(4), 1617–1625 (2013). https://doi.org/10.1016/j.chb.2013.01.008

Wang, J., Antonenko, P.D.: Instructor presence in instructional video: effects on visual attention, recall, and perceived learning. Comput. Hum. Behav. **71**, 79–89 (2017). https://doi.org/10.1016/j.chb.2017.01.049

Development of an Eye-Movement Training System that Can Be Easily Used by Students Alone in Special Instructional Classrooms

Kosei Inoue[1]([✉]), Saizo Aoyagi[2] [iD], Satoshi Fukumori[3], Michiya Yamamoto[1] [iD], Yukie Isaka[4], and Katsuya Kitade[5]

[1] Kwansei Gakuin University, Sanda 669-1330, Hyogo, Japan
gqn06487@kwansei.ac.jp
[2] Komazawa University, Setagaya 154-8525, Tokyo, Japan
[3] Kagawa University, Takamatsu 761-0396, Kagawa, Japan
[4] Kokufu Elementary School, Izumi 594-0071, Osaka, Japan
[5] Vision Training Center JoyVision, Kobe 650-0021, Hyogo, Japan

Abstract. As a result of inexperienced eye movements, children or students may suffer from learning disabilities or encounter difficulties playing sports. In previous studies, we have developed an eye-movement training system using an eye tracker and indexes to assess eye movement. In this study, we developed a prototype for an eye-movement training system for students in special instructional classrooms in elementary school. In particular, we developed video-creation formats and game-like interface so that students can use the system alone easily in special instructional classrooms. The results of the field evaluation demonstrated the system's effectiveness in elementary school.

Keywords: vision therapy · eye-movement training · eye tracker · gaze interaction · special instructional classrooms

1 Introduction

In recent years, the number of students with learning disabilities has increased in Japan. According to a survey by the Ministry of Education, Culture, Sports, Science and Technology (MEXT), it was 18.4% in 2012, but it increased up to 28.7% in 2022 [1]. Special educational support is required for these children, and as a part of this, special instructional classrooms have been established to provide that [2]. However, special instructional classrooms and the special educational support there have not spread sufficiently, so MEXT prepared guidance web for unfamiliar teachers [3] and published a collection of practical examples [4] in 2020.

The students there suffered from various kinds of learning disabilities, such as difficulties in learning and behavioral aspects. In this study, we focused on eye-movement training, which is expected to be effective for learning such as reading and writing. Eye-movement training is reported to be effective in improving learning and behavior by promoting eye movements in addition to visual acuity [5].

© The Author(s), under exclusive license to Springer Nature Switzerland AG 2024
H. Mori and Y. Asahi (Eds.): HCII 2024, LNCS 14691, pp. 59–71, 2024.
https://doi.org/10.1007/978-3-031-60125-5_5

Authors have already developed an eye movement assessing and training system using a PC and an eye tracker, developed an original index to evaluate eye movements during eye-movement training, and demonstrated its effectiveness by comparison with assessments by experts [6, 7]. In this study, we propose a system that allows students to perform eye-movement training alone in special instructional classrooms.

2 Concept

The availability of eye-movement training using PCs and eye tracking devices in special education classrooms would be an effective solution for students with learning difficulties. However, to propagate this kind of system, it is necessary to consider that teachers are not accustomed to special instructional classrooms and that the teaching materials used there are created through trial and error to fit each student. In addition, contrary to the national standard, one teacher is assigned to every 13 students [8], but, currently, a teacher must be in charge of an immense number of students [9] – for example, about 90 students in our case. Based on this, we propose the following eye-movement training system for special instructional classrooms.

1. Teachers install an eye-movement training system on the desks of special instructional classrooms.
2. Students there conduct eye movement assessment/training by their own will and by following teachers' advice.
3. The students who want to use the system can use it alone.
4. In 3, students can use the system in an enjoyable way as if they are watching attractive videos or playing games but not in the assessment procedure.
5. In 3, we make the assessment accurate and precise in order to measure daily eye movement and the training procedure.
6. In 3–5, we make it available to record a log of system usage in each class and for each student.

Item 1 enables us to operate the system in typical special instructional classrooms without preparing specific facilities. Items 2 and 3 are essential in ensuring little or no increase in teachers' workload because students can use the system alone or with slight teacher assistance. Item 4 is used to promote the system's use by students themselves. Item 5 is necessary to make the system as an assessment and training tool. Item 6 is useful for personal instruction by recording, checking, and analyzing students' attitudes in daily use.

3 System Development

3.1 Hardware Development

Before developing the system proposed in Sect. 2, we first considered item 1 so that we could install the system on a desk in a regular elementary school classroom. Here, we checked the desk size (600 mm × 400 mm according to the old JIS standard, 650 mm × 450 mm according to the new JIS standard) and used a 17.3-inch display (cocopar,

JSJ-173). We used a mini-PC (Intel, NUC11PAHI5) that could be attached to the VESA mount on the back of the display. An eye tracker (Tobii, Eye Tracker 5) and a web camera (Logitech, C922n) were connected to the PC, making it possible to capture gaze and videos.

Additionally, we developed an enclosure to house this hardware. This enclosure was designed to minimize sharp corners for safety during use in special instructional classrooms, evoke a sense of desire for use by students, as proposed in item 2, and eliminate the appearance of a typical inspection device as in item 4. Consequently, we designed a friendly, rounded enclosure as depicted in Fig. 1. This enclosure was 3D printed and housed components such as the aforementioned display and PC. Additionally, we applied a soft, warm acrylic coating as shown in Fig. 2.

Fig. 1. Hardware design.

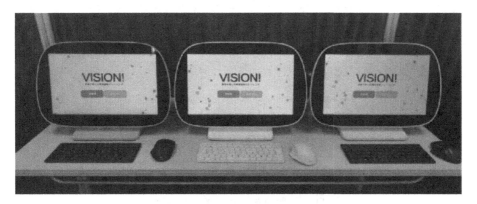

Fig. 2. Overview of the eye-movement training systems.

3.2 Software Development and Operation Confirmation

We installed Windows 10 as an OS on the mini-PC. The development was done using Unity 2020.3.18f1 from Unity Technologies and Tobii Unity SDK for Desktop. For items

3 and 4, we developed a software capable of playing MP4-format videos and measuring gaze during eye-movement training while watching videos. Instead of introducing gaze interaction, where gaze may be lost for some time, we adopted video watching. This decision was aimed at encouraging continuous training by making the system enjoyable during daily use. Furthermore, the software allowed users to store multiple videos, enabling them to freely select from a list of videos they wished to play (Fig. 3).

Fig. 3. A screenshot of video list.

Figures 4 and 5 illustrate examples measured in using this hardware and software. The display resolution was 1920 × 1080 pixels, with the top-left corner of the display serving as the origin for plotting the coordinates of the gaze point. In Fig. 4, the plotted values represent the x and y coordinates of the gaze point when the object of fixation jumps from right to left, showing the movement of the gaze point. Similarly, in Fig. 5, the plotted values represent the x and y coordinates of the gaze point when the object of fixation moves from right to left, demonstrating the movement of the gaze point.

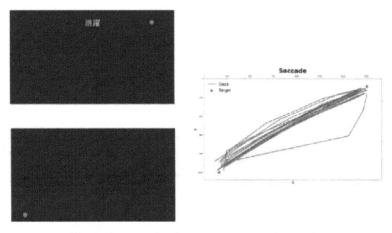

Fig. 4. An example of measurement smooth saccade.

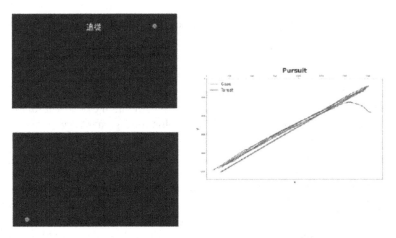

Fig. 5. An example of smooth-pursuit measurement.

Furthermore, we implemented a system in which one account is issued per classroom where the system is installed. This allows each student to create and select their own user profile, enabling the storage of individual usage history and other related data to comply with item 6. The video contents of the saccadic eye-movement training and pursuit eye-movement training are created, as shown in Figs. 6 and 7, respectively. These videos feature targets such as characters that participants can track with their eyes to engage in the respective training exercises.

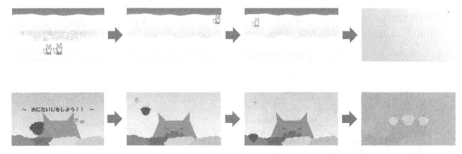

Fig. 6. Examples of the video for saccade training (up: fox, down: demon slaying)

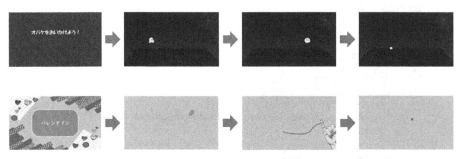

Fig. 7. Examples of the video for pursuit training (up: ghost, down: Valentine's Day)

3.3 Mini-game for Gaze Measurement

To ensure accurate eye tracking measurements, even when a child is using the system by themselves, as proposed in item 5, it is crucial to maintain the head within the range where eye tracking is feasible. Therefore, we develop mini-games to guide the position of the head appropriately, as shown in Figs. 8 and 9, because many children in special instruction classrooms tend to have ADHD. In Fig. 8, the head position is represented by the meat and frying pan, with the range of measurement displayed by the stove. By moving the head to the position where the meat is cooking on the stove, the head position is appropriately adjusted. Similarly, in Fig. 9, the facial puzzle panel is used to guide the movement of the head position, encouraging it to fit into the panel accurately.

On December 13 and 14, 2022, a two-day experiment was conducted in a special instructional classroom in Izumi City Kokufu Elementary School, Osaka, Japan, to determine whether the system could be adequately used, especially whether the developed mini-game could be properly integrated into eye tracking. One of the authors described this experiment to the participants, and parents' consent was obtained. Over the course of the experiment, over 80 children came to the classroom. About 20 of the students participated in this experiment.

During this experiment, the authors acted as experimenters, providing verbal instructions and explanations of the system without adjusting the positions of chairs or tilting the displays. As a result, all children were able to position their heads within the designated range and performed the training (Fig. 10). Additionally, it was observed that the

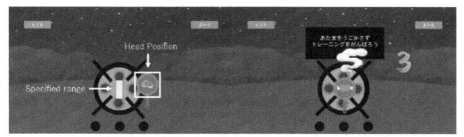

Fig. 8. Implemented head position guidance scene (grilled meat).

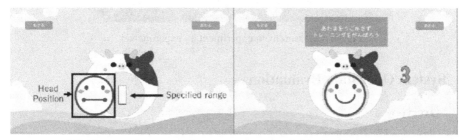

Fig. 9. Implemented head position guidance scene (face panel).

children enjoyed the interactive experience of objects moving in correspondence with their head movements (Fig. 11).

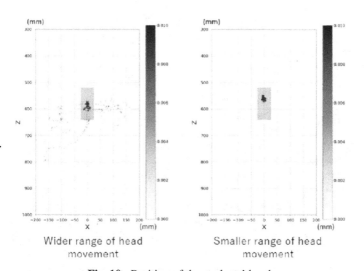

Fig. 10. Position of the students' head.

Fig. 11. Measurement experiment by experimenter.

4 System Operation Evaluation

4.1 Overview

In Sect. 3, we developed a system that satisfies items 1–6. We installed the system in a special instructional classroom of Izumi City Kokufu Elementary School and conducted an operation evaluation. Here, after only explaining how to use the system in advance, we did not go to the site during the period, and we allowed the children to use the system by themselves without specifying the type of video, number of training sessions, and training time (Fig. 12). We prepared one video each for training and measurement, as shown in

Fig. 12. Experimental scenery in Kokufu Elementary School.

Figs. 6 and 7, respectively, with three types each for saccadic eye movements and smooth-pursuit eye movements. The operational period spanned 7 weeks from January 30, 2023, to March 20, 2023, totaling 35 days, excluding weekends and holidays.

4.2 Evaluation of Measurement Accuracy

First, we evaluated the measurement accuracy from January 30 to February 13. Here, we calculated the ratio of measurement (measured frames/total frames) by judging whether the users' heads were in the range of measurement. We also compared the results with the cases of full assistance (experimenters adjusted chair positions and display tilts, performed in July 2022) and verbal assistance (experimenters offered advice for properly using the system, performed in December 2022). In full assistance, 23 training sessions were conducted by 23 participants, and in verbal assistance, 100 training sessions were conducted with 24 participants. In this no-assistance evaluation, 135 training sessions were conducted with 24 participants. The results are shown in Fig. 13. The average ratios of measurement for full assistance, verbal assistance, and no-assistance were 93.3%, 88.7%, and 75.8%, respectively. Excluding the three individuals who exhibited extremely low ratio of measurement in the no-assistance evaluation, the average was 81%. Figure 14 illustrates the actual measurement examples. According to the introduction of the mini-game developed in Sect. 3, eye tracking accuracy was at the same level compared to full or verbal assistance. Thus, the development of an eye-movement training system that children could use by themselves proved to be successful.

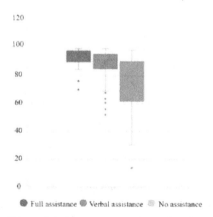

Fig. 13. Results of the ratio of measurement depending on types of assistance.

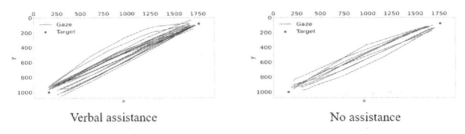

Verbal assistance   No assistance

Fig. 14. Examples of gaze measurement results with or without assistance.

4.3 Operation Results

As shown in Sect. 4.2, accurate gaze tracking was achieved. Consequently, the system was operated until March 20, 2023. Throughout this operational period, 31 individuals participated in the training, totaling 368 training sessions. Figure 15 illustrates the number of training sessions per user. Seventeen children utilized the system seven times or more (approximately once a week) on average. Additionally, approximately 90 children attended the special needs education class that year.

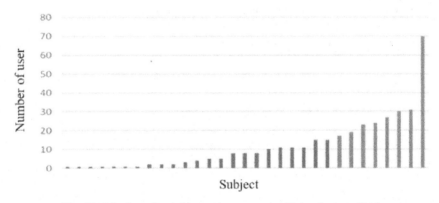

Fig. 15. Number of training sessions per user. (Color figure online)

To assess the training status, we conducted an analysis focusing on the measurement data of eight students (highlighted in orange in Fig. 15) who had a high number of training sessions and consistently used the system throughout the period. The results of this analysis are summarized in Table 1.

Here, we labeled the eight individuals from the collaborators with a high number of training sessions as A to H. We utilized the S_{eo}, developed in previous research [6, 7], as an index for the effectiveness of training. Additionally, we calculated the correlation coefficient between the number of training sessions and the values of the index for each student. Here direction 1 was from top right to bottom left. Direction 2 was the opposite.

Because a lower S_{eo} value indicates better eye movement, it is desirable to observe a negative correlation with the training period. However, in the results of this operational

Table 1. Eye movement characteristics of frequently used users.

Saccade	Number of training	Number of saccades	Analyzable data	S_{eo} Minimum	S_{eo} Max	Direction 1 S_{eo} correlation coefficient	Direction 2 S_{eo} correlation coefficient
Individual A	70	42	69/84	1.06	8.90	−0.03	0.26
Individual B	31	24	56/48	0.63	1.73	−0.08	0.29
Individual C	30	16	24/32	1.11	3.84	0.59	0.41
Individual D	27	22	23/30	0.74	2.60	0.03	−0.13
Individual E	24	14	24/28	0.94	4.47	0.23	0.50
Individual F	23	14	24/28	1.17	2.00	0.38	0.42
Individual G	19	12	20/24	0.95	2.27	−0.05	0.46
Individual H	17	11	14/22	0.96	5.53	0.49	0.33

evaluation, small correlation was observed. In this special instructional classroom, eye-movement trainings without our system have been performed, and this experiment was conducted at the end of the fiscal year. So, the eye movement abilities of the students may have already improved beyond the level of those with learning difficulties.

Another reason for this was the lack of concentration of students in training. This resulted in the inability to accurately measure participants' real capabilities. For instance, Table 1 shows several instances of data that were not analyzable; for example, only 75% of the data were suitable for the analysis of training effects in the case of participant C, and only 63% of the data were suitable for participant H. To verify whether the children were concentrating during the measurements, we compared the data when the eye movement error values were small and when they were large in the daily measurements of participant A (Fig. 16). The comparison suggested that the eyes may not have moved the specified number of times on certain days.

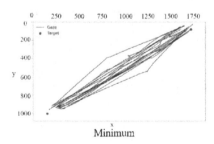
Minimum

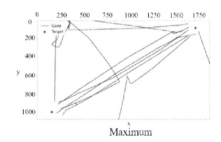
Maximum

Fig. 16. Comparison of measurement results when the value of eye movement error is at its minimum and maximum (saccade).

5 Conclusion

In this study, we proposed an eye-movement training system that can be used by individual students in special instructional classrooms, developed the system, conducted operational evaluation experiments, and demonstrated its effectiveness. In particular, we proposed a system where students could perform eye movement assessment and training while watching videos using a PC, and an eye tracking device was effective. According to the repeated operational evaluations and ongoing problem-solving efforts, we successfully developed a system that students can use alone easily. Although the teaching materials in special instructional classrooms are still evolving, we hope this system will be widely used to overcome difficulties in reading and sports skills at an early stage.

References

1. Ministry of Education, Culture, Sports, Science and Technology (MEXT) Elementary and Secondary Education Bureau Special Support Education Division: Results of a Survey on Students with Special Educational Needs Enrolled in Regular Classes, MEXT Elementary and Secondary Education Bureau Special Support Education Division (online) (in Japanese). https://www.mext.go.jp/content/20230524-mext-tokubetu01-000026255_01.pdf. Accessed 16 Feb 2024
2. MEXT Elementary and Secondary Education Bureau Special Support Education Division: Elementary School Curriculum Guidelines, MEXT Elementary and Secondary Education Bureau Special Support Education Division (online). (in Japanese). https://www.mext.go.jp/a_menu/shotou/new-cs/1387014.htm. Accessed 16 Feb 2024
3. MEXT Elementary and Secondary Education Bureau Special Support Education Division: A Guide for Teachers of Special Instructional Classrooms for the First Time. MEXT (online). (in Japanese). https://www.mext.go.jp/tsukyu-guide/common/pdf/passing_guide_02.pdf. Accessed 16 Feb 2024
4. MEXT: Practical Case Studies of Project to Improve Expertise about Developmental Disabilities for Teachers of Special Instructional Classroom, MEXT (online). (in Japanese). https://www.mext.go.jp/a_menu/shotou/tokubetu/main/006/h29/1421549.htm. Accessed 16 Feb 2024
5. Dawkins, H., Edelman, E., Forkiotis, C., Williams, R.: Suddenly Successful Student and Friends, The Writing Team (2012)
6. Kita, R., Yamamoto, M., Kitade, K.: Development of a vision training system using an eye tracker by analyzing users' eye movements. In: Stephanidis, C., et al. (eds.) HCI International 2020 – Late Breaking Papers: Interaction, Knowledge and Social Media. HCII 2020. LNCS, vol. 12427, pp. 371–382. Springer, Cham (2020). https://doi.org/10.1007/978-3-030-60152-2_28
7. Fukumori, S., Kita, R., Aoyagi, S., Yamamoto, M., Kitade K.: Development of assessment indices for an eye-movement test and vision training. Trans. Hum. Interface Soc. **24**(2), 121–132 (2022). (in Japanese)

8. MEXT Elementary and Secondary Education Bureau Special Support Education Division: Current Status of Special Instructional Classrooms, Ministry of Education, Culture, Sports, Science and Technology Elementary and Secondary Education Bureau Special Support Education Division (online). (in Japanese). https://www.mext.go.jp/component/a_menu/education/micro_detail/__icsFiles/afieldfile/2019/03/06/1414032_09.pdf. Accessed 16 Feb 2024
9. Nakao, A., Aoyagi, S., Yamamoto, M., Kitade, K., Isaka, Y.: Development of a vision training system for children in coaching classes for children with special needs. In: Proceedings of the Human Interface Symposium 2023, pp. 549–552 (2022). (in Japanese)

Development of Learning Support System for Acquisition of Convincing Argument Methods

Akio Kobashi[1]([✉]), Tomoya Horiguchi[1], and Tsukasa Hirashima[2]

[1] Graduate School of Maritime Sciences, Kobe University, Kobe, Japan
akio0121kobac@gmail.com

[2] Graduate School of Advanced Science and Engineering, Hiroshima University, Higashihiroshima, Japan

Abstract. We developed and evaluated a learning support system for learning logical reasoning. Focusing on the ability of convincing argument, we formulated a method of improving the convincing power of deductive and abductive arguments, then defined seven educational models based on the method called "Argument Unit." We implemented a system in which learners assemble the argument structure of a given document with nodes of proposition and links of their relationship. The system then compares the structure with Argument Units and gives appropriate feedback to learners if the structure is incomplete. We conducted an experiment for evaluating the effectiveness of learning with the system. Nine university students learned a set of ways of making a convincing argument and took pre-/post-test. Both tests included 5 learning tasks. Post-test also included 5 transfer tasks. As a result, in learning tasks, scores were significantly higher in the post-test than in the pre-test. On the other hand, in transfer tasks, scores were also significantly higher in the post-test than in the pre-test. This result indicated a certain degree of learning effect in the system-based learning immediately after learning. However, the results of the task-by-task analysis suggest that the effectiveness of this system varies greatly depending on the type of argument units handled in tasks. In upcoming research, we plan to analyze whether the learning effect is maintained after a certain period of time has elapsed after learning with the system in this experiment.

Keywords: E-learning and e-education · logical reasoning · learning support system

1 Introduction

In recent years, logical thinking skills have tended to be emphasized in education. There are many different types of logical thinking skills, among which the ability to make arguments is particularly important in debate and academic writing [1]. The purpose of this research is to design and develop a learning support system that promotes the acquisition of more convincing argument methods. In this research, we assume that logical correctness in argument leads to more convincing arguments.

H. Mori and Y. Asahi (Eds.): HCII 2024, LNCS 14691, pp. 72–88, 2024.
https://doi.org/10.1007/978-3-031-60125-5_6

Various learning support systems have been developed in the research of argument learning. Many of these systems often use the Toulmin model to teach the construction of arguments (hereinafter referred to as argument structures) [2, 3]. The Toulmin model is a model of argument that does not depend on a specific area of expertise, and it expresses the elements of argument, such as claims, data, warrants, qualifiers, and backings, as well as the relationships among them. A warrant (hereinafter referred to as rule) is a general rule that applies to relatively many things, and new propositions (claims) can be derived by applying a rule to known propositions (data). In addition, the model may include backing, which is the element that proves the validity of the warrant, and rebuttal, which narrows the scope of the warrant's applicability.

Kitamura et al. proposed a model called "Triangle Logic Model," which narrows down the elements of the Toulmin model to three: claim, data, and warrant, and have conducted a series of studies on learning support systems based on this model. For example, the system proposed in the literature [4] allows learners to learn the structure of a proper argument by considering propositions that apply to the elements of claim, data, and warrant and creating argument structures. In addition, learners' structures are automatically diagnosed, and feedback is returned if they are incorrect. The system based on "Triangle Logic Model" is almost the only system that can return feedback in learning arguments. However, when making an argument, the reliability of each element of the model (propositions as data and general rules as warrants, etc.) is often insufficient. To the best of the author's knowledge, there are currently no research focusing on such aspects of argument and developing learning support systems. In this research, therefore, we formulate a method to improve the convincing power of arguments, focusing on the arguments based on two types of logical reasoning, deductive and abductive reasoning. Based on the formulation, we developed a learning support system that facilitates the acquisition of methods to improve the convincing power of arguments by logical reasoning and conducted an experimental evaluation of its learning effectiveness.

2 Research Design

2.1 Purpose

The purpose of this research is to formulate a method to improve the convincing power of arguments by deduction and abduction, to develop an interactive learning support system based on the formulated method, and to experimentally evaluate the learning effects obtained by using the learning support system.

2.2 Materials and Methods

First, based on the Toulmin model, we formulated a method to improve the convincing power of arguments. Factors that make an argument less convincing include the nature of the logical reasoning used in the argument and the insufficient reliability of the data or rules used. Deductive reasoning (hereinafter referred to as deduction) and abductive reasoning (hereinafter referred to as abduction) are two types of logical reasoning often used in argument. When there is a rule that leads from a premise (hereinafter referred to antecedent) to a conclusion (hereinafter referred to consequent), deduction is defined as reasoning that asserts that the proposition in the consequent is true using the facts in the antecedent as data. Abduction, on the other hand, is defined as reasoning that asserts that the proposition in the antecedent is true using the facts in the consequent as data. If the data and rules are correct, then a proposition derived by deduction is always logically true, while a proposition derived by abduction is not always true. This is because it is possible to explain the cause of the occurrence of the fact used as data by a proposition other than the claim, regardless of the truth of the claim. In short, arguments by abduction are less convincing than those by deduction [5]. It is also clear that regardless of the logical reasoning used, if the data and rules that make up the argument are unreliable, the argument will be less convincing. We have defined methods to reinforce data, rules, and arguments by abduction that are not sufficiently reliable, respectively, in order to improve the convincing power of the argument as a whole. The argument structure created by improving the convincing power with these methods was called an "Argument unit" (hereinafter referred to as "AU") in this research. We defined seven types of argument units. In the next section, we will demonstrate a formulated method that improves the convincing power of arguments.

Basic Argument Structure. First, we introduce basic arguments by deduction or abduction. In the rule "If A, then B," claim B is derived from data A by deduction. (Fig. 1, the red figures represent claims, and the same is true in the following figures). On the other hand, claim A is derived from data B by abduction (Fig. 2). In the figures, the proposition connected to the root of the arrow is data and the proposition connected to the tip of the arrow is a claim. The followings are reinforcements that improve the convincing power of these structures.

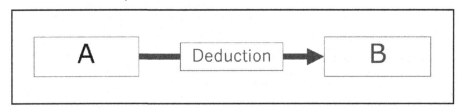

Fig. 1. Basic argument structure by deduction (Color figure online)

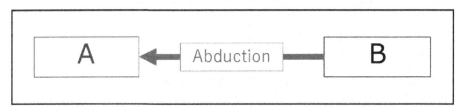

Fig. 2. Basic argument structure by abduction (Color figure online)

Limitations on the Scope of Application of the Rules. In general, it is expected that narrowing the scope of application of a rule used to derive a claim increases the accuracy of the argument, which improves the convincing power of the argument. In this research, this method of reinforcing unreliable rules is called "Limitations on the scope of application of the rules" (hereinafter referred to "rule imitation"). This corresponds to "rebuttal" in the Toulmin model. In addition, whether the basic argument is an argument by abduction (Fig. 3) or abduction (Fig. 4), the convincing power can be improved by reinforcing the argument with "rule limitation." The red boxes in Fig. 3 and Fig. 4 represent a conjunction (A and C).

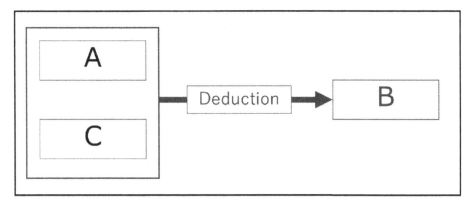

Fig. 3. Deduction: rule limitation (AU-1) (Color figure online)

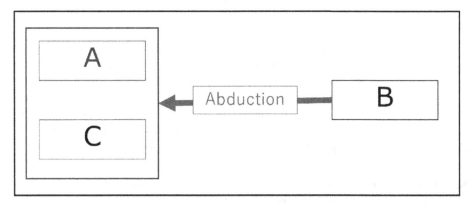

Fig. 4. Abduction: rule limitation (AU-4) (Color figure online)

Reinforcing Data. If a proposition of data for the basic argument is not sufficiently reliable, it is expected that the basic argument will be more convincing if the proposition of data is reinforced by another proposition from which it is derived. In this research, this method of reinforcing unreliable data is called "Reinforcing data." In addition, whether the basic argument is an argument by abduction (Fig. 1) or abduction (Fig. 2), the convincing power can be improved by reinforcing the argument with reinforcing data. Either deduction or abduction can be used to reinforce the data. Therefore, there are four possible combinations of reasoning methods in the basic argument and the reinforcement part of the argument (Figs. 5-1, 2, 3, 4). Among those four types of arguments, however, an argument that uses deduction when reinforcing the data used to derive a claim by abduction in the basic argument (Fig. 5-4) does not necessarily improve the convincing power of the basic argument. This is because the data of the reinforcement part will be able to explain the cause of the occurrence of the data of the basic argument, regardless of whether the claim is true or false.

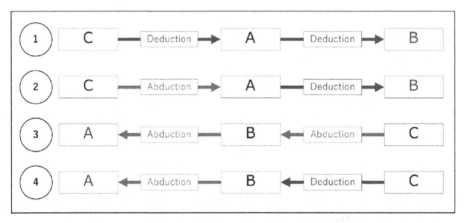

Fig. 5. Reinforcing data (1: Deduction: Reinforcing data by deduction (AU-2), 2: Deduction: Reinforcing data by abduction (AU-3), 3: Abduction: Reinforcing data by abduction (AU-5))

Adding Facts of Data. When the reasoning method of the basic argument is abduction, and the reliability of a claim derived from data is low, it is expected to improve the convincing power of the basic argument by adding another fact that can be derived from the claim as data. This is called "Adding facts of data" (hereinafter referred to "Adding data"). This method reinforces the argument by abduction. In an argument in which claim A is derived from data B by abduction in Fig. 2, the convincing power of claim A can be improved by adding data C and using data C and the rule "If A, then C" as shown in Fig. 6.

Negating Rival Proposition. When the reasoning method of a basic argument is abduction, it is expected that the convincing power of the basic argument will be improved by citing another proposition (hereinafter referred to "rival proposition.") from which data used to derive a claim can be derived, and then negating that rival proposition. This is called "Negating rival proposition." This method reinforces the argument by abduction. In an argument in which claim A is derived from data B by abduction in Fig. 2, the reliability of claim A is relatively increased by using rival proposition C and the rule "If C, then B" and then using the rule "If D, then not C" to negate proposition C, as shown in Fig. 7.

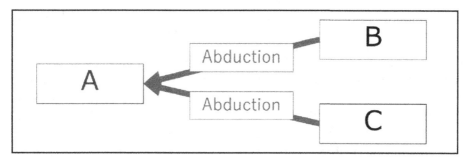

Fig. 6. Abduction: Adding facts of data (AU-6)

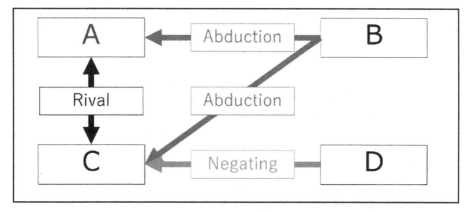

Fig. 7. Abduction: Negating rival proposition (AU-7)

2.3 The Argument Unit

The structure created by adding the rules and propositions necessary to improve convincing power to a basic argument (i.e., a claim accompanied by a rule and data that directly derive it) described in Sect. 2.2 is called an "Argument unit" in this research. We defined seven types of argument units (Table 1).

Table 1. The argument unit

Unit_id	Unit_name	Base argument	Reinforcing method
AU-1	Deduction: Rule limitaion	Deduction	Rule limitaion
AU-2	Deduction: Reinforcing data by deduction	Deduction	Reinforcing data
AU-3	Deduction: Reinforcing data by abduction	Deduction	Reinforcing data
AU-4	Abduction: Rule limitaion	Abduction	Rule limitaion
AU-5	Abduction: Reinforcing data by abduction	Abduction	Reinforcing data
AU-6	Abduction: Adding facts of data	Abduction	Adding facts of data
AU-7	Abduction: Negating rival proposition	Abduction	Negating rival proposition

The argument unit represents the smallest unit of argument that derives a claim from data in a sufficiently convincing way, and complex argument structures can be created by combining multiple argument units. In addition, when supporting the argument learning, if an argument structure (or its substructure) constructed by a student is identified as an incomplete structure of one of the argument units, educational information can be explicitly provided on what reinforcements should be added to make it a complete structure (i.e., an argument that is sufficiently convincing).

3   Experiment Design

3.1   Hypothesis

In order to verify the validity and usefulness of the author's framework in supporting the learning of argument, we developed a learning support system based on the framework and conducted a learning experiment by using it to evaluate its effectiveness with the following hypotheses.

1. Learning with the learning support system will improve the ability to create argument structures in tasks the learners did once.
2. Learning with the learning support system will also improve the ability to create argument structures in tasks the learners did for the first time.

3.2   Learning Support System

In this study, we developed an interactive learning support system based on the formulated method described in Sect. 2.2. Figure 8 shows the operation screen of the system. Subjects read a given text and create argument structures in the text in the system.

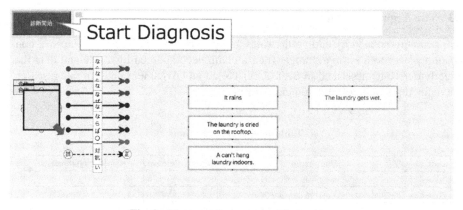

Fig. 8. The operation screen of the system

This system has the function that asks subjects to create argument structures as a graph using proposition nodes (claim and data) and links (deduction, abduction, rival and negation) that indicate the relationship between them. This system also has the function that diagnoses the argument structures created by the subjects by matching it against the argument unit and gives appropriate support based on the argument units depending on the errors (errors in the argument structure itself or lack of convincing power). In the next section, we will introduce the components used in the system and the contents of the support.

3.3   The Components Used in the System

The subject uses three types of components in the system: Proposition nodes, Reasoning links, and Limitation boxes.

Proposition Nodes.   The propositions written in a text are displayed as nodes as shown in Fig. 9. In addition, only the node of the proposition of claim is indicated in red letters. When the subjects do a task and create its argument structure, just the right number of proposition nodes necessary to create the argument structure are displayed on the screen at the beginning of the task.

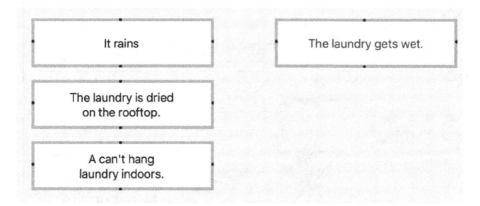

Fig. 9. Proposition nodes

Reasoning Links.   In the system, there are four types of links that indicate relationships between propositions. "Deduction link" (Fig. 10-a) is used to make an argument or reinforce an argument by deduction. When this link is connected to proposition nodes, as shown in Fig. 10-a, it indicates the deductive derivation of proposition A, which is the consequent of the rule (If B, then A), from proposition B, which is the antecedent of the rule. On the other hand, "Abduction link" (Fig. 10-a) is used to make an argument or reinforce an argument by abduction. When this link is connected to proposition nodes, as shown in Fig. 10-a, it indicates the abductive derivation of proposition A, which is the antecedent of the rule (If A, then B), from proposition B, which is the consequent of the rule. In both of these links, subjects connect the root of the arrow to a proposition node that is data and connect the tip of the arrow to a proposition that is derived or reinforced. Therefore, in both of these links, the tip of the link is always connected to the proposition node of claim, which is the proposition to be derived or reinforced. When the subject tries to connect the root of the link to the proposition node of claim, the link is automatically disconnected with the instruction, "You cannot connect the root of the link to claim, please connect it to the tip of the arrow."

"Rival link" (Fig. 10-c) and "Negation link" (Fig. 10-c) are used for reinforcement by the argument unit 7 "Abduction: negating rival proposition" introduced in Sect. 2. When these links are connected to propositions, as shown in Fig. 10, they indicate that propositions A and B, which can be derived from proposition D by abduction, are rival propositions, that proposition A is true while proposition B is false, and that proposition C negates proposition B. In principle, these links can be connected only in the form shown in Fig. 10-c. If a subject connects these links in a form other than Fig. 10-c and then tries to receive a diagnosis from the system, these links are automatically disconnected with the instruction, "Please connect the links correctly." At the beginning of a task, each type of link is displayed more than the number of links needed to create the correct argument structure.

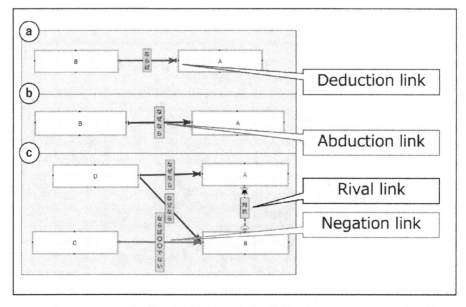

Fig. 10. Reasoning links

Limitation Box. When subjects reinforce their arguments using the rule limitation method introduced in Sect. 2, they use the "Limitation box" shown in Fig. 11. When subjects enclose the propositions enclosed with a limitation box as shown in Fig. 11, it indicates the conjunction of them "A and C." It can enclose only propositions that are the antecedents of a rule. Therefore, when connecting it to deduction link, it is connected to the root of the link, and when connecting it to abduction link, it is connected to the tip of the link. If the subjects connect it in the opposite direction to these links, these links are automatically disconnected with the instruction "The direction of the link connecting to the limitation box is wrong". At the beginning of a task, it is displayed more than the number of limitation boxes needed to create the correct argument structure.

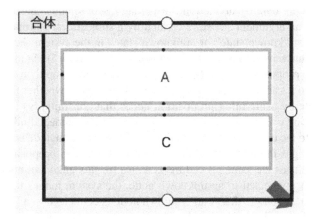

Fig. 11. Limitation box

3.4 Diagnosis and Feedback by System

The system matches an argument structure created by a subject against the correct one. Then it diagnoses whether or not the claim in the task is correctly derived in the structure and whether or not it is a sufficiently convincing argument structure. If necessary, it provides feedback based on the argument units that instructs the subject to modify the argument structure. The followings are a specific diagnostic procedure. After creating the argument structure, a subject presses the "Start Diagnosis" button shown in the upper left corner of Fig. 3-1. The system then starts to diagnose it and displays the feedback. Four types of diagnoses are made by the system: 1. Diagnosis of illegal propositions or reasoning links, 2. Diagnosis of limitation box errors, 3. Diagnosis of insufficient reinforcement errors, 4. Diagnosis of the insufficient number of data errors, and 5. Diagnosis of lack of rival proposition errors.

Diagnosis of Illegal Propositions or Reasoning Links. First, in an argument structure created by a subject, the system diagnoses whether there are any combinations of propositions and links that are not included in the correct structure. If so, the system gives feedback. Specifically, when propositions that should not be connected are connected, feedback is given that "there is no relationship between the propositions." Also, if a link between propositions is connected in the opposite direction of the correct structure, feedback is given that "the direction of the link is opposite."

Diagnosis of Limitation Box Errors. This is a diagnosis and feedback based on the argument units 1 "Deduction: Rule limitation" and the argument units 4 "Abduction: Rule limitation." If the limitation box created by the subject does not include an appropriate proposition, or if it includes an inappropriate proposition, the subject will be informed of this.

Diagnosis of Insufficient Reinforcement Errors. This is a diagnosis and feedback based on the argument units 2 "Deduction: Reinforcing data by deduction," the argument units 3 "Deduction: Reinforcing data by abduction" and the argument units 5 "Abduction: Reinforcing data by abduction." It is diagnosed whether there is insufficient reinforcement in an argument structure created by a subject. Each proposition node is pre-assigned either "known state" or "unknown state" in the system (hereafter, a node assigned known/unknown state is called "known/unknown node"). At the beginning of the diagnosis, the proposition nodes (including the claim) that should be derived or reinforced by other nodes are in unknown state. The system checks whether these nodes can be in known state by using other proposition nodes that are (initially) in known state. That is, for checking whether an unknown node can be known node, it finds a proposition node connected to the unknown node by a link. If this proposition node is a known node, the system re-assigns the unknown node to known state. If this proposition node is an unknown node, it tries the same procedure as above for this unknown node. (Note that if no other link is connected to an unknown node, the system judges the node cannot be in known state. Also note that if an unknown node is connected to a Limitation box, the above procedure is done about each proposition node in the box.) If there exist the proposition nodes (including the claim) that cannot be in known state, the feedback is given that these propositions are still in unknown state and that they should be derived or reinforced with other proposition nodes in known state.

Diagnosis of the Insufficient Number of Data Errors. As explained in Sect. 2.2, in an argument structure in which a claim is derived by abduction, there may be multiple data from which the claim is directly derived. If an argument structure created by a subject lack any of the above data, the system instructs the subject to check whether there are any other data in the text of the task from which the claim is derived, in addition to the data from which the subject derived the claim. This feedback is based on the argument unit 6 "Abduction: Adding facts of data."

Diagnosis of Lack of Rival Proposition Errors. In a task of an argument structure that improves the convincing power of an argument by negating a rival proposition against the claim, as explained in Sect. 2.2, if an argument structure created by a subject lacks this proposition, the subject is instructed to check whether there is any rival proposition in the text of the task from which the data can be derived. The subject is then instructed to negate this rival proposition. This feedback is based on the argument unit 7 "Abduction: Negating rival proposition."

3.5 Subjects

Subjects were nine undergraduate or graduate students affiliated with Kobe University. The experiment was conducted individually and on the same computer in the laboratory (iMac, Retina 4K, 21.5-inch, 2019).

3.6 Tasks

The topics of the texts used in the tasks were scientific articles in which rules between propositions were easy to understand, mystery works in which abduction was often used, and commentaries on historical events. In addition, in order to cover all the argument units and to make the argument structure and the rules between propositions easier to understand, we partly modified the original texts to create the experimental texts for five learning tasks (Tasks L-01–L-05) and for five transfer tasks (Tasks T-01–T-05.) (The text for each task was approximately 500 characters in Japanese.) The learning task was a task that subjects were given when they learned the argument unit with the system. On the other hand, the transfer task was a task that the subjects did for the first time after learning with the system. The argument units handled in the learning tasks and the transfer tasks are shown in Table 2. Except for the task L-03 and T-03, a pair of tasks with the same task number (e.g., L-01 and T-01) handled the same type of argument unit. Due to the difference of source texts, the number of proposition nodes in some transfer tasks was larger and more difficult than that in learning task with the same task number. In addition, due to the difference of source texts, in the task T-03, a different argument unit was handled from task L-03.

Table 2. The argument units handled each number of tasks

Learning task num	Argument Unit				
L-01	AU-1	Deduction: Rule limitaion	AU-2	Deduction: Reinforcing data by deduction
L-02	AU-1	Deduction: Rule limitaion	AU-3	Deduction: Reinforcing data by abduction
L-03	AU-5	Abduction: Reinforcing data by abduction		
L-04	AU-4	Abduction: Rule limitaion	AU-6	Abduction: Adding facts of data
L-05	AU-7	Abduction: Negating rival proposition		
Transfer task	Argument Unit				
T-01	AU-1	Deduction: Rule limitaion	AU-2	Deduction: Reinforcing data by deduction
T-02	AU-1	Deduction: Rule limitaion	AU-3	Deduction: Reinforcing data by abduction
T-03	AU-5	Abduction: Reinforcing data by abduction	AU-4	Abduction: Rule limitaion
T-04	AU-4	Abduction: Rule limitaion	AU-6	Abduction: Adding facts of data
T-05	AU-7	Abduction: Negating rival proposition		

3.7 Procedure

First, subjects received a tutorial explaining arguments, logical reasoning, and argument units. Next, as a pre-test, they did five learning tasks (with a time limit of 10 min per task, post-test as well) on the system. During the pre-test, they did not receive any feedback from the system (post-test as well). Then, in a learning session, subjects did five learning tasks on the system (with a time limit of 15 min per task). During the learning session, subjects were allowed to have the system diagnose their argument structure as many times as they wished to receive feedback. Finally, as a post-test, subjects did 5 learning tasks and 5 transfer tasks on the system. The learning task in the post-test is referred to as "Post-test 1", and the transfer task in the post-test is referred to as "Post-test 2."

4 Result and Discussion

4.1 Scoring Method

In tests, the argument structures created by the subjects were scored based on reasoning links and the limitation boxes.

First, if there was a reasoning link in the argument structure that had the same propositions (or limitation boxes) at both ends as those of a reasoning link in the correct argument structure, two points were awarded, regardless of the type and direction of them. Then, if the type or direction of them didn't match, one point is deducted. On the other hand, if there was no reasoning link in the correct argument structure that has the same propositions (or limitation boxes) at both ends as those of a reasoning link in the argument structure the subject created, one point was deducted.

Next, if at least one proposition that should be placed in the limitation box was placed in the limitation box in the argument structure created by the subject, two points were awarded. Then, one point was deducted for each proposition that should be placed in that limitation box but was not placed. In addition, one point was deducted for each proposition that should not be placed in that limitation box but was placed.

4.2   Comparison of Total Score and Total Score Rate

The total score (Table 3) and total score rate (Table 4) for each test (pre-test, learning session, post-test 1, and post-test 2) for each subject are as follows. The total score and total score rate refer to the score and score rate for all tasks in each test (5 learning tasks in the pre-test, learning session, and post-test 1, and 5 transfer tasks in post-test 2).

Table 3. The total score for each test

Total score	Full Score	S-01	S-02	S-03	S-04	S-05	S-06	S-07	S-08	S-09	Mean	S.D.	Median
Pre-test	30	19	14	16	11	15	3	8	19	14	13.222	5.191	14
Learning session	30	19	19	26	23	30	26	16	27	26	23.556	4.613	26
Post-test1	30	27	22	27	17	30	27	27	27	24	25.333	3.841	27
Post-test2	34	18	14	20	23	28	15	28	25	20	21.222	5.167	20

Table 4. The total score rate for each test

Total score rate	Full Score	S-01	S-02	S-03	S-04	S-05	S-06	S-07	S-08	S-09	Mean	S.D.	Median
Pre-test	30	0.633	0.467	0.533	0.367	0.500	0.100	0.267	0.633	0.467	0.441	0.173	0.467
Learning session	30	0.633	0.633	0.867	0.767	1.000	0.867	0.533	0.900	0.867	0.785	0.154	0.867
Post-test1	30	0.900	0.733	0.900	0.567	1.000	0.900	0.900	0.900	0.800	0.844	0.128	0.900
Post-test2	34	0.529	0.412	0.588	0.676	0.824	0.441	0.824	0.735	0.588	0.624	0.152	0.588

We compared the mean of the total scores and the mean of the total score rates of all subjects between the pre-test and post-test. In the comparison between pre-test and post-test 1, scores of the learning task are used, while in the comparison between pre-test and post-test 2, the score rate of the transfer task is used. First, using Wilcoxon signed rank test (all the following tests are Wilcoxon signed rank test), we compared the mean of all subjects' total score in the learning task between the pre-test and the post-test 1 (Table 3). The results showed that the mean of all subjects' total score of the post-test 1 is significantly higher than that of the pre-test ($p = 0.014$.) Next, we compared the mean of all subjects' total score rate in the transfer task between the pre-test and the post-test 2 (Table 4). The results showed the mean of all subjects' total score rate of the post-test 2 is marginally significantly higher than that of the pre-test ($p = 0.050$.) These results support hypothesis 1 "Learning with the learning support system will improve the ability to create argument structures in tasks the learners did once" and hypothesis 2 "Learning with the learning support system will also improve the ability to create argument structures in tasks the learners did for the first time" in the post-test conducted immediately after the learning.

4.3 Comparison of Score and Score Rate in Each Task

The scores and score rates for each task number are shown in Table 5 and Table 6. In the analysis of the results of each task, there are tasks in which most of the subjects had high scores, while there are tasks in which most of the subjects had low scores. Furthermore, in the learning and the transfer tasks, tasks with the same task number (e.g., L-01 and T-01), except for the task (L-03 and T-03), handle the same type of argument units. Therefore, it is possible to evaluate the learning effect of each type of argument unit by comparing each task number.

Table 5. Mean of score for each learning task number

Mean of score	L-01	L-02	L-03	L-04	L-05
Pre-test	4.889	4.000	2.889	-2.222	3.667
Learning session	5.889	5.889	4.000	2.222	5.444
Post-test1	5.889	5.444	4.000	3.000	7.000
Post-test2	6.889	4.889	3.778	-1.333	7.000

Table 6. Mean of score for each transfer task number

Mean of score rate	T-01	T-02	T-03	T-04	T-05
Pre-test	0.815	0.667	0.722	-0.370	0.458
Learning session	0.981	0.981	1.000	0.370	0.681
Post-test1	0.981	0.907	1.000	0.500	0.875
Post-test2	0.861	0.815	0.630	-0.222	0.875

L-01 (T-01) and L-03 (T-03). L-01 (T-01) is a task handling the argument unit 1 "Deduction: Rule imitation" and the argument unit 2 "Deduction: Reinforcing data by deduction." The results of the comparison of the mean of score between pre-test and post-test 1 ($p = 0.1058$) and the mean of score rate between pre-test and post-test 2 ($p = 0.733$) showed no significant difference in both cases. On the other hand, since L-03 (T-03) is a task that handle different argument units in some parts (the learning task handles the argument unit 5 "Abduction: Reinforcing data by abduction", the transfer task handles the argument unit 5 "Abduction: Reinforcing data by abduction" and the argument unit 4 "Abduction: Rule limitation"), scores and score rates between the learning task and the transfer task cannot be compared. The results of the comparison of the mean of the score between pre-test and post-test 1 showed no significant differences (p = 0.1814.) These results suggest that the scores and score rates at the pre-test were so high that no significant difference appeared due to the ceiling effect.

L-02 (T-02). L-02 (T-02) is a task handling the argument unit 1 "Deduction: Rule imitation" and the argument unit 3 "Abduction: Reinforcing data by Abduction." The results of comparison showed that the mean of the score of the post-test 1 is marginally significantly higher than that of the pre-test (p = 0.08897). On the other hand, the result of the comparison of the mean of score rate between pre-test and post-test 2 showed no significant difference (p = 0.4452.) In other words, the learning effect was observed in the learning task L-02, but no learning effect was observed in the transfer task T-02. It is assumed that there is the following reason why no learning effect was observed before and after the learning in the comparison of the transfer task T-02. The argument structure of this task handles argument unit that include reinforcement by abduction. It also handles argument unit that include limitation in the rules for deriving claims. Therefore, when subjects did this task, it was necessary to be aware of connecting the reasoning links in the opposite direction of the rules between the propositions and narrowing the scope of application of the rules. Hence, it is assumed that it is difficult to transfer what was learned in the learning task to the transfer task.

L-04 (T-04). L-04 (T-04) is a task handling the argument unit 4 "Abduction: Rule imitation" and the argument unit 6 "Abduction: Adding facts of data." The results of comparison showed that the mean of the score of the post-test 1 is significantly higher than that of the pre-test (p = 0.008433). On the other hand, the result of the comparison of the mean of score rate between pre-test and post-test 2 showed no significant difference (p = 0.370.) In other words, the learning effect was observed in the learning task L-04, but no learning effect was observed in the transfer task T-04. It is assumed that there is the following reason why no learning effect was observed before and after the learning in the comparison of the transfer task T-04. The argument structure of this task handles argument unit that include reinforcement by abduction. Furthermore, unlike the other tasks, it handles an argument structure in which the claim is contained within a limitation box, as shown in Fig. 12.

Therefore, when subjects did this task, it was necessary to be aware of connecting the reasoning links in the opposite direction of the rules between the propositions and narrowing the scope of application of the rules. In addition, it was necessary to be aware of both the rules for deriving the claim directly and the rules for deriving it indirectly using limitations box. Hence, it is assumed it is difficult to transfer what was learned in the learning task to the transfer task.

L-05 (T-05). L-05 (T-05) is a task handling the argument unit 7 "Abduction: Negating rival proposition." The results of comparison showed that the mean of the score of the post-test 1 is significantly higher than that of the pre-test (p = 0.0131). The results of comparison showed that the mean of the score rate of the post-test 2 is significantly higher

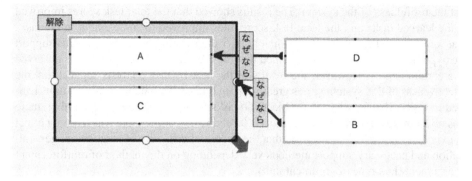

Fig. 12. The argument structure of Task L-04

than that of the pre-test ($p = 0.05583$.) In other words, learning effects were observed both in the learning task and in the transfer task. This result suggests the following. Unlike the other tasks, subjects use rival link and negate link when creating argument structures, as shown in Fig. 13. Therefore, it has a specific structure that is very different from other argument units. Hence, it is assumed that this task was easy to identify the argument unit handled in this task even if the topic changed.

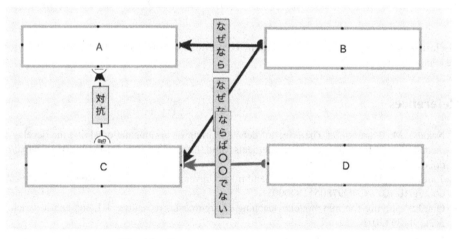

Fig. 13. The argument structure of Task L-05

5 Conclusion

In this research, we formulated two hypotheses (Learning with the learning support system will improve the ability to create argument structures (1) in tasks the learners did once and (2) in tasks the learners did for the first time) and conducted an experiment to test the usefulness of the system. The results showed that the total task scores improved in the learned tasks and the total task score rates improved to some extent in the tasks that were new to the subjects immediately after the learning. The above results support the hypotheses. Therefore, it is assumed that the usefulness of the system was observed to a certain degree. However, the results of the task-by-task analysis suggest that the effectiveness of this system varies greatly depending on the type of argument units handled in tasks. That is, when the subjects do tasks for the first time after learning, there was no learning effect as to some tasks (L-02 and L-04), while there was learning effect as to another (L-05). This suggests that the degree of difficulty of acquisition, generalization and necessary support methods vary depending on the method of reinforcement of argument (i.e., type of argument unit).

In upcoming research, we plan to analyze whether the learning effect is maintained after a certain period of time has elapsed after learning with the system in this experiment. We also plan to conduct a more detailed analysis of the difficulty level of mastery of each argument units and the necessary support methods to acquire them. In addition, there were cases, in this experiment, in which the semantic content of the text used in some tasks had an unexpected influence on the difficulty level of the task. Therefore, in the analysis of the difficulty level of mastery of each argument unit, we will design the experiment in such a way that the influence of the semantic content on the difficulty level of the task will be eliminated as much as possible.

Acknowledgments. This work was supported by JSPS KAKENHI (Grant Number 21H03565).

Disclosure of Interests. The authors have no competing interests to declare that are relevant to the content of this article.

References

1. Nakano, M., Maruno, S.: The effect of debate training on argumentation skills: the developmental process for Japanese college students. Stud. Learn. Soc. **3**(1–2), 4–12 (2013). https://doi.org/10.2478/sls-2013-0001
2. Toulmin, S.: The Use of Argument. Cambridge University Press, Cambridge (1958). https://doi.org/10.1017/CBO9780511840005
3. Qin, J.: Applying Toulmin model in teaching L2 argumentative writing. J. Lang. Learn. Teach. **3**(2), 21–29 (2016)
4. Kitamura, T., et al.: Development of a learning environment for logic-structure-assembling exercises and its experimental evaluation. Trans. Jpn. Soc. Artif. Intell. **32**(6), C-H14_1–12 (2017). https://doi.org/10.1527/tjsai.C-H14
5. Paavola, S.: Abduction as a logic and methodology of discovery: the importance of strategies. Found. Sci. **9**, 267–283 (2004). https://doi.org/10.1023/B:FODA.0000042843.48932.25

Comparing Human Versus Avatar Instructors of Different Ethnicities: Effects on Student Learning Outcomes Using a Virtual Learning Platform

Joshua M. Mosonyi[✉], Gabriella Hancock, and James D. Miles

California State University, Long Beach, CA, USA
joshua.mosonyi01@student.csulb.edu

Abstract. The process of education is changing in the modern world with an increased emphasis on e-learning environments that employ avatar agents as teachers. As such it is unclear how avatars compare to human instructors in online learning platforms in metrics such as comprehension, trust, usability, mental effort and engagement. 110 students were recruited to assess the effect on these metrics in an asynchronized online learning study to compare human instructors with avatar instructors and include African -American, Asian, Hispanic and White representations for each of the manipulations. We overall found no statistically significant effect for comprehension nor any of the metrics apart from the interaction between ethnicity and instructor type on trust scores. We discussed potential reasons for this and suggested further studies.

Keywords: education · avatar · diversity · e-learning. · comprehension · usability · mental effort · engagement · trust

1 Introduction

1.1 Global Education and the Emergence of E-Learning Environments

The access to a quality education is considered a fundamental human right according to the United Nations, who have established specific parameters and goals to achieve a worldwide baseline standard in education [1]. Despite this, many countries still struggle severely to provide equitable access to education, which inhibits individuals from moving up social hierarchies and enjoying greater economic and social prosperity [2]. Education is one of the most powerful tools for reducing poverty and promoting economic growth in society, and countries with high levels of educational attainment and literacy levels tend to have lower poverty rates and higher levels of economic prosperity that benefit all members of society [3].

Educational attainment is also one of the most reliable predictors for health, wealth and longevity [4]. It is also crucial to consider that high schools and universities function as institutionalization facilities, playing a critical role in shaping and transmitting political and cultural values to their students, who will need to cooperate with others in society

H. Mori and Y. Asahi (Eds.): HCII 2024, LNCS 14691, pp. 89–117, 2024.
https://doi.org/10.1007/978-3-031-60125-5_7

in the future [5]. As such, schools, and universities ideally aim to enable individuals to learn about various political and social systems and provide them with sufficient information to build their own political beliefs and values among valuable life skills that are advantageous in the market. Emile Durkheim [6], one of the founding mothers of academic sociology, argued that education serves as an extended socialization mechanism that instructs individuals on how to function in society and how to best conduct their lives. Similarly, Pierre Bourdieu coined the term social capital to refer to the cultural, attitudes and behaviors that are valued by the educational institutions which are then broadcasted into society more widely [7]. A quality education is therefore an essential ingredient for the thriving of human life in society as it opens doors to new opportunities and perspectives and empowers individuals to reach their full potential, which ultimately leads to greater prosperity for both individuals and communities at large.

Unfortunately, the quality of education can vary widely depending on factors such as race, ethnicity, class, gender, and geographic location [8]. In the United States, for example, marginalized groups such as low-income students or students of color frequently receive a much lower-quality education than their more privileged peers [9]. Sociological research has shown that socioeconomic status (SES) is a powerful predictor of educational outcomes as a whole and that children from low-SES backgrounds are more likely to experience academic difficulties, drop out of school, and have limited access to post-secondary education [10]. The so-called digital divide, which is defined as the gap in access to technology and digital resources between different SES groups, has become an increasingly growing area of study in education as access to technology is now esteemed a crucial factor in educational equity since modern education is slowly adding layers of online material to the learning experience [11].

The increase in online material is likely due to the rise of the internet in the late 20th and early 21st centuries which led to a shift towards online education and distance learning, with many universities and colleges offering online courses and degrees [12]. It is generally predicted that this trend will only continue to grow in the near future and ultimately reach hitherto unprecedented levels of accessibility of quality learning materials at a global scale [13]. The necessity for more and better quality virtual learning platforms became particularly noticeable to the public during the COVID-19 pandemic which accelerated the trend towards online education, with many schools and universities shifting to remote learning only in order to prevent the spread of the virus [14]. The growth of e-learning platforms is expected to revolutionize the way education is delivered and received, and aims to benefit millions of people who would otherwise be unable to access traditional brick-and-mortar institutions.

This becomes more evident as technology continues to advance as new modes of instruction are expected to emerge which challenge the way traditional classrooms facilitate learning experiences. In a sense education has gone full circle, where there now seems to be an increasing trend that emphasizes less on written material and rather on personal and direct oral instructions as in ancient Rome and Greece. William James [15] lectures for instance, were dutifully transcribed and rendered by a member of the audience, in which in one part he actually verbally states that he stood behind a podium lecturing, whereas today it would be more likely that someone would record such a lecture and make it available for students to watch it online rather than reading it from a book. The development of Massive open online course (MOOCs), that offer quality university level education for free to the public has become very popular [16]. Additionally, the use of Extended Reality (XR) and Virtual Reality (VR) technologies, can create immersive virtual classrooms in which students and teachers can interact with each other through personalized avatars, creating a more engaging and interactive learning experience [17].

With the help of avatars, students could in the future attend virtual field trips, explore numerous museums and historical sites, and conduct scientific experiments in a safe virtual lab. The use of virtual reality and avatars creates a whole host of possibilities for students, particularly those who may not have the opportunity to travel or visit such locations in person. In addition, avatars can be used to facilitate gamification and interactive simulations in education that can motivate students to actively, rather than passively, participate in the learning process. This approach to e-learning can be very interesting and beneficial for students who struggle with traditional lecture-based methodologies, as it provides a more hands-on and interactive learning experience.

Avatar technologies has also the potential to enhance student learning outcomes by providing a more stimulating and interactive environment where avatars could provide a sense of presence and embodiment in scenarios where physical contact perhaps may not be possible. In a seminal work published by Foster [18] the researcher proposed that the safety of students in universities and high schools located in high-crime areas could be improved by providing online avatar-based classroom experiences. He cited an example which is the University of Peroria, located in a vicinity of many strip clubs and atrocious violent crime that endanger students. By using avatars instead, he argues that students can attend classes from the safety of their own homes and reducing the risk of physical or social harm.

1.2 The Role of Avatars and Embodiment in Pedagogical Cyber Space

The word avatar etymologically is a Sanskrit word that refers the descent or physical appearance of a "spiritual" deity [19]. As such, the theological system of Hinduism proposes an emanationist view of the world which teachers that humanity is already trapped in a sort of virtual reality and chained to physicality by ignorance and lack of virtue [20]. Although the Hindu perspective of avatars is not the subject of the current inquiry yet it is still interesting to note that the first appearance of the term avatar was closely tied to the topic of education itself as the said avatar appearance of a Hindu deity always took place in order to instruct a dutiful devotee [21]. Avatars from a modern perspective refer to a digital icon or figurative representation of a particular person in cyber space [22]. In contemporary pedagogy avatars become ever more prevalent as the previously mentioned technologies, along with phone application that children use to learn and acquire skills become increasingly popular [23].

Recent investigations that examine the impact and potential applications of avatars in cyberspace have already yielded unique and interesting results that can help elucidate patterns of behavior in human nature that are more difficult to detect in real-world settings. One such instance comes from a study that looked at the role of gender on help seeking behaviors by Lehdonvital and colleagues [24]. It is well documented, that in most of parts of the world, men are significantly less likely to seek out help due to social expectations of the male gender role, yet the study found that although this trend is still present in virtual environments when men use male avatars, this effect disappears when men "embody" female avatars in virtual reality, as they now were much more likely to seek for psychological help. This clearly suggests that avatar appearance in virtual environments and cyberspace itself can have a significant and unexpected impact on human behavior.

Another study investigated how teachers embody their presence in virtual environments through the camera and how this relates to their teaching styles [25]. The data revealed that teachers used their body deliberately as an instrument through various movements and gestures to sustain the attentional presence and increase engagement of students. It would be very interesting to see whether these movements, if facilitated by an avatar which is often rendered with less detail (i.e., fewer movable joints and body parts) could be accurately captured by an avatar or whether they perhaps even more clearly communicate gestures than real video material alone.

It is important to note, however, that in cyberspace, individuals are at greater liberty to choose how to represent themselves, particularly when designing digital avatars, since unlike in the physical world where appearance are mostly governed by genetics and lifestyle choices, avatars can be designed in a manner by which an avatar appears, sounds and behaves to ones liking. Nonetheless, this liberty also can lead to quite problematic social issues and behaviors, such as the so-called "digital blackface", which is a phenomenon in which a non-black person uses digital avatars to present themselves as a black individual [26]. As such behavioral adaptations, such as the use of black slang and vernacular in online conversation and other types of cultural appropriation can perpetuate and ultimately create harmful stereotypes that are not conducive to the health of a multi-ethnic society. Unfortunately, this behavior has been widely documented in numerous cyber spaces, such as social media platforms, online games and virtual reality environments and therefore highlights the importance for individuals to be cognizant and respectful about the manner in which they represent themselves in cyberspaces and how their behaviors might affect others [27].

1.3 Avatar and Comprehension

Comprehension is the ability to understand, remember and grasp the true meaning of a piece or collection of information [28]. The study of the underlying mechanisms of comprehension are a rather complicated phenomenon that span the cognitive, behavioral, biological, and social sciences [29]. From a cognitive perspective comprehension is an extremely complex symposium of multiple interacting components such as memory, attention, perception, and inference [30]. The ability to comprehend information is depended on the ability to decode and understand the meaning of a message (whether a lecture, a written text or other form of semiotic meaning) and to use critical thinking to form an understanding of the subject matter at hand. Comprehension, as one might have guessed it, is therefore an essential component of education, particularly in online remote education where comprehension can be at times difficult to assess.

A recent study that compared online courses to traditional face-to-face courses found that students reported that they felt like they learned less in online classes, were treated with more respect in in-person courses and overall rated online courses less highly than in-person courses and overall gave online classes significantly lower satisfaction ratings [31]. As such, subjective assessments of comprehension were significantly lower in online learning environments and satisfaction rates were rated as significantly lower. During the COVID-19 pandemic similar perceptions have been documented by educational psychologists [32].

Daniels and Lee [33] conducted a systematic interview study aimed at identifying the impact of physical characteristics of human teachers versus avatars on student learning. The overall findings of the interviews were mixed, as some students reported finding avatar teachers more engaging, and therefore leading to greater comprehension while others found them to be distracting. However, some students did not report any preference for either teacher type as long as the material was delivered effectively.

It is important to note that online learning environments can have various benefits over traditional classrooms which could facilitate greater comprehension. For instance, students can rewatch lectures, rewind certain moments that they might have missed during class, take more time during note taking activities and rewatch lectures several times during intense revision periods. Online lectures also enable students to work at their own schedule and at times where they feel inspired or ready to soak information in.

To further investigate the use of avatar based education on e-learning, Talit and colleagues [34] designed a study in which students either attended a real museum tour or were presented the same tour in virtual reality using avatars. The results of the study are rather counter-intuitive as the results showed that students who attended the virtual museum tour had a significantly better recall of events and objects presented than those who attended the real museum tour. Additionally, students who attended the virtual museum tour reported a greater perceived presence that was as much or in some cases even more than those who attended the real museum tour. Avatars could therefore enhance comprehension by providing visual cues within a deeply immersive learning environment and this effect could be further enhanced by giving visual cues to students who suffer from learning disabilities as information can be presented in a more accessible and engaging way.

Mizuho and colleagues [35] are so fond of the use of avatars in online learning environments that they developed a systematic ecological approach that is designed, according to them, to maximize comprehension in e-learning environments. They propose a novel form of remote lecturing style in order to teach a class using avatars that change their appearance at different time intervals. The reasoning behind this idea was linked to studies that indicated that memory performance is enhanced through environmental changes. The researchers divided a 90-min lecture into four parts and used a different avatar for each quarter of the span and then looked at comprehension rates in comparison to a 90 min lecture used with just one avatar. The researchers found that students performed significantly higher with the avatar changes than with the one avatar alone.

1.4 Avatar and Trust

Trust, which is ontologically very difficult to describe, is generally defined or character-ized by researchers in the social sciences as an individual's (or in some instances group of individuals) believe in the reliability, truthfulness, competence and ethical conduct of a person or entity [36]. A more frequently cited definition might be that trust is 'a psy-chological state comprising the intention to accept vulnerability based upon the positive expectations of the intentions or behavior of another' [37]. As such trust is a founda-tional pillar for the flourishing of human life in society ranging from the formation of interpersonal relationships to everyday business transactions and the evermore prevalent interactions that humans have with their creations (i.e., technology)[38].

Researchers usually believe that trust is a multi-dimensional construct that is medi-ated by numerous deeply interdependent factors. Some of these factors are for instance familiarity, competence, communication style and consistency [39]. Oftentimes, how-ever, systematic biases can emerge and led to stereotypes that view certain groups of individuals in an untrustworthy manner and can become problematic since previous research has shown that trust judgements based on the appearance of an individual's alone can be very inaccurate and biased, which in turn, if cascaded to a wider societal scale, can lead to a foundational biases that disrupt social interaction within society [40]. This is even more problematic if we consider that neurological evidence suggests that appearance-based judgments occur on a subconscious level and are based on certain facial and bodily characteristics which therefore illumines that this problem might be biologically rooted [41].

MacArthur [42] conducted a study in which he examined first impressions and found that morphology significantly impacts trust scores during first impressions and that there are clear cut preferences in morphological representations among individuals. In this study, he found that anthropomorphic representations ranked significantly higher than zoomorphic and techno-morphic visual representations, and therefore highlighting the importance of paying attention to the synthetic embodied representations that human beings utilize in online telecommunication environments.

In terms of education, particularly for remote online learning environments, trust is an essential component to facilitate a fruitful and enjoyable learning experience for both the teacher and student. A lack of trust inhibits open and truthful communication, as students might be reluctant to share their ideas or contribute to the classroom discussions which as a byproduct ultimately leads to a deprived learning experience and in the long run likely also inhibits the realization of the students potential.

Now it is interesting to consider for a moment how individuals would form a trusting relationship with an avatar instructor. As mentioned earlier, it is likely that in the future experts might share their technical abilities in virtual or extended reality environments that might use avatars over camera recordings due to its potential of full embodied representation. One question that arises here is whether students, or individuals in general are more trusting of "real" people than of avatar-based representations of people. The answer perhaps might lead people on a superficial level of reflection to say that people would trust human representation more, however, one must also consider that many corporations purposefully chose to hide behind the use of an icon (i.e., avatar, mascot or cartoon character) to represent the entity at large and influence consumer behavior in a favorable way that is mediated primarily on trust [43].

Furthermore, Chae and colleagues [44] found that avatar trust building in e-learning environments is strongly mediated by the attractiveness of the avatar itself and argues that social desirability and trust is therefore influenced by attractiveness, even in e-learning environments. Avatars often exaggerate human features that regulate the perceived attractiveness and trustworthiness (two concepts that are in themselves related to one another) such as increased eye size, lip size, and exaggerated gestures which in the real world have evolved to convey information to people and are seen as markers of trustworthiness.

Yet, it is not fully clear whether avatars would be purely beneficial in terms of the development of trust in e-learning environments. Recent advancements in artificial intelligence and computer-generated imagery have made it possible to create realistic images that can be difficult to discern from real photographs or videos. Yet researchers have shown that once people become aware that an image has been generated by a computer or AI, they may become less likely to trust the content provided even if it was not meant to educate [45]. This is an important consideration for a variety of reasons in educational settings as the trust in the accuracy and authenticity of visual content is crucial for students to develop trust in the institution, and if students are skeptical or uncertain about the source or reliability of an image, they may be less likely to believe or accept the information presented.

To our knowledge there has been no study that has looked at a direct comparison between human instructors and avatars in online learning environments that assessed trust in avatars with human instructors.

1.5 Avatars and Mental Effort

Another important concept that pertains to online education is the study of mental effort, which refers to the amount of cognitive resources, including attention, working memory among others individual must exert in order to complete an activity or process presented information [46]. Mental effort can be affected by numerous external factors, such as task complexity, novelty of the concept and familiarity among internal factors such as individual differences in motivation, personality, and cognitive ability [47]. In remote education, mental effort is an important concept to consider for the design of online material and platforms so that the technology will ideally be an invisible component so as to not take anything away from the learning experience. As such it is generally recommended that educational platforms must be easy to navigate to reduce cognitive load and if possible, use various forms of media such as videos, images and animations to present information in a manner that is engaging and accessible to students [48]. It is also essential during lectures to communicate with students and provide feedback to them in order to gauge their mental effort, which is often, as previously mentioned, secondarily mediated through gestures and bodily movements of the instructors. These are often not as easily communicable in online environments as they are in "real-world" classroom environments [49]. In a lecture hall or a seminar room teachers can actively monitor student reactions and gauge for engagement or if students require further clarification on the subject at hand, whereas in remote learning environments such as via zoom for instance students often have their cameras disabled or are in general are harder to gauge all at once. However, using avatars, such escapism on part of the student would perhaps be less possible.

To our knowledge there have been no systematic investigations of avatars effect on mental effort and avatar uses in online learning environments. However, there has been some research done to see whether anxiety is increased or decreased when students and teachers employ avatars. As such anxiety is often marked by increased negative affect and heightened arousal, which at times have been linked to mental effort [50]. The results vary, and perhaps are culturally mediated as in one study English as a second language learners in Turkey exhibited and reported no greater or lesser anxiety when having class conducted online versus in person [51] whereas in a research study conducted in Japan that Japanese learners felt much more likely to speak up in zoom classes when they or their teacher were using an avatar and reported overall less anxiety [52].

It is therefore interesting to see whether avatars would either be distracting and take away from the learning experience and thereby increasing the mental effort that needs to be exerted to process the content of the lecture or whether the avatar's features would add to the experience and making the information easier to process. It is possible that avatars can reduce mental workload by presenting information in a way that is more visually appealing, and in a sense exaggerated it which makes it more memorable than seeing a human instructor. In other class room settings it could also assist learners overcome their shyness or anxiety by masking themselves with a digital avatar and therefore become more likely to ask questions in a traditional classroom setting.

1.6   Usability and Avatars

Closely related to the concept of mental effort is also the topic of usability. Usability, roughly speaking, is the level or extend to which a product or system is usable by its intended user base in order to achieve specific goals as efficiently and effectively as possible with the greatest amount of satisfaction [53]. The academic study or concept of usability emerged in the 1940s when human factors psychologist began to deal with the evermore complex technological landscape that human beings have to interact with [54]. These days usability is part and parcel of big business and almost any cooperation has incorporated the systematic evaluation of usability into their practices [55]. It is critical for online platforms to be designed with usability in mind to ensure that students can successfully navigate the system by developing a good information hierarchy and thereby enable them to complete tasks as efficiently and effectively as possible.

The potential benefits avatars may add to the usability of online learning platforms is that in immersive learning environments embodiment perhaps increases the satisfaction of the user experience and decreases mental load, as students would have to be fully present in the classroom environment when using a headset. Likewise, the novelty among with the customizability of the experience might also lead to greater satisfaction in students. It also important to note at this point that user satisfaction is a very subjective phenomena and it is unclear whether the recording of a human instructor would yield greater satisfaction rates when compared to an online avatar.

Avatar-based education technologies that allow users to create unique online personas have shown to enable educators to present activities that are difficult to demonstrate with a static picture images alone and have been found to be particularly useful for patients with low literacy levels as shown by Wonggom and colleagues [56]. In their meta-analysis, the researchers showed that avatar-based education interventions in patient education can have a positive effect on various healthcare outcomes, including improved knowledge, self-care behaviors, and self-efficacy in patients who suffer from chronic diseases. In e-learning environments we could also therefore assume that the use of avatar images for teachers, avatar-based technology could also provide a more engaging and interactive experience for students as avatars could demonstrate activities and concepts that would be difficult to convey through text, PowerPoint slides or static images alone, and therefore could be used to personalize the learning experience. This technology may be particularly beneficial for students with low literacy, young students or students who struggle with traditional learning methods.

A study by Wang, Chignell, and Ishizuka [57] also found that avatars can have a positive impact on learner motivation and concentration during learning and students ranked the overall usability of e-learning avatars as very helpful when used in conjunction to eye trackers that adapt to their behaviors which in turn can enhance the functionality and usefulness of e-learning avatars. The researchers also noted that early evaluations have shown that learners pay attention to the explanation from avatar agents and find feedback about their own eye movements useful. With advancements in eye tracking technology, more sophisticated and socially aware avatars may in the near future make e-learning available to supplement classroom education.

1.7 Avatar Engagement

Engagement, from a human factor's perspective refers to the degree of involvement, interest, arousal and motivation an individual exhibits when interacting with a person, product, service or experience [58]. It is a critical component in the study of psychology, marketing, education and human-computer interaction [59]. Secondarily, it has also been associated strongly with the promotion of learning, behavioral and attitudinal changes [60]. Engagement within the context of online learning environments is critical to capture and sustain the attention of students and promote a learning experience that induces feelings of interest and active participation on behalf of the students.

Now it is interesting to examine whether avatars and regular teachers may engage with students differently and whether students would engage with avatars differently than they would with a video camera. Students often report that they feel insecure about their appearance when being captured on camera, particularly when they are aware of the lecture being recorded, avatars on the other hand might be a way by which this problem could be circumvented [61]. By comparing the instructor type of avatar vs human instructors, we could gain deeper insights into what teaching strategies are most effective at keeping students engaged and motivated.

As such, previous studies have found that attributes of humanness (i.e., whether an entity is human or not) involve different brain mechanisms and circuitry when people think they are engaging with a human person versus a virtual avatar [62]. The study detected that the mere belief that a virtual avatar of a person was just a digital avatar resulted in significantly less arousal levels than believing that it was a human person that acted the avatar out, therefore resulting in different arousal levels.

Park [63] also examined the effectiveness of avatars in increasing interest in educational material and highlighted that avatars were more effective than a read text alone in increasing interest in the learning material. This finding is consistent with previous research that has suggested avatars can enhance engagement and interactivity in educational settings. However, Mazlan and Burd [64] found no significant difference between avatars and written material in terms of increasing interest in educational material. These mixed findings highlight the need for further research to explore the effectiveness of avatars in different educational contexts and populations.

However, it is important to look at the duality of such matters and some of the potential problems that can come from the use of avatar in e-learning environments. It could be for instance that avatars do not provide the same level of emotional connection and empathy as human teachers do in person or via a video and therefore taking away from the engagement of the experience. Students perhaps also could think of the avatars as a gimmick and become less interest in the content being taught. Additionally, avatar technologies have also not yet fully developed to a level that it can be adequate to real world settings and therefore it is unclear whether engagement would increase.

1.8   The Role of Ethnicity in E-Learning Environments:

One frequently neglected component of studies that investigate the role of avatars on e-learning environments is the role of teacher's ethnicity. It is important to note that the scientific literature on avatars as a whole has primarily focused on using white male avatars, despite the fact that the user base for virtual environments is diverse [65]. This lack of diversity in avatar representation is concerning as it perpetuates the exclusion of marginalized groups and undermines the potential benefits of virtual environments for individuals who do not identify with the standard avatar prototypes. Additionally, this homogenous representation may also lead to an inaccurate understanding of how students interact with and fundamentally perceive avatars, as it perhaps fails to account for potential differences in how people from diverse backgrounds may respond to different avatar representations in teachers. As such, it is essential to broaden the scope of our current avatar research to include a much more diverse range of avatars that reflect the varied identities and experiences of virtual environment users.

A research paper for instance examined the representation of gender and race in massively multiplayer online games (MMOs) [66]. The study examined 417 unique characters that appeared over 1,000 times in 20 h of recorded content from four popular MMOs and found that white male characters were overrepresented, while female and racial minority characters were significantly underrepresented. Another study examines racial diversity in avatar design and discussions about race in Whyville.net, a large-scale virtual world with over 1.5 million players and found that the racial diversity of resources available for avatar construction was severely limited [67].

There is also fairly strong evidence that Black and other minority students score higher on achievement tests when assigned to at least one teacher that is of their ethnic background [68]. It is hypothesized that is can come from in-group preferences, a cultural understanding and communication style and the role that the teacher acts as a role model.

However, there also seem to be differences across trust measures that are based on inter-ethnic interactions and facial features alone [69]. The study found that ethnicity characteristics affect trustworthiness judgments that in a sample of two Caucasian and two Asian instructors that trust perception generalized across face-ethnicity but that differences in trustworthiness judgments of other-ethnicity faces exhibited a bias towards their own ethnicity. It also found that negative ethnicity stereotypes can influence social judgments of faces when no positive facial expression cues are present.

This effect becomes more interesting as trust, which we mentioned earlier, tends to be influenced by facial expressiveness, yet research clearly indicates that not all facial expressions by all ethnicities are processed similarly. For instance, Gingras [70] found that pain experienced by African-Americans is systematically underestimated by participants of all ethnic groups, including African-Americans themselves and concludes that there are variations in examining facial communication that are based on ethnicity. This is very closely related to the concept of cultural responsiveness which has become an important area of study in sociology of education [71] and refers to the ability of teachers to recognize and value the cultural background and experiences of their students and that teachers who are culturally responsive might be better able to create inclusive and supportive learning environments for all students.

One study that looked at avatar use in higher education institutions in Saudi Arabia, which is a highly gender-segregated classroom environment has shown that female students' learning experiences can be positively shaped by avatars that are ethnically similar [72]. The study looked at the experiences of female instructors teaching a MOOC course on the Rwaq platform, a popular online learning platform in Saudi Arabia. The objective was to develop a safe social interaction environment with learners in online learning within MOOCs and evaluate whether avatars could alleviate issues of gender-segregation for female lecturers in online learning courses within MOOCs in higher education in Saudi Arabia, and found that most students provided supportive feedback on the avatar experience and indicating the need for more female Arabian instructors.

Hodgson [73] designed a study that used the same class material and lecture verbatim found no significant different outcomes between western and non-western teachers but suggested that the user experience and perception is favored towards Caucasian. It could be the case teachers of color may face unique challenges in online teaching, such as navigating cultural differences and building rapport with students they have never met in person. Likewise, it has also been found that black and Hispanic students reported lower levels of engagement and satisfaction with online learning compared to white students and researcher proposed that this may be due in part to differences in access due to cultural barriers [74].

Efforts to improve the usability, comprehensiveness, trust, and usability and engagement in online learning environments should therefore be designed with the needs of more diverse students at mind and therefore include a focus on addressing issues of equity and access.

1.9 Research Question

To address the aforementioned research questions, the study was designed to assess comprehension, usability, trust, engagement, and mental effort of students in an asynchronized learning platform that compares avatars instructors with human instructors and whether the human or avatar instructors were African-American, Asian, Hispanic, White. We hypothesize that there is a significant effect of instructor type will have on the usability, comprehension, trust, and mental effort of students and also suggest that there will be a main effect of the instructors ethnicity. To analyze this phenomenon, we will use a 2 (Type of Instructor: Human vs. Avatar) x 4 (Ethnicity: African-American, Asian, Hispanic, White) ANOVA.

2 Methods

The present study investigated the effects of instructor ethnicity and type (Human vs. Avatar) on students' comprehension and perceptions of usability, mental effort, engagement, and trust in an asynchronized college psychology course. A 4 (African-American, Asian, Hispanic, White) x 2 (Human vs. Avatar Instructor) between subjects ANOVA will be conducted to analyze the data. As such, human instructors refer to webcam recorded instructors, whereas avatars instructors refer to instructors generated via the Animazeme application (see Figs. 2 and 3).

The independent variables are the type of instructor (Human vs. Avatar) and type of ethnicity (African-American, Asian, Hispanic, White). A visual representation of the avatar manipulations can be seen in Fig. 3. Our dependent variables are trust as measured by the modified Trust in Automation Scale, mental effort, as measured by the Paas mental effort rating scale, comprehension which was measured by a 20-item quiz based on the material of a cognitive psychology memory lecture. We also administered a learning engagement questionnaire to assess general online learning engagement and used the System Usability Scale to measure usability [75].

2.1 Participants

Out of the CSULB student sample a total of 110 individuals were recruited. 87 were female (79.1%), and 4 participants (3.6%) in the sample identified as non-binary and the remaining 19 individuals (17.3%) were male. The age of participants ranged from 18-39 with a mean age of 19.65 (SD = 3.192) years.

7.3% of the sample reported to never have taken an online class before, 11.8% reported to have taken one, another 11.8% to have taken two, 16.4% reported to have taken three, 11.8% reported to have taken four, 1.8% reported to have taken five, 8.2% to have taken six, and 30.9% to have taken seven or more online classes.

In terms of racial and ethnic composition, the group was diverse. About 24.5% of individuals identified as White, 13.6% as African-American, and 21.8% as Asian. A smaller percentage, 0.9%, identified as Hawaiian or Pacific Islander. A significant portion, 29.1%, identified as "Hispanic or other", while 22% did not want to disclose their racial or ethnic background.

Participants were required to be in the age range of 18–65 years old to ensure that they are within the target population for the present study and have normal or corrected vision. The participants were screened for being fluent in English in order to complete the study and assessment.

For the final sample, after having accounted for the systematic Qualtrics error that did not capture all the data during the first quarter of the project (see discussion) the comprehension group consisted of the full sample of 110 participants, the usability sample had 99 participants, the trust scores consisted of a sample of 100, the engagement sample had 99 participants and the mental effort sample had 96 participants (Fig. 1).

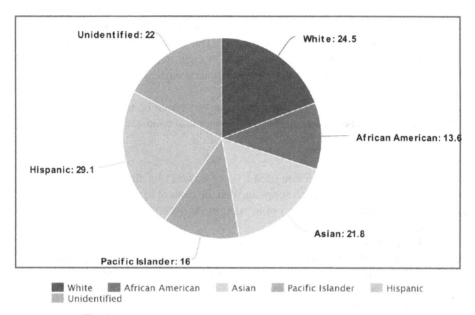

Fig. 1. A pie chart distribution of the sample's ethnic background

2.2 Materials

Metrics and stimuli

System Usability Scale (SUS). - The System Usability Scale (SUS) was adopted from Lewis [75] to assess the usability of the different conditions. The SUS is a widely used questionnaire that measures usability and user satisfaction with a system. The scale consists of 10 items, each rated on a 5-point Likert scale, and produces a score between 0 and 100.

Modified Trust in Automation Scale. - The Modified Trust in Automation Scale was adapted from Jian et al. [76] used to assess participants' trust in the avatar instructor. This scale measures participants' trust in an automated system, and was modified to be used in the context of an avatar instructor. The scale consists of 10 items, each rated on a 5-point Likert scale.

Pre-test questions -. Prior to the lectures, participants were asked a series of 5 pre-test questions to assess their general knowledge of the psychological sciences.

Transcripts -. The transcripts were taken from a real-world class in Cognitive Psychology and rendered at a verbatim level to ensure that all recording are the same class word for word.

PAAS scale for mental effort -. The Paas scale for mental effort was adopted from Paas and Merriënboer [77] and is used to assess the mental effort required to complete the lectures. The Paas scale measures the level of cognitive load, or mental effort, required to complete a task. The scale consists of six items, each rated on a 7-point Likert scale.

Learning Activity Engagement measurement -. The Learning Activity Engagement measurement was used to assess participants' general engagement to online instructional material which his measurement is a self-report questionnaire that assesses the level of engagement during general learning activity. The scale was adopted from Henrie, Halverson and Graham [78]. The scale consists of eight items, each rated on a 7-point Likert scale but only capture data that relate to general engagement and not immediate engagement.

Quiz -. A set of 20 questions was developed that was based on the material presented alone that required no previous knowledge of the topic at hand and consisted of 4 items multiple choice items.

Software

Microsoft PowerPoint -. The lecture used a set of PowerPoint slides from a real-world Cognitive Psychology class which supplemented the content of the lecture by providing additional visual aids and information to support the lecture material (Version 2022, Microsoft, Redmond, VA, US).

Animaze Me Application -. In order to manipulate the avatar of the instructor, the lectures were presented by either a human instructor or an avatar instructor. The avatar instructors were created using the Animaze Me app, which allowed for the creation of 3D animated avatars that could be customized to represent different ethnicities and genders (Holotech, Studios, San Francisco, US).

Adobe Premiere Pro -. The video editing software ensured that all lectures were of similar quality, length and rendered at the same quality and that the audio and video were synchronized. In order to ensure that the quality of the audio and video recordings was consistent across all lectures, the Zoom recordings were standardized using the same audio and video settings for all lectures. The audio was also adjusted to ensure that the volume was consistent across all lectures (Version 2022, Adobe, San Jose, US).

Qualtrics - The study was designed using Qualtrics, an online survey platform that allowed for the creation and distribution of surveys and questionnaires (Qualtrics, Provo. UT, US).

2.3 Procedure

Participants were recruited from California State University, Long Beach's SONA system, and received 1 credit for their participation. Participants were directed to Qualtrics and presented with a consent form that informed them about the purpose of the study.

Following the consent form, participants were asked to provide demographic information, including age, gender, race/ethnicity, and educational background. After clicking to provide their consent, participants then underwent a pre-screen to assess their level of prior knowledge of the material to be covered in the lectures, and were then randomly assigned to one of eight experimental conditions. The conditions were one of the four types of ethnicities (African-American, Asian, Hispanic, White) and one of the two types of instructor types (Human Instructor, Avatar Instructor). The participants then watched a 35-min long lecture about a selected topic in cognitive psychology (memory) taken from a zoom class.

After the experimental session, participants were given a 20-question multiple-choice task to complete. The task was designed to assess participants' comprehension of the material provided. The task was the same for all participants and was used to ensure that all participants had a similar level of knowledge prior to the lectures. Next, after the multiple-choice task, participants were randomly assigned to complete the System Usability Scale (SUS), Learning Activity Engagement measurement, Paas scale for mental effort, Modified Trust in Automation Scale, and demographic questionnaire. Participants were not informed of the order of these questionnaires to prevent any potential biases. After completing all questionnaires, participants were debriefed and given the opportunity to ask any further questions. Participants were thanked for their participation and given 1 credit for their participation in the study.

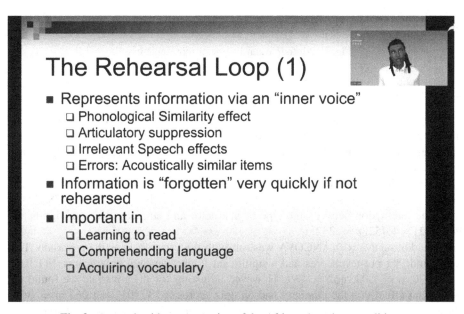

Fig. 2. A sample video presentation of the African-American condition.

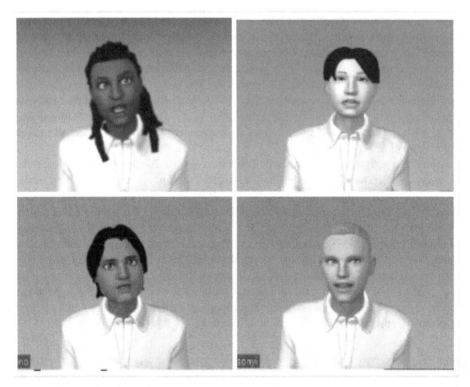

Fig. 3. All four avatar instructor representations.

2.4 Results

Comprehension Results. A 2 × 4 between-subjects ANOVA was performed to assess the effect of ethnicity and instructor type comprehension via quiz scores. A Levene's homogeneity of variance test was not significant and therefore suggests that equal variances can be assumed, $p = .963$. Overall, we found no statistically significant of ethnicity did not significant impact quiz scores, $F(7, 102) = 1.1.138$, $p = .364$. The effect of the instructor type on quiz scores was also not significant, $F(1, 102) = .074$, $p = .785$ Likewise, the interaction between the type of instructor and ethnicity was non-significant $F(3, 102) = 1.452$, $p = .232$.

An additional 2 × 4 ANCOVA was run with pretests scores as the covariate. The test found that pre-test scores had a significant impact on final quiz scores, $F(1,101) = 10.170$, $p = .002$, $\eta p2 = .091$. However, adjusting for the covariate we found no significant effect that the ethnicity had on quiz scores, $F (3, 101) = 1.063$, $p = .368$. We also found no significant that of instructor had on quiz scores, $F (1, 101)$, $.045$, $p = .952$. The interaction for ethnicity and type was also not significant, $F (3,101) = 1.601$, $p = .194$. Indicating that that pre-existing knowledge did not influence the quiz scores when manipulating ethnicity and instructor type. However, it is important to note that the mean for all pre-test scores were generally very low with only 1.4 questions, on average, being answered correctly.

Modified Trust in Automation Scores. To assess trust the modified Trust in Automation scores were analyzed using a 2 × 4 between subjects ANOVA. The Levene's test of homogeneity of variance was not significant, therefore equal variances can be assumed, $p = .330$. There was no significant effect of the instructor's ethnicity on trust scores, (F(3, 92) = 0.127, $p = .944$). We also found overall no statistically significant effect for type of instructor on trust scores, F(1, 92) = .312, $p = .578$). However, we did find a significant interaction between trust scores and the type of ethnicity and type of instructor on trust scores, F(3, 92) = 4.179, $p = .008$, $\eta p^2 = .120$). A post-hoc pairwise comparison using the Bonferroni correction revealed that Asian Avatars Instructors (M = 3.57) scored significantly lower on trust scores than Human Asian Instructors (M = 14.07), $M_{diff} = -10.5$, $p = .006$. Conversely, for African-American instructors we found the opposite effect with African-American Avatar instructors (M = 13.30) being trusted significantly more than Human African-American Instructors (M = 4.46), $M_{diff} = 8.84$, $p = .033$ (see Fig. 4). There was however no significant interaction across ethnicities and type (i.e., Asian Avatar vs. Human African American) for any of the groups, p > .05.

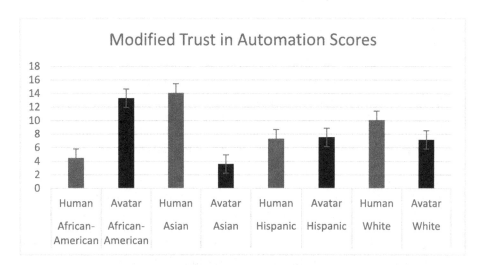

Fig. 4. The Mean differences across all groups on modified trust scores.

A 2 × 4 ANCOVA was performed that examined whether participants ethnicity had a significant impact on trust scores. The test revealed that participants ethnicity had no significant impact on trust scores, F(1,91) = 1.686, $p = .197$. Our model therefore still detected no effect for ethnicity (F(3,91) = .081, $p = .970$) and type of instructor (F(1,91) = .442, $p = .508$ on trust scores. The interaction between ethnicity and type of instructor was still significant, F(3, 91) = 4.50, $p = .005$.

Mental Effort Scores. For the assessment of mental effort, we used the PAAS Scale and employed a 2x4 ANOVA test as the homogeneity of variance assumptions had been met with a non-significant Levene's test of $p = .066$. There was no statistically significant effect of ethnicity on mental effort scores, F(3, 88) = 0.725, $p = .540$. There was also no significant effect of instructor type on mental effort, $F(1, 88) = 1.405, p = .239$. There was also no statistically significant interaction between instructor ethnicity and type of instructor on mental effort scores, $(F(3, 88) = 1.988, p = 0.122)$.

System Usability Scores. For the measure of perceived usability, scores were analyzed using the System Usability Scale, we also employed a 2x4 between subjects ANOVA. The Levene's test for homogeneity of variance was not significant (p = .535). There was no statistically significant effect based of ethnicity of instructor on usability scores $F(3, 91) = .541, p = .656$, and no effect for type of instructor $F(1, 91) = 1.759, p = .188$. Finally, there was also no significant interaction of ethnicity and type on usability scores, $F(3,91) = .461, p = .710$.

Engagement Survey. A frequencies statistical analysis was employed to document the most common responses individuals reported in the engagement survey to see how individuals generally behave on virtual learning platforms. When watching an instructional video, participants reported that they typically pause the video for the following reasons: 25.3% needed time to think and reflect on what they just watched, 24.2% wanted to write a note, 31.3% were distracted or needed a break, 8.1% searched for additional information using the web or a textbook, and 2.0% selected "other" to specify a different reason.

In response to the question "When watching an instructional video, I typically navigate forwards because…," 27.3% of participants indicated that usually fast forward when the content is found to be irrelevant, boring, or already known to them, while 28.3% reported that they wanted to get the gist of the content before watching the entire video to decide whether to continue. Additionally, 34.3% preferred to study the video at their own pace by jumping around, and 1.0% chose the "other" option.

The analysis for the question "When watching an instructional video, I typically highlight section of the video because…" reveals that 26.3% of participants highlight sections of the video because they zoned out or got distracted and want to make sure they did not miss anything. Additionally, 27.3% highlight sections of the video because they did not understand the explanation the first time, and 30.3% do so because it helps them remember the content. Only 6.1% of respondents highlighted sections of the video to understand the path that was taken to get to the end goal, and 1.0% selected "Other, please specify here."

"When watching an instructional video, I typically annotate on the video itself because…" reveals that 17.2% of participants usually annotate to add relevant information that is not on the video, 52.5% annotate to remember something important for an assignment or test, 18.2% summarize the video to save study time, and 3.0% chose the "Other" option to specify their own reasons.

"When watching an instructional video, I typically search the filmstrip and/or transcript because…" shows that 23.2% of participants do so to locate a specific piece of information to navigate to, 36.4% do it to better understand what is being said in the video, 14.1% like to read the transcript while watching the video, and 17.2% are looking for a keyword.

For the question "When watching an instructional video, I typically change the playback speed (faster and/or slower) because…" is as follows: 49.5% of respondents chose "The speaker is talking too slow or fast," 26.3% chose "Speeding up the playback saves me time," 12.1% chose "I am familiar with the content," and 3.0% selected "Other, please specify here."

3 Discussion

This study aimed to investigate the effect of ethnicity and instructor type on comprehension, usability, mental effort, trust, and engagement using. The following section will discuss each of the metrics in greater detail.

Comprehension. For the comprehension analysis we found that there was overall no significant difference in comprehension between avatars and human instructors, nor did the ethnicity of the instructor or interaction between type of instructor and ethnicity influence comprehension scores in a meaningful way. As such, participants scored essentially equally across all conditions with all mean average scores averaging out between 10.4–12 out of 20 possible correct answers. These findings suggest that there is a rather low number of correct responses, and therefore also highlights the fact that comprehension was generally low across conditions. There could be various reasons for these findings, particularly as the lecture consisted of an advanced level portion of a lecture in a memory topic in theoretical cognitive psychology, and as such might be harder to comprehend in one session alone. It is important to note that participants also scored very low on the pre-test questions, which assessed their prior knowledge in psychological science. This suggests that they may not be familiar with the general psychological literature, as the average number of correct responses in the pre-test questions was only 1.3 questions. Participants who signed up for the study might therefore not have been interested, familiar, or motivated enough to learn about the advanced level material, as it did not align with their current goals or was simply too complex for them to comprehend in one session alone and therefore could potentially account for the low performance on comprehension scores. It worthwhile to note that the low scores in pre-tests are not unexpected as participants were mostly sampled from a freshman PSY 100 course, and therefore had little to no existing knowledge in psychological science.

The study's finding clearly indicates that ethnicity and instructor type do not play a role in comprehension, which is particularly interesting since instructors exhibited individual differences in the manner by which they communicated. Although the material was delivered verbatim (i.e., word for word), each instructor still had a unique pacing, distinct ethnic accents (i.e., for instance African American speaker had an AAVE/African-American Vernacular English accent) which consists of differences in which words are pronounced, and varying levels of nonverbal communication in which they delivered the content material.

Our findings that avatars had no significant effect on comprehension scores when compared to human instructors, may align with the mixed results reported by Daniels and Lee [33]who found that some students found avatar teachers more engaging, others may found them to be less effective in delivering the material, which could have contributed to the lack of a significant difference in comprehension between avatar and human teachers and others were indifferent to them. It is possible that the effectiveness of avatars as instructional tools could depend on individual student preferences, the subject matter being taught, and the overall context of the learning environment in which student learns.

In contrast to Mizuho's study, our research found that avatars had no significant effect on comprehension when compared to human instructors. One possible reason for this discrepancy could be differences in the methods used to measure comprehension. Mizuho's study utilized a unique approach of changing avatars at different intervals, which may have increased engagement and retention in the learners [35]. On the other hand, this study primarily focused on traditional instructional methods, without utilizing the full potential of avatar technology by systematically switching the avatars instructor at specific intervals during class.

Additionally, it could also be indeed that comprehension is simply not influenced by the appearance or use of either an avatar or instructor, and that the virtual learning experience is primarily mediated by the content alone with the only potential difference of attending to trust in the creation of virtual avatars. Please note that we carefully rendered all lectures so that they are visually the same lecture verbatim. However, it remains to be answered whether the lack of an effect on comprehension would remain if the experiment were to extend over multiple testing days, perhaps even a semester long, as opposed to one lecture on its own.

Our study therefore suggests that the material itself is more important than the idiosyncratic individual differences of the lecturers themselves. Future studies could incorporate easier material that does not require a general understanding of psychological terminology and manners of speaking.

Trust. Our findings on trust revealed no significant influence of instructor type or ethnicity or trust scores on trust scores. However, the measure did indicate a significant influence that the interaction of instructor type and ethnicity on trust scores. It was observed that the Human Asian instructors scored higher than the Avatar Asian instructor. On the other hand, the effect of African-American instructors was in the opposite direction, as the Human African-American Instructors scored significantly lower in trust scores than the Avatar African-American instructor.

These findings are quite surprising as they suggest that participants generally trusted Asian human instructors more than Asian avatar instructors, whereas the opposite effect was observed for African-Americans instructors, who were significantly less trusted as a human versus as an avatar instructor. These findings suggest that there are quite clear differences in the manner by which trust is formed in online learning platforms and that avatars might be beneficial to use for some ethnic groups and less so for others. The reason for this effect is unknown, particularly as we also found no greater in-group trust preferences across ethnicities when controlling for the ethnicity of the participant. These findings also disagrees with the general literature which suggests that there generally tends to be greater ingroup preferences in trust [69]. Yet we also found no significant interaction between the ethnicity of the participants, the ethnicity of the instructor and the type of instructor when assessing baseline trust scores.

Our findings on trust were consistent with MacArthur's [42] results who found that morphology mediates and impacts trust in first impression in online telecommunication environments. Our study, which focused on the impact of teacher type and ethnicity on trust metrics within an educational context, did find similar results; specifically, as our study found that trust was significantly impacted by the instructor type in conjunction to the ethnicity, with participants reporting lower levels of trust for the Avatar Asian instructor compared to the Human Asian instructor and vice versa in the African-American condition. These findings suggest that factors beyond morphology, such as cultural biases and stereotypes, may perhaps play a role in shaping trust in educational settings, especially when the avatar or human being is of an underrepresented minority. It is perhaps possible that the morphologies of certain ethnic groups, due to scarcity of customizability led to these observed trust scores.

The findings that trust judgments are biased based on the human or avatar appearance alone emphasizes the importance of considering the potential biases that may emerge in avatar-based e-learning environments as trust judgments can be inaccurate and biased based on appearance alone and thus highlights the importance of considering the potential biases that may arise, particularly with regards to ethnicity. The findings on trust judgments becomes even more prevalent when considering that all groups scored equally on comprehension scores, indicating that the effect may perhaps be modulated primarily by trust perceptions. The subconscious nature of appearance-based judgments further emphasizes the need for greater awareness of the role that ethnicity plays in the future of online environments.

Mental Effort. Mental effort was not influenced by the instructor type or ethnicity. There was almost a one-to-one correlation between PAAS scores and the instructor type which is interesting to consider since this contrasts with the research conducted by Hirata [52] where Japanese learners reported lower arousal levels (which as discussed earlier is associated to a degree with mental effort) and with feeling more comfortable speaking up in Zoom classes when their teacher or themselves were represented by an avatar. As our findings are, to our knowlege, the first to assess mental effort, the findings therefore conclude that in asynchronous courses neither the instructor type, nor the ethnicity of the instructor influence mental effort. This effect, however, could be due to the very nature of our study of the asynchronous course itself, since mental effort perhaps might be increased or decreased during live classes that require greater interaction with fellow students and the instructor and as such might influence mental effort. Our results are, however, to an extent, consistent with the study by Bozkurt [51] in Turkey, where English as a second language learners showed no significant difference in arousal and anxiety levels when attending online or in-person classes. As such, these diverse findings suggest that cultural factors may perhaps play a role in how individuals perceive and respond to different forms of online learning, but the impact of avatars and ethnicity type on mental effort is not universal.

As our findings suggest that the instructor type does not have a significant effect on mental workload, we might be able in the future to use avatars as viable options for instructors in online learning environments. Again, since our study, is the first to investigate the impact of avatars on mental effort, our findings therefore do not suggest that mental effort suffers or is improved using avatars and therefore could be used without having to attend to this metric as a factor of concern. Our findings, which also showed that usability was not impacted by teacher type (human vs. teacher), suggest that avatar-based education technologies could be a viable alternative to traditional teaching methods without compromising the usability of the e-learning platform. The use of avatars did not result in any significant differences in terms of user satisfaction, ease of use, or perceived learning outcomes. The findings of the current investigation therefore supports the view that avatars, when designed well, could offer an immersive, engaging, and interactive experience for students without negatively impacting the usability of the platform as a whole.

Usability Scores.   Our findings for usability also yielded no significant effect that the instructor type and ethnicity of the instructor had on usability scores which suggests that neither the type of instructor nor the ethnicity of the instructor shape or influence perceptions of usability in online learning platforms. The current usability findings are important to consider as universities and students could feel reassured that the quality of education is not perceived less satisfactory, nor the usability in virtual learning platforms diminished by the instructors ethnicity. Likewise, our study also suggests that avatars could be used in lectures where it was perhaps not possible to record the presenter and replace him or her with an avatar. As such, our results differs from the findings of Wang, Chignell and Ishizuka [57] as they found that avatars used in e-learning environments had a positive impact on the learning experience and usability as a whole. However, their study also included the recording of eye-tracking data and physiological measurements to which the instructor's avatars automatically responded in real time and as such generating a much more immersive experience for students whereas we just examined the effects of students comprehension in an asynchronous course. More research is therefore needed to fully understand the impact of avatar-based education interventions on usability and learning outcomes in different educational contexts. As such, it would be essential to assess this phenomenon in a fully immersive e-learning environments via virtual reality.

Engagement.   As our study did not directly look at the effect of ethnicity and type of instructor on engagement but rather used a survey to map out general tendencies and behavior in virtual learning platforms, we cannot make definite claims about the effect of instructor type and ethnicity on engagement. We conducted a frequencies analysis to average out the responses to questions such as "why do you usually take notes during lectures", and scored their answers "preparing for an exam" and as to why they generally feel the need to fast forward or rewind during asynchronous courses. Future studies should use metrics that capture data that are more immediately related to engagement and not attempt to capture data about general student behaviors. For instance, the survey on engagement could ask "During the lecture I just watched I did/did not pause the video" because "…" instead of asking for general student learning behaviors such as "Usually I take notes during lectures because" I want to study for an exam ", since this does not pertain to the research condition at hand and therefore would make it impossible to determine whether students took notes in one of the conditions or did not since this was not specifically asked by the questionnaire. To effectively inquire about a phenomenon, it is crucial to articulate questions that are unambiguous and specifically relevant to the subject matter. Furthermore, it is essential to differentiate between questions that inquire about general behavior and those that seek to understand immediate behaviors. Likewise, there is no way in telling as to whether participants did fast forward during a particular condition or whether participants fast forward when something occurs, as the question were framed in a manner that asks what usually motivates them to fast forward when they do fast forward.

3.1 Limitations and Future Studies

One major limitation of our study is that it does not capture the full diversity of the human spectrum of ethnicities. The current study only looked at African-Americans, Asians, Hispanic, and White instructors. However, there are many other ethnicities and subgroups within ethnicities that might be relevant to our findings. For instance, Asian instructors could also mean Indian, Turkish, or Eastern Russian instructors and as such excludes a whole gamut of diversity. Future studies should therefore account for regional differences and include more ethnic sub-groups (such as Native American, Pacific Islander, Indian, etc.) to overcome these issues.

The study was also conducted on young college students in California, who were mostly female, which is arguably the biggest predictor for the assessment of liberal population that values diversity and equity [79], and as such it may not be surprising that there were biases in the study. It would be questionable if this would translate across different states, countries, and cultures as our previously mentioned example in Saudi Arabia [72] showed a significant benefit in having a female Middle Eastern teacher over other ethnic groups.

Future studies should include lectures that compare video to no video, avatar to no avatar, and the effects of ethnicity on the scores above. It would be very interesting to see whether the video had any impact on the scores at all, and if just having a blank zoom screen would have yielded similar results. This could be further enhanced by the use of eye-tracking data to see how long individuals actually looked at the instructors.

Additionally, we also suggest that future studies could use a standardized audio feed for all conditions to further limit regional differences and examine the appearances of avatars and instructors alone. As such, voice actors that use a standardized General American dialect might be able to perform a lecture that could be lip-synced to videos to examine the effect of visual stimuli on learning experiences.

Studies should also use and compare the type of instructor and ethnicity of the instructor in more immersive virtual or extended reality environments and in live online classes. In such environments, presence is immediate, and students would have no choice but to attend fully to the instructor and therefore the effect on mental effort, usability, trust and comprehension might be more prevalent.

Finally, in any research study, it is important to acknowledge and address the limitations of the study in order to provide an accurate assessment of the results. In the current study, we have identified a significant limitation that affects the validity and reliability of the data collected. Specifically, we have discovered a systematic error that appeared in the Qualtrics survey platform that we used to collect data. This error has resulted in a large amount of data not being recorded properly, which has compromised the integrity of the results. We believe that this error occurred due to a technical issue with the software and recording equipment. As such, during the first quarter of the data collection period, one of four the questionnaires was not displayed. So, one of either the PAAS Scale for Mental Effort, SUS, Engagement, or Trust was not properly collected. As a result, for each case, 10–15 participants had to be removed and separate data files created to minimize this effect. The final participant number for the PAAS score was 96, for the SUS 99, and for the trust scores 99. All 110 participants quiz scores that assess comprehension were recorded and no data were lost here. Obviously, this loss of data is a significant influence on the result of the study, particular for ethnicity since the study was already underpowered, and analysis might have detected a significant effect if the study collected all the data.

3.2 Conclusion

In this current study, we sought to investigate the influence of the instructor's human or avatar presentational form and ethnicity on various aspects of online learning, including comprehension, usability, trust, engagement, and mental effort. Additionally, we also aimed to address the gaps in the literature by considering the role of ethnicity in online learning environments. Our results indicated that, with the exception of one metric, there were no significant differences between human and avatar instructors nor between ethnicities across the studied parameters. We did, however, observe an interaction between the type of instructor and ethnicity on learners' perceived trust of the instructor. Specifically, Human Asian Avatar instructors were rated as significantly more trustworthy than Avatar Asian instructors. On the other hand, African-American instructors were rated as significantly less trustworthy than human instructors when compared to their avatar counterparts.

These findings are important for the general research literature as they highlight the role of appearance and ethnicity in shaping learners' trust and perceptions of online instructors. Moreover, they suggest that educators and developers of online learning platforms should consider the potential biases that may arise due to appearance and ethnicity and take steps to mitigate them.

In conclusion, our study adds to the existing research literature on online learning and provides insights into the impact of instructor appearance and ethnicity on learner outcomes. We hope that our findings will encourage further research in this area and inform the development of more inclusive and effective online learning environments (Table 1).

Appendix

Table 1. Appendix. 1. Tables for Comprehension Frequencies

When watching an instructional video, I typically navigate forwards because...	Frequency	Percent
I find the content to be irrelevant, boring, or already known to me	23	31.5
I want to get the gist of the content before I watch the entire video, to know what to expect and decide whether to watch it	24	32.9
I prefer to study the video at my own pace by jumping around, instead of watching linearly.	25	34.2
Other please specify here	1	1.4
Total	73	100.0

When watching an instructional video, I typically highlight section of the video because...	Frequency	Percent
I zoned out or got distracted, and want to make sure I did not miss anything	20	27.4
I did not get the explanation the first time	24	32.9
It helps me remember the content	23	31.5
I can start from the end goal and understand the path that was taken to get there	5	6.8
Other please specify here	1	1.4
Total	73	100.0

When watching an instructional video, I typically annotate on the video itself because...	Frequency	Percent
I want to add relevant information that is not on the video	15	20.5
I want to remember something important for an assignment or test	35	47.9
I summarize the video to save study time	20	27.4
Other please specify here	3	4.1
Total	73	100.0

When watching an instructional video, I typically search the filmstrip and/or transcript because...	Frequency	Percent
To locate a specific piece of information to navigate to	25	34.2
To better understand what is being said in the video	26	35.6
I like to read the transcript while watching the video	9	12.3
I am looking for a keyword	13	17.8
Total	73	100.0

When watching an instructional video, I typically change the playback speed (faster and/or slower) because...	Frequency	Percent
The speaker is talking too slow or fast	45	61.6
Speeding up the playback saves me time	19	26.0
I am familiar with the content	7	9.6
Other please specify here	2	2.7
Total	73	100.0

References

1. Bajaj, M.: Human rights education: Ideology, location, and approaches. Human Rights Q., 481–508 (2011)
2. Banerjee, R., Mishra, V., Maruta, A.A.: Energy poverty, health and education outcomes: evidence from the developing world. Energy Econ. **101**, 105447 (2021)
3. Cvecic, I., Sokolic, D., Mrak, M.: Higer education and economic prosperity at regional level. Revista Portuguesa de Estudos Regionais **50**, 9–25 (2019)
4. Orazem, P.F., King, E.M., Hoque, M.M., Montenegro, C.E.: Education and Longevity. Handbook of Labor, Human Resources and Population Economics, pp. 1–32 (2022).
5. Bulmer, M.: The Chicago school of sociology: Institutionalization, diversity, and the rise of sociological research. University of Chicago Press (1986)
6. Durkheim, E.: Education and sociology. Simon and Schuster (1956)
7. Woolcock, M.: Social capital: A theory of social structure and action. JSTOR (2004)
8. Flynn, S., Brown, J., Johnson, A., Rodger, S.: Barriers to education for the marginalized adult learner. Alberta J. Educ. Res. **57**(1), 43 (2011)
9. McWhirter, E.H.: Perceived barriers to education and career: Ethnic and gender differences. J. Vocat. Behav. **50**(1), 124–140 (1997)
10. Jury, M., Smeding, A., Stephens, N.M., Nelson, J.E., Aelenei, C., Darnon, C.: The experience of low-SES students in higher education: Psychological barriers to success and interventions to reduce social-class inequality. J. Soc. Issues **73**(1), 23–41 (2017)
11. Wei, L., Hindman, D.B.: Does the digital divide matter more? Comparing the effects of new media and old media use on the education-based knowledge gap. Mass Commun. Soc. **14**(2), 216–235 (2011)
12. Bejerano, A.R.: The genesis and evolution of online degree programs: Who are they for and what have we lost along the way? Commun. Educ. **57**(3), 408–414 (2008)
13. Dhawan, S.: Online learning: A panacea in the time of COVID-19 crisis. J. Educ. Technol. Syst. **49**(1), 5–22 (2020)
14. Rajab, M.H., Gazal, A.M., Alkattan, K., Rajab, M.H.: Challenges to online medical education during the COVID-19 pandemic. Cureus, **12**(7)(2020)
15. James, W.: The varieties of religious experience, vol. 15. Harvard University Press (1985)
16. Baturay, M.H.: An overview of the world of MOOCs. Procedia Soc. Behav. Sci. **174**, 427–433 (2015)
17. McVeigh-Schultz, J., Isbister, K.: The case for "weird social" in VR/XR: a vision of social superpowers beyond meatspace. In: Extended Abstracts of the 2021 CHI Conference on Human Factors in Computing Systems, pp. 1–10 (2021)
18. Foster, A.L.: Professor Avatar. Education Digest: Essential Readings Condensed for Quick Review **73**(5), 12–17 (2008)
19. Long, J.D.: A Hinduism without walls? Exploring the concept of the avatar interreligiously. In: Theology Without Walls, pp. 227–233. Routledge (2019)
20. Rambachan, A.: A Hindu theology of liberation: Not-two is not one. State University of New York Press (2014)
21. Khin, H.M.: A study of Hindu concepts about gods and goddess. Dagon Univer. Res. J. **11**, 58–64 (2020)
22. Nowak, K.L., Fox, J.: Avatars and computer-mediated communication: a review of the definitions, uses, and effects of digital representations. Rev. Commun. Res. **6**, 30–53 (2018)
23. Lee-Cultura, S., Sharma, K., Papavlasopoulou, S., Retalis, S., Giannakos, M.: Using sensing technologies to explain children's self-representation in motion-based educational games. In: Proceedings of the Interaction Design and Children Conference, 541–555 (2020)

24. Lehdonvirta, M., Nagashima, Y., Lehdonvirta, V., Baba, A.: The stoic male: How avatar gender affects help-seeking behavior in an online game. Games and Culture **7**(1), 29–47 (2012)
25. Bolldén, K.: Teachers' embodied presence in online teaching practices. Stud. Contin. Educ. **38**(1), 1–15 (2016). https://doi.org/10.1080/0158037X.2014.988701
26. Erinn, W.: Digital blackface: How 21st century internet language reinforces racism (2019)
27. Freelon, D., Bossetta, M., Wells, C., Lukito, J., Xia, Y., Adams, K.: Black trolls matter: racial and ideological asymmetries in social media disinformation. Soc. Sci. Comput. Rev. **40**(3), 560–578 (2022)
28. Just, M.A., Carpenter, P.A.: The psychology of reading and language comprehension. Allyn & Bacon (1987)
29. Mar, R.A.: The neuropsychology of narrative: Story comprehension, story production and their interrelation. Neuropsychologia **42**(10), 1414–1434 (2004)
30. Graesser, A., Golding, J.M.: And comprehension. Handbook Reading Res. **2**, 171 (1984)
31. Bergstrand, K., Savage, S.V.: The Chalkboard versus the avatar: comparing the effectiveness of online and in-class courses. Teach. Sociol. **41**(3), 294–306 (2013). https://doi.org/10.1177/0092055X13479949
32. Badriyah, B., Rahmawati, E.: Students' problems of reading comprehension during online learning in the period of Covid-19 Pandemic. In: Proceedings of the 2nd International Conference on English Language Education, ICONELE 2020 (2020).
33. Daniels, D., Lee, J.S.: The impact of avatar teachers on student learning and engagement in a virtual learning environment for online STEM courses. In: Learning and Collaboration Technologies. Novel Technological Environments: 9th International Conference, LCT 2022, Held as Part of the 24th HCI International Conference, HCII 2022, Virtual Event, June 26–July 1, 2022. Proceedings, Part II, 158–175 (2022)
34. Tatli, Z., Altinişik, D., Şen, H., Çakıroğlu, Ü.: Learning via virtual and real museums: a comparative study on presence and retention. Inter. J. Virtual Personal Learn. Environ. (IJVPLE) **11**(1), 38–53 (2021)
35. Mizuho, T., Amemiya, T., Narumi, T., Kuzuoka, H.: Virtual omnibus lecture: investigating the effects of varying lecturer avatars as environmental context on audience memory. In: Proceedings of the Augmented Humans International Conference 2023, pp. 55–65 (2023)
36. Evans, A.M., Krueger, J.I.: The psychology (and economics) of trust. Soc. Pers. Psychol. Compass **3**(6), 1003–1017 (2009)
37. Rousseau, D.M., Sitkin, S.B., Burt, R.S., Camerer, C.: Not so different after all: a cross-discipline view of trust. Acad. Manag. Rev. **23**(3), 393–404 (1998)
38. Hardin, R., Cook, K.S.: Trust and society. Compet. Struct., 17–46 (2000)
39. Gurviez, P., Korchia, M.: Proposal for a multidimensional brand trust scale. In: 32nd Emac-Conference-Glasgow, Marketing: Responsible and Relevant, pp. 438–452 (2003).
40. Foddy, M., Platow, M.J., Yamagishi, T.: Group-based trust in strangers: The role of stereotypes and expectations. Psychol. Sci. **20**(4), 419–422 (2009)
41. Marzi, T., Righi, S., Ottonello, S., Cincotta, M., Viggiano, M.P.: Trust at first sight: evidence from ERPs. Soc. Cognit. Affect. Neurosci. **9**(1), 63–72 (2014). https://doi.org/10.1093/scan/nss102
42. MacArthur, K.: Dispositional Trust Response to Morphological Differences in Synthetic Representative Agents (2021)
43. Pairoa, I., Arunrangsiwed, P.: The effect of brand mascots on consumers' purchasing behaviors. Inter. J. Econ. Manag. Eng. **10**(5), 1702–1705 (2016)
44. Chae, S.W., Lee, K.C., Seo, Y.W.: Exploring the effect of avatar trust on learners' perceived participation intentions in an e-learning environment. Inter. J. Hum.-Comput. Interact. **32**(5), 373–393 (2016)

45. Weisman, W.D., Peña, J.F.: Face the uncanny: The effects of doppelganger talking head avatars on affect-based trust toward artificial intelligence technology are mediated by uncanny valley perceptions. Cyberpsychol. Behav. Soc. Netw. **24**(3), 182–187 (2021)

46. Mulder, L. B. J., de Waard, D., Brookhuis, K.A.: Estimating mental effort using heart rate and heart rate variability. In Handbook of Human Factors and Ergonomics Methods, pp. 227–236. CRC Press (2004)

47. Cennamo, K.S.: Learning from video: Factors influencing learners' preconceptions and invested mental effort. Educ. Technol. Res. Developm., 33–45 (1993).

48. Van Nuland, S.E., Rogers, K.A.: The anatomy of E-Learning tools: Does software usability influence learning outcomes? Anat. Sci. Educ. **9**(4), 378–390 (2016)

49. Ni, A.Y.: Comparing the effectiveness of classroom and online learning: teaching research methods. J. Public Affairs Educ. **19**(2), 199–215 (2013)

50. Howells, F.M., Stein, D.J., Russell, V.A.: Perceived mental effort correlates with changes in tonic arousal during attentional tasks. Behav. Brain Funct. **6**, 1–15 (2010)

51. Bozkurt, B., Aydin, S.: The impact of collaborative learning on speaking anxiety among foreign language learners in online and face-to-face environments. Inter. J. Virtual Personal Learn. Environ. **13**, 1–16 (2023). https://doi.org/10.4018/IJVPLE.316973

52. Hirata, Y.: Do avatar-assisted virtual classrooms work for students with low speaking confidence?: a qualitative study. Interact. Technol. Smart Educ. (2023). https://doi.org/10.1108/ITSE-10-2022-0142

53. Harte, R., et al.: A human-centered design methodology to enhance the usability, human factors, and user experience of connected health systems: A three-phase methodology. JMIR Hum. Factors **4**(1), e5443 (2017)

54. Hawkins, F.H.: Human factors in flight. Routledge (2017)

55. Sundbo, J., Sørensen, F.: Introduction to the experience economy. In: Handbook on the Experience Economy, pp. 1–18. Edward Elgar Publishing (2013)

56. Wonggom, P., Kourbelis, C., Newman, P., Du, H., Clark, R.A.: Effectiveness of avatar-based technology in patient education for improving chronic disease knowledge and self-care behavior: Aasystematic review. JBI Evidence Synth. **17**(6), 1101–1129 (2019)

57. Wang, H., Chignell, M., Ishizuka, M.: Improving the usability and effectiveness of online learning: how can avatars help? Proc. Human Factors Ergon. Soc. Annual Meeting **49**(7), 769–773 (2005)

58. Nes, L.S., Segerstrom, S.C., Sephton, S.E.: Engagement and arousal: Optimism's effects during a brief stressor. Pers. Soc. Psychol. Bull. **31**(1), 111–120 (2005)

59. Doherty, K., Doherty, G.: Engagement in HCI: conception, theory and measurement. ACM Comput. Surv. (CSUR) **51**(5), 1–39 (2018)

60. Sawesi, S., Rashrash, M., Phalakornkule, K., Carpenter, J.S., Jones, J.F.: The impact of information technology on patient engagement and health behavior change: A systematic review of the literature. JMIR Med. Inform. **4**(1), e4514 (2016)

61. Mallia, Ġ.: "I don't like seeing myself" and other stories: reasons for camera (non) use during online lectures. Commun. Technol. Educ. **104** (2021).

62. Burkhardt, H., Schoenfeld, A.H.: Improving educational research: toward a more useful, more influential, and better-funded enterprise. Educ. Res. **32**(9), 3–14 (2003)

63. Park, S.: Chapter 10—Virtual avatar as an emotional scaffolding strategy to promote interest in online learning environment. In: Tettegah, S.Y., Gartmeier, M. (eds.), Emotions, Technology, Design, and Learning, pp. 201–224. Academic Press (2016). https://doi.org/10.1016/B978-0-12-801856-9.00010-4

64. Mazlan, M.N.A., Burd, L.: Does an avatar motivate? 2In: 011 Frontiers in Education Conference (FIE), T4J-1-T4J-6 (2011). https://doi.org/10.1109/FIE.2011.6142700

65. Dietrich, D.R.: Avatars of whiteness: Racial expression in video game characters. Sociol. Inq. **83**(1), 82–105 (2013)

66. Waddell, T. F., Ivory, J.D., Conde, R., Long, C., McDonnell, R.: White man's virtual world: a systematic content analysis of gender and race in massively multiplayer online games. J. Virtual Worlds Res. **7**(2) (2014)

67. Kafai, Y.B., Cook, M.S., Fields, D.A.: "'Blacks deserve bodies too!'": design and discussion about diversity and race in a tween virtual world. Games Culture **5**(1), 43–63 (2010). https://doi.org/10.1177/1555412009351261

68. Arora, R.: Race and ethnicity in education. Routledge (2018)

69. Birkás, B., Dzhelyova, M., Lábadi, B., Bereczkei, T., Perrett, D.I.: Cross-cultural perception of trustworthiness: the effect of ethnicity features on evaluation of faces' observed trustworthiness across four samples. Personality Individ. Differ. **69**, 56–61 (2014)

70. Gingras, F., et al.: Pain in the eye of the beholder: variations in pain visual representations as a function of face ethnicity and culture. British J. Psychol. (2023)

71. Khalifa, M.A., Gooden, M.A., Davis, J.E.: Culturally responsive school leadership: A synthesis of the literature. Rev. Educ. Res. **86**(4), 1272–1311 (2016)

72. Adham, R., Parslow, P., Dimitriadi, Y., Lundqvist, K.Ø.: The use of avatars in gender segregated online learning within MOOCs in Saudi Arabia—A Rwaq case study. Inter. Rev. Res. Open Distributed Learn. **19**(1) (2018). https://doi.org/10.19173/irrodl.v19i1.3139

73. Hodgson, E.E.: Learning from video examples: Does instructor ethnicity (Western/Non-Western) affect test performance and self-efficacy of students from Vocational education? [Master's Thesis] (2020)

74. She, L., Ma, L., Jan, A., Sharif Nia, H., Rahmatpour, P.: Online Learning satisfaction during COVID-19 pandemic among chinese university students: the serial mediation model. Front. Psychol. 12 (2021). https://www.frontiersin.org/articles/https://doi.org/10.3389/fpsyg.2021.743936

75. Lewis, J.R.: The system usability scale: Past, present, and future. Inter. J. Hum.-Comput. Interact. **34**(7), 577–590 (2018)

76. Jian, J.-Y., Bisantz, A.M., Drury, C.G.: Foundations for an empirically determined scale of trust in automated systems. Int. J. Cogn. Ergon. **4**(1), 53–71 (2000)

77. Paas, F.G., Van Merriënboer, J.J.: The efficiency of instructional conditions: an approach to combine mental effort and performance measures. Hum. Factors **35**(4), 737–743 (1993)

78. Henrie, C.R., Halverson, L.R., Graham, C.R.: Measuring student engagement in technology-mediated learning: a review. Comput. Educ. **90**, 36–53 (2015)

79. Woolpert, S.: The Face of the Democratic Party (2019)

Examining the Relationship Between Playing a Chord with Expressions and Hand Movements Using MediaPipe

Chika Oshima[✉][iD], Taiyo Takatsu, and Koichi Nakayama

Saga University, Saga, Japan
sj5872@edu.cc.saga-u.ac.jp

Abstract. This paper examined whether hand movements are responsible for expression in a piano performance. A player played a chord 100 times each with 12 different performance expressions, which consisted of three articulations (tenuto, heavy staccato, and light staccato) and four-level dynamics. The landmarks' coordinates of her right fingers, wrist, elbow, and shoulder estimated as she played the chord (12×100 times), judged by MediaPipe Pose and Hands, were used for machine learning training and testing. In the results for the learning model, the testing accuracy rate was 0.99. In each performance expression, F1-scores were 0.94–1.00. This suggested a relationship between performance expressions and hand movements. Moreover, when the player happened to play a different, unintended type of expression, her landmarks' coordinates were close to those when she had aimed exactly to play that type of performance expression.

Keywords: Piano · MIDI · Machine learning

1 Introduction

In classical music performance, players reproduce the performance expected by the composer of the piece based on sheet music information and the performers' own unique approach and interpretation. During piano lessons, teachers guide pupils to execute appropriate performance expressions. Usually, pupils memorize how to play these expressions using their own ears and physical senses and then try to acquire the expressions reliably by continuing to reproduce them at home when practicing. However, in real-world situations, it is difficult to reproduce those expressions that have not yet been acquired.

With the above in mind, we aimed to develop a system that supports the acquisition of performance expressions during home practice. A simple method is to take home video data recorded during a lesson. The video includes not only the pupil's performances but also the teacher's comments; hence, it is possible for the pupil to review what was taught. However, it is questionable whether objectively photographing the pupil's fingers and hand movements are sufficient

H. Mori and Y. Asahi (Eds.): HCII 2024, LNCS 14691, pp. 118–131, 2024.
https://doi.org/10.1007/978-3-031-60125-5_8

for their attempts to acquire the performance expressions during their home practice sessions.

Performance expressions, described simply, are determined by a combination of factors, such as the speed of the key-press and -release, and the length of time a key is pressed. To press and release a key, appropriate finger movements, joint angles, and muscle tension and relaxation are required from just before the key is pressed until it is released.

It is likely that, just before pressing a key, piano players anticipate the physical sensations of their fingers and hands about to press the key. However, they do not carefully calculate and check their "shape," which consists of the height and movement of their fingers and hands. In contrast, although the pupil may be unable to recall even the physical sensations during home practice, first knowing the required shape of their fingers and hands may allow them to gradually recall the resulting physical sensation.

As the first stage of research, this paper examines how the movements from the fingertips to the shoulder are responsible for controlling key presses and releases for a certain performance expression (articulation and dynamics). We used MediaPipe [1] for hand tracking. MediaPipe is an open-source framework provided by Google. The MediaPipe Pose [2] and Hand [3] Landmarker task detects the landmarks of the human body, including the hands, in an image or video and can output these as image coordinates operated with a machine learning model. In this way, MediaPipe can acquire numerical data on human movements using a home video camera. Using MediaPipe may also be useful for supporting piano practice at home, which is the goal of this research.

Despite its advantages, there are some concerns about the recognition accuracy of MediaPipe. The hand tracking solution implemented in MediaPipe uses a machine learning pipeline consisting of several models working together. One is a palm detector model (BlazePalm) [4]. In this model, the palms are used to estimate bounding boxes based on a trained palm detector, because it is difficult to detect hands with articulated fingers [5]. Although MediaPipe has high accuracy in gesture recognition, there are some concerns it may have low accuracy related to piano performances in which the palm is not visible to the camera [6]. This study employs a playing method without crossing or covering the fingers and examines the relationship between performance expressions and hand movements.

2   Experimental Method

2.1   Acquire Performance Data

Piano performance data were acquired in two ways. The data of hand movements from the fingertips to the shoulder were acquired using MediaPipe. The velocities of striking and releasing a key, and the duration from striking the key to releasing it, were acquired using Musical Instrument Digital Interface (MIDI) data.

The data acquired using MediaPipe Pose and Hands were used to clarify the relationship between performance expressions and hand movements. MediaPipe

Pose is a library that detects human body poses and movements by estimating 33 three-dimensional pose landmarks [2]. MediaPipe Hands recognizes the shapes and movements of hands by estimating 21 three-dimensional pose landmarks [3].

Each landmark is composed of x-, y-, and z-coordinates. The x- and y-coordinates are normalized to the image width and height [0.0-1.0]. The z-coordinate represents the depth information. In MediaPipe Pose, the z-coordinate represents the landmark depth, with the depth at the midpoint of the hips being the origin [2]. In MediaPipe Hands, the z-coordinate represents the landmark depth, with the depth at the wrist being the origin. The smaller the value, the closer the landmark is to the camera [3].

The data acquired via MIDI were used to numerically confirm the actual performance expressions under each condition (see Sect. 2.2). MIDI describes performance information in digital form. When a performer plays on a MIDI instrument, a variety of messages are generated; of these, the following were used in this paper:

Note On Message Indicates that a particular note starts playing.
> **Note On**
>> The key was pressed.
> **Note Number**
>> Which key was pressed.
> **Velocity**
>> How fast the key was pressed (almost volume).

Note Off Message Indicates that the note stops playing.
> **Note Off**
>> The key was released.
> **Note Number**
>> Which key was released.
> **Velocity**
>> How fast the key was released (change sound attenuation).

2.2   Twelve Kinds of Chords

Figure 1 shows a C chord (consisting of C (Do), E (Mi), and G (So)) that a player (the paper's first author) played on the piano using her right hand. As shown in Table 1, the chord was played in 12 different ways, with different articulations and dynamics. Regarding articulations, Jones [7] says, *"Articulation is the key to breathing life into each note and conveying feelings that words alone can't express."*

In this experiment, the term "tenuto," in the articulation column, refers to holding the applicable note for its full length, although the term also has several other meanings [8]. Furthermore, there are many parts of piano pieces that should be played tenuto, even if there is no tenuto mark. The dictionary meaning of "staccato" indicates that the marked note should be shortened to half of its written note value (length). However, in actual piano pieces, there are various types of staccato playing techniques [8]. In this experiment, two types of staccato were employed: a very short and light staccato ("light staccato"), and a slightly longer and heavier staccato ("heavy staccato").

In addition, symbols such as p (piano), mp (mezzo piano), mf (mezzo forte), and f (forte) are usually written on the score to indicate playing softly, moderately soft, moderately loud, and loudly, respectively [9], as relative changes of tone and volume. In this experiment, these four symbols were used to indicate four levels of tone and volume.

Fig. 1. The player played a C chord on the piano using her right hand.

Table 1. Twelve kinds of chords were played in different ways (abbreviations).

Articulation	Soft, quiet ⟸⟹ powerful, loud			
	Piano	Mezzo Piano	Mezzo Forte	Forte
	(p)	(mp)	(mf)	(f)
Tenuto	TP	TMP	TMF	TF
Light Staccato	LP	LMP	LMF	LF
Heavy Staccato	HP	HMP	HMF	HF

2.3   Data Recordings

The C chord (see Fig. 1) was played 100 times each with 12 different performance expressions (see Table 1). The player played the chord once every 4 s, using a metronome for timing. These data were recorded over several days; therefore, the player's clothing was different, and the position of the camera was also slightly different from day to day.

A digital piano, Kawai MP11SE, was used for the recordings. The MP11SE can output the velocity of releasing a key (note off velocity: 0~127). Many other keyboards and silent pianos that output MIDI data in their silent mode only output 0 or 64 (releasing the key) as the note off velocity value.

The digital piano was placed in a soundproof room. As shown in Fig. 2, a camera was set in front of the player to record video from the front. The player was asked to always keep her left hand on the keyboard, although only the right hand was used to play the chord. MediaPipe's recognition rate can improve when both hands are kept on the keyboard and within the camera's shooting frame.

Similarly, the player's chin was always kept within the camera's shooting frame, to stabilize the recognition rate.

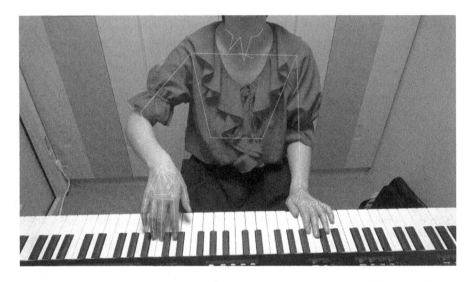

Fig. 2. A camera was placed in front of the player.

2.4 Classifying Performance Data Using Machine Learning

Of the landmarks (x-, y-, and z-coordinates) output by MediaPipe Pose, the landmarks of the right hand's wrist, elbow, and shoulder were used. By contrast, all of the right hand's landmarks (x-, y-, and z-coordinates) output by MediaPipe Hands were used. These landmarks' coordinates were used as training and/or test data in machine learning by two methods, as explained below.

Preprocessing MediaPipe Data. A stream of images of the player playing the chords was input to MediaPipe. Then, using MediaPipe Pose, 33 three-dimensional landmarks were detected at 30 fps to yield body landmarks rendered on the images. Similarly, using MediaPipe Hands, 21 three-dimensional landmarks were detected to yield hand landmarks rendered on the images. Numerical coordinate data for each landmark was output to comma separated values (CSV) files at a rate of 30 times per second.

First, we found the image where the player's hand began moving while demonstrating each type of performance expression. Since the chord was played once every four seconds, the data corresponding to 12,000 images from the first image were used as data for 100 performances.

Moreover, for the MediaPipe Pose data, all coordinates other than the land-marks of the right hand's wrist, elbow, and shoulder were deleted. Among the MediaPipe Hands data, the landmark coordinate data for the left hand were deleted.

LSTM. Long short-term memory (LSTM) [10], which is a deep recurrent neural network architecture, was used for the classification of time-series performance data obtained with MediaPipe. To implement LSTM, the library uses Tensor-Flow [11] because it produces better results than Pytorch [12].

Learning Method. First, the data for all 100 iterations of 12 different perfor-mance expressions were combined. Then, 80% of the randomly selected coordi-nates' data was used for training, while the remaining 20% was used for testing. In total, there were 144,000 sets of data because there were 12,000 images (30 fps × 4 s × 100 times) for each type of performance expression. The results of the test show how many times out of these 28,800 (20%) were classified as the expected (correct) performance expression.

2.5   Visually and Numerically Investigate Differences Between Images

As MIDI data for each performance expression were analyzed and outlier data were found, the time series of images of a performance with outlier data were compared visually with those of mean data. If the difference between the two types of performance were visually unclear, their similarities were investigated based on the x- and y-coordinates of each of the 24 landmarks (see Sec. 2.4).

First, each value was standardized using Equ. 1.

$$z = \frac{x - \mu}{\sigma}, \tag{1}$$

where z is a standardized value. x indicates each coordinate value for the 24 landmarks. μ and σ indicate the mean and the standard deviation of the five coordinate values of each landmark (because there five images), respectively.

Then, the movement trajectory of each landmark in the time series was com-pared between the two performances (outlier data and the mean data in a per-formance expression type) using a method [13] based on Euclidean distance.

The $v = (v_i, v_i')$ is a vector in a two-dimensional space. The distance between two vectors v_i, v_i' is defined as shown below.

$$D(v_i, v_i') = \sqrt{(x - x')^2 + (y - y')^2} \tag{2}$$

Then, the distance between two time series vectors $D(L, L')$ is defined as shown below.

$$D(L, L') = \sqrt{\sum_{i=1}^{n} D(v_i, v_i')^2} \tag{3}$$

Finally, the mean value of $D(L, L')$ at 24 landmarks was calculated in each data set.

3   Results

3.1   Note on Velocity

Figure 3 shows the note-on velocity results for the 100 iterations of 12 different performance expressions using a boxplot. The boxplot comes from five statistics: minimum value, second quartile, median value, third quartile, and maximum value. The figure shows that the median values increased as assumed volumes of p, mp, mf, and f changed.

In practice, the median values of mp and mf differed greatly depending on the performance expression (tenuto, heavy staccato, light staccato). For example, the median value of Heavy-staccato Mezzo Forte (HMF) was almost the same as the values for Tenuto Forte (TF) and Light-staccato Forte (LF).

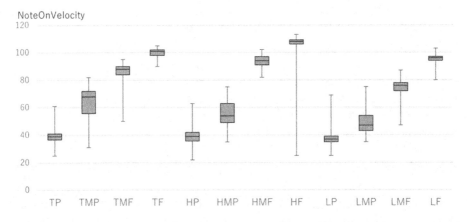

Fig. 3. Note-on velocity of 100 iterations for 12 different performance expressions.

3.2   Note Off Velocity

Figure 4 shows the note-off velocity results for the 100 iterations for 12 different performance expressions using a boxplot. The median values for Light-staccato (LP, LMP, LMF, and LF) were around 80. However, the median values of HMF and Heavy-staccato Forte (HF) were also around 80.

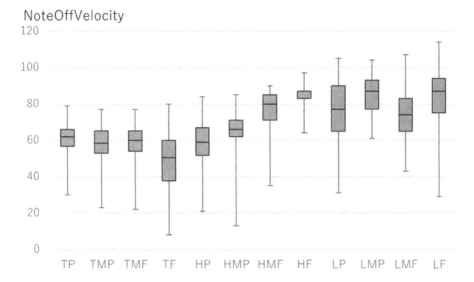

Fig. 4. Note-off velocity of 100 iterations for 12 different performance expressions.

3.3   Length of Time the Key Was Kept Being Pressed

The length of time that the key remained pressed can indicate the times from the note-on to note-off. Figure 5 shows the mean values for the lengths of time C, E, and G were each played using 12 different performance expressions. The values of Tenuto (TP, TMP, TMF, and TF) were the longest of the three articulations, as assumed. The values of Heavy-staccato (HP, HMP, HMF, and HF) led to longer key presses than the values of Light-staccato (LP, LMP, LMF, and LF).

3.4   Results of Learning

Table 2 shows the evaluation of the model created by coordinate data obtained using MediaPipe, in terms of precision rate, recall rate, and F1 score. The F1 scores ranged from 0.94 to 1.00. The testing accuracy rate was 0.99.

3.5   Comparisons Among Images

The player tried to maintain the same expression for 100 iterations of the same performance expression. Therefore, the movements of the arms and hands did not change much during the 100 iterations. However, as shown in Fig. 4, some unexpected note on velocity values were recorded for each performance expression. For example, although the median value for HF was 108, there was also a minimum value of 25 in the HF data. This section examines whether factors that caused unexpected performance expressions can be revealed by the coordinates of the landmarks by comparing the images.

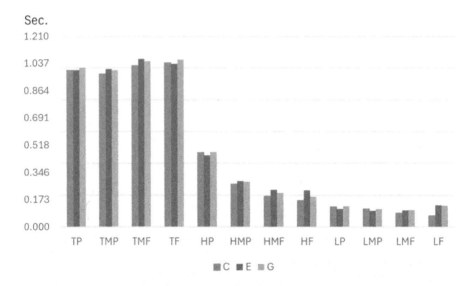

Fig. 5. Average length of time that the key remained pressed over 100 iterations for 12 different performance expressions.

Figures 6–8 show the images of hand movements before and/or after pressing the keys. The middle row of Fig. 6 shows the images of hand movements when the player pressed a C note with note-on velocity 25 as HF (HF-min), despite the median velocity of HF (HF-med) being 108. In HF, the player rotated her elbow from the outside to the inside to produce a louder volume; in other words, to press the keys more quickly. Therefore, both the HF-min and HF-med, as indicated in the images in the bottom row of Fig. 6, show that the player's elbow started from a high position.

By contrast, when the player pressed C in the HF-min, compared to HF-med, she closed her arm (indicated by the blue circle) and hit her thumb diagonally into the key (indicated by the red circle). Because her thumb could not press the key from a straightforward position, potential energy that started from the elbow was not transmitted to the thumb as it tried to hit the C key, so the velocity of the C key became slower.

The middle row of Fig. 7 shows the images of hand movements when the player hit a C note with a note-on velocity of 61 as Tenuto Piano (TP-max), despite the median velocity of TP (TP-med) being 39. The velocity of 61 is the same as the median velocity of Tenuto Mezzo Piano (TMP-med), shown at the top of Fig. 7. Just 0.2 s before the keystroke, TP-max's wrist is lower than that of TP-med and TMP-med (indicated by the red circle). It becomes difficult to hit the key when one's wrist is down. Therefore, with TP-max, we can see she hit the G key with a grasping motion by bending her little finger (indicated by the blue circle). In TP-med, her wrist was lowered after pressing the keys, compared to TMP-med (indicated by the yellow circle).

Table 2. Precision, recall, and F1-score.

	Precision	Recall	F1-score
TP	1.00	0.95	0.97
TMP	0.94	1.00	0.97
TMF	1.00	1.00	1.00
TF	1.00	1.00	1.00
HP	1.00	1.00	1.00
HMP	1.00	1.00	1.00
HMF	1.00	1.00	1.00
HF	1.00	1.00	1.00
LP	1.00	1.00	1.00
LMP	1.00	1.00	1.00
LMF	0.95	0.95	0.95
LF	0.94	0.94	0.94

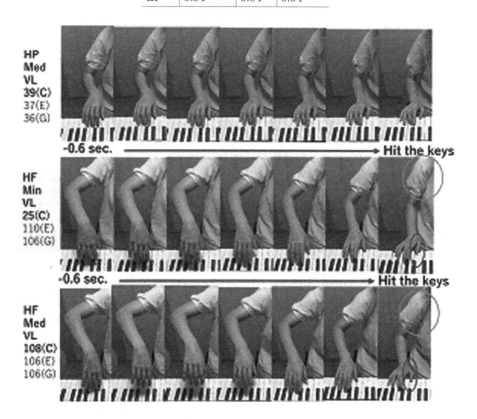

Fig. 6. Hand movements of HP-med, HF-min, and HF-med.

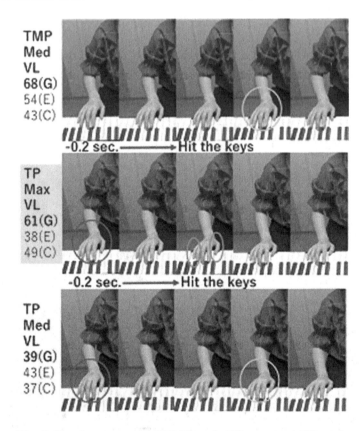

Fig. 7. Hand movements of TMP-med, TP-max, and TP-med.

The middle row of Fig. 8 shows the images of hand movements when the player hit a G note with note-on velocity of 75 as Light-staccato Mezzo Piano (LMP-max), despite the median velocity of LMP (LMP-med) being 47. Even when comparing LMP-max and LMP-med with images, it is not clear why the velocity of the G note was larger.

Therefore, we compared the similarity between LMP-max and the median velocity of Light-staccato Mezzo Forte (LMF-med), and between LMP-max and LMP-med, based on the x- and y-coordinates of each of the 24 landmarks in each of the five images arranged in a time series (see Sect. 2.5).

In the results, the similarity (distance) between LMP-max and LMF-med was 5.79, and between LMP-max and LMP-med it was 6.03. Namely, LMP-max was more similar to LMF-med than to LMP-med.

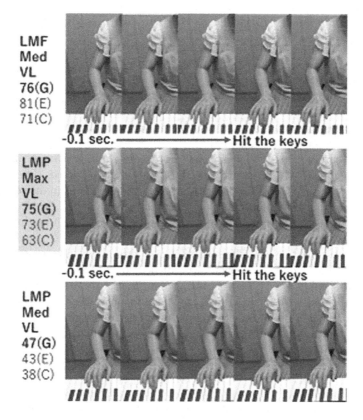

Fig. 8. Hand movements of LMF-med, LMP-max, and LMP-med.

4 Discussion

The results of the machine learning showed that there is a relationship between the coordinate values of each landmark in the time series and the performance expression, although these results were only for one player. Several times during these performances, as the MIDI data showed, she unintentionally played with another type of performance expression. When this happened, some differences in hand movements could be seen visually in the images and numerically in the coordinates, highlighting the differences between an expected expression performance and an unintentional expression performance.

The effects of these differences in the movements for expressions are explainable (see Sect. 3.5), but these explanations are currently limited to the first author's knowledge and estimates. It will be meaningful to practice by imitating one's own hand movements when a pupil played an expected expression during a lesson. What is even more important is knowing the intention of that set of movements. However, it may be difficult for a pupil to compare the images of their hand movements and notice meaningful differences and intentions in them. These are issues to consider as the piano learning support system using MediaPipe is constructed.

5   Conclusion

A player played a chord 100 times using 12 different performance expressions, and the coordinates of landmarks of right hand, wrist, elbow, and shoulder were obtained as image data using MediaPipe. To investigate whether performance expressions can be classified based on coordinate data, a learning model was created using 80% of the coordinate data, randomly selected. The results of testing showed that the model can estimate 12 different performance expressions from the coordinates of landmarks (F1 scores ranged from 0.94 to 1.00). This suggested a relationship between the coordinate values of each landmark in the time series and the performance expression.

In the future, we will analyze hand movements when the note-off velocity values were unintended. Moreover, we will develop a system using MediaPipe that supports home practice by acquiring images of a pupil's performance with a suitable expression during a piano lesson and once they take this information home. Through repeated experiments using the system, we will clarify the appropriate support method for mastering performance expression on the piano.

References

1. Lugaresi, C., et alet al.: Mediapipe: a framework for building perception pipelines, arXiv:1906.08172 (2019)
2. Google MediaPipe, Pose landmark detection guide. https://developers.google.com/mediapipe/solutions/vision/pose_landmarker. (Accessed 28 Jan 2024)
3. Google MediaPipe, Hand landmark detection guide. https://developers.google.com/mediapipe/solutions/vision/hand_landmarker. (Accessed 28 Jan 2024)
4. Zhang, F., et al.: Mediapipe hands: On-device real-time hand tracking. arXiv:2006.10214 (2020)
5. Bazarevsky, V., Zhang, F.: On-Device, Real-Time hand Tracking with mediaPipe. https://blog.research.google/2019/08/on-device-real-time-hand-tracking-with.html. (Accessed 28 Jan 2024)
6. Wu, E., Nishioka, H., Furuya, S., Koike, H.: Marker-removal networks to collect precise 3D hand data for RGB-based estimation and its application in piano. In: Proceedings of the IEEE/CVF Winter Conference on Applications of Computer Vision, pp. 2977-2986 (2023)
7. Jones, T.: The Art of Piano Articulation: Mastering Musical Expression. https://tamecajones.com/. (Accessed 28 Jan 2024)
8. Creative Piano Teacher: The Long and Short of Articulations: How to Correctly Interpret Piano Articulations, https://creativepianoteacher.com/. (Accessed 28 Jan 2024)
9. Take Note: Learn How to Read Sheet Music: Dynamics, Articulations and Tempo, https://blog.sheetmusicplus.com/. (Accessed 28 Jan 2024)

10. Guan, Y., Plötz, T.: Ensembles of deep lstm learners for activity recognition using wearables. Proc. ACM interactive, Mobile, Wearable Ubiquitous Technol. **1**(2), 1–28 (2017)
11. TensorFlow. https://github.com/tensorflow/tensorflow. (Accessed 28 Jan 2024)
12. Pytorch, https://pytorch.org/. (Accessed 28 Jan 2024)
13. Yanagisawa, Y., Akahani, J., Satoh, T.: Shape-based similarity query for trajectory of mobile objects. In: Chen, M.-S., Chrysanthis, P.K., Sloman, M., Zaslavsky, A. (eds.) MDM 2003. LNCS, vol. 2574, pp. 63–77. Springer, Heidelberg (2003). https://doi.org/10.1007/3-540-36389-0_5

Instructor Avatars and Virtual Learning: How Does Instructor Type and Gender Affect Student Perceptions and Learning Outcomes?

Kyle Phillips, Gabriella Hancock, and James D. Miles[✉]

California State University, Long Beach, CA 90840, USA
Kyle.Phillips@student.csulb.edu, {Gabriella.Hancock,
Jim.Miles}@csulb.edu

Abstract. This study investigated the impact of instructor gender (male versus female), type (human versus avatar), and lesson difficulty (easy and difficult) on the usability, trust, engagement, and comprehension of a virtual learning platform system. The study utilized animation software to create virtual male and female instructors and embedded them into a university psychology lecture on memory. Comprehension was evaluated through the use of multiple-choice tests, while usability, trust, and engagement were measured using the System Usability Scale, Trust in Automation Scale, and Paas Mental Effort Scale questionnaires, respectively. The results indicated no causal effect between instructor gender or type on comprehension, usability, and engagement. However, the study did reveal a significant effect of lesson difficulty on trust in the instructor, such that trust in the instructor was significantly higher following the difficult lesson. Implications of these findings pertain to the educational design of virtual classrooms.

Keywords: Avatar Instructors · Education · Instruction · Trust · Usability · Engagement

1 Introduction and Literature Review

In recent years, virtual instruction has become increasingly prevalent, with a surge in popularity following the COVID-19 Pandemic. While this increased popularity has provided new opportunities for remote learning and educational access, concerns have arisen about the effectiveness of virtual instructors compared to their in-person counterparts [1]. As virtual education's popularity grows, it is crucial to understand how the medium can be presented to best facilitate learning outcomes and engage students. Previous research has suggested that leadership characteristics have an effect on task complexity and follower engagement [2]. However, the extent to which this effect is influenced by instructor gender and instructor type has not been extensively explored. Therefore, this study aims to examine the interactions between instructor type, instructor gender, and lesson difficulty on student engagement and learning outcomes in virtual instruction. By investigating these interactions, this study can inform policymakers, educators, and

H. Mori and Y. Asahi (Eds.): HCII 2024, LNCS 14691, pp. 132–147, 2024.
https://doi.org/10.1007/978-3-031-60125-5_9

learners about how to optimize virtual instruction to promote student engagement and effective learning outcomes. What follows is a review of the literature on each variable manipulated in the study and followed by the methodological approach and results.

1.1 Instructor Type

Studies have compared the effectiveness of in-person and virtual instructors with positive results. For example, a study on design students has found that virtual instruction, or instruction through a video telecommunication device promoted student self-efficacy and design novelty by producing a smaller priming effect [3]. However, data on the effectiveness of virtual teaching across the U.S. during 2021 has shown that average test scores for math and English in virtual-only classrooms were lower than in-person only [4]. One aspect that could lend itself to better student outcomes in online lessons is avatar virtual instructors (AVIs). AVIs, computer-generated models that overlay and mimic the fluid movements of virtual instructors, have the potential to be more engaging than in-person or purely virtual instructors. While the literature on AVIs is very small, they can be compared to animated pedagogical agents, which are defined as "intelligent computer characters that guide learners through an environment" [5 (pg.112)], where avatar instructors may be considered a type of animated pedagogical agent. Studies have shown that avatar instructors can improve learner motivation and interest due to presenting information in a novel and engaging manner [6].

While select and nascent studies on avatar instructors suggest they can be more engaging and effective than human instructors, there is little evidence to suggest that they are seen as more trustworthy. Studies have shown that tests of perceptions of trustworthiness in avatar instructors are dependent on their degree of human likeness [7]. This finding is further demonstrated by a study that showed people were more likely to trust an avatar instructor if they appeared to share an ethnicity [8]. These findings suggest that while avatar instructors may have some advantages in terms of engagement and effectiveness, they may not be perceived as more trustworthy than human instructors. However, the issue of trustworthiness is a complex one and may depend on a variety of factors, such as the type of material being presented and the context in which it is being presented. Additionally, little evidence exists on virtual instructors and their interaction with usability scores, such as if there are any confounding effects from different types of instructors on different systems. Further research is needed to fully understand the advantages and limitations of avatar instructors compared to human instructors.

1.2 Instructor Gender

Research has shown that students may have different perceptions of instructors based on gender [9]. In that study, students perceived male instructors as being more competent, while perceiving female instructors as being more supportive and nurturing and admitted that they would put more effort into the male instructor's class given the higher perception of competency. In the context of virtual instruction, gender may also influence how students perceive an AVI such as students perceiving a female AVI as being more nurturing and approachable than a male AVI, or vice versa. This perception could potentially impact student engagement and learning outcomes. Additionally, the use of an AVI may also impact how gender is perceived. Research has shown that students may expect animated characters to act stereotypically in line with their portrayed gender [10], which could potentially impact how students interact with the instructor and their learning outcomes.

Further research is needed to explore the potential interaction between gender and the difficulty of the material being taught in relation to instructor effectiveness. Previous research on instructor gender and perceived effectiveness without a difficulty component are equivocal, with some showing a bias toward competence in male instructors [11], while others show no effect [12]. This suggests that gender bias may interact with the difficulty of the material being taught and impact student evaluations of instructor effectiveness depending on the sample and methodology.

1.3 Lesson Difficulty

Numerous studies across different domains have shown that learning and performance are significantly affected by the level of difficulty of the content being presented. Specifically, research consistently reveals that individuals tend to exhibit poorer performance on more demanding material when compared to easier material. A study found that participants who were presented with more complex texts had significantly lower levels of comprehension than those who were given simpler texts [13]. Similarly, in another study [14], learners who were exposed to more difficult instructional material in a computer programming class performed worse on post-tests than those who were given easier material. These findings have important implications for education and training, as they suggest that the level of difficulty must be carefully considered when designing curricula and assessments to ensure optimal learning outcomes.

The complexity of content within a lesson may impact the level of trust students have in their instructor. Trustworthiness is a multifaceted concept that incorporates perceived ability, benevolence, and integrity [15]. In the present study, participants will not be familiar with the instructor and cannot be certain that there is no element of deception involved in the study. Consequently, they will most likely assess the instructor's perceived ability as the primary indicator of trustworthiness. This assessment may lead to different trust scores across lesson conditions, as more challenging material may be viewed as a stronger indicator of competence and thus elicit greater trust.

Research on course difficulty has alluded to a balance between challenging intuitive material to maximize engagement [16]. A study of college students found that perceptions of lesson difficulty correlated to worse student performance such that students who perceived the lesson as more difficult performed more poorly. This finding is consistent with prior research that has emphasized the importance of appropriately challenging content for promoting learning outcomes [17]. It is important to note that the perception of challenge is subjective and highly influenced by individual differences in experience. Despite prior research suggesting that high perceived difficulty can have negative effects on student outcomes, a study that deliberately manipulated difficulty levels revealed that students who received instruction in material above their competency level performed better on tests than those who received material slightly below their competency, after a 15-week period [18]. These results suggest that exposure to more difficult material, when supported by favorable conditions, may have beneficial effects on student outcomes.

Certain perceptions about the difficulty of a course may be a confound to assessing usability, as a study with an introductory biology class showed that female students who perceived the class the be difficult in a post-questionnaire were also more likely to respond that they intended on leaving the major entirely which may allude to a resistance to the system itself over a single course, however, it is unclear if this finding generalizes to males [16]. Additionally, animation as a medium may be linked to perceptions of childishness, as the most common form of children's television is animated [19]. This statistic raises the possibility that participants who view animated courses may assume that they will be of low difficulty and, as a result, may underestimate the attention needed for the class and perform poorly. Therefore, it is essential to consider how different types of instructors, including their gender, may interact with lesson difficulty to influence student engagement and learning outcomes. By testing the effects of various virtual instructors across varying levels of difficulty, it is possible to gain a more comprehensive understanding of their potential effectiveness in online learning contexts. This understanding can help inform the design of online classes to promote better outcomes for learners.

1.4 Hypotheses

Performance

1. Participants will have higher comprehension in the low-difficulty condition than in the high-difficulty condition as demonstrated by higher comprehension scores.
2. Participants will have higher comprehension scores in the male instructor condition than in the female instructor condition as demonstrated by higher comprehension scores.
3. Participants will have higher comprehension scores in the avatar instructor condition than in the human instructor condition as demonstrated by higher comprehension scores.

Trust

1. Trust in the instructor will be higher in the difficult lesson condition than in the easy lesson condition as demonstrated by higher ratings on the modified trust in automation scale.
2. Trust in the instructor will be higher for male instructors than female instructors as demonstrated by higher ratings on the modified trust in automation scale.
3. Trust in the instructor will be higher in the human condition than in the avatar condition as demonstrated by higher ratings on the modified trust in automation scale.

Usability

1. Usability will be perceived as greater in the easy lesson condition than in the difficult lesson as demonstrated by higher ratings on the System Usability Scale (SUS).
2. Usability will be perceived as greater in the female condition than in the avatar condition as demonstrated by higher ratings on the SUS.
3. Usability will be perceived as greater in the human condition than in the avatar condition as demonstrated by higher ratings on the SUS.

Engagement

1. Engagement will be higher in the difficult lesson condition than in the easy lesson as demonstrated by higher PAAS scale scores.
2. Engagement will be higher for male instructors than female instructors as demonstrated by higher PAAS scale scores.
3. Engagement will be higher in the avatar condition than in the human condition as demonstrated by higher PAAS scale scores.

2 Methods

2.1 Participants and Design

Participants were 9 CSULB College students enrolled in the PSY 100 course recruited online through Sona Systems (Sona Systems, Tallinn, Estonia) participant recruitment platform, with 3 CSULB Human Factors Master's students recruited via word of mouth. PSY 100 students were incentivized to participate in this study as a class assignment but were not directed to any specific study. Master's students were sent a link to the study via email or Discord if they expressed interest in participation but were not incentivized. 19 participants were also recruited using Amazon Mechanical Turk and were paid $4 for their time.

The experiment used a 2 (INSTRUCTOR TYPE: AVI, virtual) x 2 (INSTRUCTOR GENDER: male, female) x 2 (LESSON DIFFICULTY: easy, difficult) mixed model design. The between-subjects factors were the type of instructor and instructor gender, while the within-subjects factor was lesson difficulty. Instructor type was manipulated by creating avatar overlays of human virtual instructor videos and comparing them to each other (see Fig. 1). Instructor gender was manipulated by recruiting a male and a female master's student and having them record videos portrayed as the male and female instructors (see Fig. 1). The difficulty of the videos was determined by whether the nature of the material was more introductory and foundational to memory concepts (easy) or more advanced, presupposing an established understanding of the more fundamental concepts of memory (difficult).

These manipulations were tested for their effects on participant comprehension, engagement, trust in the instructor, and usability of the system. Comprehension of the material was assessed using a 12-question multiple-choice test per lesson. Each question had 4 options and one correct answer, the questions for each level were created to assess participants' understanding of the key concepts presented in the video lessons. The tests were reviewed by experts in the field of memory research to ensure their validity and appropriateness for the study's research questions. The measure was therefore engagement, trust, and usability were assessed by the PAAS scale of mental effort, the trust in automation scale, and the system usability scale respectively; the order of these scales was randomized to protect against order effects. The order in which the easy and difficult lessons were presented was also randomized and recorded as a covariate. Participants watched two 15-min lessons, one easy and one difficult, but were given a single instructor type (human male instructor, human female instructor, animated male instructor, or animated female instructor). Participants were randomly assigned to one of the four instructor groups and completed a comprehension test and three questionnaires to measure usability, trust, and engagement for each lesson.

2.2 Materials

The study materials consisted of computer-based video memory lessons presented through Qualtrics (Qualtrics, Provo, UT, US). Two lessons, one easy and one difficult, were created for each instructor type (male and female). The lessons were based on a university psychology lecture concerning memory, covering topics such as the working memory model, incidental learning, and memorization [20]. The lessons were transcribed and re-recorded by Master's students who portrayed the male and female instructors. The instructors used the same script and recorded it separately on Zoom, the videos were edited for length then duplicated and transformed into animated versions using the Animaze software (Holotech Studios, San Francisco, CA), making four videos in total.

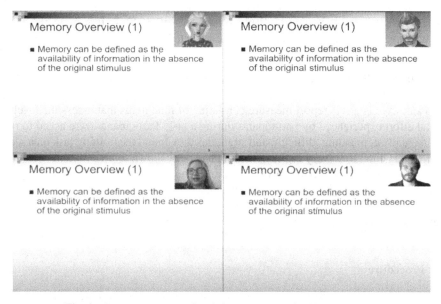

Fig. 1. A screen capture of each instructor type in the easy lesson.

Questionnaires. Usability, trust, and engagement were measured using three questionnaires: the System Usability Scale (SUS), a modified version of the Trust in Automation Scale (TIAS), and the Paas Mental Effort Scale (PAAS).

System Usability Scale. The SUS is a widely used questionnaire that measures the perceived usability of a system or product [21, 22] The SUS consists of 10 items, each rated on a 5-point Likert scale ranging from "strongly agree" to "strongly disagree." The items are designed to capture the user's overall perception of the system's ease of use, efficiency, learnability, and satisfaction. The SUS has been shown to have good reliability and validity across a variety of settings and applications [2].

The SUS was administered to all participants after they completed each lesson. The SUS was chosen as a measure of system usability because of its ease of use, wide availability, and established validity and test-retest reliability [22]. The results of the SUS were used to assess participants' perceptions of the usability of the online learning module.

The Trust in Automation Scale. A modified version of the Trust in Automation Scale (TIAS) was employed in this study to evaluate participants' trust in the automated instructor, in which the participants were requested to rate the instructor instead of the "system". The TIAS is another widely used and validated measure of trust in automation [2]. It consists of 10 items that assess various dimensions of trust, such as reliability, dependability, and confidence in the system. Participants rated their agreement with each item on a 7-point Likert scale, ranging from 1 (strongly disagree) to 7 (strongly agree). The scale has been used in a variety of domains, including aviation, healthcare, and transportation, but has been shown to reliably skew positively [243. In this study, the TIAS was administered after the participants had completed each lesson to assess their trust in the instructor after each condition.

Paas Mental Effort Scale. PAAS was used to measure the engagement expressed by participants during the learning task, the study used the Paas scale for mental effort [25]. The Paas scale is a self-report measure consisting of nine items that assess the level of mental effort experienced by participants during a task. Participants were asked to rate how mentally demanding, difficult, and strenuous they found the training task on a scale from 1 (very low) to 9 (very high). The scale has been shown to be a reliable and valid measure of mental effort across various domains, in particular, the scale has shown good internal consistency, with Cronbach's alpha, test-retest reliability, and good inter-rater reliability [26]. These measures of reliability indicate that the Paas Mental Effort Rating Scale is a reliable tool for measuring mental effort during learning tasks.

2.3 Procedure

Participants provided informed consent and completed a demographics questionnaire before being randomly assigned to one of four instructor groups: human male instructor, human female instructor, animated male instructor, or animated female instructor. Then, they were randomly assigned to which difficulty condition they would complete first. Each participant first watched a 15-min lesson consisting of presentation slides with content on memory, with about 10% of the computer screen being taken up with a video of the instructor, centered in the top right corner. After the lesson was completed participants were presented with the corresponding comprehension test to that lesson's difficulty level. SUS, TIAS, and PAAS scales were then administered in a randomized order to protect against order effects. This process was repeated for the other difficulty condition and its corresponding comprehension test followed again by the SUS, TIAS, and PAAS scales in random order. Upon completion of the study, participants were thanked for their time and provided with the researcher's contact information for any follow-up questions.

Data Analysis. All statistical analyses were conducted using IBM SPSS Software (version 29, IBM Analytics, Armonk, NY, USA). A probability value of p <.05 was assumed for all analyses.

Dependent variables:Comprehension test scores Trust in Automation ratingSUS rating PAAS rating.To determine whether instructor type, instructor gender, and lesson difficulty influence comprehension, trust, usability, and engagement, four separate 2 (Instructor Type: Avatar vs. Human) x 2 (Instructor Gender: Male vs. Female) x 2 (Lesson Difficulty: Easy vs. Difficult) mixed model ANCOVAs with repeated measures on the third factor were conducted for each dependent variable as listed above. Condition order and participant type (CSULB vs. MTurk) were included as covariates.

3   Results

In this study, a total of 51 participants were recruited for data collection. However, data from 8 participants were excluded due to a technical error with the Qualtrics program, which displayed an older and incomplete version of the study. Additionally, 12 participants were excluded from the analysis due to their participation time being less than the required 20 min. After applying these exclusion criteria, the final sample consisted of 12 participants recruited from CSULB, with a mean age of 22 years (SD = 4.4yrs), including 8 female participants, and 19 participants recruited from MTurk, with a mean age of 32 years (SD = 8.9yrs), including 9 female participants (Table 1).

Table 1. Demographics of included participants

Ethnicity	CSULB	Recruited via MTurk	Avg. Age (yrs)	Male/Female
Total	12	19	29	14/17
White	5	10	30	9/6
Black/African American	1	3	35	0/4
American Native	1	2	30	0/3
Asian	1	2	25	3/0

Comprehension. A 2 (Instructor Type: Avatar vs. Human) x 2 (Instructor Gender: Male vs. Female) x 2 (Lesson Difficulty: Easy vs. Difficult) mixed model ANCOVA with repeated measures on the third factor was conducted to examine the effects of instructor type, instructor gender, and lesson difficulty on comprehension. It was hypothesized that participants would have higher comprehension scores in the avatar condition, which was not supported by the results $F(1, 25) = 0.85$, $p = .77$. Additionally, it was hypothesized that participants would have higher comprehension scores in the male condition, which was not supported by the results, $F(1, 25) = .00$, $p = .99$. Finally, it was hypothesized that participants would have higher comprehension scores in the low difficulty condition, which was not supported by the results, $F(1, 25) = 0.24$, $p = .63$.

The covariates of participant type (CSULB vs. MTurk) and order did not significantly affect the results, $F(1, 25) = 0.85$, $p = .77$ and $F(1, 25) = 0.12$, $p = .91$, respectively. Therefore, there was no evidence to support the hypothesis that instructor type, instructor gender, or lesson difficulty affects comprehension in this study.

Trust. A 2 (Instructor Type: Avatar vs. Human) x 2 (Instructor Gender: Male vs. Female) x 2 (Lesson Difficulty: Easy vs. Difficult) mixed model ANCOVA with repeated measures on the third factor was conducted to examine the effects of instructor type, instructor gender, and lesson difficulty on trust in the instructor. It was hypothesized that participants would have higher trust scores in the high-difficulty condition, which was supported by the results, $F(1, 25) = 48.77, p < .001$, $\eta_p^2 = .66$ with participants reporting higher trust in the instructor following the difficult lesson when compared to the easy ($M_{diff} = 18.9$, $p = < .001$) as illustrated in Fig. 2. Additionally, it was hypothesized that participants would have higher trust scores in the avatar condition, which was not supported by the results $F(1, 25) = 0.14$, $p = .90$. Furthermore, it was hypothesized that participants would have higher trust scores in the male condition, which was not supported by the results, $F(1, 25) = .06, p = .80$.

The covariate of participant type (CSULB vs. MTurk) was significantly related to trust in the instructor, $F(1, 25) = 27.78, p = <.001$, $\eta_p^2 = .53$, where Mturk participants reported higher trust in the instructor compared to the CSULB participants ($M_{diff} = 23.41, p <.001$) as seen in Fig. 3. There was a significant interaction between participant type and lesson difficulty $F(1, 25) = 42, p = < .001, \eta_p^2 = .63$. The interaction was such that the Mturk participants had high trust in both the easy and difficult lessons ($M_{diff} = 1.95$) while the CSULB participants had low trust in the instructor after the easy lesson, and higher trust after the difficult lesson ($M_{diff} = 45.58$), as shown in Fig. 4. The covariate of order did not significantly affect trust in the instructor $F(1, 25) = 0.51$, $p = .48$. Therefore, the results provide support for the hypothesis that lesson difficulty affects trust, but no evidence to support the hypotheses that instructor type or gender affect trust.

Usability. A 2 (Instructor Type: Avatar vs. Human) $\times$ 2 (Instructor Gender: Male vs. Female) $\times$ 2 (Lesson Difficulty: Easy vs. Difficult) mixed model ANCOVA with repeated measures on the third factor was conducted to examine the effects of instructor type, instructor gender, and lesson difficulty on perceived usability. It was hypothesized that participants would have higher SUS scores in the avatar condition, which was not supported by the results $F(1, 25) = 1.44$, $p = .24$. Additionally, it was hypothesized that participants would have higher SUS scores in the male condition, which was not supported by the results, $F(1, 25) = .10, p = .75$. Finally, it was hypothesized that participants would have higher SUS scores in the low difficulty condition, which was not supported by the results, $F(1, 25) = 0.80, p = .38$.

The covariates of participant type (CSULB vs. MTurk) and order did not significantly affect the results, $F(1, 25) = 0.04$, $p = .84$ and $F(1, 25) = 0.87$, $p = .36$, respectively. Therefore, there was no evidence to support the hypothesis that instructor type, instructor gender, or lesson difficulty affect usability in this study.

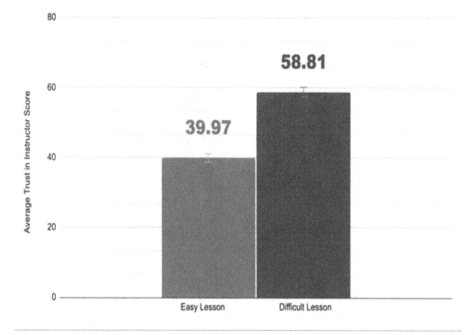

Fig. 2. Main effect of lesson difficulty on trust in the instructor scores. Error bars are standard deviations.

Engagement. A 2 (Instructor Type: Avatar vs. Human) × 2 (Instructor Gender: Male vs. Female) × 2 (Lesson Difficulty: Easy vs. Difficult) mixed model ANCOVA with repeated measures on the third factor was conducted to examine the effects of instructor type, instructor gender, and lesson difficulty on engagement. It was hypothesized that participants would have higher PAAS scores in the avatar condition, which was not supported by the results $F(1, 25) = .65$, $p = .43$. Additionally, it was hypothesized that participants would have higher PAAS scores in the male condition, which was not supported by the results, $F(1, 25) = .18$, $p = .68$. Finally, it was hypothesized that participants would have higher PAAS scores in the low difficulty condition, which was not supported by the results, $F(1, 25) = 0.2, p = .66$.

The covariates of participant type (CSULB vs. MTurk) and order did not significantly affect the results, $F(1, 25) = 0.93$, $p = .76$ and $F(1, 25) = 0.83$, $p = .37$, respectively. Therefore, there was no evidence to support the hypothesis that instructor type, instructor gender, or lesson difficulty affect engagement.

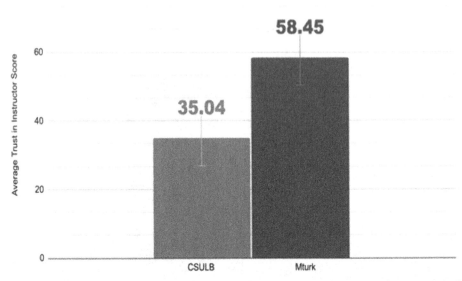

Fig. 3. Main effect of participant type on trust in instructor scores. Error bars are standard deviations.

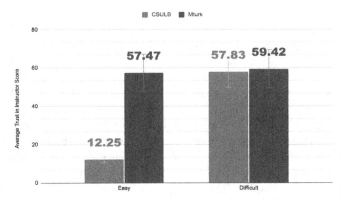

Fig. 4. Significant interaction between participant type and lesson difficulty on trust in instructor scores. Error bars are standard deviations.

4 Discussion

The present study aimed to investigate the impact of instructor type (avatar virtual instructor vs. human instructor), instructor gender (male vs. female), and content difficulty on engagement, trustworthiness, comprehension, and usability in the context of easy and difficult lessons.

Comprehension. Contrary to the hypothesis, instructor type, instructor gender, and lesson difficulty did not have a significant impact on comprehension in this study. This finding is inconsistent with previous research that showed difficulty having a main effect on testing scores [13]. However, this difference may be due to differences in manipulations, as the previous study manipulated "text difficulty" which was defined as a "complex interaction of text complexity and reader characteristics" (pg. 604). In this study, as participant characteristics were not factored into the testing criteria, it provides a more direct comparison of lesson difficulty and comprehension. Future studies may look to further strengthen this comparison by manipulating the difficult lesson to be more reliant on the information of the easier lessons to build complexity. Another possibility is that the easy and difficult lessons were too similar in difficulty, or that the difficult lesson did not require as much compounding knowledge as previously thought. This finding is supported by the fact that the average grade for both lessons was nearly identical at 46%.

The lack of significant effect of instructor gender on comprehension may be due to the one-sided nature and short duration of instruction. Previous literature that found an effect of gender on comprehension suggests that the effect is found after a full academic year, with a shared gender between students and teachers [27]. Future studies may investigate classes that are taught with virtual avatars for an extended period of time, such as a semester.

The finding that there was no significant difference in test outcomes for different instructor types suggests that learning is not dependent on whether the instructor presents themselves with an avatar or their own face. This finding has implications for platform designers and educators, showing that avatar instructors are just as effective as human instructors in terms of student comprehension.

Trust. The results showed a large main effect of trust on lesson difficulty ($\eta_P^2 = .66$) where participants reported higher trust scores following the difficult lesson compared to the easy lesson. These findings could reflect the perceived competency of the instructor, such that when instructors teach more difficult material, they are perceived as more competent and trustworthy, as suggested by previous literature [15]. Participant type (CSULB vs. MTurk) also had a significant main effect on trust in the instructor where MTurk participants reported higher trust scores compared to CSULB participants. When considering participant type, it makes sense that MTurk participants would rate the instructor's trustworthiness in both the easy and difficult lessons as roughly equivalent, as they are far less likely to have specific knowledge of memory lesson content, making it necessary to trust the instructor's authority [27]. There was a significant interaction between participant type and lesson difficulty on trust in the instructor. MTurk participants reported high trust in both the easy and difficult lessons, while CSULB participants had low trust in the instructor after the easy lesson and higher trust after the difficult lesson. This pattern is understood when considering that PSY 100 students, who were the majority of the CSULB participant pool, would have been in-between MTurk participants and Master's students in terms of familiarity with memory and therefore would have lowered the perceived competency of the instructor due to this familiarity. As PSY 100 is an introductory course, it is not likely that these students would have special knowledge of memory, but as data from PSY 100 participants were collected towards the end of the semester, it is likely they would have been exposed to some of the fundamentals of memory processing, such as the kind that was covered in the easy condition here. This exposure may have led to a greater familiarity of general terminology, thereby making the instructor's relatively greater competence less evident in the easy condition, but not necessary improving test scores over the general population (Mturk). The results show that trust in instructor was about equal for the CSULB and MTurk participants after the difficult lesson, which is consistent with the explanation that PSY 100 participants would not have had the familiarity of terms in the difficult condition that they had with the easy condition, and therefore had a similar evaluation of competency and trustworthiness to MTurk participants. Further research should measure student engagement, performance, and trust in instructors to investigate this relationship more thoroughly.

Instructor gender did not affect the trustworthiness of instructors, which aligns with the literature that gender does not influence trustworthiness [12]. The use of computer-generated avatars by instructors did not affect their credibility in the classroom, as instructor type did not significantly impact their perceived trustworthiness, supporting the conclusion that use of avatar instructors in online learning systems are viewed as equally trustworthy when compared to human instructors.

Usability. The study found no significant effects of instructor type, instructor gender, or lesson difficulty on the perceived usability of the online learning system. This result contradicts the hypothesis that participants would rate usability higher when the lesson was easy, taught by a female instructor, and using a human instructor. There are a few possible explanations for these findings. Firstly, participants may have been more focused on the lesson content than on the website features. Secondly, given that at least 39% (CSULB) of the participants in this study had recently experienced two years of online schooling as a result of COVID-19 [29], it is plausible that their familiarity with online learning platforms may have mitigated the impact of the study's manipulations, leading to the Qualtrics platform being perceived as intuitive and its usability not being influenced by instructor characteristics or lesson difficulty. These findings suggest that instructor type, instructor gender, and lesson difficulty may not impact the perceived usability of the system.

Engagement. The results indicate that instructor type, instructor gender, and lesson difficulty did not have a significant impact on engagement. These findings do not support the hypothesis that participants would report higher engagement scores in the high-difficulty condition, possibly because the information presented in both lessons was equally novel and therefore equally engaging. The mean engagement score, rounded to the nearest tenth, was 6.7 out of 9 for both the easy and difficult conditions, suggesting that participants reported a moderate level of engagement in both conditions, without a significant difference between them. The results also did not support the hypothesis that the avatar instructor would be perceived as more engaging. While the literature did support the idea that animated pedagogical agents, which are similar to virtual avatars, could be more engaging to learners due to their novelty [6]. That study was conducted in the year 2000, so it is possible that animated or computer-generated avatar teaching agents are no longer seen as novel and therefore do not create a significant effect. Lastly, the results did not support the hypothesis that the male instructor would be perceived as more engaging. It is worth noting again that previous studies have reported conflicting results regarding the impact of gender on engagement. For instance, some studies have reported that male instructors are perceived as more engaging than female instructors

[9], while others have found no significant gender effects [12]. Therefore, the present study adds to the literature by providing evidence that instructor type, instructor gender, and lesson difficulty do not significantly impact engagement in a learning system.

4.1 Limitations and Future Directions

Sample Size One Limitation of This Study is the Relatively Small Sample Size. While the findings of this study provide useful insights, the small sample size weakens the conclusions about the causal relationships between the independent and dependent factors and limits the generalizability of the results. It is possible that a larger and more diverse sample could have yielded different results, and future studies should consider using a larger sample to increase the generalizability of the findings.

Gender-Neutral Instructor A limitation of the instructor types used in this study is that they fall along the gender binary, and do not include the representation of non-binary individuals. It is possible that a gender-neutral or androgynous instructor could have led to different outcomes, as the literature shows that students prefer instructors that exhibited both male and female characteristics [12]. This direction may be particularly important for those who have had negative associations or experiences with instructors of a particular gender, or as students are taught by instructors who identify across the gender spectrum. Future studies should consider the impact of instructor gender on the effectiveness of mindfulness interventions and explore the use of a gender-neutral/androgynous instructor and/or manipulate gender across a greater spectrum than the traditional gender binary only to provide a more inclusive representation.

Online Testing The research was limited by the lack of control and observation over participants' environment and behavior, leading to potential confounds and biases. Without the ability to ensure accurate adherence to the study protocol and collect nonverbal cues and social interactions, this study may not have obtained the full experimental control necessary to draw valid conclusions. Additionally, self-selection bias may arise, as certain types of people may choose to participate, leading to a non-representative sample. Future studies may benefit from incorporating in-person data collection methods to ensure that attention is effectively paid to the experimental manipulation.

Biased Subject Pool. The study's subject pool may be biased as participants were recruited from psychology classes. About 3 (10%) of the participants were Master's students in psychology with a high likelihood of familiarity with the lesson topics, and 9 (29%) were in an introductory psychology class with low likelihood of familiarity with lesson topics. However, any familiarity could have influenced their performance on memory tests and limited the findings' generalizability. To reduce potential biases, future studies could recruit participants from a more diverse range of academic disciplines.

5 Conclusion

The current study aimed to examine the influence of instructor type, instructor gender, and lesson difficulty on engagement, trustworthiness, comprehension, and usability. The results indicate that instructor type, instructor gender, and lesson difficulty did not significantly impact comprehension, usability, or engagement. However, a significant main effect was found between trust and lesson difficulty, which was mediated by participant type. This suggests that trust in the instructor and perceived instructor expertise are positively correlated, and the latter is mediated by a learner's familiarity with the topic being taught. However, high trust in the instructor did not correspond to high student performance or system usability. This finding highlights the implication that trust in the instructor may not necessarily result in better student outcomes. Although the absence of significant effects from other manipulations may appear unexpected, further research with a larger and unbiased sample, as well as other instructor genders, is necessary to further understand these effects. This study provides useful insights for educational designers who want to modify the appearance of the instructor for a course without impacting student perceptions or outcomes. Overall, the findings suggest that the use of avatars and the alteration of instructor appearance do not compromise the quality of the learning experience for students and may offer greater flexibility and accessibility for teachers.

References

1. Anthony Jnr, B., Noel, S.: Examining the adoption of emergency remote teaching and virtual learning during and after COVID-19 pandemic. Int. J. Educ. Manag. **35**(6), 1136–1150 (2021)
2. Vila-Vázquez, G., Castro-Casal, C., Álvarez-Pérez, D.: From LMX to individual creativity: Interactive effect of engagement and job complexity. Int. J. Environ. Res. Public Health **17**(8), 2626 (2020)
3. Schauer, A.M., Fillingim, K.B., Pavleszek, A., Chen, M., Fu, K.: Comparing the effect of virtual and in-person instruction on students' performance in a design for additive manufacturing learning activity. Res. Eng. Design **33**(4), 385–394 (2022)
4. Halloran, Jack, Okun, J., Oster, E.: Pandemic schooling mode and student test scores: Evidence from US states. National Bureau of Economic Research (2021)
5. Woolf, B.P.: Collaborative inquiry tutors. Building Intelligent Interactive Tutors, pp. 298–336 (2009)
6. Dehn, D.S.M., Van Mulken, S.: The impact of animated interface agents: a review of empirical research. Inter. J. Hum.-Comput. Stud. **52**(1), 1–22 (2000)
7. MacArthur, K.: Dispositional Trust Response to Morphological Differences in Synthetic Representative Agents. Electronic Theses and Dissertations (2021)
8. Baylor, A. L., Kim, Y.: Pedagogical agent design: The impact of agent realism, gender, ethnicity, and instructional role. Intell. Tutoring Syst. 592–603 (2004)
9. Rezvani, R., Miri, P,: The impact of gender, nativeness, and subject matter on the English as a second language university students' perception of instructor credibility and Engagement: a qualitative study. Front. Psychol. 12 (2021)
10. Thompson, T. L., Zerbinos, E:. Gender roles in animated cartoons: has the picture changed in 20 years? Sex Roles **32**(9–10), 651–673 (1995)
11. MacNell, L., Driscoll, A., Hunt, A.N.: What's in a name: exposing gender bias in student ratings of teaching. Innov. High. Educ. **40**(4), 291–303 (2014)

12. Freeman, H.R.: Student evaluations of college instructors: effects of type of course taught, instructor gender and gender role, and student gender. J. Educ. Psychol. **86**(4), 627–630 (1994)
13. Spencer, M., Gilmour, A.F., Miller, A.C., Emerson, A.M., Saha, N.M., Cutting, L.E.: Understanding the influence of text complexity and question type on reading outcomes. Read. Writ. **32**(3), 603–637 (2018)
14. Andres, H.P.: Active teaching to manage course difficulty and learning motivation. J. Further Higher Educ., 1–16 (2017)
15. Lee, M.A., Alarcon, G.M., Capiola, A.: I think you are trustworthy, need I say more? the factor structure and practicalities of trustworthiness assessment. Front. Psychol. **13**, 9 (2022)
16. England, B.J., Brigati, J.R., Schussler, E.E., Chen, M.M.: Student anxiety and perception of difficulty impact performance and persistence in introductory biology courses. CBE—Life Sci. Educ. **18**(2) (2019)
17. Lodge, J. M., Kennedy, G., Lockyer, L., Arguel, A., Pachman, M.: Understanding difficulties and resulting confusion in Learning: An integrative review. Front. Educ. **3** (2018)
18. Namaziandost, E., Esfahani, F.R., Ahmadi, S.: Varying levels of difficulty in L2 reading materials in the efl classroom: impact on comprehension and motivation. Cogent Educ. **6**(1), 1615740 (2019)
19. Bedekar, M., Joshi, P.: Cartoon Films and its impact on children's mentality. Res. Rev. Inter. J. Multidisciplinary **05**(06), 13–18 (2020)
20. Vu, J.: Memory [Lecture]. California State University, Long Beach, CA (2022)
21. Brooke, J.: SUS: A quick and dirty usability scale. Usability Eval. Ind. **189** (1995)
22. Lewis, J.R.: The system usability scale: Past, present, and future. Inter. J. Hum.-Comput. Interact. **34**(7), 577–590 (2018)
23. Jian, J.-Y., Bisantz, A.M., Drury, C.G., Llinas, J.: Foundations for an empirically determined scale of trust in Automated Systems (1998)
24. Gutzwiller, R.S., Chiou, E.K., Craig, S.D., Lewis, C.M., Lematta, G.J., Hsiung, C.-P.: Positive bias in the 'Trust in Automated Systems Survey'? an examination of the jian et al. (2000) scale. In: Proceedings of the Human Factors and Ergonomics Society Annual Meeting, **63**(1), 217–221 (2019)
25. Paas, F.G.W.C.: Training strategies for attaining transfer of problem-solving skill in statistics: a cognitive-load approach. J. Educ. Psychol. **84**, 429–434 (1992)
26. Paas, F., Tuovinen, J.E., Tabbers, H., Van Gerven, P.W.: Cognitive load measurement as a means to advance cognitive load theory. Educ. Psychol. **38**(1), 63–71 (2003)
27. Antecol, H., Eren, O., Ozbeklik, S.: The effect of teacher gender on Student Achievement in Primary School: Evidence from a randomized experiment. SSRN Electr. J. (2012)
28. Milgram, S.: Behavioral study of obedience. Psychol. Sci. Public Interest **67**(4), 371–378 (1963)
29. Selvaraj, A., Radhin, V., Ka, N., Benson, N., Mathew, A.J.: Effect of pandemic based online education on teaching and learning system. Inter. J. Educ. Developm. **85**, 102444. (2021)

Modeling of the Problem-Solving Process and Development of a Learning Support System for Text-Based Programming Problems

Koki Shirahige[1]([✉]), Taiki Matsui[2], Shintaro Maeda[1], and Takahito Tomoto[3]

[1] Graduate School of Information and Computer Science, Chiba Institute of Technology, Narashino, Chiba, Japan
s2381022nq@s.chibakoudai.jp
[2] Graduate School of Engineering, Tokyo Polytechnic University, Atsugi, Kanagawa, Japan
[3] Faculty of Information and Computer Science, Chiba Institute of Technology, Narashino, Chiba, Japan

Abstract. Programming story problems requires an understanding of the requirements of the problem statement and how to write source code that satisfies them. However, some learners are unable to write source code that meets the requirements of the problem statement. Therefore, we modeled the problem-solving process in programming story problems. The problem-solving process begins by organizing the information in the context of the problem statement, thinking through the abstract operations necessary to find a solution, and defining the solution. In this study, we propose a learning support method and develop a learning support system that follows this problem-solving process.

Keywords: Problem-Solving Process · Learning Support System · Text-Based Programming Problem

1 Introduction

In general programming learning, story problems are often presented to learners through lectures and reference books. The story problems require learners to understand the requirements from the question text and to write source code that satisfies them. An example of such a learning activity would be to organize the information about the situation presented by the problem statement, think about the processing required to find the solution, and then write the source code. However, in normal programming lectures, learners submit their own source code to the professor, who then assesses whether the submitted source code satisfies the requirements of the problem statement. However, the professor rarely assesses the solution process itself, namely, how the solution was found. It is also difficult for professors to understand and evaluate the process of writing source code from the problem statement to writing the source code for each learner, and it is difficult to evaluate which process the learner is having difficulties with in solving story problems in programming tasks. Therefore, it is not possible for professors to provide support according to the learner's state of understanding. In this situation, we consider that there are two types of learners: those who cannot think of a solution from the problem statement (learners (A)), and those who cannot write source code that satisfies the requirements of the problem statement even if they think of a solution (learners (B)).

We previously developed a learning support system [2] for learners (A) that encourages thinking to derive solutions from problem statements by utilizing the problem-solving process model by Tsukasa et al. [1] Based on the evaluation results, a certain level of learning effectiveness was suggested for learners (A). However, considering the context of learning to program, it is important to support not only learners (A) but also learners (B). In other words, it is desirable to support both understanding of the solution and to assist learners until they can write source code based on that solution.

Therefore, in the present study, in addition to the previously developed learning support method for learners (A), a new learning support method targeting learners (B) is proposed. The method deals with knowledge specific to the programming domain required for writing source code, which has not been dealt with before, and models the problem-solving process in the story problem of programming tasks. Specifically, the proposed method uses a processing structure that applies an operation structure to the quantitative relationship between an operation structure that transforms abstract operations, which require the organization of the processing necessary to find a solution, into concrete operations that construct the actual source code, and a solution structure that represents a sequence of flows to find a solution.

This paper proposes and develops a new learning support system that implements the proposed operation and processing structures and incorporates them into the previously developed systems.

2   Modelling of Problem-Solving Processes in Mathematics and Mechanics

Tsukasa et al. [1] modeled the problem-solving process as the process of deriving a target solution from a problem statement in mathematics and mechanics (Fig. 1). This model consists of three parts: the surface structure creation process, the formulation structure creation process, and the solution derivation process. The process of creating a surface structure refers to the process of generating a surface structure representing the relationships between objects and attributes that exist in the problem statement. The process of formulation structure creation refers to the process of applying quantitative relationships to the surface structure to generate a formulation structure that allows attributes to be quantitatively represented. The solution derivation process refers to the process of generating the goal structure, which is the solution, and the goal structure is the structure containing the solution to the problem by adding transformations using numerical relationships to the formulated structure. A structure that expresses a series of quantitative relationships used to find the solution to the solution derivation process is the solution structure. The numerical relationships in the solution structure are only part of the situation that the problem targets, and the constraint structure is the structure that expresses all the numerical relationships that exist in the target situation.

Learning along the three processes in the model of the problem-solving process described above leads learners to a series of thinking activities in which they read information from the problem statement, think about quantitative relationships, and arrive at a solution. Therefore, we believe that by working through this learning activity, learners will be able to think about the solution from the problem statement.

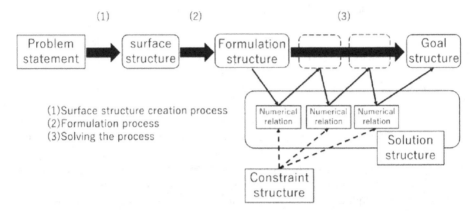

Fig. 1. Problem-solving process in the realms of mathematics and mechanics

2.1 Surface and Formulation Structures

Figure 2 shows the surface and formulation structures. In problem statements for fields such as mechanics, there may be objects and attributes that are explicitly included, such as "ball" (object) and "release quietly" (attribute) in the statement "release the ball quietly". This relationship between objects and attributes is represented as a surface structure. In this example, the formulation structure is the structure that transforms the attribute "release quietly" into an expression that can be used in formulas and numerical relationships, such as "velocity V0(T = 0)".

2.2 Constraint Structure

Figure 3 shows part of the constraint structure, which is the structure that describes all the numerical relationships present in the problem, including those that are not necessary to find a solution to the problem, by connecting the input–output attributes corresponding to the numerical relationships with lines. For example, the constraint "vector decomposition" requires three attributes: "slope inclination", "block vertical gravity", and "block slope direction gravity component". In the constraint structure, the three attributes and the "vector decomposition" constraint are connected by lines and expressed as quantitative relationships between the attributes.

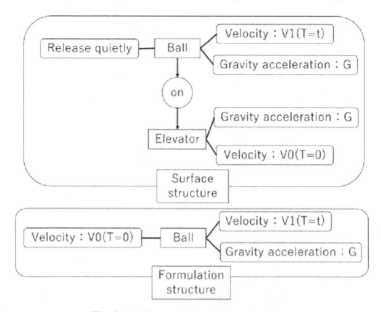

Fig. 2. Surface and formulation structures

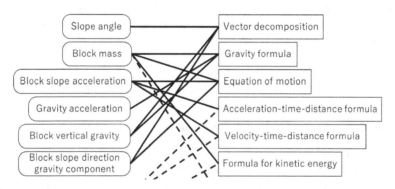

Fig. 3. Constraint structure

2.3 Solution Structure

Figure 4 shows the solution structure, which expresses a series of flows leading to a solution by arrows connecting input attributes to numerical relationships and numerical relationships to output attributes. For example, the numerical relationship "$v1^2 - v0^2 = 2AS$" can be used by using "block initial velocity", "block slope directional acceleration", and "travel distance" as input attributes. The output attribute "block slope directional acceleration" can also be obtained by using "$v1^2 - v0^2 = 2AS$".

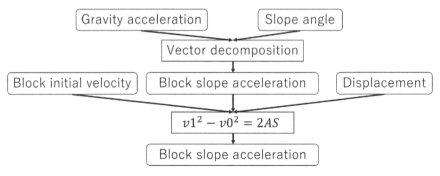

Fig. 4. Solution structure

3 Application of the Problem-Solving Process to Programming Tasks

We previously proposed a learning support method [2] for promoting understanding of how to solve story problems in programming tasks by using the problem-solving process proposed by Tsukasa et al. [1] in fields such as mathematics and mechanics. The method defines a formulation structure that represents the relationships between objects and attributes that are present in the problem statement. A structure expressing the attributes and the relational expressions comprising the attributes is then defined as a constraint structure. Using attributes and relational formulae, a structure expressing a sequence of steps for finding a solution is defined as a solution structure. Our previously developed learning support system allows learners to create these three structures in sequence and to understand the sequence of steps for finding a solution from a problem statement.

3.1 Formulation Structure Creation Screen

Figure 5 shows the formulation structure creation screen. This screen presents the learner with a problem statement and as well as a list of words present in the problem statement. Learners are required to categorize these words as either objects (red blocks) or attributes (blue blocks) and to connect them with each other using lines to show their relationships.

For example, in Fig. 5(i), the words "bathing ticket" and "number of bathing tickets purchased" are presented. The learner selects "bathing ticket" and assigns it as an object, and similarly selects "number of bathing tickets purchased" and assigns it as an attribute. Next, because the learner judges that "number of tickets purchased" is relevant as an attribute of "bathing ticket" in this example, they connect these words using these a line.

The formulation structure creation screen compares the correct answer with the learner's answer and supports the learner if they answered incorrectly by providing feedback. Specifically, it compares three aspects: the correctness of objects (red blocks), the correctness of attributes (blue blocks), and the correctness of the connection relationships between the objects and attributes. As another example, in Fig. 5(ii), the learner answers that "discounted price of a bathing ticket" is an object, but the correct answer is that it is an attribute. When a word is mistakenly identified as an object in the response, feedback is provided as follows: "There is 1 incorrect block assigned as an object." Similarly, if the learner does not connect "discounted price of a bathing ticket" to "bathing ticket" but instead to "swimming pool ticket", the system would determine that there is one point to which a line should not be connected and one point to which a line should be connected. In this case, the feedback provided would be "There is one point where lines must not be connected and one point where lines must be connected." This feedback leads the learner to think about the appropriate assignment of objects and attributes and the connection of relationships between words.

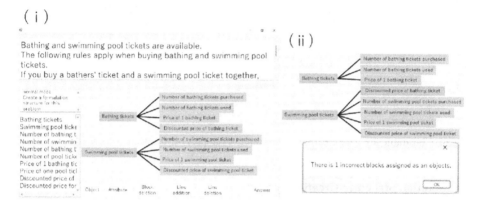

Fig. 5. Formulation structure creation screen (i) and examples of wrong answers and feedback (ii) (Color figure online)

3.2 Constraint Structure Creation Screen

Figure 6 shows the constraint structure creation screen. This screen presents the learner with a template and formulation structure for the attributes and the relational expressions that make up the attributes. The learner is required to select the attributes that apply to the relational expression with reference to the formulation structure.

For example, in Fig. 6(i), an attribute is presented with a letter assigned to it. The learner selects "H" (the total price for an undiscounted bathing ticket), "A" (the number of bathing tickets purchased), and "G" (the price of one bathing ticket) to create the relational expression "H = A*G". This expresses the need to calculate A*G in order to determine H.

The constraint structure creation screen compares the correct answer with the learner's answer, and provides support if the learner answered incorrectly by providing feedback. Specifically, it sequentially compares the left side of the relational expression as the "attribute sought" and the right side as the "expression of attributes needed to determine the left side." If the left-hand side is incorrect, the number of incorrect parts is displayed, and the colors of the incorrect parts are changed. If the right-hand side is incorrect, the incorrect relational expression is displayed. For example, in Fig. 6(ii), the learner inputs "H = B*G" (using "B", the number of bathing tickets used), but the correct answer is "H = A*G", so the equation on the right-hand side is incorrect. In this case, the system provides the following feedback: "The right-hand side of the following equation is incorrect: H = B*G." This feedback helps the learner to understand which attributes they are using incorrectly in the relational expression and to think about the correct attributes to use in the relational expression.

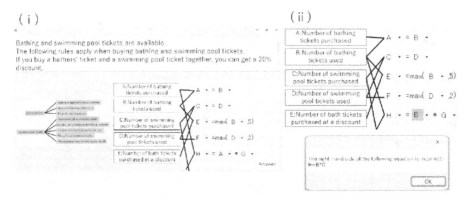

Fig. 6. Constraint structure creation screen(i) and examples of wrong answers and feedback(ii)

3.3 Solution Structure Creation Screen

Figure 7 shows the solution structure creation screen. In the solution structure creation screen, a model of the constraint structure and solution structure is presented to the learner. Learners are required to create a structure representing a sequence of steps for seeking a solution by referencing the constraint structure and selecting the attribute sought, the relational expression for obtaining the attribute, and the attributes used in the relational expression.

For example, Fig. 7(i) asks for the "cheapest total price for a swimming pool ticket and a bathing ticket". In this example, the learner enters "Q" (the cheapest total amount) at the end of the solution structure. To determine "Q", it is necessary to use the relational expression "Q = min(O,P)", so the learner selects this relational expression in the step preceding "Q". Furthermore, this relational expression requires two attributes: "O" (the total amount without a discount) and "P" (the total amount with a discount). Therefore, the learner selects "O" and "P" as attributes in the step preceding "Q = min(O,P)".

The solution structure creation screen compares the correct answer with the learner's answer, and provides supports to the learner if they answered incorrectly by providing feedback. Specifically, it compares the following three aspects: the "attribute sought", the "relational expression for obtaining the attribute", and the "attributes used in the relational expression". For example, in Fig. 7(ii), the learner selects "O" for both attributes in the step preceding the relational expression "Q = min(O,P)". However, the correct attributes for this relational expression are "O" and "P", which are the wrong attributes to use in the relational expression. The system judges correctness based on the relational expression listed below and changes the color of the combo box to red if the answer is incorrect or blue if the answer is correct. In this case, after determining which part is incorrect, feedback is displayed saying "The attribute for finding the relational equation is incorrect" and the color of the incorrect combo box is changed to red. This feedback helps the learner to understand which relational equations and attributes are incorrect from the attributes they ultimately seek, and leads them to thinking about the correct sequence of steps for finding the solution.

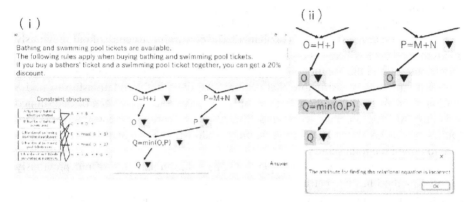

Fig. 7. Solution structure creation screen(i) and examples of wrong answers and feedback(ii)

3.4 Challenges in Using the System for Programming

In fields such as mathematics and mechanics, as explored in Tsukasa et al. [1], when there is a numerical relationship such as $F = ma$, the method of finding the value of a is considered to be obvious, since the values of F and m can be found if they are fixed. However, when a programming task involves the specific task "assign the higher value of a and b to c", the method of finding the value of c is non-trivial, as different learners may have different ways of determining the value of c. Therefore, finding a solution to a programming task requires knowledge specific to the programming domain, in addition to knowledge of the domain the problem is targeting. However, our previously proposed method was based on the problem-solving processes proposed by Tsukasa et al., which have been applied only in the fields of mathematics and mechanics, and have not been used for knowledge specific to the programming domain [1].

Therefore, in addition to our previously proposed method, this study deals with knowledge specific to the programming domain and models the process from the problem statement to writing the source code. In addition, support is proposed for learners' activities throughout the process of writing source code, from the problem statement to the source code based on the modeled content.

4   Modeling the Problem-Solving Process in Text Problems for Programming Tasks

In addition to our previously proposed method [2] for promoting understanding of solution methods, the present study deals with knowledge specific to the programming domain and models the problem-solving process in story problems in programming tasks (Fig. 8). The part of the process shown in the left side of Fig. 8 is identical to the problem-solving process of Tsukasa et al. [1]. In the present study, an operational and processing structure was added to this process to model the problem-solving process in the story problem of a programming task. This paper describes the constraint and solution structures, whose structural content has been changed from our previously proposed learning method, as well as the newly added operation and processing structures, in order to realize learning in line with modeling.

First, the constraint structure is explained. The constraint structure of our previously proposed method has been to obtain the quantitative relationship necessary to obtain the attribute that is the solution as a relational expression. In this study, however, the constraint structure is a structure that requires the quantitative relationship to find a solution as an abstract operation. For example, "Mr. A's total score" can be determined by adding "Mr. A's language score" and "Mr. A's math score". The constraint structure requires this as an abstract operation, namely, "add Mr. A's language score and math score to obtain the total score".

Next, the solution structure is explained. The solution structure of our previously proposed method has been structured to represent a series of steps for finding a solution using relational expressions obtained by the learner in the attribute and constraint structure. However, in the present study, the numerical relationships used in the solution structure are changed to abstract operations because what the learners are looking for in the constraint structure is an abstract operation. For example, in the task "output the higher total score between Mr. A's and Mr. B's total scores", the final attribute "the higher total score between Mr. A's and Mr. B's total scores" needs to be determined. The solution structure describes an abstract operation for finding this attribute, namely, "find the higher value of the total scores between Mr. A's and Mr. B's total scores". Since the operation also requires the input attributes "Mr. A's total score" and "Mr. B's total score", these two attributes are described. The solution structure is the structure that represents the sequence of steps in which attributes and abstract operations are connected by arrows to find a solution.

Next, the operating structure is explained. Figure 9 shows the constraint structure and the operation structure. The operation structure is a structure in which the numerical relationships obtained in the constraint structure are converted into concrete operations. Learners describe numerical relationships in the operational structure, such as "assign the higher value of A and B to C", but in the abstract operation state, the method of finding the value varies from learner to learner and the way to find the value is not self-evident. The structure that translates this numerical relationship into concrete operations such as "if A > B then C = A, else C = B" is the operation structure. In the operation structure, this abstract operation is converted into the concrete operation "if E > F then G = E. else G = F" and the abstract and concrete operations are expressed by connecting them with lines.

The processing structure is described next. The processing structure is shown in Fig. 10. The processing structure is a structure in which the operation structure is applied to the numerical relationships of the solution structure. A solution structure is a structure that expresses the process of finding the final value to be obtained from the input values or values explicitly stated in the problem statement. However, the solution structure uses a formulation structure, which combines the numerical relationships of the constraint structure and is implicit about specific operations. We therefore considered that the source code could be constructed by applying the specific operations obtained in the operation structure to the solution structure and creating a processing structure.

For example, in Fig. 10, "G" is the endpoint that is the final attribute to be output. For the specific operation of determining "G", it is connected by an arrow from "if E > F then G = E, else G = F". The input attributes used for "if E > F then G = E, else G = F" are "E" and "F", so the input attributes and concrete operations are connected by arrows.

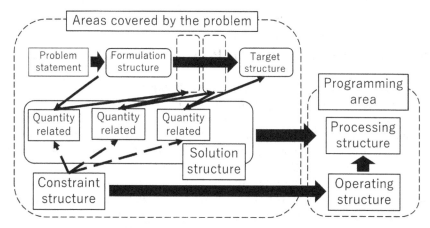

Fig. 8. Problem-solving processes in story problems in programming tasks

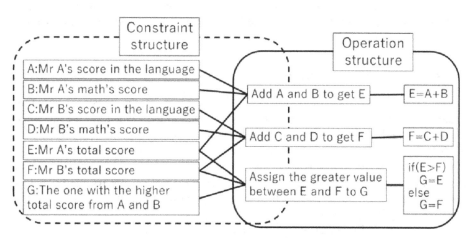

Fig. 9. Constraint structures and operation structures

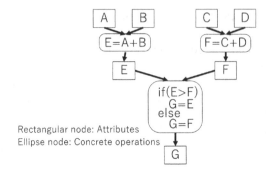

Fig. 10. Processing structure

5 System Implementation of the Proposed Method

This study modeled the problem-solving process of story problems in programming tasks and developed a learning support system according to the model. The system consists of five screens: the formulation structure creation screen, the constraint structure creation screen, the solution structure creation screen, the operation structure creation screen, and the processing structure creation screen. In the formulation structure creation screen, the learner performs the same tasks as in the screen of our previously developed system [2]. In the create constraint structure and create solution structure screens, the learner also creates a structure for the processing part that was represented by a relational expression in the previous system but changed to an abstract operation. The system allows learners to view structures created before the structure they are creating. Learners can create structures by looking at the structures they have created. This paper describes the newly added operation structure creation screen and processing structure creation screen, in addition to the constraint structure creation screen and solution structure creation screen, which have been changed from those in the previous system.

5.1 Constraint Structure Creation Screen

Figure 11 shows the constraint structure creation screen. In the constraint structure creation screen, the part of our previously developed system that requires relational expressions has been changed to a process that requires abstract operations. This enables the learner to ask for the source code, which is a concrete operation, in the operation structure creation screen described below. On this screen, the learner is presented with a template showing attributes and abstract operations. Learners are required to select the attributes that fit the template. This creates a constraint structure that expresses the processing required to find the solution.

For example, in Fig. 11(i), the model is presented as "assign the larger value between □ and □ to □" (where □ refers to a drop-down selection). The learner selects "E" (Mr. A's total score), "F" (Mr. B's total score), and "G" (the higher total score between Mr. A's and Mr. B's total scores) that fit the template.

The constraint structure creation screen compares the input and output attributes with the correct answers and uses feedback to support learners who answer incorrectly. If an output attribute is incorrect, the system displays the feedback "Some output attributes are incorrect." If the input attribute is incorrect, the system displays the feedback "The input attribute for the following operation is incorrect" and lists the relational expression for which the input attribute is incorrect. For example, in Fig. 11(ii), the learner uses "A" (Mr. A's language score), "C" (Mr. B's language score), and "E" (Mr. A's total score), and inputs "add A and C to get E". The user also uses "B" (Mr. A's math score), "D" (Mr. B's math score), and "F" (Mr. B's total score), and inputs "add B and D to get F". However, because the input attributes are incorrect, the system gives the feedback "The input attributes for the following operations are incorrect: Add A and B to get E Add C and D to get F." This feedback leads the learner to think about the input–output attributes that fit the template of the abstract operation and the abstract operation required to find the solution.

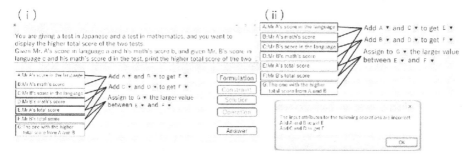

Fig. 11. Constraint structure creation screen(i) and examples of wrong answers and feedback(ii)

5.2 Solution Structure Creation Screen

Figure 12 shows the solution structure creation screen. In this screen, the part where relational expressions are input into our previously developed system has been changed to allow for input of abstract operations. This is because the constraint structure has been changed from a process of finding relational expressions to a process of finding abstract operations. On this screen, a model of the solution structure is presented to the learner. Learners are required to apply attributes and abstract operations to a model of the solution structure. For example, in Fig. 12(i), the learner enters "G" at the end of the structure because the problem requires that they "output the value with the higher score". In addition, "assign to G the larger value between E and F" is entered as the operation leading to 'G'.

The solution structure creation screen compares the "attributes sought", the "abstract operations for seeking attributes", and the "attributes used for abstract operations" with the correct answers and uses feedback to assist learners who answer incorrectly. For example, in Fig. 12(ii), the learner answers "B" (Mr. A's math score) and "F" (Mr. B's total score) as the attributes used to "assign the larger value of E and F to G". However, the correct attributes are "E" (Mr. A's total score) and "F" (Mr. B's total score), which is the wrong attribute to use for an abstract operation. In this case, the system makes a decision on the correctness of the answer based on the item below and changes the color of the combo box to red if the answer is incorrect. After determining the incorrect part, feedback is displayed saying "Input attribute is incorrect" and the color of the incorrect combo box is changed to red. This feedback leads the learner to think about which abstract operations and attributes are erroneous from the attributes they ultimately seek and the correct sequence of steps for finding a solution using abstract operations.

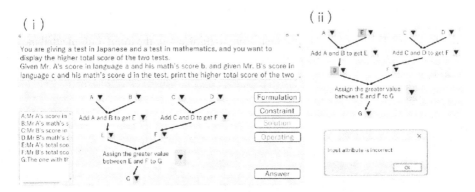

Fig. 12. Solution structure creation screen(i) and examples of wrong answers and feedback(ii)

5.3 Operation Structure Creation Screen

Figure 13 shows the operation structure creation screen. In this screen, learners are presented with source code templates, such as "if(? > ?)", and abstract operations created by learners in constraint structures, such as "find the larger value between E and F and assign it to G". Learners are required to combine models and enter variables and values.

For example, in Fig. 13 (i), the task is presented to create a code that is a concrete operation to realize the abstract operation "Assign the larger value of E and F to G". To express this abstract operation in concrete terms, the learner chooses "if (? > ?)" and inputs the condition as "E > F". Next, as a process within the "if" block, the learner chooses "? = ?" and enters "G = E". In addition, a block is presented for the "else" statement, and as a process in this block, the learner selects "? = ?" and inputs "G = F". Since "G = E" and "G = F" are nested conditional branches, pressing the arrow buttons at the end of each block moves it to the left or right to express the nesting.

The operation structure creation screen compares the correct answer with the learner's answer, and presents feedback to assist the learner if they answered incorrectly. Specifically, learners compare three aspects: the "template to use", the "applicable attributes", and the "block position". For example, in Fig. 13(ii), the learner assigns "B" (Mr. A's math score) and "D" (Mr. B's math score) as the attributes used for the condition of the if statement. However, the attribute used for the if statement is incorrect. In this case, the user receives feedback "The selected attribute is incorrect" and the color of the incorrect combo box is changed to red. This feedback leads the learner to think about the correct attributes to translate abstract operations into concrete operations.

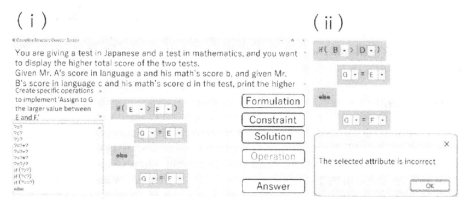

Fig. 13. Operation structure creation screen(i) and examples of wrong answers and feedback(ii)

5.4 Processing Structure Creation Screen

Figure 14 shows the processing structure creation screen. This screen presents the learner with the solution structure with the processing part hidden and the specific operations created by the learner. Learners are required to apply specific operations to the solution structure. In Fig. 14(i), arrows emanate from "E" (Mr. A's total score) and "F" (Mr. B's total score), presenting a solution structure that leads to "G" (the higher total score between Mr. A's and Mr. B's total scores) via the processing part. The learner uses "E" and "F" and selects the block "if E > F then G = E, else G = F" as the process for determining "G" and applies it to the process part shown in blue in the solution structure.

The processing structure creation screen compares the learner's answers to the correct answers for specific operations, and provides support to the learner if they answer incorrectly by giving feedback. For example, in Fig. 14(ii), the learner enters "E" and "F" as input attributes. In addition, the specific operation chosen for the output attribute "G" is "F = C + D". However, the correct answer would be to select "if E > F then

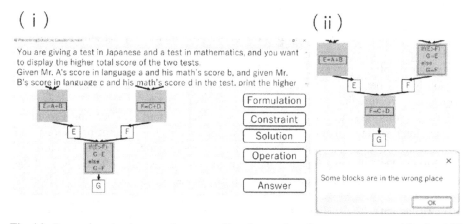

Fig. 14. Processing structure creation screen(i) and examples of wrong answers and feedback(ii)

$G = E$, else $G = F$". In this case, the system displays feedback "Some blocks are in the wrong place" and changes the color of the incorrect part to red. This feedback leads learners to think about the correct sequence of steps for finding a solution using specific operations.

6 Discussion

It should be noted that we have not discussed at what granularity the operations proposed in this study should be described. For example, the operation "assign the greater of A and B to C" in Fig. 9 can be broken down in more detail into several operations, such as "assign the value of A", "assign the value of B", "compare A and B", and "if B is greater than A, assign to C". Furthermore, if we consider the "swap two values" operation found in common sorting algorithms, this too can be described at different granularities, such as "store the largest value in the array at the end of the array" or "assign'" Thus, the granularity of operations in programming is not uniquely defined and various granularities are possible. Therefore, in the description of operations, it is important to consider the granularity at which the operations are expressed.

Currently, since this study targets learners studying programming in lectures, we consider that the knowledge (scope) that learners have learned in lectures as an appropriate granularity of operation. For example, if learners have studied assignment in programming lectures, they can treat "assign" as an operation. Similarly, if a learner has learned swapping, they will be able to treat "swap two values" as an operation. In this way, we believe, the degree to which learners have learnt in lectures can be set as the appropriate granularity of operation.

Another remaining issue is the difficulty for learners to learn operations. This was not considered in this study; however, Kento et al. [3] have already proposed a learning method for acquiring a functionally significant set of codes (which they define as parts). The developed system is therefore aimed at learners who have already mastered the operations required to find the solution.

7 Conclusion

In this study, the problem-solving process of story problems in programming tasks is modeled and a learning support system is developed according to the model. The modeled problem-solving process consists of a formalized structure that applies quantitative relationships to the relationships between objects and attributes in the problem statement, a constraint structure that creates abstract operations necessary to derive solutions from attributes, a solution structure representing a sequence of steps for obtaining a solution, an operational structure that transforms abstract operations into specific operations, and a processing structure that applies the operational structure to the solution structure.

Future tasks include verification and evaluation of the learning effectiveness of the developed system and discussion of the granularity of the operations described in Sect. 6.

Acknowledgments. This study was supported by JSPS KAKENHI Grant Numbers JP22K12322, JP21H03565, and JP20H01730.

References

1. Tsukasa, H., Syozou, A., Akihiro, K., Jun'ichi, T.: A formulation of auxiliary problems. Jpn. Soc. Artif. Intell. **10**(3), 413–420 (2016). (in Japanese)
2. Koki, S., Taiki, M., Takahito, T.: Development and evaluation of a learning support system that encourage the understanding of the solution by formularization for programming sentences. Jpn. Soc. Inf. Syst. Educ. Spec. Paper Symp. **37**(7), 1–8 (2023). (in Japanese)
3. Kento, K., Takahito, T., Tomoya, H., Tsukasa, H.: Proposal of the expandable modular statements method for structural understanding of programming, and development and evaluation of a learning support system. Trans. Jpn. Soc. Inf. Syst. Educ. **36**(3), 190–202 (2019). (in Japanese)

Information in Business and eCommerce

Characteristics and Relationships of Consumer Individual Demographics Regarding TV Commercial Advertising Effectiveness

Seira Aguni and Yumi Asahi[✉]

Graduate School of Management, Department of Management, Tokyo University of Science, 1-11-2, Fujimi, Chiyoda-Ku, Tokyo 102-0071, Japan
asahi@rs.tus.ac.jp

Abstract. In Japan, where economic disparity is widening due to the increase in the number of single parents, the increase in the number of non-regular employees, and the impact of the spread of new coronavirus infection, purchase intentions for specific products are declining. This is due to TV advertising, and the failure of TV advertisers to create TV ads that match the interests of individual consumers. Although viewing intention for TV ads is decreasing, viewing intention for TV ads that match individual consumer interests is significantly higher. However, from the perspective of TV ad creators, it is time-consuming to create TV ads that match the interests of individual consumers, and they have not been able to create such TV ads. In this study, we investigated the effects of TV ads on purchase intention for each individual attribute of consumers who watch TV ads and found a targeting aid for creating TV ads that match the interests of individual consumers.

Keywords: TV ads · effect or effectiveness of advertising · Personal Attributes

1 Introduction

This study focuses on the social problem of declining consumer spending. The causes for this are thought to be related to the decline in annual household income [1] and the increase in single-parent households [2] and informal employment [3]. On the other hand, consumers' willingness to purchase has been maintained [4]. We believe that these contrasting phenomena are related to a decrease in purchase intentions for specific products [5], and that this is caused by a decline in the accuracy of targeting in TV advertising [6]. The purpose of this study is to improve targeting accuracy to increase consumers' purchase intentions for specific products by clarifying the characteristics of the differences in purchase intentions for each product within individual attributes depending on whether they watch TV ads.

2 Theory and Hypothesis

In the realm of consumer life activities, "working," "spending," and "raising" are considered areas that change over time. People go through over a decade of student life, then enter the workforce, get married, have children, raise them, and grow old. Even though individuals may not change apart from their age, how others perceive them changes. This change in perception has a significant impact on self-construction. I consider the classification based on changes people experience to be in occupation, household income, and number of children. When people start working, their occupation changes from being a student. With employment comes the change in occupation from being a student, enabling them to earn money themselves, and the priority of money usage shifts towards maintaining their own lives. With promotions at work, household income changes. As household income changes, the priority of money usage shifts towards maintaining their own lives and indulging in luxuries due to the newfound financial comfort. Getting married changes from being single to being part of a couple. Then, with births, the number of children changes. As the number of children changes, the priority of money usage shifts towards the family's life and the children. Therefore, the commonality among changes in occupation, household income, and number of children is that priorities in money usage are set. According to Aronson's (2014) theory of social norms, people tend to adjust their behavior based on the actions of others and social expectations [7]. Based on this theory, it can be assumed that as adults, as superiors, and as parents, people adjust their money usage based on social expectations. From this theory, it is hypothesized that the priority of money usage is adjusted based on social expectations, and there are commonalities in the adjusted attributes for each. Therefore, the following hypothesis is proposed:

H1: Among the seven items, there is similarity in purchase intentions for products in occupation, household income, and number of children. Consumer household financial assets indicate economic stability. Economic stability reflects the extent of financial comfort. According to Case (1991), as household wealth increases, consumption also increases [8]. Therefore, the following hypothesis is proposed:

H2: Consumer purchase intentions for products based on household financial assets show that the high-asset group shows interest in many products, while the low-asset group shows interest in few products. Family composition represents the income of the entire household, directly affecting the purchasing power of products. This suggests how much budget the family allocates to each product. Therefore, the following hypothesis is proposed:

H3: Among the seven items, there is similarity in purchase intentions for products in family composition, occupation, and gender/age. Demand varies by residential area. Going to commercial facilities to purchase products and using online shopping sites lead to various differences. For example, going to commercial facilities allows customers to see actual products. Additionally, when customers see products that they have seen in TV advertisements and have a favorable impression of, they are more likely to have positive feelings about the products due to the exposure effect proposed by Zajonc (1968). Therefore, seeing the product increases the frequency of contact with the product, making it easier to promote purchasing behavior [9]. Therefore, the following hypothesis is proposed:

H4: Urban residents show interest in more products.

3 Data and Analysis Method

3.1 Data

For measuring the effectiveness of television advertising, we will use survey data and advertising data provided by Nomura Research Institute [10]. The survey was conducted targeting men and women aged 20 to 59 in the Kanto region, comprising one metropolis and six prefectures, from January 21 to April 1, 2023, with a sample size of 2500.

3.2 Analysis Method

The analysis method consists of the following three items. The analytical procedure and characteristics of the semi-parametric DID estimation method are explained based on Hoshino (2009) [11]. DID stands for Difference-in-Differences and is a statistical method.

1. First, a semi-parametric DID estimation method with looser assumptions than the general DID estimation method is conducted. The DID estimation values are tested using Welch's t-test, which tests the difference in means without assuming equal variances between the viewing group and the non-viewing group. The explanatory variables are the time variables representing the two survey dates and the treatment variable representing the presence or absence of TV advertising viewing. The objective variable is the change in purchase intention due to the presence or absence of TV advertising viewing.
2. Next, the DID estimation values calculated from the semi-parametric DID estimation method are divided into positive, 0, and negative values. This is defined as dichotomization. If the DID estimation value is positive, it indicates a positive effect of advertising on purchase intention, meaning that purchase intention improved after TV advertising viewing. If the DID estimation value is 0, it indicates no change in the effect of advertising on purchase intention, meaning that purchase intention did not change after TV advertising viewing. If the DID estimation value is negative, it indicates a negative effect of advertising on purchase intention, meaning that purchase intention decreased after TV advertising viewing.
3. Finally, the trichotomized DID estimation values are classified by the number of positive and negative values for each product category. For each product category, products for which positive values are indicated in the DID estimation are classified as comprehensive type, products for which negative values are indicated in the DID estimation for two or more products are classified as selection-preference type, products for which positive values are indicated in the DID estimation for one product are classified as narrowed-down type, products for which negative values are indicated in the DID estimation for one product are classified as single-deletion type, and products for which negative values are indicated in the DID estimation for all products are classified as indifferent type.

This study aims not to indicate the degree of increase in purchase intention, but to indicate the ups and downs of purchase intention in trichotomized form, classify the number of positive and negative values for each product category, and make it easier to see the commonalities among consumers' individual basic attributes by focusing on them.

This study's main analysis method, the semi-parametric DID estimation method, is explained in detail. The analytical procedure of the semi-parametric DID estimation method is as follows:

1. First, consumers are classified into two groups based on TV advertising viewing.
2. Then, among the DID estimation methods that compare the difference in purchase intention between these two groups, the method used here uses unobserved individual attributes that are not influenced by TV advertising viewing as covariates to measure the advertising effect while correcting for the influence [11].

If the estimated value is positive, it means an improvement in purchase intention, and if it is negative, it means a decrease in purchase intention. This analysis method is characterized by its ability to handle various data flexibly, its ease of understanding what caused the results while considering external influences, its ability to estimate the impact of intervention, and its ability to be used in combination with other methods. The DID estimation method compares the results of both groups before and after the change to estimate the effect.

Next, a comparison is made between the semi-parametric DID estimation method and other methods. Compared to the parametric method of regression analysis, it is more flexible. While regression analysis requires specific model assumptions to be met, the semi-parametric DID estimation method can be used to analyze with looser assumptions. Compared to non-parametric methods such as matching and kernel density estimation, it is considered to have higher model estimation accuracy and improve the reliability of estimation results.

An explanation is provided for the difference between parametric DID estimation methods and semi-parametric DID estimation methods. Parametric DID estimation methods assume a specific functional form for the model. For example, the use of a linear regression model is common. In contrast, the semi-parametric DID estimation method relaxes the assumption about the functional form. This means that it does not make specific assumptions about the functional form and uses a more flexible model. One of the characteristics of the semi-parametric DID estimation method is that it can perform analysis with looser assumptions. This loose assumption means that it can estimate the effects of time and regional effects non-parametrically.

Therefore, the semi-parametric DID estimation method is more flexible and robust than conventional methods for estimating advertising effects. It does not require determining a functional form that fits the data, is particularly useful for analyzing non-linear effects and effects that change over time, is less dependent on model assumptions, and can be applied to various data. Considering these flexibility and accuracy, the semi-parametric DID estimation is used to estimate the advertising effects.

4   Analysis Results

4.1   Analysis of Each Product's DID Estimation Values for the Attributes (Occupation, Household Income, Number of Children)

First, to examine H1 regarding the commonalities among the three attributes, the semi-parametric DID estimation method was used to calculate the DID estimation values for occupation, household income, and number of children. These three attributes were then classified into positive, neutral, and negative categories using dichotomization, and the results were further classified based on the number of products showing positive effects. From Fig. 1, it can be observed that all three attributes can be classified, and there is a commonality where the preference for two or three options is higher in the selection-preference type, while the preference for one option is higher in the narrowing-down type, supporting H 1.

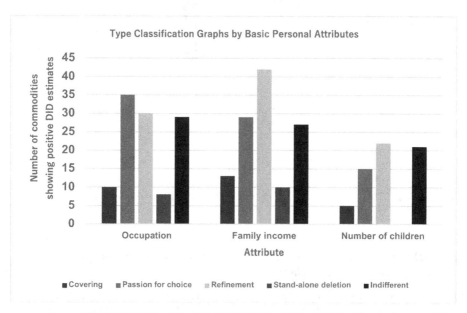

Fig. 1.   Type Classification Graphs by Basic Personal Attributes.

4.2   DID Estimation Values for Each Product by Household Financial Assets

The purchase intentions for each product were divided into eight categories based on household financial assets, and the DID estimation values for each product were calculated. The results were classified into three categories: positive, zero, and negative, and the number of products showing positive DID estimation values for low and high asset groups was compared to the total.

From Fig. 2, it can be seen that the number of products showing positive DID estimation values is lower for the group with financial assets of 20 million yen or more compared to the total. Similarly, the number of products showing positive DID estimation values is lower for the group with financial assets of 1 million yen or less compared to the total. Therefore, the characteristics of each household's financial assets indicate that the group with higher financial assets and the group with lower financial assets have fewer products showing positive DID estimation values, while the groups with financial assets of 5 to 10 million yen and 10 to 20 million yen have more products showing positive DID estimation values compared to the total. This suggests that there is a regularity in the attributes based on household financial assets, supporting H2 to some extent.

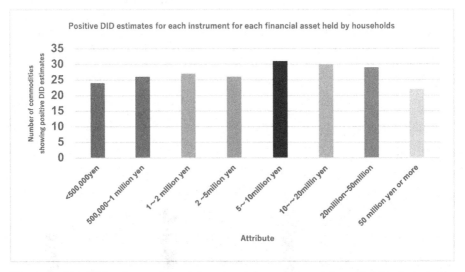

Fig. 2. Positive DID estimates for each instrument for each financial asset held by households.

4.3 DID Estimation Values for Each Product by Household Composition, Occupation, and Gender/age

In H3, DID estimation values for each product were calculated for household composition, occupation, and gender/age. The results were classified into positive, zero, and negative values, and a type of classification was conducted based on the number of products showing positive values.

As a result, although DID estimation values for each product were calculated, when classified into three categories and grouped by the number of products showing positive values, there were more than half of the product categories that showed an equal number of products with positive DID estimation values in terms of household composition. Therefore, classification was not possible, and H3 was not supported.

4.4 DID Estimation Values for Each Product by Residential Area

The purchase intentions for each product were divided into seven categories based on the residential area, and the DID estimation values for each product were calculated.

The results were classified into positive, zero, and negative values, and the number of products showing positive values in Tokyo, a metropolitan area, was compared to the total.

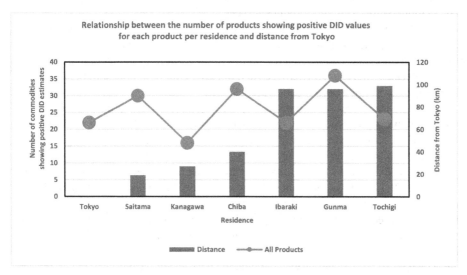

Fig. 3. Relationship between the number of products showing positive DID values for each product per residence and distance from Tokyo.

From Fig. 3, it can be seen that there is no consistency when comparing Tokyo, a metropolitan area, with other regions, and H4 was not supported. As a result, it was found that there is no consistency in residential areas regarding the number of products showing positive DID estimation values, indicating that there may not be a pattern based on individual attributes.

5   Discussion

This study aimed to investigate whether there are patterns or commonalities in consumer individual basic attributes (within and between attributes). For H1, which focused on three attributes, occupation, household income, and number of children, H1 was supported by a strong tendency to narrow down the product purchase intention to a type preferring two or three choices; for H2, it was suggested that the group with higher household financial assets had a more positive purchase intention for each product. However, this hypothesis was not supported. Specifically, the number of products that exhibited positive DID estimates for the attribute of ¥50 million or more was significantly lower than for the other attributes. Several factors could account for this. First, the level of satisfaction may be high. It is possible that those with higher household financial assets are already highly satisfied with many products and services and have lower demand for new products. Second, it could be related to investment choices. Those with higher household financial assets may choose to invest for higher returns, which may affect their willingness to purchase. Third, it could be due to diminishing marginal utility. There may be a point at which consumption demand reaches its limit and the willingness to make additional purchases declines. Finally, it may be due to increased risk aversion. Given the risks associated with new products, those with more household financial assets may be more cautious in their product choices.

For H3, although DID estimation values for each product were calculated, classification was not possible due to a majority of product categories showing an equal number of products with positive DID estimation values in terms of household composition. This could be because individual differences and biases are large in household composition, leading to a distribution across various types.

Regarding H4, there was no consistency in residential areas in terms of the number of products showing positive DID estimation values, and the hypothesis was not supported. While distance from urban areas was not supported as a factor, further investigation from various aspects is deemed necessary.

This study examined whether there are patterns or commonalities within and between consumer individual basic attributes, focusing on the attributes of occupation, household income, and number of children. The study presented H1 regarding commonalities between the three attributes, and using a semi-parametric DID estimation method for each attribute, calculated DID estimation values for each product and classified them into positive, zero, and negative values. Based on the number of products showing positive values, a type of classification was conducted. As a result, strong tendencies towards preferring 2 or 3 choices and narrowing down choices were found across the three attributes, supporting H1. It is considered that this is because when selecting products while considering others or oneself, and thinking about one's own preferences, there is a tendency to narrow down choices when one can clearly grasp what the other person likes or what one likes. This is based on the mentalization theory proposed by Fonagy (1997), which suggests that understanding the actions and intentions of others and understanding their meaning leads to building better relationships [12]. According to this theory, it is conceivable that there is a lot of information about what the other person likes, but it is difficult to prioritize their preferences. Furthermore, regarding one's own preferences, it is based on the self-concept theory proposed by Rogers (1959), which suggests that understanding one's own characteristics and preferences and forming an identity [13]. It was considered that consumers who tend to prioritize their preferences in terms of the priority of money usage purposes show a strong tendency to prefer 2 or 3 choices or to narrow down choices in these three attributes. The commonality between occupation, household income, and number of children can be said to be established by the theory of empathy towards others and self-concept towards oneself.

Considering whether there are patterns or commonalities within and between consumer individual basic attributes, H2 was presented for individual patterns, calculating the number of positive purchase intentions for high-income groups and low-income groups for each household financial asset. Regarding the place of residence, H3 compared the number of positive purchase intentions for each prefecture and Tokyo, a metropolitan area. For each, DID estimation values were calculated using a semi-parametric DID estimation method, the values were classified into positive, zero, and negative values, and the number of products showing positive DID estimation values was compared. As a result, it was found that there is a pattern where the higher and lower income groups have fewer purchase intentions, and the middle-income group has more purchase intentions. Based on these results, it was considered that the lower number of products showing positive purchase intentions for the high-income group was due to their higher satisfaction levels. Regarding the consistency of residential areas, no relationship with the distance from urban areas was found, and there was no consistency. It was considered that further examination from other perspectives is necessary regarding the consistency of residential areas. For example, an examination of the relationship using train route data could be conducted. This is because it is possible to compare the convenience of access to large commercial facilities.

6 Contribution

This study makes several theoretical contributions:

1. Understanding the influence of individual attributes: Detailed understanding of how individual attributes affect purchase intentions can lead to the development of marketing strategies and effective advertising designs that take into account the heterogeneity arising from consumers' differing interests.
2. Development of marketing theory: The prioritization of money usage purposes, the consideration of what factors influence purchase intentions for products, and the length of time spent browsing the web are all factors that contribute to the development of marketing theory. This deepens the understanding of consumer behavior, leading to more effective deployment of marketing strategies and higher customer satisfaction, which can also be applied to research on customer satisfaction.
3. Consideration of individual differences: Many of the hypotheses based on the theoretical framework of this study were not supported, which may be due to the biased nature of consumer preferences and the corresponding individual differences. By considering these differences, it becomes possible to offer products that are more suitable for customer needs.
4. Methodological contribution: The focus of the methodology used in this study was not on numerical values but on the positive or negative estimation values and their quantities. This made it possible to clearly assess the characteristics within attributes.

The practical contributions of this study include:

1. Optimization of marketing strategies: Understanding the purchase intentions of each individual attribute can improve the accuracy of targeting, allowing brands to more precisely identify their target audience.
2. Improvement of customer satisfaction: Improved customer satisfaction contributes to the enhancement of a company's brand value.
3. Understanding the complexity of the market: By using demographic segmentation based on demographic information such as individual basic attributes, psychological segmentation based on consumer values, and behavioral segmentation based on web browsing time, it became possible to construct marketing strategies in a rational and beneficial manner.

7 Outlook

Future research aims to enhance consumers' purchase intentions for specific products and connect them to specific purchasing behaviors. To achieve this, it is proposed to examine the interaction between consumer attributes in terms of advertising effects on purchase intentions for each specific product category based on whether or not consumers watch TV ads, and to study the characteristics of consumers' attributes for each specific product category in terms of advertising effects on purchases based on whether or not consumers watch TV ads. By doing so, it will be possible to calculate the advertising effects without excessively subdividing the purchase intentions and purchasing behaviors among consumer attributes.

Furthermore, in order to examine the influence of internet communities, which are temporal events of TV advertising, on purchase intentions and purchasing behaviors, it is proposed to analyze the text information of internet communities to analyze what characteristics of TV advertising are improving the level of interest in products. Additionally, to examine the influence of implicit consciousness on purchase intentions based on whether or not consumers watch TV ads, it is proposed to combine implicit association tests (IAT) and explicit measurement methods (such as questionnaires) for analysis [14].

Future developments in this combination include examining interactions and interaction effects, which can lead not only to purchase intentions but also to purchasing behaviors, and simplifying the combination of attributes for each product category to improve the accuracy of targeting that enhances both.

8 Limitations

There are three main limitations to this study:

1. Attribute variation: Concerns about the sustainability of adapting strategies and research results to consumers who change over time.
2. Consideration of external influencing factors: Consideration of market conditions, different brands within the same product category, strategies of competing companies, and consumers' lifestyles, values, and preferences are necessary, but such data is not available in the survey data.
3. Difficulty in generalization: The nature of products, services, and market environments has changed significantly in recent years, making it very difficult to apply the findings to other markets or industries.

References

1. Yamaji, S.: Kobe shimbun NEXT. Average annual salary of full-time employees at corona disaster down 60,000 yen due to pay cuts and reduced overtime, 13 December 2021. https://www.kobe-np.co.jp/news/sougou/202112/0014912835.shtml. Accessed 25 Feb 2023
2. Ministry of health, Labour and welfare. Income status of various households. National survey of basic living standards 2013, 15 Jul 2014. https://www.mhlw.go.jp/toukei/saikin/hw/k-tyosa/k-tyosa13/dl/03.pdf. Accessed 25 Feb 2023

3. Cabinet office. Economic and fiscal white paper. Annual economic and fiscal report 2006, Jul 2006. https://www5.cao.go.jp/j-j/wp/wp-je06/pdf/06-00302.pdf. Accessed 25 Feb 2023
4. Dentsu. The consumption that moved hearts and minds shifted from nest egg and housing consumption to outdoor experiential consumption during the Golden Week holidays. Dentsu NEWS RELEASE, 14 Jul 2022. https://www5.cao.go.jp/j-j/wp/wp-je06/pdf/06-00302.pdf. Accessed 25 Feb 2023
5. Matsuzaki, N.: The realities of Japanese consumption: will the 100,000-yen benefit be saved without spending? Tokyo Keizai Online, 11 Jan 2022. https://toyokeizai.net/articles/-/500524. Accessed 25 Feb 2023
6. Japan Net Keizai Shimbun editorial department breaking news team. 71.2% of Gen Z have used subscriptions. Nihon Net Keizai Shimbun, 15 May 2023. https://netkeizai.com/articles/detail/8758. 25 Feb 2023
7. Aronson, E.: The social animal: an invitation to the social psychology of reading people and the world (11th ed.). Science Inc (2014).
8. Case, B., Quigley, J.M.: The dynamics of real estate prices. Rev. Econ. Stat. **73**(1), 50–58 (1991). https://doi.org/10.2307/2109686
9. Zajonc, R.B.: Attitudinal effects of mere exposure. J. Pers. Soc. Psychol. **9**(2, Pt.2), 1–27 (1968). https://doi.org/10.1037/h0025848
10. Nomura research institute. Nomura research institute marketing analysis contest 2023. Nomura research institute. Nomura Research Institute, 19 Dec 2023. https://www.is.nri.co.jp/contest/2023/index.html
11. Hoshino, T.: Statistical Science of Survey Observation Data: Causal Inference, Selection Bias, and Data Fusion (8th ed.). Iwanami Shoten (2014)
12. Fonagy, P., Target, M.: Attachment and reflective functioning: their role in self-organization. Dev. Psychopathol. **9**(4), 679–700 (1997). https://doi.org/10.1017/s0954579497001399
13. Rogers, C.R.: A Theory of Therapy, Personality, and Interpersonal Relationships: developed within a client-centered framework (Vol. 3). McGraw-Hill (1959)
14. Okubo, S., Ideno, T., Takemura, K.: The front line of consumer psychology (Vol.2)-Potential cognitive measures in consumer behavior research: applicability of the Implicit Association Test (IAT). Soc. Textile Consum. Sci. **48**(9), 578–584 (2007). https://ndlsearch.ndl.go.jp/books/R000000004-I8958642

A Study on Input Methods of User Preference for Personalized Fashion Coordinate Recommendations

Shun Hattori[1]([✉]), Shohei Miyamoto[1], Wataru Sunayama[1],
and Madoka Takahara[2]

[1] The University of Shiga Prefecture, Hikone-shi, Japan
{hattori.s,sunayama.w}@e.usp.ac.jp, tz23smiyamoto@ec.usp.ac.jp
[2] Ryukoku University, Otsu-shi, Japan
takahara@rins.ryukoku.ac.jp

Abstract. In most of the existing researches and practical e-commerce services for fashion coordinate recommendations, only one of various input methods of a user's preference has been adopted without enough arguments. Therefore, this paper conducts a deeper study on various input methods of a user's preference for personalized fashion coordinate recommendations, comprehensively by two kinds of questionnaire investigation: how well do you think that you have expressed your preference to a recommender system of fashion coordinates via an input method? and how well has a recommender system recommended fashion coordinates for you based on your preference expressed via an input method?.

Keywords: Preference Input Methods · Fashion Coordinates · Personalization · Recommender Systems · CLIP · Text-to/from-Image

1 Introduction

In recent years, a lot of researches on AI (Artificial Intelligence) for a diverse array of domains have been being conducted actively, and their application to practical services. Also for fashion products and fashion design, there are a lot of researches on IR (Information Retrieval), Recommendation, DL (Deep Learning) techniques [1–24] and their applications to practical e-commerce services [25–27].

In such a recommender system as shown in Fig. 1 to recommend fashion coordinates for a target user, there are several important factors such as

- the target user's personal preference on fashion coordinates (e.g., fashion styles such as "casual", color, shape, size, preferred items such as "skirt"),
- the other users' social evaluations on how nice a fashion coordinate looks in the target user,

Partially supported by Regional ICT Research Center of Human, Industry and Future at The University of Shiga Prefecture, and by Cabinet Office, Government of Japan.

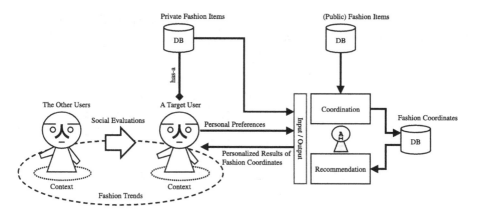

Fig. 1. An overview of personalized fashion coordinate recommender systems.

- context-awareness on how nice a fashion coordinate looks in a target context, i.e., situation, what is called TPO (Time, Place, and Occasion) in Japan, and
- fashion trends of the (current) time on how nice a fashion coordinate is incorporated fashionable items and styles of the trends into.

However, in most of the existing researches and practical e-commerce services for fashion coordinate recommendations, only one of various input methods of a user's preference has been adopted without enough arguments. For instance, in XZ [27], that is a practical application program with AI stylists for smartphones to recommend (one-week) fashion coordinates using the fashion items a target user has, the target user can do nothing but select from three kinds of keywords (specifically, "casual," "simple," and "street" for male, while "casual," "feminine," and "cool" for female) and their corresponding images (photos), as an input method of her/his preference.

Therefore, as shown in Fig. 2, this paper conducts a deeper study on various input methods of a user's preference for personalized fashion coordinate recommendations, comprehensively by analyzing two kinds of questionnaire investigations:

1. how well do you think that you have expressed your preference to a recommender system of fashion coordinates by an input method?
2. how well has a recommender system (based on Japanese Stable CLIP [28]) recommended fashion coordinates for you based on your preference expressed by an input method?

The remainder of this paper is organized as follows. Section 2 explains in detail an experimental method to conduct a deeper study on 10 kinds of input methods of a user's preference for personalized fashion coordinate recommendations, comprehensively by analyzing two kinds of questionnaire investigations. Section 3 shows some experimental results to compare 10 kinds of input methods of a user's preference for personalized fashion coordinate recommendations, with respect to their two kinds of performance, expression performance and recommendation performance. Finally, Sect. 4 concludes this paper.

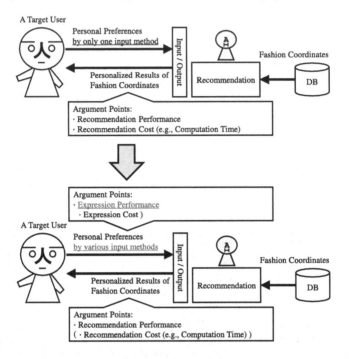

Fig. 2. Comparison between this paper and most of the existing researches.

2 Experiments

This section explains in detail an experimental method to conduct a deeper study on various input methods of a user's preference for personalized fashion coordinate recommendations, by two kinds of questionnaire investigations:

1. how well do you think that you have expressed your preference to a recommender system of fashion coordinates by one of 10 kinds of input methods?
   0. Technical Keywords (without Images) as a baseline
   1. Commonly-used Keywords (without Images)
   2. Commonly-used Keywords with Images
   3. Positive Images (without Commonly-used Keywords)
   4. Positive/Negative Images
   5. Grading Images Absolutely
   6. Comparing Images Relatively
   7. Free Description
   8. Inputting SNS Post Data for Preference Estimation
   9. Inputting Life Log Data for Preference Estimation

2. how well has a recommender system recommended fashion coordinates for you based on your preference expressed by an input method?

2.1 1st Questionnaire Investigation on Preference Input Methods

In November 2023, the 1st questionnaire investigation that consists of 2 steps was conducted for 136 subjects: 97 males and 39 females, students who study at The University of Shiga Prefecture, mainly Department of Electronic Systems Engineering, School of Engineering.

Step 1. For each of 10 kinds of preference input methods,
    (a) by an input method, a subject expresses her/his preference on fashion coordinates to a recommender system, and then
    (b) the subject absolutely selects one 5-grade evaluation on how well s/he has expressed her/his preference to a recommender system of fashion coordinates by the input method?

Step 2. Finally, a subject is given an overview of 7 kinds[1] of preference input methods in the left of Fig. 3, and then s/he relatively compares 9 kinds[2] of preference input methods as a Ranking-type question of Microsoft Forms [29] in the right of Fig. 3.

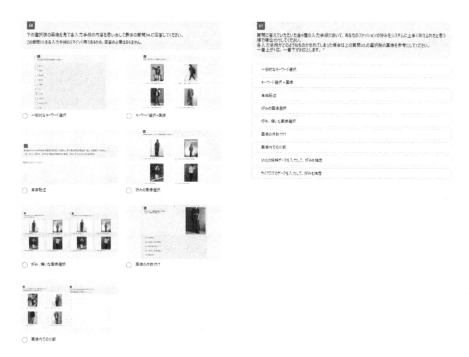

Fig. 3. Comparing 9 kinds of input methods as a Ranking-type question of MS Forms.

---

[1] Without the 3 kinds of input methods, "0. Technical Keywords (without Images)" as a baseline, "8. Inputting SNS Post Data for Preference Estimation," and "9. Inputting Life Log Data for Preference Estimation.".

[2] Without the 1 kind of input method, "0. Technical Keywords (without Images).".

0. Technical Keywords (without Images). By using the input method "0. Technical Keywords" of a user's preference, a user is shown technical keywords on fashion styles at random, and selects one or more from them. Figure 4 shows 12 technical keywords for male, while Fig. 5 shows 12 technical keywords for female. These technical keywords were found in more than one existing researches [1–7] for Japanese users searched manually by the 2nd author.

1. Commonly-Used Keywords (without Images). By using the input method "1. Commonly-used Keywords" of a user's preference, a user is shown commonly-used keywords on fashion styles at random, and selects one or more from them. Figure 6 shows 10 commonly-used keywords for male, while Fig. 7 shows 12 commonly-used keywords for female. These commonly-used keywords were found in more Web sites on fashion for Japanese users searched manually by the 2nd author.

Fig. 4. Input method "0. Technical Keywords" for male.

Fig. 5. Input method "0. Technical Keywords" for female.

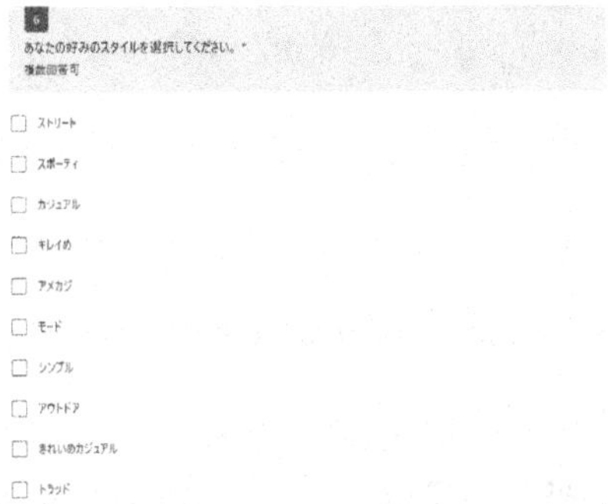

Fig. 6. Input method "1. Commonly-used Keywords" for male.

Fig. 7. Input method "1. Commonly-used Keywords" for female.

2. Commonly-Used Keywords with Images. By using the input method "2. Commonly-used Keywords with Images" of a user's preference, a user is shown not only commonly-used keywords on fashion styles but also their corresponding images at random, and selects one or more from them. Figure 8 shows 10 commonly-used keywords with images for male, while Fig. 9 shows 12 commonly-used keywords with images for female. These corresponding images to commonly-used keywords were searched from WEAR [30], that is one of the largest Web sites for fashion coordinates in Japan, manually by the 2nd author.

Fig. 8. Input method "2. Commonly-used Keywords with Images" for male.

Fig. 9. Input method "2. Commonly-used Keywords with Images" for female.

184   S. Hattori et al.

3. Positive Images (without Commonly-Used Keywords). By the input method "3. Positive Images (without Commonly-used Keywords)" of a user's preference, a user is shown not commonly-used keywords on fashion styles but their corresponding images at random, and selects one or more from them. Figure 10 shows 10 images (without commonly-used keywords) for male, while Fig. 11 shows 12 images (without commonly-used keywords) for female. These corresponding images to commonly-used keywords were also searched from WEAR [30] manually by the 2nd author, but they are different from the images shown by the input method "2. Commonly-used Keywords with Images."

Fig. 10. Input method "3. Positive Images (without Commonly-used Keywords)" for male.

Fig. 11. Input method "3. Positive Images (without Commonly-used Keywords)" for female.

4. Positive/Negative Images. By using the input method "4. Positive/Negative Images" (without Commonly-used Keywords) of a user's preference, a user is shown not commonly-used keywords on fashion styles but their corresponding images at random, and selects not only one or more positive images but also one or more negative images from them. A male user selects one or more positive images from them in the left of Fig. 12, and then he selects one or more negative images from them in the right of Fig. 12. These corresponding images to commonly-used keywords are quite the same as the images shown by the input method "3. Positive Images (without Commonly-used Keywords)."

Fig. 12. Input method "4. Positive/Negative Images" for male.

5. Grading Images Absolutely. By using the input method "5. Grading Images Absolutely" (without Commonly-used Keywords) of a user's preference, a user selects one 5-grade evaluation for each of the 10 or 12 images without their corresponding commonly-used keywords on fashion styles respectively for male or female. A male user grades 2 of 10 images (without commonly-used keywords) in Fig. 13, while a female user grades 2 of 12 images (without commonly-used keywords) in Fig. 14. These corresponding images to commonly-used keywords were also searched from WEAR [30] manually by the 2nd author, but they are different from both the images shown by the input method "2. Commonly-used Keywords with Images" and the images shown by the input methods "3. Positive Images" and "4. Positive/Negative Images."

Fig. 13. Input method "5. Grading Images Absolutely" for male.

Fig. 14. Input method "5. Grading Images Absolutely" for female.

6. Comparing Images Relatively. By the input method "6. Comparing Images Relatively" (without Commonly-used Keywords) of a user's preference, a user ranks 10 or 12 images without their corresponding commonly-used keywords on fashion styles respectively for male or female. A male user is shown 10 images (without commonly-used keywords) in the left of Fig. 15, and then he relatively compares them in the right of Fig. 15 as a Ranking-type question of Microsoft Forms [29]. These corresponding images to commonly-used keywords are quite the same as the images shown by the input method "5. Grading Images Absolutely."

Fig. 15. Input method "6. Comparing Images Relatively" for male.

7. Free Description. By the using input method "7. Free Description" of a user's preference, a user freely describes her/his preference on fashion coordinates (e.g., fashion styles such as "casual", color, shape, size, preferred items such as "skirt") in such a natural language as Japanese, shown as in Fig. 16 or Fig. 17 respectively for male or female.

Fig. 16. Input method "7. Free Description" for male.

Fig. 17. Input method "7. Free Description" for female.

8. Inputting SNS Post Data for Preference Estimation. By the using input method "8. Inputting SNS Post Data for Preference Estimation" of a user's preference, a system could automatically estimate a user's preference on fashion coordinates from her/his SNS post data. In Fig. 18, a user selects whether or not a system is inputted her/his own SNS post data so that the system could estimate her/his preference on fashion coordinates.

9. Inputting Life Log Data for Preference Estimation. By the using input method "9. Inputting Life Log Data for Preference Estimation" of a user's preference, a system could automatically estimate a user's preference on fashion coordinates from her/his life log data (e.g., sleeping time and the number of steps by Apple Watch and Fitbit etc.). In Fig. 19, a user selects whether or not a system is inputted her/his own life log data so that the system could estimate her/his preference on fashion coordinates.

Fig. 18. Input method "8. Inputting SNS Post Data for Preference Estimation."

Fig. 19. Input method "9. Inputting Life Log Data for Preference Estimation."

2.2   2nd Questionnaire Investigation on Preference Input Methods

In November 2023, the 2nd questionnaire investigation that consists of 2 steps was conducted for 49 subjects (from 136 subjects of the 1st questionnaire investigation in Sect. 2.1): 32 males and 17 females, students who study at The University of Shiga Prefecture, mainly Department of Electronic Systems Engineering, School of Engineering.

Step 1. A male subject selects 5 fashion coordinate images from among 30 ones (for 10 commonly-used keywords for male, their 3 corresponding images), while a female subject selects 5 fashion coordinate images from among 36 ones (for 12 commonly-used keywords for female, their 3 corresponding images). Here, these fashion coordinate images corresponding to commonly-used keywords were searched from WEAR [30] manually by the 2nd author, but they are different from the images shown by the input method "2. Commonly-used Keywords with Images," the images shown by the input methods "3. Positive Images" and "4. Positive/Negative Images," and the images shown by the input methods "5. Grading Images Absolutely" and "Comparing Images Relatively."

Step 2. For each of 8 kinds[3] of preference input methods, mAP (mean Average Precision) of rankings by scoring 30 or 36 fashion coordinate images by the expression results at Step 1(a) of the 1st questionnaire investigation in Sect. 2.1 and the following two kinds of similarity of Japanese Stable CLIP (Contrastive Language-Image Pretraining) [28] are evaluated as "how well has a recommender system (based on JSCLIP) recommended fashion coordinates for you based on your preference expressed by an input method?":

(1) the Language-Image similarity $\mathrm{sim}(img, kw_u)$ between each fashion coordinate image img and a subject's selecting keyword kw_u (or a corresponding keyword to a subject's selecting image), and

(2) the Image-Image similarity $\mathrm{sim}(img, img_u)$ between each fashion coordinate image img and a subject's selecting image img_u (or a corresponding image(s) to a subject's selecting keyword).

The two kinds of scores $\mathrm{score}_{kw}(img, u)$ and $\mathrm{score}_{img}(img, u)$ of each fashion coordinate image img for a subject u are defined as follows.

$$\mathrm{score}_{kw}(img, u) := \sum_{\forall kw_u} \mathrm{sim}(img, kw_u) \cdot \mathrm{weight}(kw_u, u) \qquad (1)$$

$$\mathrm{score}_{img}(img, u) := \sum_{\forall img_u} \mathrm{sim}(img, img_u) \cdot \mathrm{weight}(img_u, u) \qquad (2)$$

where $\mathrm{weight}(kw_u, u)$ stands for the weight of a keyword kw_u selected (or a corresponding keyword kw_u to a image selected) by a subject u via a preference input method, and $\mathrm{weight}(img_u, u)$ stands for the weight of an image img_u selected (or a corresponding image(s) img_u to a keyword selected) by a subject u via a preference input method.

3 Experimental Results

This section shows some experimental results to compare 10 kinds of input methods of a user's preference for personalized fashion coordinate recommendations, with respect to their two kinds of performance, expression performance and recommendation performance.

Table 1 shows the average of absolute 5-grade evaluations and relative ranks on expression performance for 10 kinds of input methods of a user's preference. The findings from the 1st questionnaire investigation are summarized as follows:

– The input methods "4. Positive Images" and "5. Positive/Negative Images" are preferred, while the input methods "0. Technical Keywords" and "9. Inputting Life Log Data for Preference Estimation" are not preferred.

---

[3] Without the 2 kinds of input methods, "8. Inputting SNS Post Data for Preference Estimation," and "9. Inputting Life Log Data for Preference Estimation.".

- The input method "0. Technical Keywords" is the worst because its keywords on fashion styles that were found in more than one existing researches [1–7] for Japanese users searched manually by the 2nd author might not be commonly-used and understandable for most subjects.
- The input method "9. Inputting Life Log Data for Preference Estimation" is the 2nd worst because most subjects might be concerned that a system

Table 1. The average of absolute 5-grade evaluations and relative ranks on expression performance for 10 kinds of input methods of a user's preference.

preference input methods		absolute evaluations			relative ranks	
0. Technical Keywords	male	2.876	± 1.092	male	(n/a)	
	female	3.077	± 1.133	female	(n/a)	
	all	2.934	± 1.104	all	(n/a)	
1. Commonly-used Keywords (without Images)	male	3.588	± 1.097	male	6.567	± 2.354
	female	3.590	± 0.966	female	6.795	± 2.296
	all	3.588	± 1.057	all	6.632	± 2.331
2. Commonly-used Keywords with Images	male	**4.299**	± 0.903	male	4.165	± 2.418
	female	**4.103**	± 0.852	female	**4.077**	± 2.217
	all	**4.243**	± 0.890	all	4.140	± 2.354
3. Positive Images (without Keywords)	male	3.928	± 1.013	male	**4.021**	± 1.958
	female	3.513	± 1.144	female	**3.897**	± 2.198
	all	3.809	± 1.065	all	**3.985**	± 2.022
4. Positive/Negative Images (without Keywords)	male	**4.113**	± 0.934	male	**3.897**	± 2.191
	female	3.923	± 0.870	female	**3.795**	± 2.142
	all	**4.059**	± 0.917	all	**3.868**	± 2.170
5. Grading Images Absolutely (without Keywords)	male	**4.227**	± 0.872	male	**3.990**	± 2.430
	female	**4.077**	± 1.036	female	4.231	± 2.253
	all	**4.184**	± 0.921	all	**4.059**	± 2.375
6. Comparing Images Relatively (without Keywords)	male	3.804	± 1.105	male	4.361	± 2.324
	female	3.846	± 1.065	female	4.769	± 2.518
	all	3.816	± 1.090	all	4.478	± 2.379
7. Free Description	male	3.722	± 1.125	male	5.536	± 2.799
	female	**4.103**	± 0.821	female	4.744	± 2.673
	all	3.831	± 1.058	all	5.309	± 2.777
8. Inputting SNS Post Data for Preference Estimation	male	3.784	± 1.092	male	5.650	± 2.458
	female	3.872	± 0.951	female	5.256	± 2.531
	all	3.809	± 1.051	all	5.537	± 2.476
9. Inputting Life Log Data for Preference Estimation	male	3.299	± 1.235	male	6.814	± 2.133
	female	2.769	± 1.180	female	7.436	± 1.789
	all	3.147	± 1.239	all	6.993	± 2.053

infringes their privacy by using their own life log data, which are not publicly generally. Meanwhile, the input method "8. Inputting SNS Post Data for Preference Estimation" is preferred more than the input method "9. Inputting Life Log Data for Preference Estimation" because most subjects might not be concerned that a system infringes their privacy by using their own SNS post data, which are not always private generally.

- "Images" are preferred more than "Text," e.g., keywords and free description, by most subjects, for preference input methods on fashion coordinates.
- The input method "7. Free Description" is preferred by female subjects, while it is not preferred by male subjects.
- The input method "3. Positive Images" is absolutely evaluated as be lower by female subjects, while it is relatively ranked as be higher by them.

Table 2. The mAP based on Language-Image similarity or Image-Image similarity of Japanese Stable CLIP for 8 kinds of input methods of a user's preference.

preference input methods	Language-Image similarity			Image-Image similarity		
0. Technical Keywords	male	**0.314**	± 0.157	male	0.309	± 0.139
	female	0.207	± 0.103	female	0.250	± 0.135
	all	**0.277**	± 0.149	all	0.289	± 0.139
1. Commonly-used Keywords (without Images)	male	**0.266**	± 0.140	male	**0.354**	± 0.172
	female	**0.216**	± 0.163	female	**0.286**	± 0.173
	all	0.249	± 0.149	all	**0.330**	± 0.174
2. Commonly-used Keywords with Images	male	**0.273**	± 0.115	male	0.297	± 0.155
	female	0.211	± 0.086	female	0.274	± 0.121
	all	0.251	± 0.110	all	0.289	± 0.143
3. Positive Images (without Keywords)	male	0.235	± 0.083	male	0.333	± 0.143
	female	0.213	± 0.104	female	**0.294**	± 0.193
	all	0.227	± 0.090	all	**0.319**	± 0.161
4. Positive/Negative Images (without Keywords)	male	0.252	± 0.108	male	0.295	± 0.130
	female	**0.286**	± 0.144	female	**0.339**	± 0.154
	all	**0.264**	± 0.121	all	**0.310**	± 0.139
5. Grading Images Absolutely (without Keywords)	male	0.239	± 0.098	male	**0.340**	± 0.157
	female	0.173	± 0.066	female	0.194	± 0.081
	all	0.216	± 0.093	all	0.289	± 0.151
6. Comparing Images Relatively (without Keywords)	male	0.241	± 0.100	male	**0.341**	± 0.162
	female	0.177	± 0.062	female	0.209	± 0.112
	all	0.219	± 0.093	all	0.295	± 0.158
7. Free Description	male	0.250	± 0.126	male	(n/a)	
	female	**0.286**	± 0.129	female	(n/a)	
	all	**0.264**	± 0.130	all	(n/a)	

Table 2 shows the mAP (mean Average Precision) based on the Language-Image similarity $\text{sim}(img, kw_u)$ of Japanese Stable CLIP and the mAP based on the Image-Image similarity $\text{sim}(img, img_u)$ of Japanese Stable CLIP, as recommendation performance for 8 kinds[5] of input methods of a user's preference. The findings from the 2nd questionnaire investigation are summarized as follows:

- The input method "0. Technical Keywords" gives the best mAP based on Language-Image similarity (however, it gives the worst expression performance in Table 1), while the input method "1. Commonly-used Keywords" gives the best mAP based on Image-Image similarity.
- The input method "4. Positive/Negative Images" robustly gives high mAP both based on Language-Image similarity and based on Image-Image similarity, while the input method "5. Grading Images Absolutely" gives the worst mAP and the input method "6. Comparing Images Relatively" gives low mAP both based on Language-Image similarity and based on Image-Image similarity.
- The mAP based on Image-Image similarity is superior to the mAP based on Language-Image similarity, while the mAP based on Image-Image similarity cannot be applied to the input method "7. Free Description" (it might be able to be applied but become too low if an image(s) is generated from a user's free description by Text-to-Image AIs [31])
- The input method "7. Free Description" gives the best mAP for female subjects, while it does not give high mAP for male subjects. Mind that similarly in Table 1, the input method "7. Free Description" is preferred by female subjects, while it is not preferred by male subjects.

Finally, Table 3 shows a comprehensive evaluation by average ranks for 8 kinds of input methods of a user's preference, with respect to their expression performance (absolute 5-grade evaluations and relative ranks) and recommendation performance (mAP based on Language-Image similarity and mAP based on Image-Image similarity). The findings from the comprehensive analysis are summarized as follows:

- "4. Positive/Negative Images" tends to be the most appropriate input method of any user preference for personalized fashion coordinate recommendations.
- The input method "7. Free Description" tends to be the most appropriate for female subjects, while the input method "2. Commonly-used Keywords with Images" tends to be the most appropriate for male subjects.
  - The input method "7. Free Description" tends to be the most appropriate for female subjects, while it is not appropriate for male subjects.
  - The input method "2. Commonly-used Keywords with Images" is second-appropriate for any subject (both male subjects and female subjects), behind the input method "4. Positive/Negative Images."

Table 3. Comprehensive evaluation by average ranks for 8 kinds of input methods of a user's preference, with respect to their expression performance (relative ranks and absolute 5-grade evaluations) and recommendation performance (mAP based on Language-Image similarity and mAP based on Image-Image similarity).

preference input methods		expression		recommend		average
0. Technical Keywords	male	(n/a)	10	1	5	6.50
	female	(n/a)	9	6	6	7.50
	all	(n/a)	9	1	7	6.50
1. Commonly-used Keywords (without Images)	male	8	8	3	1	5.00
	female	8	7	3	3	5.25
	all	8	8	5	1	5.50
2. Commonly-used Keywords with Images	male	4	1	2	6	**3.25**
	female	3	2	5	5	**3.75**
	all	4	1	4	5	**3.50**
3. Positive Images (without Keywords)	male	3	4	8	4	4.75
	female	2	8	4	2	4.00
	all	2	7	6	2	4.25
4. Positive/Negative Images (without Keywords)	male	1	3	4	7	**3.75**
	female	1	4	2	1	**2.00**
	all	1	3	2	3	**2.25**
5. Grading Images Absolutely (without Keywords)	male	2	2	7	3	**3.50**
	female	4	3	8	8	5.75
	all	3	2	8	6	4.75
6. Comparing Images Relatively (without Keywords)	male	5	5	6	2	4.50
	female	6	6	7	7	6.50
	all	5	5	7	4	5.25
7. Free Description	male	6	7	5	(n/a)	5.75
	female	5	1	1	(n/a)	**2.00**
	all	6	4	3	(n/a)	**4.00**

4   Conlcusion and Future Work

While most of the existing researches and practical e-commerce services for fashion coordinate recommendations has adopted only one of various input methods of a user's preference without enough arguments, this paper has more deeply argued about various input methods of a user's preference for personalized fashion coordinate recommendations, by conducting two kinds of questionnaire investigations and comprehensively analyzing some experimental results to compare 10 kinds of input methods of a user's preference for personalized fashion coordinate recommendations, with respect to their two kinds of performance, expression performance and recommendation performance. As a result, "4.

Positive/Negative Images" tends to be the most appropriate input method of user preference for personalized fashion coordinate recommendations.

The future work includes

- personalization of a target user's input method of her/his preference for personalized fashion coordinate recommendations, because of its dependency on her/his sexuality, the input method "7. Free Description" tends to be the most appropriate for females, while the input method "2. Commonly-used Keywords with Images" tends to be the most appropriate for males,
- more comprehensively analysis of two kinds of cost (expression cost and recommendation cost) as well as two kinds of performance (expression performance and recommendation performance) in Fig. 2.

Acknowledgment. This work was supported by KAKENHI 20K13787 and 22H03433.

References

1. Fukuda, M., Yonezawa, Y., Nakatani, Y.: Talkin closet: clothes recommendation themselves from their sales points. Proc. Hum. Interface Simposium **2010**, 617–620 (2010)
2. Kamma, Y., Marutani, T., Kajita, S., Mase, K.: Proposal of a fashion coordinate recommendation system based on fashion image keywords. IPSJ SIG Tech. Rep. **2011-HCI-142**(26), 1–7 (2011)
3. Tanabe, Y.: A study on fashion coordinating support system. Chuo University Bulletin of Graduate Studies – Science and Engineering –, vol. 43 (2013)
4. Suzuki, N., Kagawa, S.: The relationship between contemporary young women's leg fashion style and stockings/socks. J. Jpn. Res. Assoc. Textile End-Uses **56**(2), 155–162 (2015)
5. Katsura, K., Kato, M., and Shimakawa, H.: recommendation of fashion coordinates considering TPO and impression. In: Proceedings of the 15th Forum on Information Technology (FIT 2016), O-016, pp. 4-381–386 (2016)
6. Yanagida, Y.: Construction about the suitability of the fashion image term to a fashion style (The 2nd Report) - comparison of Japanese and South Korean young women. Trans. Jpn. Soc. Kansei Eng. **16**(1), 9–18 (2017)
7. Koike, S.: A study on kansei evaluation of fashion coordinate. Chuo University Bulletin of Graduate Studies – Science and Engineering, vol. 50 (2020)
8. Nishi, S., Sugihara, T., Hirano, Y., Kajita, S., Mase, K.: Design and development of the textile fashion coordination system – a communication aid for the customer and the salesclerk in real shop. In: Proceedings of the Fourth International Conference on Collaboration Technologies (CollabTech 2008), pp. 151–156 (2008)
9. Fukuda, M., Nakatani, Y.: Clothes recommend themselves: a new approach to a fashion coordinate support system. In: Proceedings of the World Congress on Engineering and Computer Science 2011 (WCECS 2011), vol. I (2011)
10. Gray, C., Beattie, M., Belay, H., Hill, S., Lerch, N.: Personalized online search for fashion products. In: Proceedings of 2015 Systems and Information Engineering Design Symposium (SIEDS 2015), pp. 91–96 (2015)
11. Liu, Z., Luo, P., Qiu, S., Wang, X., Tang, X.: DeepFashion: powering robust clothes recognition and retrieval with rich annotations. In: Proceedings of the IEEE Conference on Computer Vision and Pattern Recognition (CVPR 2016), pp. 1096–1104 (2016)

12. Bracher, C., Heinz, S., Vollgraf, R.: Fashion DNA: merging content and sales data for recommendation and article mapping. In: Proceedings of the KDD'16 Workshop on Machine Learning Meets Fashion, arXiv:1609.02489 (2016)

13. Inoue, N., Simo-Serra, E., Yamasaki, T., Ishikawa, H.: Multi-label fashion image classification with minimal human supervision. In: 16th IEEE International Conference on Computer Vision Workshops (ICCVW 2017), pp. 2261–2267 (2017)

14. Laenen, K., Zoghbi, S., Moens, M.-F.: Cross-modal search for fashion attributes. In: Proceedings of the KDD 2017 Workshop on Machine Learning Meets Fashion (2017)

15. Ota, S., Takenouchi, H., Tokumaru, M.: Kansei retrieval of clothing using features extracted by deep neural network. Trans. Jpn. Soc. Kansei Eng. **16**(3), 277–283 (2017)

16. Cardoso, A., Daolio, F., Vargas, S.: Product characterisation towards personalisation: learning attributes from unstructured data to recommend fashion products. In: Proceedings of the 24th ACM SIGKDD International Conference on Knowledge Discovery & Data Mining (KDD 2018), pp. 80–89 (2018)

17. Laenen, K., Zoghbi, S., and Moens, M.-F.: Web search of fashion items with multimodal querying. In: Proceedings of the Eleventh ACM International Conference on Web Search and Data Mining (WSDM 2018), pp. 342–350 (2018)

18. Yu, C., Hu, Y., Chen, Y., Zeng, B.: Personalized fashion design. In: Proceedings of the IEEE/CVF International Conference on Computer Vision (ICCV 2019), pp. 9046–9055 (2019)

19. Chen, W., et al.: POG: personalized outfit generation for fashion recommendation at Alibaba iFashion. In: Proceedings of the 25th ACM SIGKDD International Conference on Knowledge Discovery & Data Mining (KDD 2019), pp. 2662–2670 (2019)

20. Wu, H., Gao, Y., Guo, X., Al-Halah, Z., Rennie, S., Grauman, K., Feris, R.: Fashion IQ: a new dataset towards retrieving images by natural language feedback. In: Proceedings of the IEEE Conference on Computer Vision and Pattern Recognition (CVPR 2021), pp. 11307–11317 (2021). arXiv:1905.12794

21. Sharma, S., Koehl, L., Bruniaux, P., Zeng, X., Wang, Z.: Development of an intelligent data-driven system to recommend personalized fashion design solutions. Sensors **21**(12), 4239 (2021)

22. Ma, N., Kim, J., Lee, J.H.: Exploring personalized fashion design process using an emotional data visualization method. Fashion Textiles **9**, 44 (2022). https://doi.org/10.1186/s40691-022-00321-9

23. Noh, T., Yeo, H., Kim, M., and Han, K.: A study on user perception and experience differences in recommendation results by domain expertise: the case of fashion domains. In: Extended Abstracts of the 2023 CHI Conference on Human Factors in Computing Systems (CHI EA 2023), no. 14, pp. 1–7 (2023)

24. Ling, X., Zhenyu, J., Hong, Y., Pan, Z.: development of novel fashion design knowledge base by integrating conflict rule processing mechanism and its application in personalized fashion recommendations. Textile Res. J. **93**(5/6), 1069–1089 (2023)

25. Iwai, R., Shimizu, R., and Yamashita, H.,: Recommendation of Fashion Coordination Posts Based on Image and Linguistic Information. In: Proceedings of the 37th Annual Conference of the Japanese Society for Artificial Intelligence (JSAI 2023), 2L6-GS-3-03 (2023)

26. Sato, Y., et al.: Comment generation using a large-scale language model for fashion item recommendation. In: Proceedings of the 37th Annual Conference of the Japanese Society for Artificial Intelligence (JSAI 2023), 3D5-GS-2-02 (2023)

27. XZ. https://xz-app.jp/. Accessed 02 Feb 2024
28. stabilityai: japanese-stable-clip-vit-l-16.   https://huggingface.co/stabilityai/japanese-stable-clip-vit-l-16. Accessed 02 Feb 2024
29. Microsoft 365 Japan: [Microsoft Forms] Question Types and their Features – advance. https://www.youtube.com/watch?v=pY55LLUtkKM (2022)
30. WEAR: Fashion Coordinates. https://wear.jp/. Accessed 02 Feb 2024
31. Hattori, S., Takahara, M.: A study on human-computer interaction with text-to/from-image game AIs for diversity education. In: Mori, H., Asahi, Y. (eds.) Human Interface and the Management of Information. HCII 2023, LNCS, vol. 14015, pp 471–486. Springer, Cham (2023). https://doi.org/10.1007/978-3-031-35132-7_36

Possibility of Practicing Effectual Selling by Non-salespersons

Shinji Honge[1]([⊠]) and Chizuru Taniguchi[2]

[1] Okayama University of Science, Okayama, Japan
s.honge@ous.ac.jp
[2] Snack-Lemonade Inc., Osaka, Japan

Abstract. This research is a case study to examine the question "How can we sell without selling?" in accordance with the logic of Effectuation. For this purpose, we examined the association between the activities of employees of medical management consulting firms and Effectual Selling. We used the method of collaborative autoethnography to study, initiating at the time when she was a working graduate student at a business school, through a period of having sideline works, and to the time when she started her own company. The result may motivate practitioners to take action, since it indicates that the Effectuation logic and the "Otherish" behavior by successful other-oriented givers who are non-salespeople stimulates long-term sales achievements.

Keywords: Collaborative Work · Sales · Effectuation · Entrepreneurship

1 Introduction

With the maturing of society and the diversification of work styles, it is becoming more difficult to recruit and train salespeople year by year. For example, when a company hires university graduates, it faces following problems. First is the cost of education. It takes time for new employees hired to produce results, and during that time veteran staff become less productive. Next is the risk of lower customer satisfaction due to mistakes. Since new employees have little experience, they are likely to make more basic mistakes, including in terms of communication, which can lead to customer anxiety and dissatisfaction. Furthermore, the risk of deterioration in human relations is also a problem. Executives and sales managers sometimes have difficulty finding a balance between experienced and inexperienced employees. In addition, it is necessary to mention the high turnover rate. Inexperienced workers are more likely to feel that the industry, products, and services do not suit them, and are more likely to retire early.

In view of this situation, this research focuses on sales activities of people who are not salespeople. The role of indirect sales activities by non-salespeople is becoming increasingly important as online business meetings and information dissemination via social networking sites have become more common. This is an important role that can be considered in relation to the part-time marketer (Grönroos, 1989) in the service logic discussion. We will discuss a case study in which the theory of effectuation (Sarasvathy 2001, 2008) was learned and put into practice in its implementation.

H. Mori and Y. Asahi (Eds.): HCII 2024, LNCS 14691, pp. 197–205, 2024.
https://doi.org/10.1007/978-3-031-60125-5_13

2 Review of Prior Research

2.1 Eigyo (Japanese Sales and Marketing Style)

There are few studies in English that discuss the peculiarities of Japanese business. "Eigyo" in Japan contains both functions of marketing and sales. In Honge and Sato (2016), the following diagram shows the relationship between "Eigyo" and sales and marketing in Japan, and and focuses on the adjustment function as an important role of "Eigyo", especially by managers. The role of "Eigyo" is to coordinate activities among many departments of their own company, customer's company, even customer's customer's company, and their supplier companies. This shows that "Eigyo" is the role of co-creation of customer value while involving customers, other departments within the company, and cooperating partners (Fig. 1).

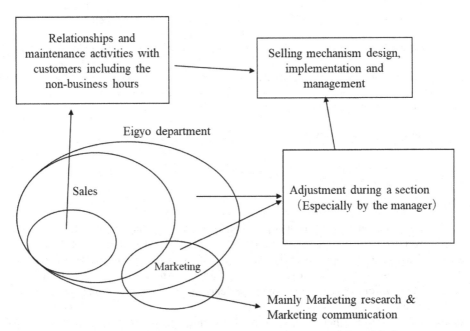

Fig. 1. Positioning of Eigyo in Japan Source: Honge and Sato (2016)

2.2 Sales in Service Research

Hartmann et al. (2018) clearly state that the role of sales no longer refers to a unilateral approach to persuading buyers to exchange products or services. Hughes et al. (2020) describe the evolution of the role of professional selling and argue that an integrated state of service and sales should be achieved. This flow of service research examines the evolution of sales, and has similarities to the role of "Eigyo" mentioned above.

2.3 Effectuation

Effectuation is a general theory of decision-making in situations of high uncertainty, discovered and proposed by Sarasvathy (2001, 2008). Although this theory was originally created through a decision-making on experiment targeting expert entrepreneurs, it has gained attention as a way of thinking for creating new businesses in recent years, as business uncertainty has increased due to the Covid-19 pandemic. Five specific principles have been identified as elements that make up the logic of effectuation. They are "Bird in Hand," "Affordable Loss," "Lemonade," "Crazy Quilt," and "Pilot in the Plane."

The principle of "Bird in Hand" is to create something new from existing means rather than ends. The principle of "Affordable Loss" is to commit based on what loss is acceptable, not on the maximizing of expected profit. The principle of "Lemonade" is not to avoid the unexpected, but rather to leverage chance. The principle of "Crazy Quilt" is to negotiate and build partnerships with all parties willing to commit. The principle of "Pilot in the Plane" is to focus on controllable activities and achieve desired outcomes. These are also theorized as a series of cycles.

2.4 Effectual Selling

Wang et al. (2020) connected the concept of Effectuation to the sales field. It defined Effectual Selling as focusing on resource integration, stakeholder interaction, and value co-creation under environmental uncertainty. The following framework is presented for Effectual Selling. The framework is a series of cycles that begin with what resources are available to the salesperson, then reach out to stakeholders to co-create customer value, and then the stakeholders make a commitment to change the salesperson's environment.

Next, we will list two studies that cite Effectual Selling. Epler and Leach (2021) shows that sales associate bricolage is more strongly associated with sales performance when the sales environment is more heavily disrupted, as in Covid-19. Edwards et al. (2022) suggested that entrepreneurial self-efficacy positively influences sales outcomes.

The research gap is that there is little research on the practice of Effectual Selling. And most sales research has focused on salespeople or sales managers, while research of people indirectly involved in sales are rare.

3 Research Questions and Methods

The research question is "How can we practice sales without selling activity?" We consider including internship students and new employees as non-salespersons. We conducted a case study through collaborative auto ethnography (CAE); a research method that combines the characteristics of autobiographical writing and ethnography while ensuring objectivity (Chang et al. 2012). In this method one recursively reflects on and describes one-self, targeting on experiences as a party in various events. It also generates new insights by questioning the experiences from multiple perspectives. One author of this paper, Taniguchi, is an employee of a medical management consulting company. At the same time, she was a graduate student attending a business school. The other author is a researcher. Taniguchi's experience as a practitioner was interviewed by the researcher and described by Taniguchi herself. The authors had repeated dialogues about the content, and analyzed the outcome as qualitative research data.

4 Case Study

4.1 Opportunity for Service Creation

While working for a medical management consulting company, Taniguchi attended a business school to study healthcare management. As a response to a class "Innovation practice" where she learned effectuation in her second year of business school, she launched "Shiroyagi/Kuroyagi", her personal business, in 2021. Effectuation does not necessarily require a purpose in creating a business. Accordingly, "Shiroyagi/Kuroyagi" was created without any particular purpose.

4.2 Thinking Process Towards Starting a Business

Effectuation emphasizes the means rather than the ends. In accordance with this, Taniguchi first extracted the "Bird in Hand" in order to grasp her own means. As a result, the following things were discovered.

Who am I?

"I am a person who wants to convey the thoughts, aspirations, and thoughts of a small business owner to his/her employees and customers."

Taniguchi interviews more than 300 medical institution managers in her day job. She knew many cases in which management's aspirations were not clearly communicated to employees, resulting in disadvantageous business conditions.

"I am a person who wants to spread Effectuation."

She learned a growth mindset in Effectuation in her class, freeing her from the assumption that she couldn't act even if she wanted to. She thought she would like to share this idea with others who have similar troubles.

What do I know?

"I know that small businesses don't have the financial resources to hire a public relations person to keep up their communications."

Who do I know?

"I know freelance designers."

Therefore, she created a new business by combining these means, working within her "Affordable Loss".

4.3 First Customer and Lemonade

Taniguchi couldn't sell her service at all at first. Her first customer was an unexpected music hall, by a request from an attendee of a university study meeting where she was on stage. She was happy to accept, but the service quickly fell apart. The amount of work was too much for the monthly budget to handle. The service was provided in an inadequate manner, and the contract was terminated after one year. She considered this to be the appearance of a "lemon" in effect and decided to make it into "Lemonade".

Taniguchi came up with the idea of creating a landing page for small businesses. She thought it would be possible to create a landing page at a low cost by creating the first page and replacing its contents. She believed that continuity was necessary to convey the thoughts of business owners, and that even small and medium-sized businesses did not want to incur high costs in order to maintain continuity. However, on the other hand, it was not her intention to lower the compensation of designers who do high-quality work. That dilemma also bothered her. Having these conditions, she came up with the idea of receiving management income as subscription fees, in return of creating low-budget landing pages.

4.4 Leverage Social Media and Her Personality

Taniguchi decided to use social media and her personality as means. By posting on social media, she was able to make many people aware of her business. She also limited her communication to what she likes and is good at, so that she can be satisfied even if she is not rewarded (even if the reaction is weak). By doing only what she could without struggling, she was able to continue without worrying about the lack of recognition. She also tried to write in gentle and kind manners, so that people would feel easy to share them. Every time she completed a product, she posted it on social media and received additional orders from people who saw it.

4.5 Sales Results of No-Selling Sales Activities

The following table summarizes the sales results of "Shiroyagi/Kuroyagi." This is the result of approximately two years of no-selling sales activity (Table 1).

Table 1. Sales Results of No-Selling Activities

type of work	Customers/Details and Number of Achievements
Lectures	Universities 8 Metaverse event 1 Special needs school 1 Management Group 1 Governmental Organization 1 Online school 3 Corporate training 8
Writing	Effectuation Practice Book Advance Care Planning Human resources for caregivers 2 Medical Care and Effectuation
Corporate PR support	Restaurants Cosmetics manufacturer Computer business enterprise
Creating Website	Researcher 3 Doctor 1 Clinic manager 1 Startup 2 Photographer 1 Music hall 1 Community 1

4.6 Establishment of Her Own Company

While Taniguchi went to making posts on social networking sites obtaining jobs one after another, one problem arose. Public organizations began to ask her about her affiliation when they requested work. Unfortunately, "Shiroyagi/Kuroyagi." Had been just a trade name of her private business, not a proper affiliation. She approached her main employer, the medical management consulting firm, though the management was not pleased her receiving work project as her own business. Taniguchi incorporated from a sole proprietorship and formed snack lemonade, Inc in December 2023. She is open to what exact services the company may provide. She intends to make decisions each time she receives a request or consultation. Meanwhile, she intends to keep spreading Effectuation. As soon as she shared the news of the company's establishment with her stakeholders. She received many comments such as, "Let's hold a party to celebrate the establishment of the company," "I would like to request a lecture," "How about a campaign?".

Taniguchi did not feel the need to start a business with a stable income as a family. However, she had a strong inner desire to try something new. At that time, people around her suggested that she should establish a company. Through her conversations with them, she realized that it was important for her to be in an environment that matched the direction she wanted to take her career as an effectuator. As a result, she did some image training and developed a concrete vision of establishing a company. She became aware of the importance of exploring new possibilities in her life. The decision to establish the company was an attempt to align herself with the way of thinking of the people she wanted to be close to. This decision was also influenced by the words of Kenichi Ohmae, a famous Japanese management consultant, who said, "If you want to change your life, change the people you associate with.

5 Considerations

The following diagram applies the case study to the cycle of Effectuation. Taniguchi used her knowledge of the "Bird in hand" principle and her social media network to discover new business opportunities. She then used social media to advertise and promote at no cost, using the "Affordable Loss" principle. She used the "Lemonade" principle to quickly respond to social media reactions. Opinions from customers and partners were directly used to improve products and improve customer satisfaction. She decides to establish a company to solve the lemon of not having an affiliation to receive her business. She has used the 'crazy quilt' principle to reach new markets and customers through collaborations and partnerships on social media. This is only possible if you have the theoretical knowledge that "the future is something to be created, not predicted." As a result, she broke away from traditional sales methods and developed a new sales strategy through social media (Fig. 2).

Taniguchi's entrepreneurial style is different from the nessesary-type of entrepreneurship, which is to respond to the needs of society and customers. It is an optunity-type entrepreneurship in the sense that she wants to create her own life and create her own opportunities. She had an internal motivation to be someone, but had not acted on it. However, she learned about Effectuation and was able to continue to act regardless of

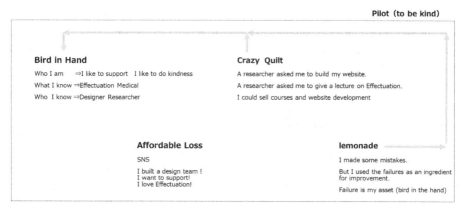

Fig. 2. Chizuru's Effectuation Cycle

the external environment. This is an example of how the concept of Effectuation can help individuals in their active career development.

Taniguchi's behavior after learning Effectuation is neither self-centered nor self-sacrificing, but rather "Otherish". The word "Otherish" is a concept coined by Grant (2013) from the words self-interest and other-interest. The "Oterish" is considered the most successful type, giving more to others than one is willing to accept, but who also calculates one's own interests as well. Takers always try to receive more than they give. Self-sacrificing givers give of their time and energy to others regardless of their own needs. Thus, this type tends to be exploited by takers. Grant (2013) states that to be the "Oterish" is to give more than you receive, but never lose sight of your own interests, and to use that as a guide to decide "when, where, how, and to whom to give (Fig. 3)."

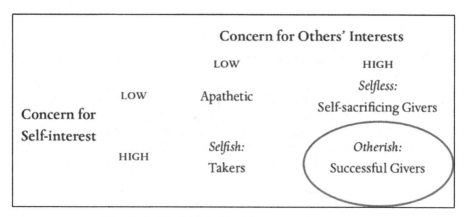

Fig. 3. Positioning of "Otherish" Source: Grant(2013)

The case study showed that by learning about Effectuation and following its principles, one can change from a "self-sacrificing giver" to an "Otherish". At the same time, the Effectual Selling framework seems promising for its application to non-sales. In addition, non-sales effectual selling is related to the original "Eigyo" role. Keeping non-salespeople doing what they love and are good at will lead to long-term sales results. Companies cannot order non-salespeople to do sales activities. Therefore, internal marketing is extremely important.

6 Conclusions, Limitations and Future Research

This study examines a case in which a non-sales company employee learned the theory of effectuation, established a private business, achieved sales results with the help of others, and established a company. A company's sales results are not solely the result of a few top salespeople. Management must come up with a mechanism to motivate ordinary employees, who are usually unnoticed, and to generate long-term sales results from their activities.

The theoretical implication of this study suggests the effectiveness of Effectual Selling in non-salespersons. The results of this study are valuable because they target non-salespeople, which has rarely been the case in sales research to date.

The managerial implication is that non-salespersons confirmed that performing the "Otherish" behaviors of successful other-oriented givers lead to long-term sales results. This provides suggestions for action for practitioners who are struggling with the current situation.

A limitation of this study is that it is based on a single case study in Japan. It is necessary to verify if the present results apply to a variety of cases. Not only qualitative but also quantitative analysis should be conducted. Future research agenda is to address the above issues by establishing a global research network. It would also be meaningful to continue this research in the areas of career development and wellbeing in the future.

References

Chang, H., Ngunjiri, F.W., Hernandez, K.-A.C.: Collaborative Autoethnography. Routledge, London (2012)

Edwards, J., Miles, M.P., D'Alessandro, S., Frost, M.: Linking B2B sales performance to entrepreneurial self-efficacy, entrepreneurial selling actions. J. Bus. Res. **142**, 585–593 (2022)

Epler, R.T., Leach, M.P.: An examination of salesperson bricolage during a critical sales disruption: selling during the covid-19 pandemic. Ind. Mark. Manage. **95**, 114–127 (2021)

Grönroos, C.: Defining marketing: a market-oriented approach. Eur. J. Mark. **23**(1), 52–60 (1998)

Grant, A.M.: Give and Take: A Revolutionary Approach to Success. Viking Press, New York (2013)

Hartmann, N.N., Wieland, H., Vargo, S., Hartmann, N.N., Wieland, H., Vargo, S.L.: Converging on a new theoretical foundation for selling. J. Mark. **82**(2), 1–18 (2018)

Honge, S., Sato, Y.: Comparison of "Eigyo" in Japan with marketing & Sales. In: Global Sales Science Institute Conference 2016 proceedings, pp. 27–33 (2016)

Hughes, D.E., Ogilvie, J.L.: When sales becomes service: the evolution of the professional selling role and an organic model of frontline ambidexterity. J. Serv. Res. **23**(1), 22–32 (2020)

Sarasvathy, S.D: Causation and effectuation: toward a theoretical shift from economic inevitability to entrepreneurial contingency. Acad. Manage. Rev. **26**(2), 243–263 (2001)

Sarasvathy, S.D: Effectuation: Elements of Entrepreneurial Orientation. Edward Elgar Publishing, Cheltenham (2008)

Wang, H., Schrock, W.A., Kumar, A., Hughes, D.E.: Effectual selling in service ecosystems. J. Pers. Sell. Sales Manage. **40**(4), 251–266 (2020)

Characteristics of Men with High Purchase Intention of Cosmetics and Approaches to Increase Their Purchase Intention

Takahide Kaneko and Yumi Asahi[✉]

Tokyo University of Science, 1-3 Kagurazaka, Shinjuku-Ku, Tokyo, Japan
Kanetaka2020@gmail.com

Abstract. The purpose of this study is to understand the characteristics of men who have a high intention to purchase cosmetics and approaches to increase their purchase intention. First, we examined the characteristics of men who have an intention to purchase cosmetics from the perspective of basic information such as age and family structure, as well as personality and purchasing behavior such as the RF scale and REC scale. Analysis from the perspective of basic information revealed that there were differences in the intention to purchase cosmetics by age group, but there were no significant differences in the intention to purchase cosmetics by family structure. Furthermore, analysis from the aspects of personality and purchasing behavior revealed that men who have purchase intentions tend to actively improve themselves and gather information at the time of purchase. Next, we considered how to approach people with a high intention to purchase cosmetics by dividing them into approaches through information gathering tools such as SNS and official websites, and approaches through purchasing methods such as drug stores and online shopping. For the analysis, we used a Bayesian network to visually grasp the causal relationships among the characteristics of male cosmetics users, information gathering tools, purchasing methods, purchasing intentions, etc. As a result of the analysis, it was found that gathering information on official websites, word-of-mouth outside of SNS, and Instagram had a significant impact on cosmetic purchase intentions. It was also found that men who use drugstores and mobile online shopping have a higher intention to purchase cosmetics. These results suggest that, along with the concept of "self-improvement," launching advertisements on word-of-mouth and Instagram outside of official websites and SNS, and focusing on sales at drugstores and mobile online shopping, are more likely to lead to the purchase of cosmetics by men.

Keywords: Digital marketing · Men's cosmetics market · Bayesian network

1 Introduction

In recent years, the male cosmetics market has been expanding. According to the literature [1], while the overall cosmetics market shrank by 89% year-on-year in 2020, the size of the cosmetics market by men expanded by 104% year-on-year in 2020. This suggests that the needs of the cosmetics industry may be changing depending on the gender and

H. Mori and Y. Asahi (Eds.): HCII 2024, LNCS 14691, pp. 206–216, 2024.
https://doi.org/10.1007/978-3-031-60125-5_14

attributes of customers, and that understanding the market and implementing effective advertising strategies are extremely important issues for companies planning to expand their markets.

However, there are several previous studies on marketing strategies for cosmetics, but most of them focused on female users. For example, Study [2] focused on women from the 2020 Insight Signal single-source data and described the impact of the presence and number of children on purchase intentions. Study [3] also describes digital marketing of cosmetics based on an interview questionnaire to female college students.

Based on the above research background, this study will focus on the following two points.

1. Understanding the characteristics of male cosmetics users

We will examine the characteristics of male users who intend to purchase cosmetics, in terms of basic information such as age, place of residence, and family structure, as well as personality and purchasing behavior such as RF scale and REC scale.

2. Capture approaches to male users

We will consider how to approach male users who have high intention to purchase cosmetics by using information gathering tools such as SNS and official websites, and by using purchasing methods such as drugstores and online shopping.

2   Analysis Method

2.1   Data Used

Table 1 shows the source, type, treatment, and duration of the data used in the analysis.

Table 1. Summary of data used

Data Source	Insight Signal 2023
Data Summary	Questionnaire data targeting men and women in their 20s to 50s. The data includes "stimulus data" such as TV viewing history, Web browsing history, and subscription history to magazines and newspapers, as well as "purchase data" such as product recognition, purchase intention, purchase experience, and repeat status from the same subjects
Data period	January 2023–April 2023

2.2 Basic Tabulation

Based on the data, we tabulated whether respondents had the intention to purchase cosmetics. As a result, 90% of women have the intention to purchase cosmetics, while only about half of men do (Figs. 1 and 2).

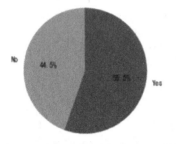 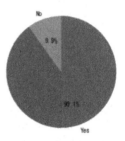

Fig. 1. Male intention to purchase cosmetics　　**Fig. 2.** Female intention to purchase cosmetics

2.3 Analysis Procedure

1. Understanding the characteristics of male cosmetics users

We examined the characteristics of men who intend to purchase cosmetics, in terms of basic information such as age and family structure, as well as personality and purchasing behavior. As indicators of personality and purchasing behavior, this study used the RF Scale and the REC Scale, which are proposed in literature [4], to measure what consumers tend to seek to gain and what they tend to avoid in their purchasing behavior. The REC scale, proposed in literature [5], is a 12-item measure that captures the degree to which consumers are rational, emotional, and affective in their purchasing behavior, based on the idea that rationality and affectivity are independent of each other. Table 2 and 3 below present the questionnaire items for evaluating the RF scale and REC scale.

Table 2. RF scale questionnaire items

RF_01	When trying to accomplish important things, I feel like I can't act as expected.
RF_02	I feel that I have made progress towards success in my life so far.
RF_03	I get excited immediately when I find an opportunity related to something I like.
RF_04	I often imagine how I will achieve my hopes and aspirations in the future.
RF_05	I believe that I am a person who actively strives to get closer to my "ideal self."
RF_06	I often followed the rules and regulations made by my parents.
RF_07	Sometimes I got hurt by not being careful.
RF_08	I worry about making mistakes.
RF_09	I often think about how to prevent failures in my life.
RF_10	I believe that I am a person who actively tries to fulfill my duties and responsibilities.

Table 3. REC scale questionnaire items

REC_01	I often take advantage of bargain sales when shopping.
REC_02	I buy what's trending.
REC_03	Before I go, I do a lot of research to find out which store I can buy from.
REC_04	I pay particular attention to the mood and emotion of the item before I buy it.
REC_05	I keep my purchases to the bare minimum.
REC_06	When I buy something, I buy what the store clerk recommends.
REC_07	When I shop, I buy brands that are often advertised.
REC_08	I buy with particular emphasis on practicality and ease of use.
REC_09	I buy especially for the look and feel and ease of use.
REC_10	I decide what to buy after comparing as many things as possible.
REC_11	When something new comes out, I buy it before others do.
REC_12	I just buy things that are cheap and economical.

2. Approaching male users

We examined how to approach male users who have a high intention to purchase cosmetics by dividing the approaches into two categories: approaches through information-gathering tools such as SNS and official websites, and approaches through purchasing methods such as drugstores and online shopping. We used a Bayesian network to visually capture the causal relationships among the characteristics of male users of cosmetics, information-gathering tools, purchasing methods, and purchase intentions.

2.4 Bayesian Networks

This section describes the fundamentals of Bayesian networks used in this study and BayoLinkS used in the analysis. A Bayesian network is a method for analyzing causal relationships in data. It is a method for graphically organizing causal relationships among a large number of events by determining the strength of causal relationships based on the magnitude of the conditional probability, which is the probability that one event will cause another event to occur if it occurs. The name "Bayesian" is derived from the Bayes' theorem proposed by Thomas Bayes, which is the basic idea behind the strength of causal relationships based on conditional probabilities. It is also called a "Bayesian network" because the analysis results are represented as a network diagram. In this study, analysis was conducted using BayoLinkS, software for constructing Bayesian networks provided by NTT Data Mathematical Systems Corporation [6]. In this study, Greedy Search was used as the algorithm for constructing Bayesian networks. Greedy Search is a method that starts with no parents for each individual node, calculates evaluation values while adding parents one by one, and terminates the search when the evaluation values do not improve even after adding parents. The analysis was also conducted using AIC (✳) as the information criterion and pairwise elimination as the method for removing missing values.

$$ML = \sum_{i=1}^{n} \sum_{j=1}^{r_i} \sum_{s=1}^{s_i} N_{ijk} log\left(\frac{N_{ijk}}{N_{ik}}\right)$$

$$AIC = -2\left(ML - \sum_{i=1}^{n}(r_i - 1)s_i\right) \cdots (\text{②})$$

n : Number of nodes
r_i : Number of states of node X_i
s_i : Number of states of parent node of node X_i
N_{ijk} : (j, k) component of the cross tabulation table for node X_i
N_{ik} : $\sum_{j=1}^{r_i} N_{ijk}$
N : Sample size

3 Analysis Results

3.1 Understanding the Characteristics of Male Cosmetics Users from the Aspect of Basic Information

The percentages of intention to purchase cosmetics were compared by age, marital status, and presence of children. Regarding age, the percentage of respondents in their 30s exceeded 60%, while the percentage of respondents in their 50s was below 50%, indicating differences by age group (Fig. 3). The percentage of never-married respondents was slightly lower than the other groups, but there was no significant difference (Fig. 4). There was little difference between the two groups in terms of the presence or absence of children (Fig. 5). In a previous study [2], the presence or absence of children and the number of children had an effect on the intention to purchase cosmetics when focusing on women, but the results for men suggest that, on the contrary, neither marital status nor the presence of children has any relationship with the intention to purchase cosmetics.

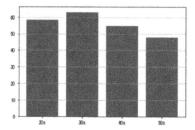

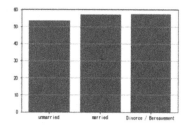

Fig. 3. The percentage of men who intend to purchase cosmetics by age group

Fig. 4. The percentage of men who intend to purchase cosmetics by marital status

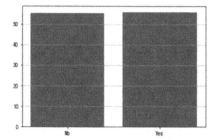

Fig. 5. The percentage of men who intend to purchase cosmetics by presence of children

3.2 Understanding the Characteristics of Male Cosmetics Users in Terms of Personality and Purchasing Behavior

We compared personality and purchasing behavior indicators, such as the RF and REC scales, by whether or not consumers intended to purchase cosmetics. First, we examined the characteristics of male consumers who intend to purchase cosmetics by using the RF scale, an index that measures what consumers aim to gain or avoid in their purchases. The results showed that a significant difference was revealed in RF_04 (I often imagine how I will realize my hopes and aspirations in the future) and RF_05 (I think I am a person who actively strives to realize my hopes, wishes, and aspirations and get closer to my "ideal self"), depending on whether or not I have the intention to purchase cosmetics (Fig. 6, 7).

Next, by using the REC scale, which is a measure of rationality and emotionality in purchasing behavior, we examined the characteristics of men who intend to purchase cosmetics. The results show that the respondents' intention to purchase cosmetics shows a large difference in REC_03 (I will check carefully before going to a store to see what I can get for my money) and REC_10 (I will decide what to buy after comparing as many items as possible), depending on whether or not they intend to purchase cosmetics (Fig. 8, 9).

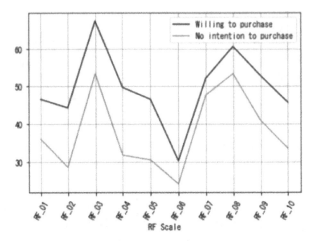

Fig. 6. Percentage of respondents who answered that the RF scale applies to them

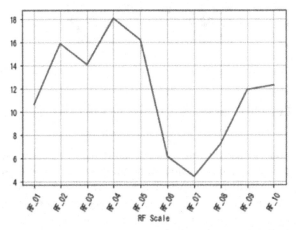

Fig. 7. Difference in the percentage of respondents who answered that the RF scale applies to them

3.3 Understanding the Media in Which Men with High Intentions to Purchase Cosmetics Gather Information

This section examines the factors that influence purchase intention and how men who are considered to have high purchase intention gather information on cosmetics, leading to purchase. In this study, we attempted to understand causal relationships visually using a Bayesian network. In this analysis, the causal relationship was set as shown in Fig. 10 below.

The following are the results of the Bayesian network. These results suggest that word of mouth and information gathering on Instagram, other than official websites and SNS, have a significant impact on purchase intentions (Fig. 11).

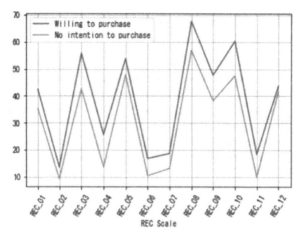

Fig. 8. Percentage of respondents who answered that the REC scale applies to them

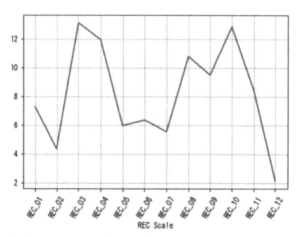

Fig. 9. Difference in the percentage of respondents who answered that the REC scale applies to them

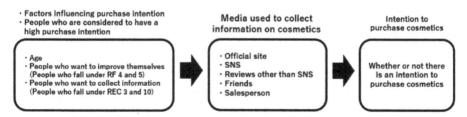

Fig. 10. Bayesian networks for understanding media used to collect information on cosmetics

3.4 Understanding the Means of Purchase Used by Men with High Intent to Purchase Cosmetics

This section examines the factors that influence purchase intention, what kind of purchasing means are often used by men who are considered to have high purchase intention, and whether these factors lead to purchases. As in the previous section, we attempted to visually understand the causal relationship using a Bayesian network. In this analysis, the causal relationship was set as shown in Fig. 12 below.

The following are the results of the Bayesian network. The results suggest that men who use drugstores and mobile online shopping also have high intentions to purchase cosmetics (Fig. 13).

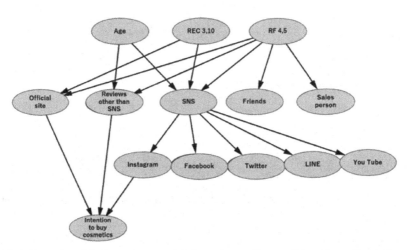

Fig. 11. The results of the Bayesian network for understanding media used to collect information on cosmetics

Fig. 12. Bayesian networks for understanding means of purchase

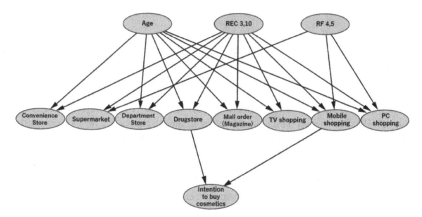

Fig. 13. The results of the Bayesian networks for understanding means of purchase

4 Conclusion

The purpose of this study was to understand the characteristics of men with high purchase intention for cosmetics and approaches to increase their purchase intention. First, we examined the characteristics of men with high intention to purchase cosmetics in terms of basic information such as age and family structure, as well as personality and purchasing behavior such as RF and REC scales. The results of the basic information analysis showed that there were differences in purchase intention for cosmetics by age, but not so much by family structure. Analysis of personality and purchasing behavior revealed that men who intended to purchase cosmetics tended to be more proactive in self-improvement and information gathering at the time of purchase. Next, we examined how to approach the group with high purchase intention by dividing the approaches into two categories: approaches through information-gathering tools such as SNS and official websites, and approaches through purchasing methods such as drugstores and online shopping. We used a Bayesian network to visually capture the causal relationships among the characteristics of male users of cosmetics, information-gathering tools, means of purchase, and purchase intentions. The analysis revealed that information gathering through word of mouth and Instagram, other than official websites and SNS, has a significant impact on purchase intention for cosmetics products. In addition, we found that men who use drugstores and mobile online shopping also have high purchase intentions for cosmetics.

These results suggest that the concept of "self-improvement," together with word-of-mouth and Instagram advertising outside of official websites and SNS, and a focus on sales at drugstores and mobile online shopping, have a high likelihood of leading to male purchase of cosmetics. Future research should examine the causal relationship between purchase intention and the development of cosmetics products in more detail to clarify what kind of products are sought after and what kind of marketing strategies are most likely to lead to purchases.

References

1. Intage Corporation: Even the Corona Disaster has grown! Men's cosmetic purchases. Koronaka demo nobita! Dansei no kesyouhin kounyuu (in Japanese)
2. Koumura, N., Kaneko, Y.: Analysis of the influence of consumers' aesthetics and the presence of children on the demand for basic cosmetics. Kisokesyouhin no zyuyou ni syouhisya no biisiki to kodomo no umu ga ataeru eikyou no bunseki (in Japanese). Doshisha Women's University
3. Ohmoto, I.: Perspectives on the latest marketing in the cosmetics business - mainly from the field of digital marketing. Kesyouhinbizinesu ni okeru saisinma-kethingu heno siza ~omoni dezitaruma-kethingu no genba kara (in Japanese). Showa Women's University
4. Ishii, H.: Sensory and evaluation mechanisms in consumer behavior. Syouhisyakoudou ni okeru kankaku to hyouka mekanizumu (in Japanese). Chikura Shobo, p. 220
5. Sugimoto, T.: New psychology for understanding consumers. Shin syouhisya rikai no tameno shinrigaku (in Japanese). Fukumura Shuppan, p. 166
6. NTT Data Mathematical Systems Corporation. BayoLinkS Manual (2023)

Factor Analysis of Purchasing a Third-Category Beer

Kazuki Seto and Yumi Asahi$^{(\boxtimes)}$

Graduated School of Management, Department of Management, Tokyo University of Science,
1-11-2, Fujimi, Chiyoda-ku, Tokyo 102-0071, Japan
8623509@ed.tus.ac.jp, asahi@rs.tus.ac.jp

Abstract. There is a beer known as the third beer in Japan. This beer has been sold at a lower price than others due to the difference in tax rates. Taking this advantage, its sales volume continued to grow until 2020. However, the price advantage will gradually disappear, due to the increase in tax rates until 2026. It is said that third beer sales volume is going to decline. So, it is important to find purchasing factors other than price in third beers and translate them into products. This paper analyzes the customer demographics of "Honkirin," a representative third beer product, to derive factors for purchasing a third beer. Based on these findings, we will also propose ideas and promotions for new third beer products. First, we extracted questionnaire items that were relevant to purchase intention for "Honkirin" by using a t variable selection method called Boruta. Then, latent class analysis was conducted, assigning samples to six classes based on the samples' answer patterns to the selected items. After that, a chi-square test was applied for each class to identify the class which significantly contained samples with purchase intention toward "Honkirin". After testing, we examined the overall response patterns of each class and their web usage to derive the needs and behavioral features of Honkirin's potential customers. Finally, based on the findings from the analyses, we summarized product ideas and promotion methods for third beer that would survive after the loss of price advantage.

Keywords: Third beer · Purchasing factors other than price in third beer · Boruta · Latent class · Chi-squared test

1 Introduction

1.1 Japanese Beer Market

There are three main types of beer-type beverages in Japan. They are beer, law malt, and third beer. They are classified according to the amount of malt used as an ingredient and whether or not it is used. Japan has a liquor tax law with different tax rates for each type, item, alcohol content, and other factors. Since the liquor tax law was revised in 1953, beer has been maintained at a high tax rate as a luxury item. Therefore, to avoid the tax burden, beer companies have developed alcoholic beverages that fall outside the definition of beer with a high tax rate [1]. These are law malt beer and third-category beer.

Total sales of all beer types have been decreased, partly because young people are turning away from alcoholic beverages [2]. However, there is one type of beer whose sales volume has grown until 2020 [3]. That is the third beer (Figs. 1 and 2).

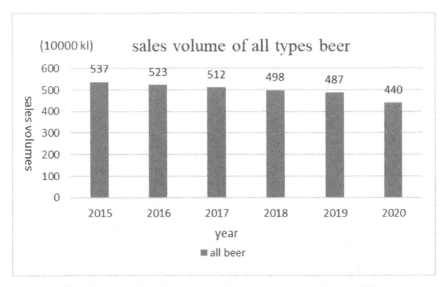

Fig. 1. Change in all beer types of sales volume from 2015 to 2020.

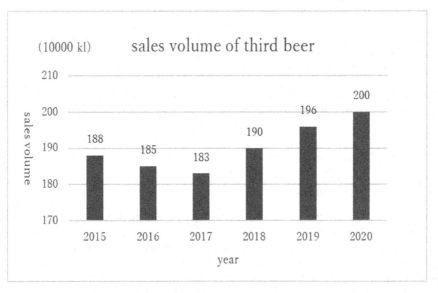

Fig. 2. Change in third beer sales volume from 2015 to 2020.

1.2 A Third Beer

A third beer is a beer-flavored alcoholic beverage made by adding another alcohol to law malt beer (less than 50% malt) or without malt as an ingredient. This drink was developed in response to another increase in the tax on law malt beer in 2003, to market an alcoholic beverage with a cheap tax rate. To the present, it has been sold at a lower tax rate and a lower price than the other two beer types. Taking this advantage, a third beer is the only beer type that has seen an increase in sales volume in recent years.

1.3 Disappearance of Price Advantage

In 2018, the Ministry of Finance changed the Liquor Tax Law to change the situation where different tax rates on the similar beverages are affecting sales volume and product development [3]. From this decision, the tax rates for beer, law malt beer, and third-beer will be unified in 2026. The Fig. 3 shows the changing in tax rates for each beer category. It will be changed in stages in fiscal years 2020, 2023, and 2026. This change will result in a gradual increase in the tax rate for third beers, and the price advantage will gradually disappear. The first phase of the tax hike, which took place in October 2020, increased the tax by 9.8 yen per 350 ml. It resulted in a price increase from 106.7 yen to 117 yen per 350 ml bottle. This reduced the sales share of third beers. They were the most affected by the tax rate changing compared to other types of beers [5]. And second tax hike in October 2023, the rate was increased by approximately 9.8 yen per 350 ml. This revision also reduced purchasing third beers [6].

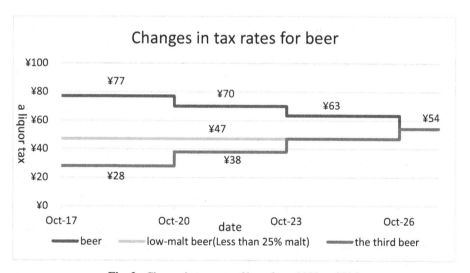

Fig. 3. Change in tax rate of beer from 2020 to 2026.

From these changes, third beer continues to shrink its sales. Ozawa [5] estimated that even with the changes in 2026, third beer will further reduce its sales volume share of alcoholic beverages.

1.4 Purpose of This Study

Through previous studies, a third beer is expected to decrease its sales volumes and a shakeout outside the major brands. To survive, it is important to find purchasing factors other than price in third beers and to utilize these needs in products. Therefore, the purpose of this paper is to derive potential needs for a third beer by analyzing the customers' features of products representing the third beer called HonKirin. It was sold 300 million bottles (350 ml volume) in the first year of sales. Based on the findings from analyses, we also propose ideas and advertising methods for new third beer products.

2 Flow of This Study

The following is the flow of this study. In the study, all data processing and analyses were performed using Python 3.11.5. First, we conduct data processing and basic analysis. A variable selection method using a random forest called Boruta is employed in the analysis. Using this method, we succeeded in extracting items from the provided questionnaire data that were relevant to questionnaire data on purchasing intentions for Honkirin. Second, we derive the features of customers with high purchase intention toward Honkirin and identify their potential needs for a third beer. A latent class analysis is conducted on the extracted data, and the sample is classified into six classes by response pattern. Then, A chi-square test is used to identify the classes with significantly higher purchase intention for Honkirin. After that, we analyze the response trends and web usage of these classes. Finally, based on the results of these analyses, we propose ideas for new third beer products and promotions that do not lose against the difficult situation.

3 The Data Summary

In this study, we used questionnaire data from the NRI Marketing Analysis Contest provided by Nomura Research Institute, Ltd. The sample in the data consisted of 2,500 men and women between the ages of 20 and 60, with approximately same ratio of sexes. And there are a total of 1,415 questions in the data.

The following is a summary of the questionnaire items used in analyses. The basic analysis and the main analysis used questionnaire data that asked about basic consumer attributes such as age and marital status, product recognition and purchase intentions for beverage products, and consumer values, including those related to purchase intentions for Honkirin. In addition, data on the frequency of web usage was used in the main analysis. This data asked about the frequency of use of each 33 social media in a week.

4 Data Processing and Basic Analysis

4.1 Data Processing

Data processing was performed before starting the analysis. To analyze the relevant features of customers with have purchase intention or not, we represented the presence or absence of purchase intention as binary data. Therefore, the data on purchasing intention toward Honkirin was processed as shown in Table 1.

Table 1. Changes in questionnaire data on purchase intention of Honkirin due to processing.

Category	data	processed category	processed data
Really want to buy	1	Want to buy	1
Want to buy	2		
Neither	3	Not want to buy	0
Not want to buy	4		

The data from the sample that did not respond to this questionnaire was excluded. After processing, we found that there were 720 samples with purchase intention and 1612 samples without purchase intention.

4.2 Basic Analysis

The basic analysis was to extract consumer features that were highly relevant to whether or not they intend to purchase Honkirin. We applied a variable selection method using a random forest called Boruta [7]. The purpose of the basic analysis was achieved by extracting items from the questionnaire data that had some relationship to the purchase intention of Honkirin. Having purchase intention toward Hon Kirin or not (no purchase intention: 0, having purchase intention: 1) was used as the objective variable. We used questionnaire data on 230 items regarding basic consumer attributes (age, gender, etc.), consumer values, channel usage frequency, channel usage status, consumption values toward REC scale and beverage products, and purchase status as explanatory variables.

Questionnaire Items Extracted by Basic Analysis. Table 2 shows the variables extracted by the analysis. 13 variables were extracted by Boruta from the 230 variables.

Checking the Validity of Variable Selection by Boruta. Table 3 is a Comparison of the classification accuracy of random forests before and after variable selection. The results showed that the accuracy was higher when only the selected variables were classified as explanatory variables. From this result, it can be said that we can select variables that had more influence on purchase intention.

Table 2. List of extracted survey items.

Variable	Contents of variable
AGE	Your age
PS_CAT_01	How much non-alcoholic beer or cocktails did you drink in a month?
PI_CAT_01	How much non-alcoholic beer or cocktails would you like to drink in a month?
PI_CAT_03	How much energy drink would you like to drink in a month?
PI_CAT_34	How much chilled cup coffee would you like to drink in a month?
PI_CAT_37	How much mineral water would you like to drink in a month?
PS_CAT_44	How much beer did you drink in a month?
PI_CAT_44	How much beer would you like to drink in a month?
PS_CAT_45	How much like low-malt beer or third beer did you drink in a month?
PI_CAT_45	How much like low-malt beer or third beer did you drink in a month?
PS_CAT_46	How much chuhai or cocktail did you drink in a month?
PI_CAT_46	How much chuhai or cocktail would you like to drink in a month?
PI_CAT_47	How much health drink would you like to drink in a month?

Table 3. Comparison of classification accuracy before and after variable selection

	before extracting	after extracting
Accuracy	0.8	0.82
recall_score	0.58	0.76
f1_score	0.67	0.75

5 Main Analysis

We analyzed how the sample with purchase intention for "Honkirin" answered to the selected questionnaire items and clarified their features.

5.1 Latent Class Analysis

We classified samples into classes based on their answer patterns to the survey extracted items, to facilitate analysis of their answers. Latent class analysis was used as the analysis method. This analysis can handle quantitative and qualitative data simultaneously. It is also very convenient because the number of classes can be determined and assigned to classes from the perspective of statistical information [8].

Determination of the Number of Classes and Assignment to Each Class. We set the number of classes, and each sample was assigned to an appropriate class after conducting this analysis. Table 4 shows the BIC and AIC scores. The number of classes was selected

Table 4. Comparison of BIC and AIC values by class

The number of classes	BIC	AIC
4 classes	15212.92	15808.74
5 classes	12038.39	12784.55
6 classes	792.43	−104
7 classes	−3584.57	−2537.71

Table 5. Table showing the probability of belonging to each class and assignment by samples

sample	c1	c2	c3	c4	c5	c6	class
1380653	45%	0%	0%	**55%**	0%	0%	4
1380708	6%	0%	0%	**94%**	0%	0%	4
1380873	0%	**100%**	0%	0%	0%	0%	2
1380926	**95%**	0%	0%	0%	0%	5%	1

based on small AIC and BIC values, yet not causing overfitting. We decided the number of classes to 6. Next, the probability of belonging to each class was calculated for each sample, and an assignment was made to the class with the highest probability of belonging. Table 5 shows some examples of it.

5.2 Chi-Square Test

We conducted this analysis to determine whether there were differences in purchase intention toward Honkirin among the classes. For this purpose, we used the chi-square test to examine whether the ratio of the total sample regarding purchase intention was significantly different from those of each class.

Preparation for Test. Seven tabulations were made regarding purchase intention toward Honkirin in each class. The results are shown in Table 6. Using these tabulations, examinations were conducted for each class group and all. The null hypothesis was "there is no relationship between each class and purchase intention" and the alternative hypothesis was "there is a relationship between each class and purchase intention". The null hypothesis was rejected if the p-value was less than 0.05.

Result of the Test. The results are shown in Table 7. In all tests, the p-values were below 0.05, which resulted in the rejection of the null hypothesis. It was clear that purchase intention toward Honkirin varies significantly by class. Thus, it can be said that samples in classes 1, 3, and 4 have the purchase intention, and the samples belonging in Classes 2, 5, and 6 have no purchase intention toward Honkirin as a whole.

Table 6. Table showing the number of samples having purchase intention toward Honkirin or not in each class.

	the number of people who have purchase intention	the number of people who don't have purchase intention
class1	205	30
class2	67	248
class3	72	35
class4	168	135
class5	62	764
class6	35	115
all	614	1340

Table 7. p-value for each chi-square tests

Test group	P-value
class1 VS. all	3.99E−62
class2 VS. all	0.000341
class3 VS. all	4.01E−14
class4 VS. all	4.99E−16
class5 VS. all	7.42E−41
class6 VS. all	0.048209

5.3 Features Analysis of Each Class by Cross Tabulation

For each class, the answer data for the survey items extracted in the basic analysis were cross-tabulated. Table 8 summarizes the answer trends for each class that can be read from the tabulation. From the table, the classes with purchase intention for Honkirin (class1, 3 and 4) had higher purchase intention for alcoholic beverages. And they had higher purchase frequency for beer. Classes 1 and 3 also had a higher purchase intention for non-alcoholic beer/cocktails. From these viewpoints, it can be said that potential customers of Honkirin are interested in alcoholic beverages in general but have a particularly strong preference for beer. Therefore, they often buy beer, and they are likely to buy other categories of alcoholic beverages along with beer. Some have purchase intention for non-alcoholic beer, it can be seen that they value not only getting drunk but also the taste and the sensation of drinking.

5.4 Analysis of Potential Customers' Web Use Frequency by Media

After Having identified the consumers who are likely to purchase the third beer, we examined the promotional methods to reach them efficiently. In this study, we analyzed

Table 8. Features of each class read from the cross tabulation

class	About purchase intentions	About purchase frequency
C1	· High purchase intention for beverage products as a whole	· Significantly high purchase frequency for beer · High purchase frequency for law malt beer/third, cocktails/chuhi
C2	· Low purchase intention for non-alcoholic beer/cocktails, law malt beer/third beer, and energy drinks · High purchase intentions for beer and cocktails/chu-hai	· No purchasing for non-alcoholic beer and third-category beer/law malt beer · High purchase frequency for beer
C3	· High purchase intention for beer, law malt beer/third beer, and cocktails/chu-hi · Significantly high purchase intention for non-alcoholic beer/cocktails	· High purchase frequency for non-alcoholic beer/cocktails, beer, law malt beer/third beer, and cocktails/chuhai
C4	· high purchase intention for law malt beer/third-category beer and cocktails/chu-hi · Significantly high purchase intention for beer · Lower purchase intention for non-alcoholic beverages	· High purchase frequency for beer and law malt beer/third-category beer · No purchasing for non-alcoholic beer/cocktail
C5	· Low Purchase intention for beverages as a whole · Significantly low purchase intention for non-alcoholic beer/cocktails, beer, law malt beer/third beer, cocktails/chu-hai	· No purchasing for non-alcoholic beer/cocktails, beer, law malt beer/third beer and cocktails/chuhai
C6	· Low purchase intention for law malt beer/third beer · High purchase intention for non-alcoholic beer/cocktails and mineral water	· No purchasing for law malt beer/third beer · Low purchase frequency Beer and cocktails/chu-hai purchased infrequency

the correlation between the presence or absence of a class with purchase intention toward Honkirin and the use of each Internet media, expressed as the Cramer linkage coefficients.

Preparation and Analysis Results. The Cramer linkage coefficient takes values between 0 and 1 and expresses the strength of the correlation between row and column elements [9]. Firstly, we processed the samples belonging to classes 1, 3, and 4 as 1 and those belonging to classes 2, 5, and 6 as 2. Then, cross-tabulated these data as row elements and the data on the use of each media as column elements. The correlation between these two elements was then derived by calculating the Cramer linkage coefficient. The formula for calculating the coefficients(V) is shown below (Table 9).

$$V = \sqrt{\frac{x^2}{n(\min[k, l] - 1)}} \tag{1}$$

Table 9. Variables of Eq. (1)

Variable	Contents of variable
x^2	Chi-square values
n	Actual frequencies
k	Number of columns in cross tabulation table
l	The number of index in cross tabulation table

Table 10. List of calculated Cramer's linkage coefficients

media	Cramel coefficients(V)
Twitter	0.066952002
Facebook	0.163229333
Instagram	0.111823081
Amebro	0.114166557
LINE	0.043393981
LINE VOOM	0.214269569
YouTube	0.075753662
Nikoniko video	0.131963226
LINE LIVE	0.214858941
Tver	0.128690681
Paravi	0.201600138
ABEMA	0.190740067
GYAO!	0.197329509
Spotify	0.178465917
Amazon	0.162926414
Rakuten	0.137312681
Yahoo! Shopping	0.170940739
Yahoo! JAPAN	0.073701286
Google	0.033769945
goo	0.215474156
d menu	0.175931302
Gunosy	0.175324428
SmartNews	0.154914331

(continued)

Table 10. (*continued*)

media	Cramel coefficients(*V*)
NewsPicks	0.223791103
LINE NEWS	0.149542004
Antenna	0.219397296
@cosme	0.224212555
Cookpad	0.094358507
Kakakukom	0.251670252
Taberog	0.227771245
Kurashiru	0.070171371
DELISH KITCHEN	0.106677065
D magazine	0.149401248

The calculated Cramer linkage coefficients are shown in Table 10. There were no values above 0.3, which was considered correlated. So, we focused mainly on media that took values above 0.2 as having a weak correlation.

Detailed Analysis of Media Use. From the crosstabulation table in each media with a coefficient over 0.2, the following points were observed. In the class with purchase intention, many answers used price.com, food logs, and NewsPicks in particular frequently. In addition, the number of respondents who used LINE VOOM, LINE LIVE, goo, and antenna was high among those who did use them, although the number of users themselves was low.

6 Proposing for New Product Ideas and Promotion Methods for Third Beer

In this study, we analyze the features of customers with high purchase intention toward Honkirin, which is represented by the third beer. Then, we derive their potential needs and media usage. Based on these results, we propose new product ideas for third beer, along with promotional methods to reach them.

Idea. Make products that reproduce the authentic bitterness and the feelings of beer going down your throat.

Promotion. Launch advertisements to recognize the product's name on Price.com, Eating Log, and News Picks. After that, write a series of articles about the specific features of third beer to the antenna.

About Proposed New Products Idea. From the analysis, we recognize that potential customers have strong preferences for beer and are concerned about taste and drinking experience. Therefore, we aim to create a product that focuses on these factors and gets on their consideration list when buying beer.

About Proposed Promotion Method. Based on the results of the analysis, we examined promotions that can efficiently contact potential customers and easily promote product recognition and purchase intentions. First, to promote product recognition, the product name is spread by using media with many potential customers. Then, we would like to convey more detailed product information by using curated media, which has a high percentage of potential customers, to increase their purchasing intention.

7 Discussion

Through this study, we recognized the following insights. Firstly, we recognize that customers who have purchase intentions toward Honkirin prefer beer to other beverages. It can be said that a third beer is better to be an alcoholic that feels like beer. Secondly, we recognize that customers who are likely to purchase a third beer, such as Honkirin, are attracted to the taste and physical sensations of drinking beer. From the main analysis, there are many consumers, who are likely to buy Honkirin and want to drink non-alcoholic beer or cocktails. It can be said that they are attracted to alcoholic beverages other than alcohol. Thirdly, we recognize that the weak association between purchase intention toward third beer and the media used. These findings would support efficient media selection for advertising placement.

In this study, we proposed product ideas and promotions for a third beer that would be effective for potential customers even if the price increases due to the tax hike. In the process, we have newly identified features of potential customers and their actual web usage. By using these insights, we believe new third beers having strengths other than price will reach potential customers and contribute to the recovery of the third beer market.

8 Conclusion

In this study, potential needs other than the price of the third beer were clarified by deriving customer features of Honkirin, which represents the third beer. After that, we examined the relationship between the customer features and the frequency of web usage by media. Finally, based on the features and web usage, we proposed effective product ideas and promotions for them which could survive third beer after the price getting higher. We are convinced that these results contribute to the development of attractive the third beer products that will not suffer from the tax hike.

References

1. Funai, T., Tanaka, A.: Analysis of changes in beer consumption and tax revenues due to changes to the liquor tax law in fiscal year 2017. University of Tokyo School of Public Policy "Micro Case Study" First Semester Report (2017)
2. Yumeno, T.: A study on the phenomenon of young people's desertion from beer (2023)
3. Kirin Holdings Company, Market Data and Sales Overview. https://www.kirinholdings.com/jp/investors/library/databook/alcohol/. Accessed 5 Feb 2024
4. Ministry of Finance: Liquor tax data. https://www.mof.go.jp/tax_policy/summary/consumption/d08.htm. Accessed 5 Feb 2024

5. Ozawa, T., Suenaga, H., Sugimoto, N.: Share of sales to change with a single liquor tax. Japan Center for Economic Research, Research Paper (2021)

6. Research on Changes in the Beer Market Due to Liquor Tax Reform! Macromill Independent Analysis Report. https://www.macromill.com/service/report/research-report/094/. Accessed 5 Feb 2024

7. Kursa, M.B., Jankowski, A., Rudnicki, W.R.: Boruta – a system for feature selection. Fundamenta Informaticae **101**(4), 271–285 (2010)

8. Iwa, T.: Introduction to Latent Class Models, Econometrics One-Step Work Course (3). https://www.jstage.jst.go.jp/article/ojjams/24/2/24_2_345/_pdf. Accessed 5 Feb 2024

9. Cramér, H.: The two-dimensional case. In: Mathematical Methods of Statistics, p. 282. Princeton University Press, Princeton (1946)

The Impact of Information from Company Marketing Platforms on Consumers' Brand Image and Intention to Use Car-Sharing Services

Mone Takasu[✉] and Yumi Asahi

Graduate School of Management, Department of Management, Tokyo University of Science, 1-11-2, Fujimi, Chiyoda-Ku 102-0071, Tokyo, Japan
mone.3071@gmail.com, asahi@rs.tus.ac.jp

Abstract. In this study, with the expansion of the car-sharing market, awareness of the challenges of promoting car-sharing to young people, and the complexity of branding measures in overall marketing. Expanding the definition of brand value as a research background, factor analysis and structural equation modeling were conducted on data from a questionnaire survey conducted on college students, The brand value of car sharing was modeled. The results showed that variation in the three factors influenced consumers' usage intentions. We also conducted a simple cross-tabulation analysis of whether and how the observed usage intentions differ depending on the marketing platform that the company has, and found that the transmission by the company has a positive impact on improving consumers' usage intentions, and that the way in which this impact is exerted differs by platform type. The results show that the impact of firms' communication has a positive impact on consumers' usage intentions, and that this impact varies by platform type.

Keywords: marketing · car-sharing · branding

1 Introduction

1.1 Research Background

Car sharing refers to the sharing (lending and borrowing) of cars between providers who want to make effective use of cars they own and users who want to use cars without owning them (i.e., without incurring maintenance costs). Car sharing has the advantage of being able to use a car only when you want to and at affordable rates. Car sharing is also mentioned as a specific measure in the "Global Warming Prevention Plan" approved by the Cabinet in October 2021. Due to these economic and environmental factors, the car sharing market in Japan is increasing every year, and as of March 2022, there were 51,745 vehicles, 2,636,121 members, and 20,371 car sharing stations in Japan [1]. While there have been many studies focusing on the car-sharing industry, most of them have been limited to analyzing the characteristics of users and non-users in order to improve car-sharing services, and there are still few studies that elucidate the relationship between consumers and car-sharing from the perspective of branding. However, the growing importance of branding and the expansion of its definition have increased the complexity and difficulty for companies in developing branding strategies. This study focused on this gap and conducted a survey analysis.

1.2 Research Objectives and Outline

From our experience participating in industry-academia projects, we have learned that the car-sharing industry is actually aware of the challenges of expanding the car-sharing market for young people. Therefore, this study aims to formulate a model of the relationship between brand value and consumers' intention to use a product or service when they purchase it, based on questionnaire data from college students and other young adults, in order to prove that brand value building is an important factor for companies to improve consumers' intention to use their products and services, and that information disclosed by companies to consumers on brand value and consumers' intention to use their products and services is important for companies to improve their brand value and consumers' intention to use their products and services [2]. The purpose of this study is to prove that brand value is an important factor for companies to improve consumers' intention to use their products and services, and to analyze how information disclosed by companies to consumers affects brand value and consumers' intention to use their products and services, and to discover branding methods that can improve consumers' intention to use their products and services.

In order to achieve the above objectives, we conducted research and analysis on the following three research questions: First, "What are the components of brand value in the car sharing industry? The second is "Do consumers' brand values actually influence their intention to use a car-sharing service, and if so, what is the relationship between these elements? If so, how can the relationship between each factor be numerically modeled? The third question is, "Does the disclosure of information from companies to consumers change the brand value that consumers perceive in companies and their intention to use their products and services? For each of the platforms on which companies provide information, we investigated the change in usage intentions and brand value held by consumers toward the company before and after viewing or listening to the information, and investigated and analyzed whether the information provided by each platform has an impact on consumers' purchasing intentions.

1.3 Theory

According to "Managing Brand Equity" by Aaker (1991), a brand equity model exists as a framework for understanding and evaluating the value and effectiveness of brands in brand management. The brand equity model includes four elements: Brand Awareness, Brand Association, Brand Loyalty, and Brand Perceived Quality. Brand Awareness is the degree to which the brand has penetrated the customer's consciousness, Brand Association is the customer's psychological connection to and image of the brand, Brand Loyalty is the degree to which the customer is a repeat customer of the brand, and Brand Perceived Quality is the degree to which the customer is a repeat customer of the brand.

Brand Perceived Quality evaluates the brand value of a company or product by measuring how customers perceive the quality of a branded product or service. Aaker also uses these four factors to measure (1) price premium, (2) customer satisfaction/loyalty, (3) perceived quality, (4) leadership/popularity, (5) perceived value, (6) brand personality, (7) organizational association, (8) brand awareness, (9) market share, and (10) market price and distribution Ten measurement measures of coverage are derived. Since these factors influence a brand's success and competitiveness in the marketplace, it is clear that improving brand value is of great importance to a company [3].

Since Aaker's research proved the importance of improving brand value, research on branding has been conducted frequently even today, and Aaker's brand equity model is widely accepted as an indicator for companies to promote branding and has been applied in various Aaker's brand equity model is widely accepted as an indicator for companies to promote branding and has been applied and used in various studies.

Keller (2003a) classifies "brand knowledge" into eight categories: (1) name recognition, (2) external and internal attribute understanding, (3) benefits, (4) visual images, (5) thoughts, (6) emotions, (7) attitudes, and (8) experiences [4].

Feldwick (1996) used (1) price and demand measures: a. Brand share and brand value premium (the relationship between the relative value of a brand and its market share), b. Price elasticity (how demand changes with changes in price), and c. Price and distribution effects. Sales effect after removing the price and distribution effects. (2) Experimental observation method: Added brand value = the value added to unbranded goods by the brand name. (3) Brand loyalty behavior measurement: a. SOR (share of requirements) or SCR (share of category requirement). (4) Brand loyalty attitude measures: a. Indicators based on customer attitudes, such as which brand they would like to purchase next time. The above four categories are classified as follows [5].

Tanaka (2017) set the four categories of Think "Think", Feel "Feel", Image "Imagine", and Do "Act" on the first axis, while the second axis represents the brand's two relationships with its customers and the world, and is captured in a 4 × 2 matrix, as follows [6] (Table 1).

Table 1. Tanaka's (2017) brand matrix

	Brand-Self	Brand-World
Think	(1) Recognition (name recognition) (2) Attitude (3) Relationship (4) Satisfaction (5) Commitment	(6) Perceived quality (7) Perceived ability (8) Perceived social responsibility (9) Attribute evaluation (10) Reputation (11) (Concept) association
Feel	(12) Emotions (13) Experiences	(14) (sensory) association
Image	(15) Attachment/Bonding/Emotional Loyalty	(16) Personality
Do	(17) Price premium/WTP (18) Purchase frequency/market penetration (19) Purchase share (20) Reaction times (21) Behavioural loyalty	(22) Market Share (23) Customer Engagement (24) Online Behavior (25) Financial Market

According to Kubota's (2010) study, brand relationship is a concept of great importance to researchers as well as to firms, as it fosters strong psychological loyalty and can be a source of a robust customer base. Emphasis was placed on measuring brand relationships using an identification approach, stating that relationship formation for a given brand consists of three components: cognitive (building a sense of unity through identification), affective (experiencing attachment and pleasure), and evaluative (positive evaluations) The relationship formation for brands consists of three elements: cognitive (building a sense of unity through identification), emotional (experiencing attachment and joy) and evaluative (positive evaluation) [7].

In Maeda's (2008) study, based on a structural analysis of brand equity, "perceived quality" and "trust in the brand" were identified as basic values that a brand should have as a product. In addition to these, "internalization," "self-expression," and "familiarity with the brand" are pointed out as added values that go beyond product quality and function. It is emphasized that these elements play an important role in the formation of brand equity [8].

Therefore, it is important to construct a model that is appropriate for the product being handled and the characteristics of the target customers in order to implement better branding.

2   Data

2.1   Data Summary

Created by Ayana Omachi and Momonei Takasu, 4th-year students of Asahi Laboratory, Department of Business Administration, Tokyo University of Science

<Target> Mainly university students living in the Tokyo metropolitan area
<Questionnaire collection period> July 5, 2023–October 13, 2023
【Number of respondents to the survey】   379
<Questionnaire Contents> Basic information, items about BIGFIVE, items about actual car sharing usage, items about values toward car sharing, car sharing brand structure, and brand image.

2.2   Questionnaire Survey Procedures

Flow Chart for Determining the Content of Survey Items. In this study, in order to investigate brand value toward car sharing held by young people, a preliminary survey (1) was conducted among undergraduate and graduate students to understand the current status of car sharing usage, including car sharing usage, and a preliminary survey (2) was conducted to determine the scale regarding brand value surveys, and a total of more than 10 revisions of question items were made. After revising the questions more than 10 times, we conducted this survey.

Preliminary Survey (1) (Understanding of Current Situation). In an industry-academia collaboration project, we conducted a questionnaire survey on the actual use of car sharing by university students together with graduate students of the Asahi Laboratory, Department of Business Administration, Faculty of Business Administration, Tokyo University of Science.

Preliminary Survey (2) (Questionnaire Item Preparation). A questionnaire with more items for measuring brand value and content items for investigating customer personality attributes was created based on the preliminary survey (1) and references such as Kubota (2010a) (2010b) and Maeda (2008), and preliminary survey (2) was conducted. Times CarShare was selected as the platform to be viewed at this time. Times CarShare utilizes all of the specified marketing platforms and boasts the top level of registered users in the car sharing market. In the preliminary survey (1), about half of the respondents indicated that they had no experience using car sharing, which raised concerns that surveying only companies and brands with low awareness would not ensure the validity of the responses regarding brand structure and image. Therefore, in order to improve the quality of the survey responses, we decided that we should select the marketing platforms of companies that were considered to have high recognition, and selected the TV commercials of Times CarShare, which has the most registered members in Japan [9], X (formerly Twitter) [10], Instagram [11], and the company website Times Car Share [12] has the largest number of registered members in Japan. Another reason is that Times CarShare uses different ways of disseminating information on each marketing platform, which may make it easier to understand the differences between the platforms. The results of Preliminary Survey 2 (18 respondents) were used to unify the confusing expressions pointed out by respondents and to delete questionnaire items that were deemed unnecessary based on the content of the responses.

Main Survey. Based on the responses to Preliminary Survey 1) and Preliminary Survey 2), survey items were determined and questionnaires were sent to a target group of young adults, including university and graduate students and some working adults. In this survey, 379 responses were collected. This study will mainly make use of the data in this survey.

3   Analysis Results

3.1   Basic Tabulation

Actual Usage of Car Sharing. When asked to choose whether or not they have used car sharing, 21% of respondents indicated that they have rented a car by themselves, 23% indicated that they have rented a car and used it by someone other than themselves, and 56% indicated that they have never used car sharing. The fact that the majority of respondents have never used car sharing and that only 21% of all respondents are registered with car sharing suggests that there is still room for growth in the penetration rate of car sharing among young people.

Frequency of Car Sharing Use. When asked "Please select the frequency of car sharing use that most closely matches the frequency of your use of a car," 31% responded "once every three months," 28% responded "once every six months," and 24% responded "once a month." It is evident that the frequency of car sharing use is lower than the frequency of car use.

Shared Use of Car Sharing. For the segment that responded "I have rented and used a car share by myself" to the question "Please select whether you use car share or not," we asked the segment to "Please select the person with whom you share a car share most often." The results show that 74% responded "friends," 14% responded "lovers," and 12% responded "family," indicating that those who are registered and have used car sharing tend to use car sharing often with friends.

Purpose of Using Car Sharing. In the question "Please select the purpose for which you most frequently use car sharing," 64% of respondents chose "day trip," 26% "long-term trip," and 8% "other (daily shopping, etc.)," indicating that younger people tend to use car sharing for recreational purposes such as driving and traveling. This indicates that younger people tend to use car sharing for recreational purposes such as driving and traveling. This suggests that the reason car sharing is used less frequently than driving is due to the fact that the purpose of car sharing is biased toward entertainment.

Time of Use of Car Sharing. In the item "Please select the time closest to the time you use the car share service", 39% of the respondents who registered and used the car share service selected "6 to 12 h", 23% selected "12 to 24 h", and 20% selected "3 to 6 h", indicating that overall the time spent using the car share service per time was long. The results show that overall, the duration of one visit is long.

Susceptible Marketing Platforms. The question "Please select the content that most influences the way you get your information." asked respondents to indicate which of the marketing platforms that companies have that they believe are the most influential. As a result, the most common response was "X (formerly Twitter)" at 32%, followed by "TV commercials" at 30%, Instagram at 25%, and the website at 13%. These results suggest that even in today's age of widespread Internet advertising, TV commercials still have a strong influence, and that survey respondents tend to be influenced more by SNS media with relatively high update frequency and diffusion power, such as X (formerly Twitter).

Browsing Experience Rate. Please select the content that most influences you in obtaining information." For the marketing platforms selected in the question "Have you ever seen XX (each platform) in the Times?", we surveyed the percentage of respondents who had viewed each marketing platform. The results showed that the "website" had the highest rate at 40%, followed by "TV commercials" at 36%, X (formerly Twitter) at 15%, and Instagram at 6%. These results indicate that among Times' market platforms, awareness of SNS is low, suggesting that there is room for improvement in SNS measures (Fig. 1).

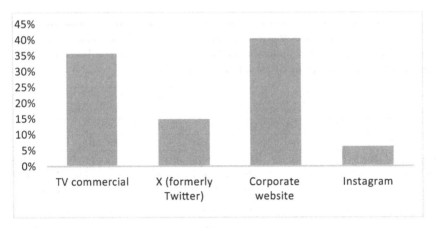

Fig. 1. Browsing Experience Rates by Marketing Platform

3.2 Analysis of Research Topic (1)

In the following, in order to elucidate "research question 1) whether brand value in car sharing consists of such components," we will analyze the data through the procedures of item analysis, factor analysis, examination of internal consistency, calculation of scale scores and correlation analysis. In the item analysis, the mean and standard deviation of the survey items are obtained to confirm the validity of the survey data itself, and inappropriate items are deleted. Next, factor analysis is used to verify whether the brand value scale is composed of two factors as hypothesized. In the examination of internal consistency, alpha coefficients are calculated for the number of factors and factor scales derived from the factor analysis, and the validity of the subscales is confirmed. In the scale score and correlation analysis, the scores of the subscales written by the mean of the items are calculated, and the correlations between the given subscale scores are calculated. The analysis was conducted primarily utilizing IBM's SPSS. [13].

What is Factor Analysis? Factor Analysis is a multivariate statistical technique used to extract common factors of multiple observed variables, thereby facilitating understanding of the structure of the data. Usually, by attributing the variation in the observed variables to a number of mutually independent latent factors, it is possible to reduce the dimensionality of the data and extract latent structure. The main objective of factor analysis is to decompose correlations among observed variables into those due to common factors and those due to idiosyncratic (unique) factors. This technique is useful in a variety of areas, such as simplifying data, extracting underlying patterns, and facilitating data interpretation. The basic mathematical model of factor analysis is expressed by the following equation

$$X = \Lambda F + U$$

where X is the matrix of observed variables, Λ is the factor loadings matrix, F is the matrix of common factors, and U is the matrix of unique factors. The factor loadings are weights that indicate how much each observed variable is influenced by the common factor, which reveals the relationship between the common factor and the observed variables. Factor analysis usually has the advantage of being easier to interpret because, unlike principal component analysis (PCA), it extracts only the common factors. In addition, factor analysis is applied in a wide range of fields, including psychology, social sciences, and economics, as a means of understanding the structure behind observed variables.

Promax Rotation. Promax rotation is one of the methods that facilitate factor interpretation in factor analysis. By rotating factors while taking into account their interrelationships in actual data, it is possible to get a more realistic view of how factors appear.

Item Analysis and Examination of Number of Factors and Factor Structure. To elucidate the brand value construct of car sharing, an item analysis of the scale was conducted, as well as an examination of the number of factors and factor structure of the data. The mean and standard deviation of the 20 items of the scale for brand composition and brand image were calculated. The following formulas are then used to check for the presence of ceiling and floor effects.

$$\text{Ceiling effect}: \text{ mean} + 1SD > 7, \text{ Floor effect}: \text{ mean} - 1SD < 1$$

As a result, a floor effect was found for five items, which were eliminated from the subsequent analysis. Next, a principal component analysis was conducted on the remaining 15 items, selecting the item on brand value held by consumers toward carsharing companies as a variable among the items in the questionnaire, and a scree plot of the factors was conducted.

Since the eigenvalues varied from 5.370, 1.494, 1.428, 1.056, and $\cdot \ \cdot \ \cdot \ \cdot$, and since the slope of the eigenvalues derived from the screen plots became smoother after the third and fourth factors, a three-factor structure was considered appropriate. Therefore, we conducted factor analysis using the main factor method and Promax rotation, again assuming a three-factor structure, and found that none of the items did not show sufficient factor loadings, and that the three factors before rotation explained 55.282% of the total variance of the 15 items.

Naming the Brand Value Scale. Next, we name each factor with reference to the characteristics of the final factor pattern derived from the above factor analysis. The first factor consisted of seven items, and the higher the value, the higher the factor loadings were for feelings toward the brand, such as "loosened up," "pleasant," and "like," among which the items with contents that would lead to familiarity. Therefore, we named it the "likeability" factor. The second factor consisted of five items, and items that were related to the impact or impression consumers felt from the brand, such as "awake," "powerful," and "dynamic," showed high factor loadings. Therefore, we named it the "Impact" factor. The third factor, consisting of three items, showed high factor loadings for items that were related to trust in the brand and a sense of security, such as "I feel attached to Times Car," "I can give a good impression to others by using Times Car," and "I trust Times Car. Therefore, we named it the "connection" factor. In the next section, we will set up a subscale based on the three factors obtained here.

Examination of Internal Consistency of Factors. Scales will be created based on the final factor structure obtained from the above factor analysis. Reliability analysis is conducted for the items included in each subscale, and internal consistency is examined by calculating the alpha coefficient. In the reliability analysis, the Corrected Item-Total Correlation, which refers to the total score and its correlation between the item in question and items "other than" the item in question, is derived. This value checks the directionality of the items included in a scale (subscale). If the Corrected Item-Total function is low or negative, it indicates that the item is not appropriate to be included in the scale. In addition, by comparing the value of Cronbach's alpha (Alpha if Item Deleted), which indicates how much the alpha coefficient would be if the item were removed, it is possible to further analyze whether the relevant scale is worthy of inclusion in the factor.

Calculation of Factor Scores. After eliminating unnecessary subscales derived from the above reliability analysis, the alpha coefficients for each subscale were calculated to examine internal consistency, and sufficient values were obtained: alpha = .735 for "favorability," alpha = .667 for "impact," and alpha = .731 for "connectedness. Next, based on the above results, the three scale scores for the "Favorability" factor, the "Impact" factor, and the "Connection" factor were calculated based on the mean scores of the items, and the correlation between the scales was analyzed.

Correlation Between Subscales. The mean score and standard deviation of each calculated subscale score and the correlation between the subscales are then calculated (Table 2).

Table 2. Aggregate values for marketing platforms and factor-by-factor estimates from structural equation modeling

	F	I	C	mean	standard deviation	αbefore deleting items	α after deleting items
F	-	0.567[a]	0.527[a]	4.615	0.97044	0.735	0.89
I		-		4.3295	0.84439	0.667	0.667
C			-	3.6676	1.23871	0.731	0.731

[a] $p < .001$ (F: favorability, I: impact, C: connectedness).

3.3 Analysis of Research Topic (2)

In the following, we utilize the brand value scale to examine research question (2), "Do brand values held by consumers actually influence usage intentions, and if so, how can the relationship between each factor be numerically modeled?" using AMOS structural equation modeling.

What is Structural Equation Modeling (SEM). It is a complex statistical method that allows the simultaneous evaluation of interactions between multiple variables. It models the relationship between latent and observed variables and helps to understand the complex structure of a phenomenon. The measurement model shows the relationship between observed variables and latent variables and quantitatively measures the concepts and characteristics expressed by the latent variables. Structural models, on the other hand, show the interactions between different latent variables and express how they affect each other. This allows complex relationships to be captured in the model; an advantage of SEM includes the ability to consider complex interactions among multiple variables at once. It also provides statistical indicators to properly model measurement error, covariance of latent variables, etc., and to evaluate the goodness of fit of the model to the data.

What is AMOS. Analysis of Moment Structures (AMOS) is statistical analysis software for performing Structural Equation Modeling (SEM), path analysis and causality evaluation, It has functions such as evaluating model adaptation, creating observation models for latent variables, and creating and visualizing path diagrams.

Relationship Between Overall Brand Value Scale and Intention to Use. Using the "Favorability" factor, "Impact" factor, and "Connection" factor found through factor analysis, structural equation modeling was conducted to determine how each factor and the brand value structure composed of these three factors affect the intention to use car sharing services. The model was formed. Among the three brand value factors, the results are significant with respect to the "favorability" and "connectedness" factors, with values of 4.615 and 4.3295, respectively. This indicates a positive influence on consumers' intention to use the brand. On the other hand, the "Impact" factor was not significant, indicating that feelings such as the strength of the impression one has of a brand do not directly affect the intention to use it. However, since the "Favorability" factor, the "Impact" factor, and the "Connection" factor all influence each other, it is possible that if customers come to have an "Impact" on a company, it may indirectly influence their intention to use the company (Fig. 2).

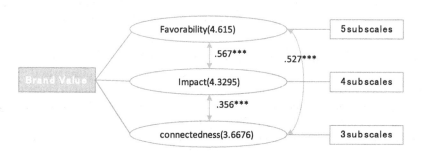

Fig. 2. Influence of each factor on intention to use

Structural Equation Modeling for Each Affected Marketing Platform. In the following, structural equation modeling was performed on the relationship between the value of the brand value scale and the value of intention to use for each marketing platform. The results are shown in the table below. The "favorability" factor was significant for TV commercials, Instagram, and the website, and was found to have a direct impact on the intention to use the brand. The "Impact" factor is not significant in any of the marketing platforms and does not directly influence the intention to use. However, it is possible that the "Impact" factor may have an indirect influence on the intention to use the platform, since the factors influence each other. The "Connection" factor was significant in the X (formerly Twitter) TV commercial and homepage, and has a direct influence on the intention to use the service. Comparing the values for TV commercials and homepages, where both the "favorability" factor and the "connection" factor were significant, it was shown that the connection factor had a greater impact on the homepage than on the TV commercials (Table 3).

Table 3. Aggregate values for marketing platforms and estimates by factor using structural equation modeling.

Marketing platforms affected	the number of people	proportion	favorable impression (Estimated value)	Impact (estimated)	connection (Estimated value)
X (formerly Twitter)	121	31.9% (%)	-	-	.636
television commercial	115	30.3% (%)	.656	-	.317
Instagram	96	25.3% (%)	.549	-	-
Corporate website	47	12.4% (1)	.669	-	.668

3.4 Analysis of Research Question (3)

In the following section, we will examine whether the disclosure of information from companies to consumers changes the brand value that consumers have for companies and their intention to use their products and services by comparing the intention to use each marketing platform before and after viewing TV commercials, X (formerly Twitter), Instagram, and websites. The results were examined by comparing the intention to use each marketing platform before and after viewing the TV commercial, X (formerly Twitter), Instagram, and the website.

Trends in the Amount of Change in Respondents' Overall Intention to Use. Focusing on the amount of change in intention to use, the mean was 0.534759 and the median was 0. This suggests that the distribution of the amount of change in the intention to use is closer to the center and that there is a small amount of positive change. The variance is slightly high at 2.783551, indicating that there is a certain amount of variation in the data on the amount of change in intention to use. Next, the mean value of the intention to use before browsing is 4.192513, with a median value of 4. This result suggests that the data for the intention to use before browsing is distributed slightly to the right, with a relatively large number of values larger than the mean. In addition, the relatively high variance of 3.224971 indicates a certain amount of variation in the data for pre-browsing intention to use. The post-viewing usage intention has a mean of 4.727273 and a median of 5. This suggests that the data for the intention to use after browsing is distributed slightly to the left, with a relatively large number of smaller values than the mean. In addition, with a relatively low variance of 2.05931, the data on intention to use after browsing has relatively little variation.

Amount of Change in Intention to Use by Intention to Use Before Browsing, and Trend in Intention to Use After Browsing. The results of the mean, variance, and median of the change in intention to use by intention to use before viewing the marketing platform are as follows. As an overall trend, both the mean and the median indicate that the amount of change in intention to use a marketing platform improves as the intention to use a marketing platform decreases prior to viewing it, indicating that information dissemination through a marketing platform is an effective strategy for those who tend to have low intention to use a marketing platform in the first place. This indicates that information dissemination through marketing platforms is an effective strategy for those who tend to have low intention to use them. On the other hand, for those who had a high intention to use the service from the beginning, such as (5, 6, 7), there is a strong tendency for it to have a negative impact. Comparing the median and the mean, we can see that in the segment where the intention of use before browsing was (2, 7), many respondents selected a number larger than the median for the amount of change in intention of use, while in the segment where the intention of use before browsing was (1, 3, 4, 5, 6), many respondents selected a value smaller than the median for the amount of change in intention of use. The variance shows that many respondents chose a value smaller than the median for the change in intention to use before browsing. The variance is higher for those who had a pre-browsing use intention of 1 (3.74), indicating that there is more variation in the data for those who have not indicated an intention to use car sharing (Fig. 3).

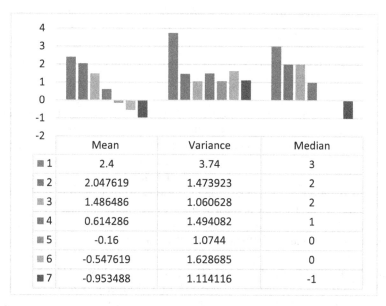

	Mean	Variance	Median
1	2.4	3.74	3
2	2.047619	1.473923	2
3	1.486486	1.060628	2
4	0.614286	1.494082	1
5	-0.16	1.0744	0
6	-0.547619	1.628685	0
7	-0.953488	1.114116	-1

Fig. 3. Trends in the Amount of Change in Intent to Use by Intent to Use Prior to Viewing

Trends in Intention to Use After Viewing by Intention to Use Before Viewing. The results of the mean, variance, and median of post-browsing intention to use the marketing platform by pre-browsing intention to use the platform are as follows. It can be seen that the higher the intention to use the platform before browsing, the higher the mean and median of the intention to use the platform after browsing. Comparing the mean and median, we see that many segments tend to have a lower median than the mean, and that overall, many respondents have a smaller value than the median. As for the variance, the segment with a pre-browsing intention to use of 1 has a high value of 3.74, indicating that there is a lot of variation (Fig. 4).

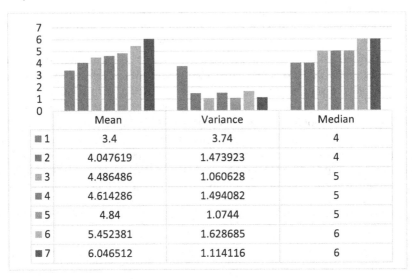

	Mean	Variance	Median
■ 1	3.4	3.74	4
■ 2	4.047619	1.473923	4
▨ 3	4.486486	1.060628	5
■ 4	4.614286	1.494082	5
▨ 5	4.84	1.0744	5
▨ 6	5.452381	1.628685	6
■ 7	6.046512	1.114116	6

Fig. 4. Trends in Intent to Use After Viewing by Intent to Use Before Viewing

Trends in the Amount of Change in Intention to Use Each Marketing Platform. Looking at the average change in intention to use each marketing platform, we see that the values indicating intention to use all marketing platforms have increased: 0.495798 for X (formerly Twitter), 0.148936 for Instagram, 0.692982 for TV commercials, and 1.021277 for corporate websites. The results show an increase in the values indicating the intention to use all marketing platforms. Among the four marketing platforms, TV commercials have the highest average value, indicating that TV commercials are the most effective in improving the overall intention to use the marketing platform. On the other hand, the median value was 1 for TV commercials and company websites, and 0 for X (formerly Twitter) and Instagram, indicating that the data is more toward the center for all marketing platforms. The variance also shows 2.999095 for Instagram, 2.423284 for TV commercials, 2.451663 for X (formerly Twitter) and Instagram, and 3.467632 for the corporate website. The results show that overall, there is a lot of variation in the data, with the website having the most variation in the numbers (Fig. 5).

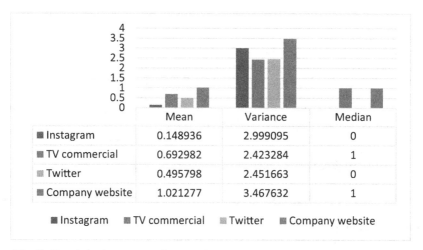

	Mean	Variance	Median
■ Instagram	0.148936	2.999095	0
■ TV commercial	0.692982	2.423284	1
▨ Twitter	0.495798	2.451663	0
■ Company website	1.021277	3.467632	1

■ Instagram   ■ TV commercial   ▨ Twitter   ■ Company website

Fig. 5. Trends in the amount of change in intention to use each marketing platform

4 Discussion

Through this study, it was found that the brand value scale of car sharing is composed of "favorability" factor, "impact" factor, and "connection" factor, among which "favorability" factor and "connection" factor have direct influence on the intention to use the service. It was also shown that the influence of the factors varied depending on the marketing platform being influenced. The results of the survey showed that the effect of information dissemination from the actual marketing platform was greater in the segment with lower original intention to use the service, and that information presentation through TV commercials and information disclosure on the website lead to higher intention to use the service in the car sharing industry, thus contributing to the creation of branding opportunities in the car sharing industry. The results of the study also proved that information presentation through TV commercials and information disclosure through websites are effective in increasing the intention to use a car sharing service.

However, this study has several limitations: first, the data population is small and the age segment of the target population is biased. The second is the issue of the questionnaire items. Due to the convenience of data collection, the choices of marketing platforms were limited to four: TV commercials, X (formerly Twitter), Instagram, and homepage. Third, respondents were limited to viewing only one marketing platform, Times CarShare. Currently, only one company utilizes all four marketing platforms, but we expect that as the market expands, many car-sharing companies will focus more on marketing. Therefore, if we could increase the number of company case studies presented to respondents in the future, we would be able to examine the relationship between car sharing and branding from a more multifaceted perspective by converting each company's scores on the car sharing brand value scale.

References

1. Consumer Affairs Agency website: "Trends in the Number of Car-Sharing Vehicles and Members in Japan." Number of Vehicle Ownership. Accessed 25 Feb 2024
2. Akutsu, Katsumura: Corporate Branding as a Process for Strengthening Organizational Capability and Its Effectiveness (2016). Accessed 25 Feb 2024
3. Aaker, D.A.: Managing brand equity: capitalizing on the value of a brand name. Free Press, New York (1991). Accessed 25 Feb 2024
4. Keller, K.L.: Brand synthesis: the multidimensionality of brand knowledge. J. Consum. Res. **29**(4), 595–600 (2003). Accessed 25 Feb 2024
5. Feldwick, P.: What is brand equity anyway, and how do you measure it? J. Mark. Res. Soc. **38**(2), 85–104 (1996)
6. Tanaka, H.: Brand Strategy Theory, pp. 1–99. Yuhikaku Publishing Co., Ltd. Accessed 25 Feb 2024
7. Kubota: Measuring Brand Relationships Using the Identification Approach and Establishing a Brand Relationship Scale (2010). Accessed 25 Feb 2024
8. Maeda: Structural Analysis of Brand Equity Based on Consumer Perception (2008). Accessed 25 Feb 2024
9. YouTube: "[Times CAR] TV Commercial Version" Is that how it is now? Arc, 30 sec. Reaction times. https://youtu.be/YjBXcu7S1uQ. Accessed 25 Feb 2024
10. Times Car Twitter. https://twitter.com/timescar_jp. Accessed 25 Feb 2024
11. Times Car Instagram. https://www.instagram.com/mobility__link/. Accessed 25 Feb 2024
12. Times Car Home Page. https://share.timescar.jp/. Accessed 25 Feb 2024
13. Atsushi, O.: Psychological and Survey Data by SPSS and AMOS Studied by Research Cases, pp. 1–107, pp. 155–197. Tokyo Shoseki Co., Ltd. Accessed 25 Feb 2024

Automatic Extraction of User-Centric Aspects for Tourist Spot Recommender Systems Using Reviews in Japanese

Fumito Uwano[✉][iD], Ran'u Kobayashi, and Manabu Ohta[iD]

Okayama University, 3-1-1 Tsushima-naka, Kita-ku, Okayama, Japan
uwano@okayama-u.ac.jp, fkddn123@s.okayama-u.ac.jp, ohta@okayama-u.ac.jp
https://de.cs.okayama-u.ac.jp

Abstract. In tourist reviews, various pieces of information are described to confirm the characteristics of tourist spots. This paper proposes a method to extract tourist spot aspects using Japanese tourist reviews automatically. The aspects of tourist spots are concepts that serve as criteria for searching the features of spots, such as "history" or "nature". Utilizing these aspects helps tourists easily find tourist spots with their characteristics. Thus, the aspects of whole spots should be readable and understandable for users. Using the Natural Language API, the proposed method extracts entities from tourist reviews on Jalan.net, a travel website. After transforming them into word vectors, the proposed method clusters them to create clusters of entities that reflect the features of the spots. Furthermore, the proposed method seeks synonyms for each cluster to extract aspects. In experiments, this paper quantitatively evaluated the automatically extracted aspects for 30 tourist spots in Okayama Prefecture in Japan. The experimental results revealed that the proposed method extracted a total of 446 aspects, of which 78.9% were deemed appropriate as aspects. In addition, the extracted aspects had been abstracted interpretably for user-centric expression to find tourist spots.

Keywords: Tourism · Recommender System · Meta-data extraction · Aspect · Review analytics

1 Introduction

Tourism informatics is now growing because of advanced AI technology and its contribution to e-tourism. There are many research topics along with how and what data the system can use. For instance, Samejima et al. proposed a planning support system for a planner, collecting case reports for tourism planning on the web and extracting topics and keywords to enable the planner to find appropriate case reports [5]. Oku et al. proposed a method for detecting the regions of substantial activity near target spots using geotagged tweets in Twitter (currently called "X") by characterizing the spots for trends, events, season, and time of day as attributes [2]. This paper is similar to the latter, focusing on extracting aspects of reviews for a tour recommendation system as an application for a user in tourism informatics.

The reviews are so valuable as to help us to purchase items and select tourist spots. However, the users are usually free to write reviews; that is, some reviews are inconsistent so that we must use data extraction and analyze the reviews. Varga et al. proposed a hotel filter recommendation method for preventing a user's overchoice and cognitive load caused by it. The method characterizes filters for relevance and uniqueness and a filter set for diversity while decreasing the size of the filter set [6]. In this work, core predicate-argument structures are extracted from the hotel reviews. For example, a predicate-argument structure with words "very delicious food", "really delicious food" and so on is tagged with a core "delicious food". Peña proposed Rich-Context, a query-based context-driven recommender system [4]. The context-driven recommender system was proposed to utilize context as critical evidence rather than additional evidence like how the previous system used [3]. The Rich Context extracts contextual information from reviews and produces a recommendation with useful side information as the contextual information of the input query.

This paper proposes an aspect extraction method for tourist reviews in a tourist spot recommender system. The aspect indicates a theme as a target of behaviour in a sentence. For example, we know the target as an aspect in Aspect-based sentiment analysis (ABSA) for which the subject has sentiment. Generally, an aspect is given before the system performs, which restricts the recommendation system from suggesting content to the users with only developer-given topics. Although the above and other existing works focused on the aspects that describe the reviews, they did not delve into the aspect from the user's perspective. This work discusses aspect extraction from the user's perspective, especially an interaction between the system and users. The given aspects may not match the user's desire. Besides recommending tourist spots with the given aspects of "meals", "nature", "history", and "souvenirs", the system needs to recommend tourist spots based on the user's experience and desire, such as "activity" for activity-loving users, for example, in order to recommend a horseback riding spot and a scuba diving spot. Furthermore, the system must have specific aspects such as "dolphins" in aquariums, which are a tourist spot's sales point. If users overlook that, the spot can attract less attention than expected. Therefore, the proposed method automatically extracts such aspects from tourist reviews.

This paper is organized as follows: Sect. 2 describes the proposed method, or automatic aspect extraction method, for tourist spots. Section 3 presents the results and discussions of automatically extracting aspects from tourist reviews. Section 4 summarises and discusses future challenges.

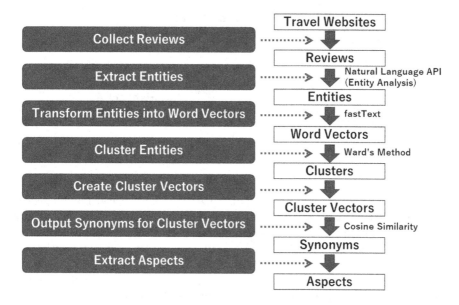

Fig. 1. Proposed Aspect Extraction Method.

2 Automatic Aspect Extraction Method for Tourist Spots

2.1 Overview

The proposed method, or an automatic aspect extraction method for tourist spots, is illustrated in Fig. 1. This method utilizes tourist reviews for tourist spots of any prefecture from jalan.net, one of the largest travel websites in Japan[1]. After collecting tourist reviews, the proposed method extracts entities for each spot from the reviews. The entities mainly consist of proper nouns such as personal names, place names, and common nouns like "restaurants" and "stadiums". The entities are transformed into word vectors, and the word vectors are clustered using Ward's method [7]. After that, the proposed method calculates the cluster vector from the word vectors in the cluster. Finally, using cosine similarity, the proposed method selects word vectors similar to the cluster vectors. Such word vectors represent aspects of the tourist spot. The proposed method generates various aspects for one tourist spot because several clusters are usually generated for one spot.

This paper explains the details in the following subsections.

2.2 Review Collection and Entity Extraction

The proposed method involves collecting tourist reviews for each tourist spot using web scraping from Jalan.net. Entities are extracted from the reviews using

---

[1] jalan.net.

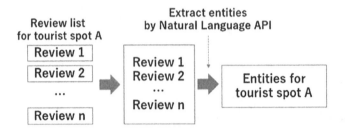

Fig. 2. Overview of Entity Extraction.

the entity analysis in the Natural Language API[2]. The Natural Language API is provided by the Google Cloud Platform (GCP) and performs various natural language processing tasks such as sentiment analysis, syntax parsing, and entity analysis. The proposed method utilizes entity analysis to extract entities and their salience (importance) information from the tourist reviews. The salience is a value between $[0.0, 1.0]$, where a value close to 1.0 indicates that the entity is important in the review. The salience values of all extracted entities sum up to 1.0. Since the number of extracted entities varies based on the review length, the average salience value is different for different reviews. Thus, this paper aggregates reviews for each spot and extracts entities from the set of reviews for each spot (refer to Fig. 2). Since the entities are clustered in the next phase, the noisy entities are removed. For each spot, entities with the top 30% salience values are extracted. The proposed method might extract the same entities. However, the same entities are removed while leaving one.

2.3   Vectorization for Word Embeddings of an Entity

Figure 3 shows a flow for transforming the entities into the word vectors using fastText[3]. The fastText is a natural language processing library that can transform words into word vectors. This paper used word vectors of the fastText pre-trained by Common Crawl[4] and Wikipedia[5]. These word vectors have 300 dimensions and represent two million kinds of vocabulary (number of words). The proposed method uses the word vector if the corresponding entity exists in the vocabulary of the pre-trained word vectors; otherwise, by following the right-hand side processes in Fig. 3, the proposed method conducts morphological

---

[2] https://cloud.google.com/natural-language/docs/analyzing-entities?hl=en.
[3] https://fasttext.cc/.
[4] https://commoncrawl.org/.
[5] https://www.wikipedia.org/.

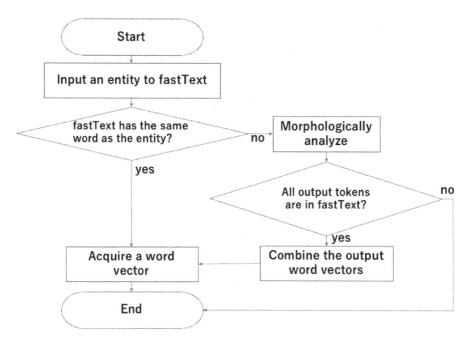

Fig. 3. Overview of transforming entities to the word vectors using fastText.

analysis. Specifically, the proposed method utilizes the morphological analyzer MeCab to break down sentences or compound words into several words (tokens). For example, "観光スポット" (tourist spot) is broken down into two tokens: "観光" (tourism) and "スポット" (spot). Note that, though "tourist" is translated into "観光客" in Japanese, there does not exist "観光客スポット" in Japanese. The Japanese language has different rules for compounding words from English. The morphological analysis helps the proposed method to find constituent tokens of the entity from the vocabulary instead of the entity itself. By summing the vectors of the constituent tokens, the proposed method calculates the word vector for the entity even if it does not exist in the vocabulary. For example, the proposed method can calculate the word vector for "観光スポット" (tourist spot) by adding up the word vectors for "観光" (tourism) and "スポット" (spot). The proposed method removes the entities if it cannot calculate these word vectors via the above processes.

2.4 Entity Clustering

The proposed method clusters the entities with similar characteristics. Since these entities are extracted from reviews of tourist spots, the clusters of these entities indicate the features of tourist spots. The proposed method utilizes Ward's method [7], a hierarchical clustering technique. Ward's method initializes each data point as a separate cluster and then iteratively merges clusters with

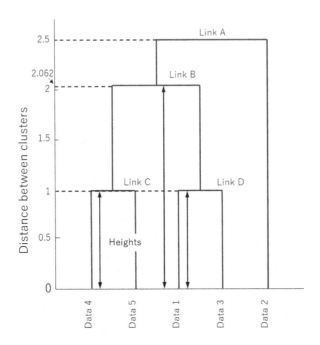

Fig. 4. An example of dendrogram (MathWorks (https://mathworks.com/help/stats/hierarchical-clustering.html), partially altered)

close distances, forming a hierarchy of clusters. Consequently, Ward's method results in all data points being merged into one cluster. Thus, the proposed method needs to select the number of clusters. We extract clusters from one level of the hierarchy to find an appropriate number of clusters. Various methods exist for selecting the number of clusters with distance or inconsistency coefficients. The proposed method utilizes the inconsistency coefficient.

Figure 4 shows an example of a dendrogram based on the output of Ward's method. The inconsistency coefficient is a value that represents the inconsistency level of the links between clusters. A higher inconsistency coefficient indicates that dissimilar clusters are merged. The inconsistency coefficient is calculated using the reference link and connected links at the lower level. For example, the proposed method calculates the inconsistency coefficient of *Link B* using *Link B*, *Link C*, and *Link D* in Fig. 4. The inconsistency coefficient of a link is 0 if it has no link at the lower level, e.g., *Link C* and *Link D*.

Specifically, the inconsistency coefficient for kth link is calculated by Eq. (1):

$$Y(k) = \frac{\text{dist}(k) - \text{mean}(k)}{\text{std}(k)}, \tag{1}$$

where $\text{dist}(k)$ represents the height of the reference link, and $\text{mean}(k)$ and $\text{std}(k)$ represent the average and the sample standard deviation of the heights of all links used in the calculation, respectively. As for *Link B*, the average height is calculated from the height of *Link B*, *Link C*, and *Link D* in Fig. 4, which is 1.354. The standard deviation is calculated to be 0.613. The standard deviation is calculated with Bessel's correction [1]. The height of *Link B* is 2.062. Substituting these values into Eq. (1), we have $Y(B) = (2.062 - 1.354)/0.613 = 1.155$. The proposed method has a threshold for the inconsistency coefficient to set the number of clusters. Specifically, the proposed method uniforms the links with the inconsistency coefficients less than the threshold. In this case, the proposed method merges the links into the same cluster. This paper set the threshold for the inconsistency coefficient by 0.99 times the maximum inconsistency coefficient of all links. For example, in Fig. 4, since the inconsistency coefficient of *Link B* is the highest among all links, the threshold is set by $Y(B) \times 0.99$. In this case, only $Y(B)$ is over the threshold, so the proposed method has three clusters for Data 4 and 5, Data 1 and 3, and Data 2.

2.5   Aspect Extraction from an Entity Cluster

Creating a List of Synonyms. After creating clusters, the proposed method calculates the cluster vectors and a list of synonyms. This paper defines the cluster vector as the average of the word vectors in cluster. The proposed method also outputs synonyms of the cluster vector from the vocabulary of the pre-trained word vectors. The list of synonyms contains three words that are most similar to the cluster vector by cosine similarity. However, the proposed method does not create a list for the clusters with less than five entities because the aspects extracted from such clusters are rarely mentioned in the reviews. The proposed method utilizes the MeCab and Juman++[6] or two morphological analyzers, to remove inappropriate words from the list of synonyms, such as particles like "の" (of) and "も" (too), or location names like "岡山" (Okayama) and "倉敷" (Kurashiki).

The conditions for output synonyms are summarized as follows. It is assumed that all output synonyms do not include any stop words (see Fig. 5). The proposed method extracts the base form of a word as a synonym if the word satisfies conditions 3, 4, and 5. Note that the second author lists the stop words in Fig. 5 deemed unsuitable as aspects.

---

[6] https://nlp.ist.i.kyoto-u.ac.jp/?JUMAN%2B%2B.

こと (things), 事 (things), もの (things), 物 (things), 観
光 (sightseeing), 市 (city), 県 (prefecture), 市内 (within
the city), 県内 (within the prefecture), すべて (all), 全
て (all), ところ (place), 所 (place), 場所 (location), 旅行
(travel), 何 (what), ある (there), いる (there), 東 (east),
西 (west), 南 (south), 北 (north), 右 (right), 左 (left),
左右 (left and right), 上 (top), 下 (bottom), 東西南北
(east, west, south, and north), 東側 (east side), 西側 (west
side), 南側 (south side), 北側 (north side), 側 (side), 前
(front), 右側 (right side), 左側 (left side), 前側 (front
side), 後ろ側 (back side), 後ろ (behind), 後 (behind), 途
中 (halfway), 近く (near), 遠く (far), そこ (there), それ
(that), ここ (here), どこ (where), あれ (that), これ (this),
名前 (name), さん (Mr., Mrs., or Ms.), とき (when), 地域
(area), 方面 (direction), 方 (direction), 一緒 (together),
客 (guest), 思う (think), 他 (other), スポット (spot), 感じ
(feeling), 考え (thought), 中 (inside), うち (inside), 最初
(first), 最後 (last), 明日 (tomorrow), 昨日 (yesterday), 私
(me), 君 (you), 僕 (me), あなた (you), 次回 (next time),
方々 (people), 今回 (this time), 今度 (next time), 大体
(mostly), ほとんど (almost), 多く (many), たち (and
others), 達 (and others) (Total of 81 words)

Fig. 5. Stop Words for Synonyms.

1 MeCab recognizes two or more tokens
2 MeCab recognizes a token and
   The part of speech is estimated as noun by at least MeCab or
   Juman++ and
   The detailed part of speech is not estimated as "地域" (area) by
   MeCab and
   The detailed part of speech is not estimated as "地名" (place name)
   by MeCab and
   The token is not estimated as an out-of-vocabulary word by
   Juman++
3 The part of speech is estimated as verb by both analyzers
4 The part of speech is estimated as adjective by both analyzers
5 The part of speech is estimated as adjective verb by both analyzers

If the synonyms are deleted due to the conditions above, the proposed method
outputs the next most similar words. However, if three or more synonyms are
deleted, the cluster is considered unsuitable for outputting appropriate synonyms
as prospective candidate aspects, and no synonyms are output.

Creating Compound Words with Suffixes. While creating the list of synonyms, the proposed method creates compound words by combining the synonyms with the suffix in the list to synonyms and add the compound words to the list. In addition, the proposed method removes the suffixes from the list. Specifically, the proposed method detects the suffixes using N-Best solutions of MeCab. The N-Best solutions are obtained as multiple candidate results by morphological analysis. The proposed method detects words whose N-Best solutions include a suffix in the top five candidates as a suffix. The compound word vectors are calculated by adding the word and suffix vectors in each compound word. For example, if the list of synonyms includes "駐車" (parking) and "場" (lot), where "場" (lot) is identified as a suffix, "駐車場" (parking lot) is added to the synonym list, and the suffix "場" (lot) is removed. The word vector of "駐車場" (parking lot) is the sum of the word vectors of "駐車" (parking) and "場" (lot). To prevent from creating wrong compound words like "海風風" (sea breeze style) from "海風" (sea breeze) and the suffix "風" (style), the proposed method does not create the compound word if the suffix is included in the synonym to be merged. Note that "海風風" (sea breeze style) does not exist in the Japanese language. Thus, the final number of synonyms in the list is not always three.

Furthermore, to prevent creating compound words that do not exist in the Japanese vocabulary, such as "動物犬" (animal dog) or "愛称声" (nickname voice), the proposed method removes words that do not appear in the search results in the Wikipedia. If the search results include an article for that word, it is considered part of the Japanese vocabulary. If not, the proposed method searches for the word in the snippets of the search results (up to 20 articles). If the word appears in ten or more snippets, the word is regarded part of the Japanese vocabulary.

Aspect Extraction from Synonym List. For clusters with a synonym list, the proposed method selects a synonym as an aspect by calculating the average of the cosine similarity between the word vectors of each synonym and the entities included in the corresponding cluster. The synonym with the highest average similarity is set as the aspect.

3   Experiments

3.1   Dataset

The experimental data are reviews at 30 spots, collected from the "Ranking for recommendation in July" of Okayama Prefecture on Jalan.net on July 5, 2022. Among the 30 spots, "倉敷美観地区" (Kurashiki Bikan Historical Quarter) has the most reviews (3,143 reviews). In contrast, "塩釜冷泉" (Shiogama Reisen) has the least reviews (116 reviews). The total number of reviews for all the spots is 19,307. The spot "岡山後楽園" (Okayama Korakuen) has the most extracted entities, a total of 494 entities excluding duplicates. The spot "石山寺（岡山県津山市）" (Ishiyama Temple, Tsuyama City, Okayama Prefecture) has the

Table 1. Rating Evaluation Criteria.

Rating	Description	Examples
A	Can be a specific aspect	"ビール" (beer), "ウサギ" (rabbit)
B	Suitable as an aspect	"飲み物" (beverage), "動物" (animal)
C	Not either	"おすすめ" (recommendation), "企業" (company)
D	Unsuitable as an aspect	"手前" (in front), "罪悪感" (sense of guilt)
E	Words not found in the Japanese vocabulary or non-independent words	"宿店" (inn store), "さ" (a Japanese character)

fewest entities, a total of 85 entities excluding duplicates. In total, 8,684 entities were extracted across all the spots, excluding duplicates.

3.2 Experimental Setup and Evaluation Criteria

In the experiment, aspects are extracted for each spot using the proposed method from the reviews of the 30 spots in Okayama Prefecture described in Sect. 3.1. The extracted aspects are then quantitatively evaluated. The evaluation analyzes whether the extracted aspects are suitable and what aspects are unsuitable. For quantitative evaluation, the extracted aspects are rated on a five-point scale: A (Can be a specific aspect), B (Suitable as an aspect), C (Not either), D (Unsuitable as an aspect), E (Words not found in Japanese vocabulary or non-independent words). Table 1 summarises the five-point scale evaluation. The second author of this paper conducts this evaluation.

As shown in Table 1, rating A includes specific words such as "ビール" (beer) and "ウサギ" (rabbit), most of which have superordinate concept such as "飲み物" (beverage) for "ビール" (beer) and "動物" (animal) for "ウサギ" (rabbit). Rating B is considered appropriate as an aspect, enabling us to analyze the tourist spots. One difference between the aspects of A and B is that the aspects of B are abstract compared with those of A. For instance, "飲み物" (beverage) and "動物" (animal) are also concerned with rating B. Other aspects of the rating B include "時間" (time), "雰囲気" (atmosphere), and "敷地" (site). "時間" (time) can lead to derivations such as "待ち時間が長い" (long waiting time) or "体感時間が短い" (short perceived time). "雰囲気" (atmosphere) has derivations like "穏やかな" (calm) or "良い雰囲気" (good atmosphere). "敷地" (site) includes derivations like "敷地が広い" (large site) or "敷地が狭い" (small site). Rating C includes words like "おすすめ" (recommendation) and "企業" (company), which can be aspects in some cases. Rating D includes words like "手前" (foreground) and "罪悪感" (sense of guilt), which are not suitable as aspects for tourist spots. Words in rating E, such as "宿店" (inn store), are not found in the Japanese vocabulary. Others like "さ" (a Japanese character with pronunciation "sa") and "の" (a Japanese character with pronunciation "no") are non-independent words whose meaning is not clear on their own.

Furthermore, this paper focuses on the named entities extracted from the identified aspects. Named entities are often specific and capture the unique features of tourist spots.

3.3 Comparative Method

The proposed method calculates cluster vectors for each cluster created from review sentences and creates a list of synonyms using the cluster vector. The aspects are estimated from the list of synonyms. In the comparative experiment, instead of extracting aspects from the list of synonyms, we extract and entity as an aspect by selecting the entity most similar to the cluster vector. Suppose the extracted aspect does not meet the conditions for output synonyms explained in Sect. 2.5, the second most similar entity to the cluster vector is estimated as an aspect. Repeating the above cycle, if aspects cannot be extracted from the top three entities in terms of similarity with the cluster vector, no aspects are extracted for that cluster. The aspects extracted by this comparative method are evaluated according to the criteria shown in Table 1, as in the proposed method. Additionally, named entities are also counted in both methods.

3.4 Results and Discussion

Table 2 shows some of the results of extracting aspects extracted using the proposed method for the 30 spots in Okayama Prefecture, while those extracted using the comparative method are shown in Table 3. In addition, the evaluation results for the aspects extracted using the proposed method are summarized in Table 4, and those for the aspects extracted using the comparative method are summarized in Table 5. Tables 2 and 3 compile the names of each spot along with the list of extracted aspects, while Tables 4 and 5 provide the number and ratio of aspects based on the ratings A to E as shown in Table 1. The tables also show the count and ratio of named entities included in these aspects.

Discussion for Aspect Extraction Using the Proposed Method. The specific information that requires actual investigation, such as "レンガ" (bricks) for spot "倉敷アイビースクエア" (Kurashiki Ivy Square), "デニム" (denim) and "町並み" (townscape) for spot "倉敷美観地区" (Kurashiki Bikan Historical Quarter), "サンバ" (samba) for spot "ブラジリアンパーク鷲羽山ハイランド" (Brazillian Park Washuzan Highland), and "ピカソ" (Picasso) for spot "大原美術館" (Ohara Museum of Art), has been extracted as aspects. Although the veracity of some of these aspects is uncertain, they have high potential as valuable aspects. In addition, compound aspects capturing the features of spots, such as "屋台店" (food stalls) for "岡山フォレストパークドイツの森" (Okayama Forest Park Germany forest), 絶叫系" (screaming rides) and 異国風" (exotic) for spot "ブラジリアンパーク鷲羽山ハイランド" (Brazillian Park Washuzan Highland), "山道" (mountain path) for "吉備津神社" (Kibitsu Jinja Shrine) have been extracted.

Table 2. Examples of Aspects Extracted Using the Proposed Method.

スポット	観点
おかやまフォレストパーク ドイツの森 (Okayama Forest Park)	チーズ (cheese), 飲み物 (beverage), ビール (beer), 雰囲気 (atmosphere), アトラクション (attraction), 雨上がり (after the rain), バーベキュー (barbecue), ウサギ (rabbit), 花 (flower), 態度 (attitude), 席 (seat), 屋台店 (food stall), 大人 (adult), 敷地 (site), パン (bread), 体験 (experience), 動物 (animal), 子供 (child), 同伴 (accompanied)
ブラジリアンパーク鷲羽山 ハイランド (Brazilian Park Washuzan Highland)	パスポート (passport), テーマパーク (theme park), スタンディングコースター (standing coaster), イベント (event), ストレス (stress), ダンス (dance), 子ども (child), サンバ (samba), スカイ (sky), フード (food), 大会 (tournament), 魅力 (attraction), 異国風 (exotic), 子供 (child), 地元 (local), 施設 (facility), 乗り物 (vehicle), 事故車 (accident car), 景色 (scenery), 斜面 (slope), 動物 (animal), 罪悪感 (sense of guilt), 絶叫系 (screaming ride), 乗る (ride), 入 園料 (entering fee), 点検 (inspection)
倉敷アイビースクエア (Kurashiki Ivy Square)	レストラン (restaurant), テーブル (table), 雰囲気 (atmosphere), カフェ (coffee shop), の人 (a person of), レンガ (brick), 夕食 (dinner), 写真 (photo), 景色 (scenery), 受付 (reception), ホテル (hotel), 建物 (Building), 売店 (kiosk), 美観 (beautiful sight), 工場 (factory), 宿泊 (accommodation), 館 (mansion), 施設 (facility)
倉敷美観地区 (Kurashiki Bikan Historical Quarter)	カンジ (feeling), ランチ (lunch), バウムクーヘン (baumkuchen), お菓子 (sweet), カメ ラ (camera), カード (card), デニム (denim), 町並み (townscape), 景色 (scenery), 子供 (child), 小物 (accessories), 部屋 (room), 映画 (movie), 駅 (station), 夕方 (evening), 周り (surrounding), 有数 (prominent), 前回 (previous), 川船 (river boat), ネコ (cat), 駐車場 (car park), 土産屋 (souvenir shop), 時間 (time), 町並み (towmscape), 美観 (beautiful sight)
吉備津彦神社 (Kibitsuhiko Jinja Shrine)	感覚 (feeling), 笑顔 (smiling), お参り (visiting), レンタサイクル (bicycle rental), 伝統 (tradition), 愛称 (nickname), 友人 (friend), 山道 (mountain road), 伝説 (legend), 神主 (priest), 鬼 (demon), 駅 (station), 神社 (shrine)
吉備津神社 (Kibitsu Jinja Shrine)	て (-), 喜び (joy), 時期 (time), ご利益 (blessing), 横 (side), 地方 (local), 娘 (daughter), 関係 (relationship), 写真 (photo), 回廊 (corridor), 桜 (cherry blossoms), 神 (god), 山道 (mountain road), 境内 (precinct of shrine), 敷地 (site), 建物 (building), 神社 (shrine)
大原美術館 (Ohara Museum of Art)	美術 (art), 西洋 (the west), 西洋 (the west), ピカソ (Picasso), 雰囲気 (atmosphere), レストラ ン (restaurant), 大地 (earth), 地元 (local), 夕方 (evenint), 大勢 (crowd), 館 (mansion), 画家 (painter), 展示 (exhibition), 作品 (work), 土産 (souvenir), 絵画 (painting), 中庭 (courtyard), 入場 (admission)
岡山後楽園 (Okayama Korakuen)	庭園 (garden), 庭園 (garden), さ (-), 整備 (maintenance), 訪問 (visit), 時間 (time), バス (bus), 抹茶 (matcha), 春 (spring), 桜 (cherry blossoms), 紅葉 (autumn leaves), 鶴 (crane), 鯉池 (carp pond), つつじ (azelea), メダカ (Japanese killfish), 見どころ (the best part), 夕 暮れ (dusk), バス停 (bus stop), ガイド (guide), 時期 (season), 価値 (value), 敷地 (site), 川 沿い (riverside), 茶店 (tea shop), 風情 (taste)
池田動物園 (Ikeda Zoo)	動物園 (zoo), 迫力 (impact), 距離 (distance), 気持ち (feeling), イベント (event), バス停 (bus stop), ウサギ (rabbit), 鹿 (deer), バス車 (bus car), 子供手 (child hand), 子供園 (childcare centre)
備中松山城 (Bitchu Matsuyama Castle)	猫 (cat), 城郭 (castle), 岩 (rock), 景色 (scenery), 駅道 (station road), タクシー (taxi), 天守閣 (castle tower), 遊歩道 (promenade), トイレ (toilet), タクシー (taxi), 若い人 (young people), 山奥 (deep in the mountains), 風情 (taste), 滞在 (visit), 駐車場 (car park), 名所 (point of interest), 登城 (entering the castle), 運動 (movement), 天守 (castle tower), 城 (castle), 戦国 (Sengoku period in Japan)
神庭の滝 (Kamba no Taki Falls)	湯原 (Yubara or a place name in Japan), 岩石 (rock), 川 (river), 子供 (child), 山道 (mountain road), 宿店 (inn store), 風景 (scenery), 夏 (summer), 見どころ (the best part), 遊歩道 (promenade), 想像 (imagination), 迫力 (impact), 間数 (number of spaces), 禁止 (prohibited), 猿 (monkey), さ (-), 駐車 (parking), 子供 (child)

* "-" indicates the aspect does not have any meanings.

However, the proposed method created wrong compound words such as "宿店" (inn store) for spot "神庭の滝" (Kamba no Taki Falls), "バス車" (bus car) and "子供手" (child hand) for spot "池田動物園" (Ikeda Zoo), all of which do not exist in the Japanese vocabulary. Note that a particle "の" should be inserted between "子供" (child) and "手" (hand) to express "child hand". These wrong compound words were created because "宿店" (inn store) is a substring of "新宿店" (Shinjuku branch), "子供手" (child hand) is a substring of "子供手当" (child allowance), and "バス車" (bus car) is a substring of "バス車庫" (bus garage). Such an issue happens in the Japanese language because one character has several meanings and can express different meanings concatenated with other characters. Additional processing is required to address this issue, e.g., using an online Japanese dictionary or performing morphological analysis on Wikipedia

Table 3. Examples of Aspects Extracted Using the Comparative Method.

スポット	
おかやまフォレストパークドイツの森 (Okayama Forest Park)	チーズたっぷり (plenty of cheese), 飲み物 (beverage), ビール (beer), 雰囲気 (atmosphere), バイキングレストラン (buffet restaurant), 雨上がり (after the rain), バーベキュー (barbecue), おもしろ自転車 (interesting bicycle), 小さなお子 (young child), できたて (freshly made), 接客態度 (customer service attitude), テラス席 (terrace seat), 店 (store), 大人分 (for adult), 食事場所 (location for dinner), パン (bread), ソーセージ手作り体験 (sausage hands-on experience), 動物 (animal), 子供たち (children), 子ども連れ (with children), 岡山市 (Okayama City)
ブラジリアンパーク鷲羽山ハイランド (Brazilian Park Washuzan Highland)	チケット (ticket), テーマパーク (theme park), メリーゴーランド (roundabout), イベント (event), 待ち時間 (waiting time), ダンス (dance), ジャングルカフェ (Jungle Cafe), サンバカーニバル (samba carnival), スカイレール (skyrail), ブラジルフード (Brazilian food), ビンゴ大会 (bingo taunament), 魅力 (attraction), 留学生風 (looks like an international student), 子人 (child person), 外側 (outer), 地元 (local), 施設 (facility), 中乗り物 (middle vehicle), 車 (car), 景色 (scenery), 斜面 (slope), 岡山県民 (Citizens in Okayama Prefecture), ふれあい動物園 (petting zoo), おしゃれ感 (stylish), 絶叫系 (screaming rides), 乗り物乗り放題 (unlimited rides), 入園料 (admission fee), 施設点検 (facility inspection)
倉敷アイビースクエア (Kurashiki Ivy Square)	レストラン (restaurant), ロビー (lobby), 町並み (townscape), キャンドルショップ (candle shop), 女性スタッフ (female staff), レンガ壁 (brick wall), 朝食バイキング (breakfast buffet), 写真スポット (photo spot), 景色 (scenery), 閉館 (closed), クラッシックホテル (classic hotel), 店 (store), 売店 (kiosk), 美観地区 (Bikan Historical Quarter), 倉敷駅 (Kurashiki Station), 紡績工場跡地 (spinning factory site), 宿泊施設メイン (mainly accommodation facility), 記念館 (memorial hall), 見学施設 (tour facility)
倉敷美観地区 (Kurashiki Bikan Historical Quarter)	カンジ (feeling), ランチ (lunch), トートバッグ (tote bag), アイス (ice cream), バッグ (bag), ポストカード (postcard), デニムストリート (denim street), 町並み (townscape), 景色 (scenery), 子供 (child), 小物 (accessories), 部屋 (room), 映画 (movie), 駅 (station), 夕方 (evening), 周り (surrounding), 老舗 (long-established store), アーケード通り (arcade street), 楽しみ方 (how to enjoy), 遊覧川舟 (sightseeing river boat), ネコカフェ (cat cafe), 駐車場 (car park), お土産物屋 (souvenir shop), 時間 (time), 途中商店街 (shopping street on the way), にぎわう美観地区 (busy Bikan Historical Quarter), 倉敷ジーンズストリート (Kurashiki Jeans Street)
吉備津彦神社 (Kibitsuhiko Jinja Shrine)	感覚 (feeling), 人柄 (personality), 吉備津 (Kibitsu or a place name in Japan), お参り (visit), レンタサイクル (bicycle rental), 伝統 (tradition), 桃太郎さん (Momotaro-san or a hero's name in Japanese folklores), 夫婦 (couple), 陶器市 (pottery fair), 桃太郎伝説 (Momotaro legend or a Japanese folklore), 神主 (priest), 鬼 (daemon), 駅 (station), 備前の国の神社 (a shrine in Bizen area)
吉備津神社 (Kibitsu Jinja Shrine)	した神社 (shrine did), 方たち (people), 喜び (joy), 時期 (season), パワースポット (spiritual place), 左手 (left hand), 地方討伐 (subjugation to a local), 娘 (daughter), 関係 (relationship), 写真 (photo), 回廊沿い (along the corridor), 桜 (cherry blossoms), 雷 (lightning), 道 (road), 境内 (precinct of shrine), 敷地 (site), 建築物 (building), 吉備津神社 (Kibitsu Jinja Shrine)
大原美術館 (Ohara Museum of Art)	現代美術 (contemporary art), 西洋絵画 (western painting), 私立西洋近代美術館 (private western museum of modern art), 意味 (meaning), ピカソ (Picasso), 雰囲気 (atmosphere), グッズ (goods), コロナ禍 (emergency for COVID-19), 地元人 (locals), 夕方 (evening), 大勢 (crowd), 倉敷美観地区 (Kurashiki Bikan Historical Quarter), オリエント館 (Orient Hall), 芸術家 (artist), 展示 (exhibition), 作品 (work), 鑑賞者 (viewer), 絵画 (painting), 中庭 (courtyard), 入場チケット (admission ticket)
岡山後楽園 (Okayama Korakuen)	岡山城と後楽園 (Okayama Castle and Okayama Korakuen), 日本三庭園 (Japan's three major gardens), 庭園 (garden), 素晴らしさ (splendor), 整備 (maintenance), 訪問 (visit), 家族旅行 (family trip), 開園時間 (opening hours), 観光ボランティア (tourism volunteer), 抹茶カフェ (matcha cafe), 春夏 (springe and summer), 桜 (cherry blossoms), 紅葉時期 (season for autumn leaves), タンチョウ鶴 (red-crowned crane), 小川 (stream), 池 (pond), ツツジ (azalea), メダカ (Japanese killifish), おすすめスポット (recommended spot), 夕暮れ (dusk), バス停 (bus stop), ボランティアガイド (volunteer tour guide), 時期 (season), 価値 (value), 気 (energy), 敷地 (site), 川 (river), 茶店屋 (tea shop store), 夜風 (night breeze)
池田動物園 (Ikeda Zoo)	動物園 (zoo), 迫力タップリ (full impact), 移動距離 (distance traveled), 気持ち (feeling), イベント (event), バス停 (bus stop), ホワイトライオン (white lion), 鹿コーナー (deer enclosure), ほか (and others), 車 (car), 手ぶり (hand gesture), 動物園 (animals)
備中松山城 (Bitchu Matsuyama Castle)	猫城主 (cat castle load), 城郭 (castle), 岩 (rock), 景色 (scenery), 幅広い道 (wide road), シャトルタクシー (shuttle taxi), 天守閣 (castle tower), 遊歩道 (promenade), トイレ (toilet), マイカー (private car), 手前 (in front), 高校生たち (high school students), 山奥 (deep in the mountains), 風情 (taste), 帰り (the way back), さんじゅーろー (Sanjuro or a cat name in Bitchu Matsuyama Castle), 城見橋公園駐車場 (car park in Shiromibashi Park), 観光案内 (tourist information), 登城 (entering the castle), 運動靴 (sports shoes), 現存天守 (existing castle tower), 日本三大山城 (Japan's three major mountain castles), 城自体 (castle itself), 武家屋敷どおり (street of samurai residences), 備中松山城 (Bitchu Matsuyama Castle)
神庭の滝 (Kamba no Taki Falls)	滝そのもの (waterfall itself), 韮山高原探勘のあと湯原インターチェンジ (Yubara Interchange after exploring Nirayama Plateau), 岩 (rock), 川魚 (river fish), 子供 (child), 山道 (mountain road), 店 (store), 景色 (scenery), 夏 (summer), 雰囲気 (atmosphere), 見どころ (the best part), 遊歩道 (promenade), 想像 (imagination), 迫力 (impact), 数 (number), 禁止 (prohibited), 楽しみのお猿 (monkey expected for something), 美しさ (beauty), 見学料金 (tour fee), 観光客 (tourist), 私達家族 (our family)

* "-" indicates the aspect does not have any meanings.

Table 4. Evaluation Results of the Aspects Extracted Using the Proposed Method.

	Total	A (ratio)	B (ratio)	C (ratio)	D (ratio)	E (ratio)
Aspects	446	238 (0.534)	114 (0.256)	34 (0.076)	38 (0.085)	22 (0.049)
		352(0.789)			94(0.211)	
Named entities	7	7 (1.000)	0 (0.000)	0 (0.000)	0 (0.000)	0 (0.000)
		7(1.000)			0(0.000)	
Ratio of named entities	0.016	0.030	0.000	0.000	0.000	0.000

Table 5. Evaluation Results of the Aspects Extracted Using the Comparative Method.

	Total	A (ratio)	B (ratio)	C (ratio)	D (ratio)	E (ratio)
Aspects	516	289 (0.560)	103 (0.200)	31 (0.060)	63 (0.122)	30 (0.058)
		392(0.760)			124(0.240)	
Named entities	53	42 (0.792)	0 (0.000)	0 (0.000)	11 (0.208)	0 (0.000)
		42(0.792)			11(0.208)	
Ratio of named entities	0.103	0.145	0.000	0.000	0.175	0.000

articles to remove such compound words. Furthermore, the proposed method also extracted the aspects like "さ" (a Japanese hiragana character) for spot "岡山後楽園" (Okayama Korakuen Garden) "の人" (a person of) for spot "倉敷アイビースクエア" (Kurashiki Ivy Square), and "て" (a Japanese hiragana character) for spot "吉備津神社" (Kibitsu Jinja Shrine). The reason for these extractions is that they were classified as nouns by either Juman++ or MeCab and were not categorized as place names. Rules such as not outputting single character hiragana words as synonyms may be necessary to resolve this problem.

Comparison of the Proposed Method and Comparative Method. The comparative method extracted more specific aspects than the proposed method because the comparative method selected entities as aspects. For instance, for spot "おかやまフォレストパーク ドイツの森" (Okayama Forest Park), the proposed method extracted aspect "チーズ" (cheese) (Table 2), while the comparative method extracted aspect "チーズたっぷり" (plenty of cheese) (Table 3). Also, for the same spot, the proposed method extracted the aspect "体験" (experience) (Table 2), whereas the comparative method extracted the aspect "ソーセージ手作り体験" (sausage hands-on experience) (Table 3). Even for already specific aspects like "チーズ" (cheese), the comparative method often added more specific information, aspects such as "チーズたっぷり" (plenty of cheese).

The experiment counted the number of named entities among the extracted aspects. According to Table 4, the proposed method extracted seven named entities out of a total of 446 aspects. The seven aspects correspond to rating A. For instance, the named entities include "ピカソ" (Picasso) for spot "大原美術館" (Ohara Museum of Art) and "湯原" (Yubara) for spot "神庭の滝" (Kamba no

Taki Falls). On the other hand, as seen in Table 5, the comparative method extracted 53 named entities out of a total of 516 aspects. 42 of the 53 entities were evaluated as A, and the other 11 entities as D. Examples include "さんじゅーろー" (name of the famous cat in Bitchu Matsuyama Castle) for spot "備中松山城" (Bitchu Matsuyama Castle) and "倉敷ジーンズストリート" (Kurashiki Geans Street) for spot "倉敷美観地区" (Kurashiki Bikan Historical Quarter), both rated A, and "吉備津神社" (Kibitsu Jinja Shrine) for spot "吉備津神社" (Kibitsu Jinja Shrine) rated D.

From Table 4, 352 out of 446 aspects extracted by the proposed method, i.e., 78.9%, were evaluated as appropriate. Similarly, from Table 5, 392 out of 516 aspects extracted by the comparative method, i.e., 76.0%, were evaluated as appropriate. These results suggest that the proposed method achieved slightly higher accuracy in extracting appropriate aspects than the comparative method, even though the comparative method extracted more aspects than the proposed method. In addition, the aspects extracted by the comparative method were more specific. By searching spots using specific aspects, we can find a limited perspective of spots, but covering many spots using such specific aspects is challenging. For example, searching for tourist spots based on the aspect of "ソーセージ手作り体験" (sausage hands-on experience) cannot provide us many tourist spots while using more abstract aspects such as "体験" (experience) allows us to find more spots associating the aspect. This ability to extract highly abstract aspects is an advantage of the proposed method.

Reducing aspects rated E can be achievable through the use of dictionaries. However, it is necessary to further consider entity extraction methods and word vector training data to improve the accuracy of automatic aspect extraction by reducing aspects rated C and D.

4   Conclusion

This paper proposed a method for automatically extracting tourist spot aspects from Japanese tourism reviews. The proposed method extracts entities from tourism reviews on the travel site Jalan.net, and calculates their word vectors using the Natural Language API. After that, the proposed method clusters the entities based on their word vectors and outputs synonyms of clusters using the cluster vectors. The above processes were repeated for each tourist spot; the proposed method created a list of synonyms to extract aspects.

In the experiment of extracting aspects for 30 spots in Okayama Prefecture, the proposed method resulted in extracting appropriate aspects, such as "ピカソ" (Picasso) for spot "大原美術館" (Ohara Museum of Art), "絶叫系" (screaming rides) and "異国風" (exotic) for spot "ブラジリアンパーク鷲羽山ハイランド" (Brazillian Park Washuzan Highland), and "桜" (cherry blossoms) and "紅葉" (autumn leaves) for spot "岡山後楽園" (Okayama Korakuen Garden). However, a few inappropriate aspects were also extracted, such as "宿店" (inn store) for spot "神庭の滝" (Kamba no Taki Falls).

In the experiment, the comparative method extracted aspects from the entities not from the synonyms, comparing results with those of the proposed method. The 352 out of 446 aspects extracted by the proposed method were evaluated as appropriate, resulting in a ratio of 78.9%. On the other hand, 392 out of 516 aspects extracted by the comparative method were evaluated as appropriate, resulting in a ratio of 76.0%. Although there was not much difference between the two methods, the proposed method performed better. In addition, the proposed method extracted more abstract aspects than the comparative method. Consequently, the proposed method can extract aspects for a more diversified search of tourist spots compared to the comparative method.

For future work, we want to explore methods for assigning weights to entities extracted multiple times before clustering and compare the extracted aspects with the proposed method. Additionally, further consideration is needed for the threshold of the inconsistency coefficient of Ward's method used in entity clustering and the thresholds used for the creation of the synonym list such as the minimum number of entities within a cluster, the number of output synonyms.

References

1. Kenney, J.F., Keeping, E.S.: Mathematics of statistics, vol. 2. Van Nostrand, New York (1947). https://catalog.hathitrust.org/Record/000579897
2. Oku, K., Hattori, F.: Mapping geotagged tweets to tourist spots considering activity region of spot. In: Matsuo, T., Hashimoto, K., Iwamoto, H. (eds.) Tourism Informatics. ISRL, vol. 90, pp. 15–30. Springer, Heidelberg (2015). https://doi.org/10.1007/978-3-662-47227-9_2
3. Pagano, R., et al.: The contextual turn: from context-aware to context-driven recommender systems. In: Proceedings of the 10th ACM Conference on Recommender Systems, RecSys '16, pp. 249–252. Association for Computing Machinery, New York (2016). https://doi.org/10.1145/2959100.2959136
4. Peña, F.J.: Unsupervised context-driven recommendations based on user reviews. In: Proceedings of the Eleventh ACM Conference on Recommender Systems, RecSys '17, pp. 426–430. Association for Computing Machinery, New York (2017). https://doi.org/10.1145/3109859.3109865
5. Samejima, M.: Topic analysis of case reports in tourism towards collaborative tourism planning support. In: Matsuo, T., Hashimoto, K., Iwamoto, H. (eds.) Tourism Informatics. ISRL, vol. 90, pp. 1–14. Springer, Heidelberg (2015). https://doi.org/10.1007/978-3-662-47227-9_1
6. Varga, I., Hayashibe, Y.: Addressing overchoice: automatically generating meaningful filters from hotel reviews. In: Neidhardt, J., Wörndl, W., Kuflik, T., Zanker, M. (eds.) Proceedings of the Workshop on Recommenders in Tourism 2021, RecTour 2021, pp. 54–68. CEUR Workshop Proceedings, September 2021
7. Ward, J.H.: Hierarchical grouping to optimize an objective function. J. Am. Stat. Assoc. **58**(301), 236–244 (1963). https://doi.org/10.1080/01621459.1963.10500845. https://www.tandfonline.com/doi/abs/10.1080/01621459.1963.10500845

Unveiling Customer-Centric Product Development: Insights from Japanese Robotics Company

Jing Zhang[1]($\boxtimes$), Xianghua Jiang[2], and Junichi Muramatsu[3]

[1] Kanazawa University, Kakuma-machi, Kanazawa, Ishikawa 9201192, Japan
`j-zhang@staff.kanazawa-u.ac.jp`
[2] Kyoto Women's University, 35 Kitahiyoshi-cho, Imakumano, Higashiyama-ku, Kyoto 6058501, Japan
[3] Gifu Shotoku Gakuen University, 1-38 Nakauzura, Gifu 5008288, Japan

Abstract. The ongoing creation of high-quality new products stands as a key driver of competitive advantage for manufacturing firms. Previous research in New Product Development (NPD) has primarily emphasized the efficiency and effectiveness of the development process, often perceiving customer relationships as a factor contributing to market uncertainty. This study explores customer-centric NPD, which centers on customer value creation. Our objective is to address two key challenges: (1) the need to balance the integration of customer value creation and NPD and (2) strategies for effectively addressing customer value creation in the NPD process (customer-centric NPD). In our case study of a Japanese robotics company, we identified several insights related to the aforementioned issues. Regarding the first challenge, we uncovered three approaches: focusing on the concentration of business scope and development processes, establishing a revenue model that encompasses both development and mass production, and offering counterproposals grounded in customer value creation. As for the second challenge, we identified facilitating factors, including the integration of R&D and marketing functions and the role and development of key personnel.

Keywords: Service-dominant logic · Customer value creation · New product development

1 Introduction

For firms, superior New Product Development (NPD) is a valuable strategy for attaining a competitive advantage [1]. Previous discussions have underscored that the success of NPD is closely tied to a firm's strategic orientation [2], its capability to efficiently activate resources [3], and its comprehension of and responsiveness to customer needs [4].

Contemporary research on NPD centers around comprehending the processes, approaches, and strategies that contribute to the creation of a strategically designed product portfolio. This portfolio aims to optimize the alignment of new products with

H. Mori and Y. Asahi (Eds.): HCII 2024, LNCS 14691, pp. 261–272, 2024.
https://doi.org/10.1007/978-3-031-60125-5_18

customer needs while minimizing the time required to bring these products to market [5]. Consequently, it is imperative for a firm to adopt a customer-focused or market-oriented approach to reduce market uncertainty. These discussions are grounded in the premise that firms generate goods or services whose value is predetermined during the development and production stages before exchange occurs [6, 7].

Since the early 2000s, service-centric perspective has proliferated in marketing and management domains, exemplified by concepts like Service-Dominant logic (S-D logic) or Service logic. These paradigms challenge the conventional notion of a firm solely determining the value of its offerings, highlighting instead the subjective evaluation of value by customers through their interaction with the firm's products or services [6, 8].

The customer's subjective determination of value in their usage of a firm's offerings constitutes a pivotal aspect of value creation within this service-centered perspective. Accordingly, corporate marketing and management should shift towards direct customer engagement in value creation (value co-creation) or the provision of offerings conducive to customer's value creation.

Significantly, firms must integrate elements that facilitate customer use during the development of offerings. While existing research predominantly focuses on incorporating customer needs into offerings through preliminary market research, limited attention has been given to assimilating potential elements supportive of value creation, emphasizing usage context, and translating these elements into product design.

This study aims to delineate the process of identifying potential elements for product development, facilitating customer value creation, and elucidating the organizational capabilities required to actualize these elements.

2 Literature Review

2.1 Customer Requirements in NPD

Marketing research and practice consider the integration of customer requirements into the NPD process pivotal for averting new product failure and ensuring innovation success [9]. The Kano Model, a prominent framework, systematically categorizes customer-perceived quality, classifying elements into must-be quality, one-dimensional quality, attractive quality, indifferent quality, and reverse quality. This classification hinges on the dynamic interplay between customer satisfaction and the physical attributes of the product. Utilizing questionnaire surveys to understand essential customer requirements, the Kano Model aids in prioritizing elements for product development and enhancement. Firms, by comprehending the nuanced relationship between customer satisfaction and specific quality attributes, can strategically align efforts to meet customer requirements effectively [10].

Furthermore, some studies focus on sales and marketing as departments gathering customer requirements and their cooperation in NPD with the Research and Development (R&D) department [11–13]. Ernst et al. (2010) investigate the impact of cross-functional cooperation among sales, marketing, and R&D on NPD performance across multiple stages, emphasizing the importance of awareness and responsiveness to customer requirements throughout the NPD process. Findings reveal that while sales–marketing cooperation is crucial in the concept development stage, it surprisingly has less impact in the implementation stage, highlighting the nuanced role of cross-functional collaboration at different NPD stages [12]. Homburg et al. (2017) examine R&D-marketing and R&D-sales cooperation in B-to-B context, finding that R&D-marketing cooperation is strongly associated with new product superiority in cost leadership strategies, high R&D power, and strong R&D collectivism. Conversely, R&D-sales cooperation has a stronger effect on new product advantage in technologically turbulent markets, differentiation strategies, and when R&D influences company-wide budget decisions [13].

2.2 Customer Participation in NPD

The preceding section discussed studies that perceive the customer as an external element and strive to integrate customer requirements into the NPD process, aiming to diminish market uncertainty. Conversely, a group of studies take a different approach, involving customers as active participants in the NPD process [14].

Customer participation manifests across NPD stages: ideation, prototype testing, and market launch. A meta-analysis by Chang and Taylor (2016) addresses the varied impact of customer participation on NPD performance. Findings reveal that involving customers in ideation and market launch stages enhances new product financial performance directly and indirectly by reducing time-to-market. However, customer participation in the development phase adversely affects financial performance by prolonging time-to-market [15].

The impact of customer participation on NPD performance is also contingent on industry characteristics [16]. Knowledge may yield lower returns in the high-tech industry due to knowledge stickiness, hindering its transfer and application [17]. The likelihood of integrating customer inputs in high-tech NPD projects is reduced, underscoring the challenges in knowledge utilization [15].

2.3 Service-Dominant Product Development Focusing on Customer Value Creation

S-D logic is a comprehensive perspective and meta-idea that delineates service and value creation by framing business and markets through the lens of two distinct logics: Goods-Dominant logic (G-D logic), primarily centered on value in exchange, and S-D logic, emphasizing value-in-context [6, 7]. G-D logic predominantly centers on developing and manufacturing tangible products, considering goods as a pivotal component in the exchange process. Conversely, the S-D logic mindset prioritizes service, defining service as a process that directly provides benefits to the other party, either independently or through goods [18]. Within the S-D logic framework, goods are perceived as a medium for providing services, with the belief that services hold a superior position compared to goods.

The S-D logic proposes a paradigm shift in the initiation of NPD. It recommends a departure from traditional customer needs and requirements, which primarily focus on the functional value of goods (value-in-exchange), to a new focus on customer value creation. This entails the generation of value-in-use or value-in-context derived from the utilization of these goods. In essence, S-D logic advocates for a reorientation in which businesses prioritize the creation of holistic and experiential value for customers. This marks a departure from the conventional emphasis solely on the functional attributes of products in the NPD process. It is acknowledged that customer value creation should be comprehended within the broader context of the customer's lifeworld [19].

2.4 Summary of Previous Studies and Positioning of This Study

This chapter systematically organizes existing research from the perspective of the role of customers in a firm's product development process. Research on integrating customer requirements into NPD typically adopts a product-centric approach known as G-D logic. Structurally, R&D and marketing functions are often segregated, with studies suggesting that proactive initiatives by the R&D department positively impact NPD performance. Investigations into customer participation typically entail limited involvement during idea generation and market testing phases, reflecting a marketing strategy aimed at managing market uncertainty and gaining a competitive advantage. Despite engaging in co-creation activities, the focus remains exclusively on the ex-ante value of the product (value-in-exchange), aligning with a G-D logic perspective.

In the past two decades, the ascendancy of service-centric thinking in the marketing and management domain has underscored the imperative to infuse customer value creation into all phases of corporate activity. While these ideas have been actively discussed in realms such as service innovation and the servitization of manufacturing [20, 21], a notable gap exists in addressing how to integrate customer value creation into the NPD process effectively. This study aims to scrutinize customer-centric (value creation-oriented) product development within the high-tech industry, characterized by high information stickiness and technology orientation. Specifically, two research questions will be addressed:

- RQ1. How can firms strike a balance between incorporating customer value creation and achieving market performance?
- RQ2. What are the key drivers for integrating customer value creation into the product development process?

3 Methodology

3.1 Case Study Research Approach

To accomplish the research objectives, a case study research methodology will be employed, with a specific focus on a Japanese robotics company referred to as Company T. The choice of a case study approach is motivated by two fundamental considerations: firstly, the study's emphasis on extracting potential elements that contribute to value creation, and secondly, the imperative to analyze diverse sources of evidence, encompassing interviews, official records, and direct observations, to address the research inquiries effectively. Case studies are deemed more appropriate for investigating such research questions when compared to alternative methods, aligning with the rationale put forth by Yin [22, 23].

The selection of Company T as the subject of the case study ensures a nuanced examination of the intricacies involved in its operations, particularly in the realm of robotics. By delving into the company's practices and strategies, the research aims to uncover insights into how value is created within the context of innovative technologies, drawing on a rich array of data sources to provide a comprehensive understanding.

3.2 Outline of the Research Subject

Company T is a pioneering Japanese technology firm, at the forefront of innovation, specializing in custom-made solutions and cutting-edge robotics. Established with a commitment to pushing the boundaries of technology, company T seamlessly integrates creativity, engineering prowess, and a forward-thinking approach into its business philosophy. Company T's business philosophy revolves around creating bespoke solutions that transcend conventional boundaries. Their commitment to technological excellence is underpinned by a dedication to understanding and addressing their customer's unique needs. By embracing a customer-centric approach, company T aims to deliver tailor-made solutions that not only meet but exceed expectations.

The company's scope encompasses a wide array of industries and applications, ranging from custom robotics to innovative products designed to enhance various aspects of daily life. Company T's expertise extends to the development of robotic systems for diverse sectors, including healthcare, manufacturing, and service industries.

3.3 Data Collection and Analysis

In pursuit of a comprehensive understanding of value creation within Company T, a multifaceted data collection approach was implemented, encompassing qualitative methods to extract rich insights. The data collection and analysis methods employed are detailed below:

Interviews. Two in-depth interviews were conducted, the first on February 14, 2023, and the second on October 19, 2023. Each interview spanned a duration of two hours. The key participants were strategically chosen, including the Chairman of the Board of Directors, one of the founders who is a pivotal figure in product development, and the General Manager of the Planning Division. These individuals possess crucial insights into the inner workings of the company's value creation processes. The interviews were meticulously recorded and subsequently transcribed for thorough textual analysis.

Archival Materials. A comprehensive review of archival materials was undertaken, including pre-released documents, the company website, and explanatory materials provided by Company T. These materials serve as valuable sources of historical context, elucidating the evolution of the company's strategies and product development initiatives.

Participant Observation. On October 6, 2023, a participant observation was conducted at the City Mobility test-ride event organized by Company T. Detailed observation notes were recorded, capturing the interactions among participants during the test-ride event and the engagement between participants and Company T employees, as well as the event operator. This method provided firsthand insights into the practical application of the company's products and the reception by the target audience.

4 Findings

4.1 Definition of Business Scope

The founder, despite his background in archaeology, assumed control of the family automobile dealership business. However, harboring reservations about affiliating with a specific manufacturer, he initiated the production of machinery through collaborations with other companies, leveraging the firm's prior expertise in machine manufacturing. Through this process, he acquired the know-how to manage production lines and ventured into manufacturing robotics, garnering significant attention. Subsequently, in response to a government official request in 2000, the company embarked on a new venture, establishing Company T, specializing in robotics. Initially producing receptionist robotics, company T, in collaboration with a university research team, achieved a breakthrough in developing a full-body model robotics. With additional funding, the founder assembled a team of passionate colleagues to collaborate with the university robotics team, culminating in the creation of integrated robotics. At this juncture, Company T emerged as an industry pioneer in integrated robot development, with a strategic focus on mobile robotics, particularly those capable of power transmission.

Company T's business scope aligns with enabling larger companies to enhance mass production, emphasizing safety and precision after dedicating resources to product development. This approach allows Company T to concentrate on developing innovative products leveraging its core technology.

The business strategy strongly emphasizes on-site working robotics capable of physically transmitting force, differentiating them from communication robots. Company T stands as the sole entity capable of manufacturing these working robotics, with the creation of a force transmission system deemed critical for competing with foreign companies. Having received robotics development requests from numerous clients globally, the engineers at Company T strategically assess suitable applications for humans and industrial robots based on client needs. The company prioritizes projects that align with cutting-edge technologies and can be mass-produced, adhering to a policy of focusing on pioneering industry-leading robots in line with its business vision and ensuring profitability through mass production.

4.2 Product Development Process

Company T's product development process, emphasizing flexibility and responsiveness to market changes, unfolds through three key phases:

Selection of Requests. When a client presents a product development need, key figures at Company T, including creators, the chairman, and engineers, assume central roles. This phase involves narrowing down requests, focusing specifically on working robotics-related projects. This strategic selection ensures that the chosen projects contribute to enhancing the company's uniqueness and competitiveness in the marketplace.

Launch NPD Projects. The initiation of NPD projects involves a key individual conceptualizing the idea, followed by the assembly of an in-house team comprising electrical, mechanical, and control experts. The team is dynamically structured for each project, accumulating valuable know-how, especially in processing highly sticky information, through participation in diverse product development initiatives. Unlike the common approach of adding applications to existing technologies, Company T prides itself on possessing the know-how to create products entirely from scratch—a distinctive strength. This approach requires a deep understanding of the genuine needs of customers and translating those needs into technological solutions. Recognizing the challenges of expressing true customer needs in robot technology, the company strongly emphasizes generating ideas, considering it a critical aspect that goes beyond technology transfer and involves cultivating the ability to invent.

Rotate the Prototyping Cycle. Company T sets itself apart from larger corporations by adopting a rapid and flexible prototyping cycle. This approach involves early prototyping, enabling the identification of issues and opportunities for improvement in the actual product, which are then incorporated into subsequent prototypes. This iterative process allows for the exploration of various variations, facilitating the efficient development of products aligned with market needs. During this phase, both theoretical considerations and real-world usage and feedback are deemed essential, underscoring the importance of a detailed understanding of the functioning of the actual product (Fig. 1).

Fig. 1. Three phases of the product development process of Company T.

4.3   Counterproposal Based on Customer Value Creation

Company T's distinctive approach to product development revolves around a customer-centric counterproposal, rooted in a unique comprehension of value creation derived from the founder's archaeological excavation experience. This perspective is prominently evident in the company's meticulous observation of actual sites where their products will be deployed.

Company T initiates the product development process by visiting sites from the project's inception, engaging directly with workers or users to solicit their insights. This proactive engagement is crucial for accurately understanding the challenges and needs of individuals actively involved in on-site work. By fostering open communication with workers or users, including engineers walking alongside them during their daily routines, Company T effectively captures authentic demands for product development.

Company T believes that without thorough on-site observation and communication, it becomes challenging to ascertain the genuine necessity of a product. Through this approach, Company T captures on-field feedback, encompassing constructive criticisms and positive insights, and incorporates them into NPD. Understanding the daily work routine is deemed essential for developing robot technology that genuinely meets the needs of on-site personnel. Therefore, true product usefulness hinges on developers actively collaborating with on-site workers and feeling the necessity for their inventions.

This approach aligns with a cultural anthropological perspective, akin to concepts found in ethnology and managerial anthropology. The founder's commitment to understanding culture and needs through direct on-site engagement, drawing from his archaeological background, reflects the incorporation of managerial anthropological perspectives into Company T's product development. For instance, when confronted with requests from clients, Company T goes beyond mere acceptance and personally visits the site to unearth the underlying problems. Emphasis is placed on precise interpreting executive directives and identifying issues from the field's perspective. This disposition, shaped by the founder's archaeological experiences, underscores the significance of field visits for comprehending genuine needs and challenges. Company T's success is attributed to this proactive understanding of the field.

"It's imperative to be on-site. Originally, during my university days, I was extensively involved in excavations. From the fragments and stones unearthed at the site, I've been reconstructing and speculating on what life might have been like. Upon seeing these fragments and stones, people often suggest that it could be a pit dwelling. However, in reality, there are few who have actually seen one. Traces of pillars, pillar holes, and hearths do emerge, but when it comes to understanding the structure during the Nara period or deducing from drawings on bronze bells, it's all speculative. It might be entirely different, you know." (Founder's Statement in Interview).

Moreover, Company T deviates from focusing on outsourcing relationships with the client, instead prioritizing direct engagement with the customer who actually use the product. This approach ensures a tangible and firsthand comprehension of the field's requirements, enhancing the effectiveness and efficiency of the company's proposals. Rather than blindly adhering to client requests, Company T's uniqueness lies in its commitment to prioritizing on-field perspectives and advancing proposals accordingly.

5 Discussion

5.1 Balancing Customer Value Creation and NPD Performance

NPD performance is characterized as the success of NPD efforts and is assessed across three dimensions: operational performance, financial performance, and marketing performance [24]. This entails evaluating the effectiveness and efficiency, economic returns, as well as aspects of customer satisfaction and loyalty in a cross-functional manner within the context of NPD.

Company T consistently strives to pioneer cutting-edge robotics that are unparalleled globally. This commitment involves deliberately investing more resources in NPD, foregoing the potential economies of scope derived from existing experience and knowledge. This stands in contrast to a risk-averse corporate management approach, which tends to favor the imitation of established businesses [25]. Notably, the development process, commencing with the value creation for users who actively use the product, demands extensive fieldwork and time to identify innovative ideas. In this context, the analysis of Company T's case study will explore three strategies for balancing the pursuit of customer value creation and NPD performance (operational performance, financial performance, and marketing performance).

1. *Improving operational performance by concentrating the scope of the business.* The operational performance of a new product is indicative of its effective and efficient development, encompassing innovation and speed to market [24]. In the case of Company T, amidst numerous development requests from clients, the company strategically accepts projects exclusively with high technical novelty. Furthermore, Company T directs its attention to the idea generation and prototyping phases, while entrusting the mass production and market introduction stages to the client. The company allocates resources to generate ideas for cutting-edge technologies and their commercialization. Company T successfully eliminates the traditional trade-off between operational performance and customer-centric product development by prioritising development time for on-site fieldwork to comprehend user value creation. This aligns with the drivers for NPD as presented in Cooper (2019) [1].

2. *Financial performance is enhanced by setting the NPD goal as a product with high prospects for mass production.* The financial performance of a new product encompasses economic returns, including sales and profits [24]. In the case of Company T, the company adopts a policy of accepting development requests with high market potential that demonstrate promising prospects for future mass production, aligning with the management vision. During the mass-production stage, company T generates revenue through royalties per unit. In other words, company T has developed a revenue model in which it collects both NPD fees and royalties. Unlike conventional NPD processes that may compromise novelty for mass production, Company T's approach strikes a balance between novelty and market potential.

3. *Market performance is enhanced through the strategic practice of making "counteroffers" to clients.* The market performance of a new product reflects satisfaction and loyalty in the customer-firm relationship [24]. From our interviews with company T, we found that when clients present development requirements with preconceived notions of product functionality, incorporating such manifested needs and features directly into the product often leads to a high probability of failure. Instead, Company T has adopted a unique approach to translating and creating NPD ideas. They focus on developing products that meet the client's expressed needs, support end-user value creation, and ensure market performance by being valued by both users and clients. Analyzing the relationship between customer-centric NPD and market performance requires a thorough examination of client value creation, in which the choice of perspective and contextual framework plays an important role [26].

5.2 Key Drivers for Integrating Customer Value Creation into the NPD Process

1. Integration of R&D and marketing functions

Existing studies that involve customers as either passive or active participants in NPD often maintain a separation between the R&D and marketing functions, leading to vertical competition within the organization [12, 13]. These studies are typically grounded in a product development paradigm primarily focusing on provider activities [27]. In the case of Company T, the objective is not merely to extend existing technology but to invent innovative products starting from user value creation. A distinctive feature of the NPD process at Company T is its transition from a B-to-B relationship to a B to B to

C relationship. In this process, the marketing function precedes by understanding customer value creation, and development ideas are generated based on this understanding. Subsequently, the technical elements required for commercialization are internally and externally sourced. As highlighted in the findings, human resources are flexibly allocated to each NPD project, fostering teamwork within a flat organizational structure that integrates R&D and marketing functions. This implies that the company consistently confronts uncertainty, underscoring the significance of establishing connections with both internal and external partners to effectively address contingencies [28].

2. Key personnel leading NPD projects

Successful and innovative NPD requires an organizational culture that fosters internal entrepreneurship and encourages risk-taking behavior [1]. In the case of Company T, the founder serves as a key figure embodying internal entrepreneurial spirit. Drawing upon his background in archaeology, the essence of NPD lies in the utilization of ethnography's strength to unveil unarticulated customer needs and transform them into technological components. As a pivotal decision-maker within the organization, the NPD leader serves as a bridge between the technology-centric R&D and customer-centric marketing functions, with the customer-focused perspective of this key individual playing a crucial role in integrating value creation into the NPD process. However, transferring such implicit knowledge and skills, essential for comprehensively envisioning and innovating NPD, presents a challenge in training individuals to see and invent within the context of NPD.

6   Conclusion

This study investigated how to address customer value creation in the NPD process for firms adopting a service-centric approach, as represented by S-D logic. Two identified issues include: (1) the challenge of balancing the integration of customer value creation and new product performance, and (2) strategies for incorporating customer value creation in the NPD process (customer-centric NPD). The case study focused on a Japanese robotics firm, Company T, within the high-tech industry. The study contributes to both service-centric research approaches and traditional NPD studies by establishing the link between customer value creation and NPD.

While service-centric discussions are prevalent in service marketing, service innovation, and the servitization of manufacturing, there has been a notable absence of comprehensive discourse on NPD, the production process for goods. Existing NPD research often incorporates customers into the development process through methods like addressing customer requirements and encouraging customer participation. Consequently, this study offers exploratory findings that bridge these two research gaps.

Practically, the study elucidates how to tackle management challenges linked to the inclusion of customer value creation, employing a case analysis of a prominent case study. For companies intending to reassess the nature of NPD using a service-centric approach, this study furnishes alternative prescriptions concerning the NPD process design and necessary organizational capabilities.

However, the application of a single-case study research methodology in this study prompts considerations regarding the generalizability of findings. Despite the study's efforts to abstract findings and address research questions, limitations exist in terms of explanatory scope and generalization. Future research should aim to enhance the robustness of findings by incorporating cases from diverse industries.

Disclosure of Interests. The authors have no competing interests to declare that are relevant to the content of this article.

References

1. Cooper, R.G.: The drivers of success in new-product development. Ind. Mark. Manage. **76**, 36–47 (2019)
2. Menguc, B., Auh, S., Yannopoulos, P.: Customer and supplier involvement in design: the moderating role of incremental and radical innovation capability. J. Prod. Innov. Manag. **31**(2), 313–328 (2014)
3. Mu, J.: Marketing capability, organizational adaptation and new product development performance. Ind. Mark. Manage. **49**, 151–166 (2015)
4. Yli-Renko, H., Janakiraman, R.: How customer portfolio affects new product development in technology-based entrepreneurial firms. J. Mark. **72**(5), 131–148 (2008)
5. Schilling, M.A., Hill, C.W.: Managing the new product development process: strategic imperatives. Acad. Manag. Perspect. **12**(3), 67–81 (1998)
6. Vargo, S.L., Lusch, R.F.: Evolving to a new dominant logic for marketing. J. Mark. **68**(1), 1–17 (2004)
7. Lusch, R.F., Vargo, S.L.: An Introduction to Service-Dominant Logic. Cambridge University Press (2014)
8. Grönroos, C.: Adopting a service logic for marketing. Mark. Theory **6**(3), 317–333 (2006)
9. Griffin, A., Hauser, J.R.: Integrating R&D and marketing: a review and analysis of the literature. J. Prod. Innov. Manag. Int. Publ. Prod. Dev. Manag. Assoc. **13**(3), 191–215 (1996)
10. Kano, N., Seraku, N., Takahashi, F., Tsuji, S.: Attractive quality and must-be quality. Hinshitsu **14**(2), 39–48 (1984). (in Japanese)
11. Joshi, A.W.: Salesperson influence on product development: insights from a study of small manufacturing organizations. J. Mark. **74**(1), 94–107 (2010)
12. Ernst, H., Hoyer, W.D., Rübsaamen, C.: Sales, marketing, and research-and-development cooperation across new product development stages: implications for success. J. Mark. **74**(5), 80–92 (2010)
13. Homburg, C., Alavi, S., Rajab, T., Wieseke, J.: The contingent roles of R&D–sales versus R&D–marketing cooperation in new-product development of business-to-business firms. Int. J. Res. Mark. **34**(1), 212–230 (2017)
14. Gruner, K.E., Homburg, C.: Does customer interaction enhance new product success? J. Bus. Res. **49**(1), 1–14 (2000)
15. Chang, W., Taylor, S.A.: The effectiveness of customer participation in new product development: a meta-analysis. J. Mark. **80**(1), 47–64 (2016)
16. Herstatt, C., Von Hippel, E.: From experience: developing new product concepts via the lead user method: a case study in a "low-tech" field. J. Prod. Innov. Manag. **9**(3), 213–221 (1992)
17. Von Hippel, E.: Sticky information and the locus of problem solving: implications for innovation. Manage. Sci. **40**(4), 429–439 (1994)
18. Lusch, R.F., Vargo, S.L., O'brien, M.: Competing through service: insights from service-dominant logic. J. Retail. **83**(1), 5–18 (2007)
19. Heinonen, K., Strandvik, T., Mickelsson, K.J., Edvardsson, B., Sundström, E., Andersson, P.: A customer-dominant logic of service. J. Serv. Manag. **21**(4), 531–548 (2010)

20. Gebauer, H., Fleisch, E., Friedli, T.: Overcoming the service paradox in manufacturing companies. Eur. Manag. J. **23**(1), 14–26 (2005)
21. Gebauer, F., Hentze, M.W.: Molecular mechanisms of translational control. Nat. Rev. Mol. Cell Biol. **5**(10), 827–835 (2004)
22. Yin, R.K.: Case Study Research, 2nd edn. Sage Publications, Thousand Oaks, CA (1994)
23. Yin, R.K.: Case Study Research and Applications: Design and Methods. Sage Publications, Thousand Oaks, CA (2018)
24. Troy, L.C., Hirunyawipada, T., Paswan, A.K.: Cross-functional integration and new product success: an empirical investigation of the findings. J. Mark. **72**(6), 132–146 (2008)
25. Morris, M.H., Schindehutte, M., LaForge, R.W.: Entrepreneurial marketing: a construct for integrating emerging entrepreneurship and marketing perspectives. J. Market. Theory Pract. **10**(4), 1–19 (2002)
26. Grönroos, C., Ravald, A.: Service as business logic: implications for value creation and marketing. J. Serv. Manag. **22**(1), 5–22 (2011)
27. Toivonen, M., Kijima, K.: Systems perspectives on the interaction between human and technological resources. Hum.-Centered Digitalization Serv., 37–56 (2019)
28. Mu, J., Thomas, E., Peng, G., Benedetto, A.D.: Strategic orientation and new product development performance: the role of networking capability and networking ability. Ind. Mark. Manage. **64**, 187–201 (2017)

**Knowledge Management
and Collaborative Work**

Decoding the Diversity of the German Software Developer Community: Insights from an Exploratory Cluster Analysis

Katharina Dworatzyk[(✉)] [iD], Vincent Dekorsy, and Sabine Theis[iD]

German Aerospace Center (DLR), Institute for Software Technology,
Cologne, Germany
{katharina.dworatzyk,vincent.dekorsy,sabine.theis}@dlr.de

Abstract. To better understand the nature of the software developer community in Germany, an open data set of 2,837 responses collected through the Stack Overflow Developer Survey was analyzed. Cluster analysis identified four sub-groups that were characterized by significant differences in sociodemographic variables, programming experience and software development specialization: the web developer (25%), the junior developer (26%), the senior developer (39%), and the research developer (10%). Cluster characteristics were associated with differences in experienced community membership, frequency of Stack Overflow visits and participation in Q&A. Senior developers with the highest level of coding experience reported the overall strongest community engagement, while research developers visited Stack Overflow least often. A positive moderate relationship between community membership and community visits and community participation provided additional evidence for the importance of the sense of (virtual) community as a psychological driving factor of community engagement. Together, these findings can contribute to developing more targeted training and community-building measures.

Keywords: software developer · virtual community · personas · cluster analysis

1 Introduction

Software engineering is a dynamic, evolving field with continual advancements in technologies, methodologies, and best practices. At the core of this evolution are the software developer communities that provide a platform for sharing knowledge and learning about technological advancements. These communities refer to a collective of individuals and organizations involved in the creation, development, use, and maintenance of software. Various forms of communities, including open-source software communities [55], local meetups [22], and members of knowledge platforms or portals [16,23], provide opportunities for knowledge exchange, which is crucial for software engineers to stay updated and competitive. In addition, they are crucial for software engineers aiming to stay abreast of

© The Author(s), under exclusive license to Springer Nature Switzerland AG 2024
H. Mori and Y. Asahi (Eds.): HCII 2024, LNCS 14691, pp. 275–295, 2024.
https://doi.org/10.1007/978-3-031-60125-5_19

technological advancements, find mentorship, collaborate, and build supportive networks [6,27].

Recent research underscores the significance of diversity within these communities. Studies indicate that understanding the composition of a community and promoting engagement and inclusion is essential to creating supportive, sustainable, and vibrant communities [25,38,45]. Semi-structured interviews, for example, highlighted that inclusion and diversity in terms of gender, ethnicity, disabilities, and age foster creativity [?]. Also, workforce diversity positively impacts on organizational competitiveness by increasing employee skills and talent, with a moderately positive relationship between age diversity and employee performance [52]. Furthermore, literature reviews showed that women's participation in open-source software (OSS) and the demographics of software development teams have a positive impact on community engagement [50], while especially increasing age diversity has a positive effect on company productivity if the company engages in creative rather than routine tasks [52]. Studies like these demonstrate how diversity regarding demographic characteristics and individual skills within a community significantly influences its quality.

In the realm of tool development for software engineers, the emphasis on understanding the community's diverse needs is also of paramount importance. The variety of tools used by developers reflects the diversity of their tasks, skills, and preferences [13]. By tailoring tools to meet these varied requirements, both functional and non-functional, the productivity and efficiency of developers can be significantly improved [26,47]. By understanding the community and its needs, working tools can be better adapted to requirements [20]. This can increase developer productivity and efficiency [9,11]. In general, creating efficient and effective software tools and workplaces benefits from studying users' needs and requirements [10]. One popular method to model different user types is constructing personas [30]. Personas are fictional characters representing common types of users and typically consist of a name, usually a photo, and demographic characteristics, skills, and abilities [5]. Designers, developers, and human factors experts apply them to get a clearer understanding of the target group they are designing products and workplaces for [8,12,28,34]. While in practice, personas are often developed qualitatively or purely on the basis of subjective perception, there are already the first successful approaches to taking quantitative data into account [40,41]

Given the critical role of diversity in fostering robust software engineering communities and the necessity of grasping user groups' diverse needs for effective tool development, a detailed examination of the current state of the software developer community, in particular in Germany, is imperative. This study aims to decode the diversity within this community through exploratory cluster analysis, seeking insights into how demographic characteristics, individual skills, and diversity factors influence community culture, engagement, and the potential for innovation.

2   Related Work

The following section provides an overview of research related to software engineering communities in Germany: the community characteristics, the role of diversity in software engineering in general, and its specific impact on this discipline. The aim is to get a clearer picture of how diversity is shaped within the German software engineering community and what impact this has.

2.1   Software Engineering Communities in Germany

In Germany, the importance of software engineering is increasing due to ongoing digitization. In 2022, the IT segment in Germany was the most profitable, with a turnover of around 46 billion euros, followed by the hardware and software sectors. Currently, there are over 90,000 companies in the IT industry with around 1.1 million employees. Nearly 35.5 billion euros were generated with software products in Germany in 2022[1]. The largest software companies include SAP, with an annual turnover of 24.71 billion euros in 2018, and DATEV, with 978 million euros in 2017, and Software AG, with an annual turnover of 879 million euros in 2017 [3]. But also many small and highly specialized software companies are based in Germany, for example, in the environment of groups in the automotive industry[2].

Software engineering takes place not only in industry but also in the research sector. While software engineering in research was largely overlooked for a long time, currently there are increasing efforts, for example in Germany, the Netherlands and the UK, to build a lively and growing research software engineering community. In contrast to previous work on software engineering, there is far more work in research software engineering that focuses on German samples. Analysis of data based on workshop participation [43, 44] showed, for example, that the software development community of the DLR[3] consists of a growing core group regularly joined by new participants. Both software engineering and research software engineering communities consist of individual groups emerging or consolidating each other primarily through international platforms and national as well as international associations.

One of the largest and best-known platforms where software engineers, as well as research software engineers, can ask and answer questions to solve programming problems is Stack Overflow[4]. The asked questions and answers can be viewed by anyone registered, while all its content is licensed under Creative Commmons. Additionally, registered users of the platform are able to rate given answers so that they can be ranked and displayed accordingly. As an international platform, it has over 14 million registered users. In one study, data visualization was applied to gain insights into the international community of

---

[1] https://de.statista.com/themen/1373/it-branche-deutschland/#topicOverview.

[2] https://www.wlw.de/de/inside-business/aktuelles/deutsche-software.

[3] www.dlr.de.

[4] www.https://stackoverflow.com/.

Stack overflow and their development over time and to identify sub-communities, their sizes, and tools used by each community. The authors identified the web development community as the biggest and most persistent one over time. In general, community members exhibit low fluctuation rates between identified sub-communities [51]. In addition, Srba and Bielikova [48] concentrated on identifying groups based on individual skills and behavior. Publicly available data on user activity was used to study the quality of contributions over time, considering how knowledgeable users were. Results indicated that when more low-quality content was posted-particularly by users who frequently ask questions without looking for answers first (known as "help vampires"), beginners who ask many basic questions ("noobs"), and users who answer many questions to gain reputation ("reputation collectors")-this lead to higher turnover rates in the community. Similarly but more in-depth, Anderson and colleagues [4] investigated that a strong relationship between the key characteristics of a question and its answers have a long-term value for a community.

Stack Overflow studies that focus more on individual factors primarily look at behavior in relation to human factors such as personality and gender. Ahmed and Srivastava [2], for example, showed that community members preferred to answer to a person from the same locality or gender. Previous work on the Stack Overflow community has very often considered the use of technical tools, the identification of sub-groups in the community, and the behavior of these sub-groups, as well as the quality of content and its impact on the community as a whole. Although initial studies show the influence of demographic characteristics such as origin or gender, there is a lack of detailed consideration of other diversity factors, particularly for the German developer community.

Like Stack Overflow, GitHub[5] is a popular community platform where especially open-source developers can exchange ideas and share their projects. This platform is often used to investigate the underlying community due to its extensive data set, but when interpreting the results, it must be borne in mind that this is a very technical user group [24]. On the other hand, GitHub data was used to examine collaboration in communities and teams. For example, to look at their development over time and to examine the influence of certain actors within a community on a development project in more detail [18]. The research utilizes GitHub data to explore how stakeholder involvement contributes to developing innovative solutions for environmental issues, emphasizing the critical role of community structures that facilitate effective communication and collaboration [31]. Similarly, Moutidis and Williams [32] conducted a study on Stack Overflow, identifying significant communities, examining the technologies these communities are interested in, and how they connect and evolve over time. These studies highlight the utility of data from large developer platforms like GitHub and Stack Overflow, offering insights into global software development practices. However, the focus on code(ing) of the GitHub platform naturally leads to corresponding data, analyses of which are less likely to provide knowledge about human characteristics, behavior, or diversity factors within the community. Consequently,

---

[5] www.github.com.

research specifically targeting the German developer community is limited, with only a few small-scale studies focusing on research software engineers. This gap points to a potential area for further research to better understand the engagement and contributions of the German developer community on these platforms.

Software engineering and developer communities in Germany are not only shaped by companies, research institutions, and international platforms but also by non-profit professional organizations. Notably, in Germany, organizations such as the Society for Informatics (Gesellschaft für Informatik, GI)[6], the Bundesverband IT-Mittelstand e.V. (BITMi)[7], which represents over 2,500 IT companies, play a significant role. The GI, in particular, has implemented robust initiatives to foster equal opportunities and gender equality both within its ranks and in the broader community GI [15]. However, up to now, their and other investigations of diversity in the developer community in Germany have concentrated on the proportion of women and girls in computer science education [42,46]. The actions of the German research software engineering community signify a pivotal shift, bridging the focus on diversity initiatives by professional organizations such as the GI and BITMi with broader academic and research practices. This advocacy has culminated in the German Research Foundation (DFG) revising its guidelines to acknowledge software development on par with traditional academic outputs. The development of the German software developer community had already been strengthened years before by the founding of the "Distributed Competence Centers for Software Engineering (ViSEK)" [19]. This project concentrated on intra- and inter-organizational learning in the software industry by building communities among software engineers through an internet portal and a regional network of SMEs.

Analyzing interactions and contributions on platforms like GitHub or Stack Overflow can offer insights into the collaborative dynamics and diversity of the software engineering community [48,51]. Leveraging open data sets related to software development projects allows for the examination of team composition, contribution patterns, and project outcomes in relation to diversity factors [48,51]. Employing data visualization techniques can help in identifying patterns and trends related to diversity within software engineering, facilitating a deeper understanding of its impact [51]. Conducting case studies on specific software engineering teams or projects can provide detailed insights into how diversity influences team dynamics and project success [48]. These qualitative and quantitative approaches allow for a nuanced exploration of diversity within the software engineering community, enabling the identification of unique diversity clusters and the analysis of their influence on software development practices. By applying these methodological approaches, researchers can decode the complexities of diversity within the German software developer community, contributing to a richer understanding of its impacts and benefits in the field of software engineering.

---

[6] www.gi.de.

[7] https://www.bitmi.de/.

In summary, the German software engineering community is shaped by the national software engineering industry, research institutes, and professional and industry associations. Efforts to build German communities have been and are currently being made by public research funding as well as research software engineering initiatives or associations. Investigations of the German software engineering community are sparse and lack generalizability. The present work aims, therefore, to explore the diversity within the German software developer community through exploratory cluster analysis. By examining demographic characteristics, individual skills, and diversity factors, we seek to provide insights into how these elements influence community culture, engagement, and the potential for innovation. Our analysis contributes to a deeper understanding of the composition of the German software developer community, offering implications for fostering more inclusive, engaging, and productive communities in the software engineering field.

3   Materials and Methods

3.1   Stack Overflow Developer Survey

To improve our understanding of the different backgrounds and development tools of German developers, an open-access data set, resulting from the annual Stack Overflow Developer Survey[8], was analyzed. The survey was conducted from mid-May to the beginning of June 2022 and mainly advertised through Stack Overflow channels.

The complete data set contained responses to questions on (1) Basic Information about participants, e.g. "Which of the following options best describes you today? Here, by 'developer' we mean 'someone who writes code'." with the response options "I am a developer by profession", "I am not primarily a developer, but I write code sometimes as part of my work", "I used to be a developer by profession, but no longer am", "I am learning to code", "I code primarily as a hobby", "None of these"; (2) Education, Work, and Career, e.g. "Which of the following describes your current job?" with response options such as "Academic researcher", "Data or business analyst", "Developer, full-stack", "DevOps specialist" or "Project manager"; (3) Technology and Tech Culture, e.g. "Which programming, scripting, and markup languages have you done extensive development work in over the past year?" with multiple response options; (4) Stack Overflow Usage and Community, e.g. "Do you consider yourself a member of the Stack Overflow community?" with response options ranging from "No, not at all" to "Yes, definitely"; (5) Demographic Information, e.g. "What is your age?"; (6) Professional Development, e.g. "Are you an independent contributor or people manager?"; and (7) Final Questions about the survey, e.g. "How do you feel about the length of the survey this year?" from 73,268 participants.

---

[8] https://insights.stackoverflow.com/survey/.

3.2   Participants

For our analysis, we selected responses from participants who indicated Germany as their current place of residence, resulting in an initial sample of 5,395 participants. Responses were excluded if participants were under 18 years old or had skipped any of the survey questions essential to the cluster analysis, which resulted in a final sample of 2,837 participants. Missing values were not replaced as the number of missing responses was substantial (46%), and the reduced data set was thought to be still large enough to meet the sample size standards recommended for cluster analysis. Recommendations that depend on the number of clustering variables vary from a minimum of 10-100 times the number of clustering variables [39], which would here correspond to a minimal sample size of 50-500 survey participants.

3.3   Data Preparation and Analysis

Prior to analysis, data were encoded and transformed into new variables where necessary. The original response option "I am a developer by profession" (see 3.1) was encoded as "yes", and all other response options in this question as "no". To reduce redundancy in the cluster analysis, the original twenty-nine individual developer jobs were summarized as higher-order categories, describing the primary focus or context of software development: "Development and programming", "Data and analytics", "Infrastructure and operations", "Management and leadership", "Education and research" or "Student". Response options to multiple choice questions were included in the analysis as separate variables with a dichotomous response format ("yes"/"no"). Ordinal categorical data were numerically encoded. For the cluster analysis, all numerical data were z-standardized and nominal data were encoded using one-hot encoding.

The prepared data set was then subjected to cluster analysis. Cluster analysis is a procedure typically used in market research to identify different consumer types [39]. Here, it was used to identify sub-groups within the German developer community and to characterize them in terms of sociodemographic aspects, use of tools and technology, and their involvement in the Stack Overflow community. Cluster analysis aims to increase the homogeneity within groups while increasing the heterogeneity between groups. As software development plays a crucial role in different areas of industries and academia, we expected to find multiple clusters.

The selection of clustering variables included socioeconomic variables, namely level of education level and yearly income, employment as professional software, coding experience in years, and the development context. To determine the appropriate number of clusters, the elbow method and a dendrogram were used. As k-means clustering can be problematic with nominal data [7], hierarchical clustering was applied using Ward's algorithm and Gower's distance. Gower's distance has the advantage that it combines Manhattan distance for numeric data and Dice distance for nominal data. When computing Gower's distance, the variables "Level of education" and "Developer by profession" were included with double weight to account for their importance. Conversely, the six variables related to "Development context" were weighted with $1/6$ to account for the fact that they were actually response options of the same multiple choice question.

To cross-validate and further explore our clustering results, the same analysis was repeated on another country-based sample from the Stack Overflow data set. The sample for cross-validation was chosen from the list of top ten countries with a focus on appropriate sample size and relative cultural similarity to the German sub-sample. Interpretation of the resulting clusters was finally based on descriptive statistics of the clustering variables and a comparison of the clusters. To test for cluster effects and differences in the clustering variables between clusters, one-way analysis of variance (ANOVA) and pair-wise comparison using Tukey's HSD were employed.

In addition to the analysis of sociodemographic variables, we visualized the use of different programming languages and other software development tools to better interpret the clusters. For programming languages, we looked at differences in use ($\geq 1\%$) for each clusters compared to the total sample to identify languages that were particularly prominent in these clusters and for development environments, frameworks and libraries, version control systems and other developers tools we visualized the relative frequency of use as radar charts to compare profiles of developers from different clusters.

As we were interested in how involved the identified developer sub-groups were in the Stack Overflow community, we analyzed the relationship between coding experience, as one of the defining clustering variables on the one hand, and the subjectively assessed level of community membership (responses ranging from -3 - "No, not at all" to 3 - "Yes, definitely"), the frequency of visiting Stack Overflow (responses ranging from 1 - "Less than once per month or monthly" to 5 - "Multiple times per day") and the frequency of participating in Q&A on Stack Overflow (responses ranging from 0 - "Never" to 5 - "Multiple times per day"), as parameters of the community involvement on the other hand. To determine the strength and direction of the relationship we used Pearson's correlation coefficient. Differences in the community variables between cluster were analyzed using ANOVA and pair-wise comparison tests (Tukey's HSD). As a last measure of community involvement differences, we compared the proportions of developers who indicated to have a Stack Overflow account for each cluster to the total sample using χ^2 test. As the time spent in the community correlates positively with the sense of community [33], we expected to find a positive relationship between coding experience and community membership. Several studies have shown that the sense of community [29] is a driving factor of community engagement, e.g. [35, 37]. Other studies have shown that the sense of community, usually discussed in the context of neighborhood communities, also plays a crucial role in virtual communities [1, 14]. Therefore, we also hypothesized a positive relationship between community membership, as one aspect of the sense of community, and the frequency of visiting Stack Overflow and participating in Q&A.

Data preparation and analysis were carried out using Python (3.9) and the following libraries: Pandas (2.0.3) [49], NumPy (1.25.1) [17], SciPy (1.11.1) [53], Scikit-learn (1.3.0) [36], Matplotlib (3.7.2) [21] and seaborn (0.13.0) [54].

4 Results

4.1 Sample Characteristics

The final sample consisted of survey responses from 2,837 participants, who mostly identified as men (95%). Half of the participants (50%) were between 25 and 34 years old, and the majority (66%) had a Bachelor's or Master's degree (see Table 1). The Dutch sub-sample, that was used to cross-validate the results of the cluster analysis, had similar characteristics (see Table 2). Similar to the German sample, most participants included in the Dutch sample (n=885) identified as men (93%). Half of the participants (50%) were between 25 and 34 years old, and the majority (75%) had a Bachelor's or Master's degree.

4.2 Cluster Analysis

Elbow method and dendrogram suggested three, four or even five clusters. The four-cluster solution was chosen to obtain clusters as homogeneous as possible without over-fitting (the fifth cluster reduced the within-cluster sum of squares only marginally). The cluster analysis (Ward's algorithm, Gower's distance) showed that the German Stack Overflow developer community could be separated into four characteristic groups (Table 1). Of these four clusters, three clusters consisted of professional developers, Cluster 1, 2, and 3, which were distinguished by a different level of education, ranging from developers mostly likely trained as "Fachinformatiker:in" (IT specialist without a university degree) in Cluster 1 over developers with a Bachelor's degree in Cluster 2 to developers with a Master's degree in Cluster 3, and a working context strongly focusing on "Development and Programming" as well as "Infrastructure and operations". Developers of Cluster 4, on the other hand, had a more diverse educational background and were less specialized regarding the context of software development but had a strong focus on "Education and Research" as well as "Data and Analytics". Similar results were obtained for the Dutch sample (Table 2)

A one-way ANOVA showed a significant difference in programming experience across clusters, $F(3, 2833) = 32.72$, $p < .001$. Developers of Cluster 3 had an on average higher programming experience (see Table 1) than developers of all other clusters ($p < .001$ for comparison with Cluster 1 and Cluster 2 and $p = .006$ for comparison with Cluster 4) and developers of Cluster 4 had significantly more programming experience than those of Cluster 2 ($p = .004$; $p > .05$ for all other comparisons). The income was also found to be significantly different across clusters, $F(3, 2833) = 34.89$, $p < .001$, and developers of Cluster 3 had the highest income ($p < .001$ for all comparisons), while the other clusters did not differ significantly ($p > .05$ for all comparisons). Similarly, there was a big difference in terms of educational level, $F(3, 2833) = 3982.28$, $p < .001$. Developers of Cluster 1 had a significantly ($p < .001$) lower level of education ($M = 1.67$, $SD = 0.68$) than developers of Cluster 2 ($M = 4.00$, $SD = 0.00$), Cluster 3 ($M = 5.10$, $SD = 0.40$) and Cluster 4 ($M = 4.34$, $SD = 1.55$). The level of education was lower for Cluster 2 compared to Cluster 3 and 4 ($p < .001$

Table 1. Sociodemographic characteristics of participants from Germany

	Total	Cluster 1	Cluster 2	Cluster 3	Cluster 4
n	2,837	696	739	1105	297
Developer by profession (%)					
Yes	90	100	100	100	0
No	10	0	0	0	100
Years of coding experience					
M	15.63	14.77	13.60	17.53	15.66
SD	8.93	9.12	7.63	9.01	9.78
Level of education (%)					
Finished school	12	43	0	0	9
College/university without degree	12	45	0	0	10
Associate degree	3	12	0	0	1
Bachelor's degree	29	0	100	3	18
Master's degree	37	0	0	84	40
Doctoral degree	7	0	0	13	22
Context of software development (%)					
Data & analytics	13	6	7	17	29
Development & programming	87	96	95	90	35
Education & research	21	16	14	19	57
Infrastructure & operations	30	32	26	29	39
Management & leadership	16	15	14	15	29
Student	1	2	2	0	4
Income (USD)					
Median	69,318	58,654	65,053	76,783	63,986
IQR	36,259	34,126	29,860	31,995	39,458
Age (%)					
18-24 years	10	22	12	2	6
25-34 years	50	43	60	48	51
35-44 years	29	24	22	36	27
45-54 years	8	7	5	11	10
55-64 years	3	3	2	3	4
>65 years	0	0	0	0	0
Gender (%)					
Man	95	94	95	95	94
Other	2	4	2	2	4
Woman	4	4	5	4	4
Accessibility (%)					
Differences in the ability to hear or see	2	3	2	1	2
Differences in the ability to type, walk or stand	0	0	0	0	0
None of the above	97	96	98	98	98
Psychological or neurological differences (%)					
Affective disorder	10	20	10	6	8
Anxiety disorder	6	11	6	4	5
Neurodiversity	12	19	12	8	12
None of the above	78	65	79	85	78

Table 2. Sociodemographic characteristics of participants from the Netherlands

	Total	Cluster 1	Cluster 2	Cluster 3	Cluster 4
n	885	146	433	244	62
Developer by profession (%)					
Yes	93	100	100	100	0
No	7	0	0	0	100
Years of coding experience					
M	15.45	15.52	14.12	17.25	17.53
SD	9.33	10.24	8.82	9.03	10.26
Level of education (%)					
Finished school	3	26	0	0	0
College/university without degree	13	74	0	0	11
Associate degree	4	0	8	0	5
Bachelor's degree	47	0	92	0	23
Master's degree	28	0	0	91	48
Doctoral degree	4	0	0	9	13
Context of software development (%)					
Data & analytics	15	7	10	21	32
Development & programming	89	98	94	88	39
Education & research	20	15	13	24	56
Infrastructure & operations	27	38	26	23	24
Management & leadership	13	14	10	13	24
Student	1	1	1	0	3
Income (USD)					
Median	66,540	63,036	63,288	78,037	71,985
IQR	46,923	41,770	40,525	48,524	56,125
Age (%)					
18-24 years	11	14	15	3	11
25-34 years	51	53	54	47	36
35-44 years	26	22	21	37	27
45-54 years	9	8	7	9	19
55-64 years	3	4	3	3	5
>65 years	0	0	0	0	2
Gender (%)					
Man	94	98	93	93	95
Other	2	3	1	2	0
Woman	5	1	6	6	5
Accessibility (%)					
Differences in the ability to hear or see	3	3	2	2	9
Differences in the ability to type, walk or stand	0	1	0	0	2
None of the above	96	96	97	97	88
Psychological or neurological differences (%)					
Affective disorder	8	8	10	5	9
Anxiety disorder	9	11	10	6	5
Neurodiversity	23	35	25	16	14
None of the above	69	57	66	79	75

for both comparisons) and also lower for Cluster 4 compared to Cluster 3 ($p <$ .001).

Differences were also found regarding the context of software development. Regarding Cluster 1, a significantly larger proportion of developers worked in the context of "Development and Programming" (χ^2 (1, $n = 696$) $= 38.14$, $p < .001$) and a smaller proportion in "Data and Analytics" (χ^2 (1, $n = 696$) $= 26.06$, $p < .001$) as well as "Education and Research" (χ^2 (1, $n = 696$) $= 9.26$, $p = .002$), but no differences were found for "Infrastructure and Operations" (χ^2 (1, $n = 696$) $= 1.08$, $p = .298$) or "Management and Leadership" (χ^2 (1, $n = 696$) $= 0.74$, $p = .389$) or the proportion of students (χ^2 (1, $n = 696$) $= 1.89$, $p = .170$) compared to the total sample. Developers of Cluster 2 as well worked more often in "Development and Programming" (χ^2 (1, $n = 739$) $= 25.58$, $p < .001$), but less often in "Data and Analytics" (χ^2 (1, $n = 739$) $= 22.84$, $p < .001$). They also worked less often in "Education and Research" (χ^2 (1, $n = 739$) $= 21.77$, $p < .001$), "Infrastructure and Operations" (χ^2 (1, $n = 739$) $= 5.53$, $p = .019$) and "Management and Leadership" (χ^2 (1, $n = 739$) $= 4.10$, $p = .043$). The proportion of students did not differ from the total sample either (χ^2 (1, $n = 739$) $= 0.04$, $p = .838$). Similar to the first two clusters, developers of Cluster 3 had a stronger focus on "Development and Programming" (χ^2 (1, $n = 1105$) $= 10.13$, $p = .001$) and, in contrast to these, worked slightly more often in "Data and Analytics" (χ^2 (1, $n = 1105$) $= 13.66$, $p < .001$) and were less often students (χ^2 (1, $n = 1105$) $= 13.73$, $p < .001$). Cluster 3 did not differ regarding the proportions of developers working in "Education and Research" (χ^2 (1, $n = 1105$) $= 1.68$, $p = .195$), "Infrastructure and Operations" (χ^2 (1, $n = 1105$) $= 0.59$, $p = .444$) or "Management and Leadership" (χ^2 (1, $n = 1105$) $= 0.90$, $p = .342$). In contrast to all other clusters, developers of Cluster 4 worked significantly less frequently in "Development and Programming" (χ^2 (1, $n = 297$) $= 545.04$, $p < .001$). Instead, they worked most frequently in "Data and Analytics" (χ^2 (1, $n = 297$) $= 66.33$, $p < .001$), "Education and Research" (χ^2 (1, $n = 297$) $= 211.07$, $p < .001$), "Infrastructure and Operations" (χ^2 (1, $n = 297$) $= 12.41$, $p < .001$) as well as "Management and Leadership" (χ^2 (1, $n = 297$) $= 37.46$, $p < .001$) and also had a higher proportion of students (χ^2 (1, $n = 297$) $= 19.07$, $p < .001$) than the overall sample.

4.3   Tools and Technology

Socioeconomic differences and differences in the development context went along with differences in tool use (Fig. 1), in particular, for Cluster 4, which was comprised of developers who mostly worked in the context of research and education. For this cluster, we observed a much stronger focus on the programming languages Python, R, and MATLAB compared to other clusters (Fig. 1a). Developers of the first cluster used programming languages that are typical of web development more frequently, such as HTML/CSS, JavaScript, PHP, and TypeScript. While the profiles of the clusters largely overlapped with respect to development environments (Fig. 1b), frameworks (Fig. 1c), and other developer tools (Fig. 1d), developers of Cluster 4 showed some special characteristics: more frequent use of IPython/Jupyter and PyCharm as well as Pandas and NumPy and less frequent use of most other developer tools such as Docker. Regarding version control systems, however, Git proved to be the standard for developers of all clusters 1e).

4.4   Community

Analyzing the relationship between coding experience and variables of community involvement, we found a weak positive relationship between coding experience and membership and participation but a weak negative relationship between coding experience and visiting Stack Overflow (Table 3). A moderate positive relationship was observed between community membership and Stack Overflow visits as well as Stack Overflow visits and participating in Q&A. Community membership and participation in Q&A also correlated positively, supporting previous findings that a stronger sense of community positively impacts community commitment. The same pattern was found when relationships were analyzed for each cluster separately. Direction and strength of the relationships were the same, with the exception of the relationship between coding experience and Stack Overflow visits in Cluster 4. In this sub-group, coding experience and Stack Overflow visits were unrelated ($r = $ -.00, $p = $ .982).

Table 3. Descriptive statistics for variables of community involvement and correlations (Pearson's correlation coefficient) with coding experience

Variable	n	M	SD	1	2	3	4
1. Coding experience	2,837	15.63	8.93	—			
2. Community membership	2,813	0.03	1.17	.09***	—		
3. Community visits	2,831	3.55	1.04	−.07***	.26***	—	
4. Community participation	2,373	1.38	1.04	.16***	.47***	.31***	—

*p < .05, **p < .01, ***p < .001

As both coding experience and community membership proved to be directly related to community engagement, differences in variables of the community involvement between clusters were tested using one-way ANOVA and Tukey's HSD. Results of the ANOVA showed significant differences for all three aspects of community involvement. The average strength of community membership (Cluster 1 - 4: $M = $ -0.11, $SD = $ 1.19; $M = $ 0.04, $SD = $ 1.17; $M = $ 0.13, $SD = $ 1.16; $M = $ -0.03, $SD = $ 1.15) differed between clusters, $F(3, 2809) = 6.08$, $p < .001$, although pair-wise comparison showed that only developers of Cluster 3 considered themselves significantly more strongly as part of the Stack overflow community than developers of Cluster 1 ($p < .001$; $p > .05$ for all other comparisons). The frequency of visiting Stack Overflow (Cluster 1 - 4: $M = $ 3.54, $SD = $ 1.07; $M = $ 3.61, $SD = $ 1.00; $M = $ 3.60, $SD = $ 1.03; $M = $ 3.21, $SD = $ 1.05) differed between clusters as well, $F(3, 2827) = 12.69$, $p < .001$; in particular developers

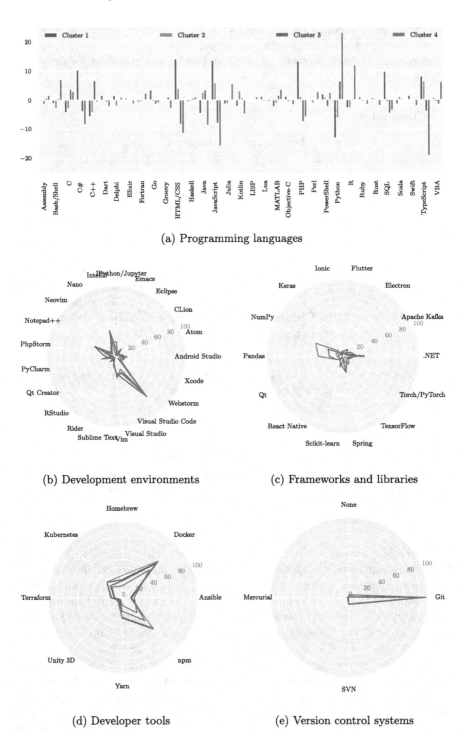

(a) Programming languages

(b) Development environments

(c) Frameworks and libraries

(d) Developer tools

(e) Version control systems

Fig. 1. Comparison of tool use over the past year for four clusters of developers.

of Cluster 4 visited Stack Overflow less often than developers of the other clusters ($p < .001$; $p > .05$ for all other comparisons). Finally, active participation in the Stack Overflow community (Cluster 1 - 4: $M = 1.26$, $SD = 0.96$; $M = 1.35$, $SD = 0.96$; $M = 1.48$, $SD = 1.10$; $M = 1.34$, $SD = 1.06$), that is, asking, answering or voting for questions, was found to be different between clusters, $F(3, 2369) = 6.22$, $p < .001$. Pair-wise comparison showed that developers of Cluster 3 were more engaged in these activities than developers of Cluster 1 ($p < .001$) but not more engaged than developers of Cluster 2 or 4 ($p > .05$ for both comparisons). Comparisons between the other clusters did not reach significance level ($p > .05$). None of the clusters were more or less likely to create a Stack Overflow account (Cluster 1 - 4: 84%, χ^2 $(1, n = 696) = 0.05$, $p = .817$; 84%, χ^2 $(1, n = 737) = 0.00$, $p = .969$; 85%, χ^2 $(1, n = 1105) = 1.13$, $p = .288$; 81%, χ^2 $(1, n = 297) = 2.42$, $p = .119$)

5   Discussion

Cluster analysis is typically used to group objects, persons, or other entities with the aim of identifying groups that share similar characteristics. For instance, in market research, cluster analysis is used to segment customers based on purchasing behaviors, preferences, and demographic factors, enabling more targeted marketing and product strategies. Similarly, here, we were able to identify four sub-groups of developers that could be used to construct the following personas:

(1) **The web developer** who is characterized by moderate programming experience and a distinct specialization in their professional developer career focusing on web development tools. The relatively low educational level is mirrored in lower income rates, suggesting that they might be high school graduates and do not have a professional degree. Nevertheless, they take on programming and development tasks, emphasizing their dedication to acquiring practical skills and experience in the domain.
(2) **The junior developer**, marked by the lowest programming experience, while having a higher educational level than the web developer, is considered to be in the early career phase. They engaged in professional software development and programming with a trend to specialization within their field.
(3) **The senior developer** has the highest programming experience and gets compensated for it more than the other personas. With an above average educational level, they are involved in many different roles, often involving lead functions. For them, the working context is slightly more diverse and requires deeper technological expertise.
(4) **The research developer** represents a niche group characterized by their substantial programming expertise and a distinct inclination towards the research context. They are characterized by a highly diverse range of educational backgrounds, with an average level suggesting a prevalence of advanced educational research degrees. The professional focus here diverges

from explicit software development roles to deeply embedded data analytics ones.

Our results thus underline the significant differences in programming experiences and the early yearly income they receive for their work across the identified clusters, with cluster three standing out for its high levels of both. The educational backgrounds vary strongly. This demonstrates diverse backgrounds and career paths within the German software developer community and is supported by the roles members in each cluster have. With this first glance at the landscape of the German developer community and its structure, we offer valuable insights for employers, educators, and developers themselves. Results emphasize the importance of suitably tailored solutions for workplace design, tool development, and educational and community-building activities. However, with this description of different groups within the community, questions now arise about their influence and connection with requirements for workplace design. As our analysis included only sociodemographic, but no psychometric or behavioral aspects, it also remains unclear whether certain personality traits can be assigned to individual groups and how this could be optimally taken into account in the training and team composition. Besides identifying sub-groups within the community, we also found relationships between coding experience and community involvement among developers in Germany, quantified by their participation in the Stack Overflow community. Findings reveal nuanced dynamics between coding experience, felt community membership, and level of community engagement. Meanwhile, "coding experience" positively correlated with "community membership" "community participation" and "community membership", in turn, with "community participation", indicating that the longer a software developer has been involved in coding, the higher the involvement in the community. Notably, "coding experience" correlated negatively with "community visits" and this relationship did not exist in research software developers. This raises questions about the factors influencing their community engagement, suggesting potential areas for further investigation, such as specific professional needs and alternative support systems. Candidate explanations for this observation could be that the more experienced developers become, the less they need the community knowledge or that, in particular, developers of the research context use other resources. Results also showed significant differences in community involvement across identified clusters where "senior developers" are more engaged in the community compared to "web developers". "Research software developers" visit the community less frequently than the other groups. Results underline the importance of coding experience for a sense of community and engagement. Overall, results highlight a complex interplay between individual experiences and community dynamics. This suggests a need for closer examination of other influencing factors in order to derive implications for community building.

5.1   Limitations

While the present study offers important insights into the diversity of the German software developer community through exploratory cluster analysis, results have to be interpreted with respect to methodological limitations and implications of the data source characteristics. First of all, it should be noted that the study relies on only one community platform and survey data from platform operators. Therefore, the sample is self-selected and biased towards one of many communities within Germany. Additionally, 46% of the initial sample was excluded due to missing responses, which could raise concerns about the potential introduction of non-response bias. The decision to not impute missing values prevented, on the one hand, skewing the data, but on the other hand, this could implicate that the present analysis could have overlooked patterns that might exist within the real world or the complete data set. Additionally, the choice of variables and clustering methods are highly exploratory and subjective. The reliance on pre-selected clustering variables, according to result interpretation, might have been influenced by confirmation bias, inadvertently supporting preconceived notions about the nature of the community. Different choices here might yield different groupings, which influences the study's reproducibility and generalizability of its conclusions. To attempt the latter, we cross-validated findings with a Dutch sub-sample, assuming cultural similarity. However, this additionally might have impacted the transferability. As we analyzed data from a survey that was not designed to address specific research questions and objectives, data on potentially important (human) factors such as attitudes, personality and preferences were not available and could, therefore, not be included in the analysis. Moreover, quality of the available data could not be assessed due to the lack of controls such as seriousness checks. Finally, single-item operationalizations of complex psychological constructs as used here might further affected the validity of our results. Nevertheless, the Stack Overflow Developer Survey data set provided an economical way to explore the German developer community in a large-scale sample.

5.2   Conclusion and Future Work

In conclusion, the present work provides some novel insights into the diversity in the German developer community, highlighting the significance of a strong sense of community. The findings underscore the importance of fostering community engagement and taking further steps to analyze diversity factors and their relation to software developer needs and requirements towards different aspects of community building and workplace design. Future research could investigate the predictors and outcomes of a strong sense of community within the software developer community, not only in large-scale online communities but also in level workplace contexts. By understanding these dynamics, organizations could benefit in terms of knowledge management strategies, enhancing workplace design, or community-building and collaboration strategies. Providing a cluster analysis based on selected variables, including demographic variables beyond education and employment status, might reveal additional insights, especially into the diversity of the developer community.

Acknowledgement. We gratefully acknowledge the HIFIS (Helmholtz Federated IT Services) team for their generous funding and support of our research. For more information on their services, please visit https://www.hifis.net/. The authors also wish to thank Stack Overflow for making the data set publicly available and the numerous respondents for participating in the survey.

Disclosure of Interests. The authors have no competing interests.

References

1. Abfalter, D., Zaglia, M.E., Müller, J., Kraler, F.: Relevanz und messung von sense of community im virtuellen kontext. In: GI-Jahrestagung (2011). https://api.semanticscholar.org/CorpusID:25722258
2. Ahmed, T., Srivastava, A.: Understanding and evaluating the behavior of technical users. A study of developer interaction at stackoverflow. Human-centric Comput. Inf. Sci. **7**, 1–18 (2017). https://doi.org/10.1186/s13673-017-0091-8
3. Aichroth, P., et al.: Wertschöpfung durch software in deutschland (2021)
4. Anderson, A., Huttenlocher, D., Kleinberg, J., Leskovec, J.: Discovering value from community activity on focused question answering sites: a case study of stack overflow. In: Proceedings of the 18th ACM SIGKDD International Conference on Knowledge Discovery and Data Mining, KDD 2012, pp. 850–858. Association for Computing Machinery, New York (2012). https://doi.org/10.1145/2339530.2339665
5. Bagnall, P.: Using Personas Effectively, pp. 221–221 (2007). https://doi.org/10.14236/EWIC/HCI2007.84
6. Bostancioglu, A.: Factors affecting English as a foreign language teachers' participation in online communities of practice: the case of webheads in action. Int. J. Lang. Educ. **4**, 20–35 (2016). https://doi.org/10.18298/IJLET.1651
7. Bruce, P., Bruce, A., Gedeck, P.: Practical Statistics for Data Scientists: 50+ Essential Concepts Using R and Python. O'Reilly Media, Inc. (2020)
8. Cajander, Å., Larusdottir, M., Eriksson, E., Nauwerck, G.: Contextual personas as a method for understanding digital work environments. In: Abdelnour Nocera, J., Barricelli, B.R., Lopes, A., Campos, P., Clemmensen, T. (eds.) HWID 2015. IAICT, vol. 468, pp. 141–152. Springer, Cham (2015). https://doi.org/10.1007/978-3-319-27048-7_10
9. Cameron, C., Wasacase, T.: Community-driven health impact assessment and asset-based community development: an innovate path to community well-being. In: Phillips, R., Wong, C. (eds.) Handbook of Community Well-Being Research. IHQ, pp. 239–259. Springer, Dordrecht (2017). https://doi.org/10.1007/978-94-024-0878-2_13
10. Courage, C., Baxter, K.: Understanding Your Users: A Practical Guide to User Requirements Methods, Tools, and Techniques. Gulf Professional Publishing (2005)
11. Deal, B., Pan, H., Pallathucheril, V., Fulton, G.: Urban resilience and planning support systems: the need for sentience. J. Urban Technol. **24**, 29 – 45 (2017). https://doi.org/10.1080/10630732.2017.1285018
12. Dotan, A., Maiden, N., Lichtner, V., Germanovich, L.: Designing with only four people in mind? – A case study of using personas to redesign a work-integrated learning support system. In: Gross, T., et al. (eds.) INTERACT 2009. LNCS, vol. 5727, pp. 497–509. Springer, Heidelberg (2009). https://doi.org/10.1007/978-3-642-03658-3_54

13. Faisal, M., Issa, G.F., Ayub, I., Asadullah, M., Joiya, U.N., Iqbal, M.: How automate requirements engineering system effects and support requirement engineering. In: 2022 International Conference on Business Analytics for Technology and Security (ICBATS), pp. 1–3 (2022). https://doi.org/10.1109/ICBATS54253.2022.9758997

14. González-Anta, B., Orengo, V., Zornoza, A.M., Peñarroja, V., Martínez-Tur, V.: Understanding the sense of community and continuance intention in virtual communities: the role of commitment and type of community. Soc. Sci. Comput. Rev. **39**, 335 – 352 (2019). https://api.semanticscholar.org/CorpusID:199004874

15. Günzler, P.: Protokoll der fachgruppensitzung der fachgruppe frauen und informatik in naumburg (2023)

16. Gupta, A., Vardhan, H., Varshney, S., Saxena, S., Singh, S., Agarwal, N.: Kconnect: the design and development of versatile web portal for enhanced collaboration and communication. EAI Endorsed Trans. Scalable Inf. Syst. **11**(2), 1–7 (2024)

17. Harris, C.R., et al.: Array programming with NumPy. Nature **585**(7825), 357–362 (2020). https://doi.org/10.1038/s41586-020-2649-2

18. Heller, B., Marschner, E., Rosenfeld, E., Heer, J.: Visualizing collaboration and influence in the open-source software community. In: Proceedings of the 8th Working Conference on Mining Software Repositories, pp. 223–226 (2011). https://doi.org/10.1145/1985441.1985476

19. Hofmann, B., Wulf, V.: Building communities among software engineers: the ViSEK approach to intra- and inter-organizational learning. In: Henninger, S., Maurer, F. (eds.) LSO 2002. LNCS, vol. 2640, pp. 25–33. Springer, Heidelberg (2003). https://doi.org/10.1007/978-3-540-40052-3_4

20. Horwood, C., Youngleson, M.S., Moses, E., Stern, A.F., Barker, P.: Using adapted quality-improvement approaches to strengthen community-based health systems and improve care in high HIV-burden sub-saharan African countries. AIDS **29**, S155–S164 (2015). https://doi.org/10.1097/QAD.0000000000000716

21. Hunter, J.D.: Matplotlib: a 2D graphics environment. Comput. Sci. Eng. **9**(3), 90–95 (2007). https://doi.org/10.1109/MCSE.2007.55

22. Ingram, C., Drachen, A.: How software practitioners use informal local meetups to share software engineering knowledge. In: Proceedings of the ACM/IEEE 42nd International Conference on Software Engineering, pp. 161–173 (2020). https://doi.org/10.1145/3377811.3380333

23. Ismail, A., Sulaiman, S.: A model for knowledge portal to support communities of practice. In: 2011 Malaysian Conference in Software Engineering, pp. 451–457. Johor Bahru, Malaysia (2011). https://doi.org/10.1109/MySEC.2011.6140715

24. Kalliamvakou, E., Damian, D., Singer, L., German, D.M.: The code-centric collaboration perspective: Evidence from github. The Code-Centric Collaboration Perspective: Evidence from Github, Technical Report DCS-352-IR, University of Victoria, p. 17 (2014)

25. Khazaei, A., Elliot, S., Joppe, M.: Fringe stakeholder engagement in protected area tourism planning: inviting immigrants to the sustainability conversation. J. Sustain. Tourism **25**, 1877 – 1894 (2017). https://doi.org/10.1080/09669582.2017.1314485

26. Kraljić, T., Kraljić, A.: ERP implementation: requirements engineering for ERP product customization. In: Themistocleous, M., Papadaki, M. (eds.) EMCIS 2019. LNBIP, vol. 381, pp. 567–581. Springer, Cham (2020). https://doi.org/10.1007/978-3-030-44322-1_42

27. Maida, C., Beck, S.: Towards communities of practice in global sustainability. Anthropology Action **23**, 1–5 (2016). https://doi.org/10.3167/AIA.2016.230101

28. Matthews, T., Whittaker, S., Moran, T., Yang, M.: Collaboration personas: a framework for understanding designing collaborative workplace tools. In: Workshop "Collective Intelligence In Organizations: Toward a Research Agenda." at Computer Supported Cooperative Work (CSCW). Citeseer (2010)

29. McMillan, D.W., Chavis, D.M.: Sense of community: a definition and theory. J. Community Psychol. **14**(1), 6–23 (1986). https://doi.org/10.1002/1520-6629(198601)14:1

30. Miaskiewicz, T., Kozar, K.: Personas and user-centered design: how can personas benefit product design processes? Des. Stud. **32**, 417–430 (2011). https://doi.org/10.1016/J.DESTUD.2011.03.003

31. Middleton, J., et al.: Which contributions predict whether developers are accepted into GitHub teams. In: Proceedings of the 15th International Conference on Mining Software Repositories, pp. 403–413 (2018)

32. Moutidis, I., Williams, H.T.: Community evolution on stack overflow. PLoS ONE **16**(6), e0253010 (2021). https://doi.org/10.1371/journal.pone.0253010

33. Oishi, S., et al.: The socioecological model of procommunity action: the benefits of residential stability. J. Personality Soc. Psychol. **93**(5), 831–844 (2007). https://doi.org/10.1037/0022-3514.93.5.831

34. Oliveira, L., Bradley, C., Birrell, S., Tinworth, N., Davies, A., Cain, R.: Using passenger personas to design technological innovation for the rail industry. In: Kováčiková, T., Buzna, Ľ, Pourhashem, G., Lugano, G., Cornet, Y., Lugano, N. (eds.) INTSYS 2017. LNICST, vol. 222, pp. 67–75. Springer, Cham (2018). https://doi.org/10.1007/978-3-319-93710-6_8

35. Omoto, A.M., Snyder, M.: Influences of psychological sense of community on voluntary helping and prosocial action. In: Stürmer, S., Snyder, M. (eds.) The Psychology of Prosocial Behavior, pp. 223–243. Wiley (2009). https://doi.org/10.1002/9781444307948.ch12, https://onlinelibrary.wiley.com/doi/10.1002/9781444307948.ch12

36. Pedregosa, F., et al.: Scikit-learn: machine learning in Python. J. Mach. Learn. Res. **12**, 2825–2830 (2011)

37. Perkins, D.D., Long, D.A.: Neighborhood sense of community and social capital. In: Snyder, C.R., Fisher, A.T., Sonn, C.C., Bishop, B.J. (eds.) Psychological Sense of Community, pp. 291–318. Springer US, Boston, MA (2002). https://doi.org/10.1007/978-1-4615-0719-2_15, http://link.springer.com/10.1007/978-1-4615-0719-2_15, series Title: The Plenum Series in Social/Clinical Psychology

38. Reed, M., Godmaire, H., Abernethy, P., Guertin, M.: Building a community of practice for sustainability: strengthening learning and collective action of Canadian biosphere reserves through a national partnership. J. Environ. Manage. **145**, 230–9 (2014). https://doi.org/10.1016/j.jenvman.2014.06.030

39. Sarstedt, M., Mooi, E.: Cluster analysis. In: A Concise Guide to Market Research. STBE, pp. 301–354. Springer, Heidelberg (2019). https://doi.org/10.1007/978-3-662-56707-4_9

40. Schäfer, K., et al.: Datenbasierte personas älterer endbenutzer für die zielgruppenspezifische entwicklung innovativer informations-und kommunikationssysteme im gesundheitssektor [data-based personas of older end users for the development of innovative information and communication systems in the health sector for specific target groups]. Zeitschrift für Arbeitswissenschaft **73**(2), 177–192 (2019). https://doi.org/10.1007/s41449-019-00150-5

41. Schäfer, K., et al.: Survey-based personas for a target-group-specific consideration of elderly end users of information and communication systems in the German

health-care sector. Int. J. Med. Informatics **132**, 103924 (2019). https://doi.org/10.1016/j.ijmedinf.2019.07.003

42. Schelhowe, H., et al.: Medienbildung für die persönlichkeitsentwicklung, für die gesellschaftliche teilhabe und für die entwicklung von ausbildungs-und erwerbsfähigkeit (2009)

43. Schlauch, T., Haupt, C.: Using knowledge exchange workshops to analyze the DLR software engineering community. In: 9th International Workshop on Sustainable Software for Science: Practice and Experiences (WSSSPE6.1) (2018). https://doi.org/10.5281/zenodo.1446474

44. Schlauch, T., Haupt, C., Meinel, M., Schreiber, A.: Analytics and insights about cultivating a software engineering community at DLR. In: 2019 IEEE Aerospace Conference, pp. 1–8. IEEE (2019). https://doi.org/10.1109/AERO.2019.8741902

45. Schmitz, C.L., Stinson, C., James, C.D.: Community and environmental sustainability. Critical Social Work **11**(3), 83–100 (2019). https://doi.org/10.22329/CSW.V11I3.5834

46. Schwarz, R., Hellmig, L., Friedrich, S.: Informatik-monitor (2021)

47. Sharon, D., Anderson, T.: Toolbox: a complete software engineering environment; top drawer. IEEE Softw. **14**, 123–127 (1997). https://doi.org/10.1109/52.582983

48. Srba, I., Bielikova, M.: Why is stack overflow failing? preserving sustainability in community question answering. IEEE Softw. **33**(4), 80–89 (2016). https://doi.org/10.1109/MS.2016.34

49. pandas development team, T.: Pandas-dev/pandas: Pandas (2023). https://doi.org/10.5281/zenodo.8092754

50. Trinkenreich, B., Wiese, I., Sarma, A., Gerosa, M., Steinmacher, I.: Women's participation in open source software: a survey of the literature. ACM Trans. Softw. Eng. Methodol. (TOSEM) **31**(4), 1–37 (2022). https://doi.org/10.1145/3510460

51. Vasilescu, B., Filkov, V., Serebrenik, A.: Stackoverflow and GitHub: associations between software development and crowdsourced knowledge. In: 2013 International Conference on Social Computing, pp. 188–195 (2013). https://doi.org/10.1109/SocialCom.2013.35

52. Verma, A.: Critical review of literature of the impact of workforce diversity (specifically age, gender, and ethnic diversity) on organizational competitiveness. Asian J. Manage. **11**, 125–130 (2020). https://doi.org/10.5958/2321-5763.2020.00020.7

53. Virtanen, P., et al.: SciPy 1.0 contributors: SciPy 1.0: fundamental algorithms for scientific computing in Python. Nat. Methods **17**, 261–272 (2020). https://doi.org/10.1038/s41592-019-0686-2

54. Waskom, M.L.: seaborn: statistical data visualization. J. Open Source Softw. **6**(60), 3021 (2021). https://doi.org/10.21105/joss.03021

55. Wen, S.-F., Kianpour, M., Katt, B.: Security knowledge management in open source software communities. In: Lanet, J.-L., Toma, C. (eds.) SECITC 2018. LNCS, vol. 11359, pp. 53–70. Springer, Cham (2019). https://doi.org/10.1007/978-3-030-12942-2_6

Operational Collective Intelligence of Humans and Machines

Nikolos Gurney[1]([✉])[ID], Fred Morstatter[3], David V. Pynadath[1,2][ID],
Adam Russell[3], and Gleb Satyukov[3]

[1] Institute for Creative Technologies, University of Southern California,
Los Angeles 90094, USA
{gurney,pynadath}@ict.usc.edu
[2] Computer Science Department, University of Southern California,
Los Angeles 90007, USA
[3] Information Sciences Institute, University of Southern California,
Los Angeles 90292, USA
{fredmors,arussell,gleb}@isi.edu
http://ict.usc.edu/ , http://www.isi.edu//

Abstract. We explore the use of aggregative crowdsourced forecasting
(ACF) [2,42] as a mechanism to help operationalize "collective intelligence" of human-machine teams for coordinated actions. We adopt
the definition for Collective Intelligence as: "A property of groups that
emerges from synergies among data-information-knowledge, software-
hardware, and individuals (those with new insights as well as recognized authorities) that enables just-in-time knowledge for better decisions than these three elements acting alone." [52] Collective Intelligence
emerges from new ways of connecting humans and AI to enable decision-
advantage, in part by creating and leveraging additional sources of information that might otherwise not be included. Aggregative crowdsourced
forecasting (ACF) is a recent key advancement towards Collective Intelligence wherein predictions (X% probability that Y will happen) and
rationales (why I believe it is this probability that X will happen) are
elicited independently from a diverse crowd, aggregated, and then used to
inform higher-level decision-making. This research asks whether ACF, as
a key way to enable Operational Collective Intelligence, could be brought
to bear on operational scenarios (i.e., sequences of events with defined
agents, components, and interactions) and decision-making, and considers whether such a capability could provide novel operational capabilities
to enable new forms of decision-advantage.

Keywords: Wisdom of the Crowd · Aggregative Crowdsourced
Forecasting · Collective Intelligence · Operational Scenarios · Hybrid
Intelligence

1 Introduction

Collective Intelligence (CI) emerges from new ways of connecting humans and
machines to enable decision-advantage, at least in part, by creating and leveraging additional sources of information that decision-makers might otherwise

H. Mori and Y. Asahi (Eds.): HCII 2024, LNCS 14691, pp. 296–308, 2024.
https://doi.org/10.1007/978-3-031-60125-5_20

not include [1,7,40]. Operational scenarios present a unique challenge for typical collective intelligence approaches. The wisdom of the crowd, the archetypal collective intelligence, works in classic applications, like predicting the weight of a cow, because the probability distributions of responses in these instances have median estimates centered near the ground truth, e.g., the weight of the cow [15,53]. Typical operational scenarios necessitate a different approach because the "crowd" is often heavily biased. For example, in a military setting operators at various levels are privileged to unique knowledge, some of which may alter their predictions in an adversarial reasoning scenario. Moreover, operational scenarios increasingly rely on input from machine intelligence, which decision-makers must integrate with human judgments. Aggregative crowdsourced forecasting (ACF) is a recent, pivotal advancement in CI methods. ACF helps decision-makers from commercial companies, government organizations, and militaries overcome the intractable problem of individual bias by collecting many predictions and integrating the best of machine intelligence into the decision process. To date, ACF has been used for risk management at a strategic level, focusing on tasks like informing policy, anticipating instability, balancing research portfolios, identifying emerging technology, and serving as an early warning mechanism for decision-making.

This document provides a preliminary exploration and evaluation of the potential use of aggregative crowdsourced forecasting as a mechanism to help operationalize "collective intelligence" for operational scenarios. After operationalizing pertinent terminology and laying out the critical research questions, we identify gaps in the research and propose ways of empirically testing solutions to the open questions.

2   Background

The insight that a group of forecasters may be more reliable than a single individual, colloquially known as *the wisdom of a crowd*, is far from new. It is in Aristotle's *Politics* [30] and was famously championed by the British polymath Sir Francis Galton. (Both use the accuracy achieved by statistical aggregation of forecasters as motivation for democracy; Aristotle waxed poetic about art judgments while Galton, more practically, used the statistical accuracy of a crowd's guesses of the dressed weight of a cow to argue that popular judgments are valuable to societies [15].) Modern technology has undeniably changed the dynamics of such crowd wisdom. Although digital technology facilitates aggregation of and eases access to crowd wisdom [27], it can also undermine it because crowd wisdom hinges on natural variation in the forecasters' information. Individual forecasters who use digital technology to change their knowledge of other forecasters' knowledge may become biased and reflect their new knowledge in their forecasts, ultimately undermining the crowd's wisdom [37]. Studying the process of crowd decision-making and how the crowd's wisdom emerges may facilitate mitigation, if not reversal, of digital technology's undermining effects on the crowd wisdom [32,52].

2.1 Collective Intelligence

Collective intelligence (CI) is a "form of universally distributed intelligence, constantly enhanced, coordinated in real-time, and resulting in the effective mobilization of skills" [32]. We are primarily interested in collective intelligence that emerges from new ways of connecting humans and AI to enable decision advantage in instances of adversarial reasoning. Decision advantages are made possible by connections that allow the collective to create and leverage information sources that decision-makers might otherwise not include in a decision process. Adversarial reasoning involves "determining the states, intents, and actions of one's adversary, in an environment where one strives to effectively counter the adversary's actions." [28].

Suran, Pattanaik, and Draheim introduce a convenient, generic framework for conceptualizing CI [52]. They posit that a CI is composed of staff with a goal they are motivated to achieve through some definable process. The "crowd" in this instance is the active staff members who contribute to the CI (some staff in a CI may be passive, e.g., beneficiaries). The CI goal is simply a desired outcome—for example, anticipating an opponent's strategy or recognizing deceptive tactics. Although it is common to think of the goal as being community-driven, individuals may also participate in a CI to achieve their own unique goals: A software engineer may commit updates to an open-source repository to improve its utility for their own project but in so doing advance the collective goal of having a robust, stable resource for a community of users. Since the authors excluded AI systems, motivation is simply the *why* behind contributions to the collective, be it intrinsic (e.g., a passion for the cause) or extrinsic (e.g., money). Lastly, the definable process of a CI describes the staff's interactions in pursuit of the goal—think of the process as the *how* that describes the way in which a CI achieves intelligence.

Each aspect of the Suran, Pattanaik, and Draheim framework builds upon extensive research—they document more than 9,000 publications in the space [52]. We are interested in the process—the how—of CI. Unsurprisingly, many publications in this space develop, review, and refine different CI processes. The project they lean on to develop the process aspect of their generalized framework looked at argument mapping tools, which diagram evidence for and against a cause, to improve online collective efforts [24]. Proper deployment of these decision support systems can improve the process of CI (i.e., lead to better outcomes) by helping staff understand the interactions that transpire during collective decision-making. Of course, decision support systems are continually improving—machine learning and artificial intelligence technologies are dramatically enhancing their capabilities. Contemporary technologies facilitate mapping interactions and enhancing the information generated by those interactions [42]. Such technologies are paving the way for operational collective intelligence.

2.2 Aggregative Crowdsourced Forecasting

We define aggregative crowdsourced forecasting (ACF) as a type of forecasting wherein predictions (X% probability that Y will happen) and rationales (why I believe it is this probability that X will happen) are elicited independently from a diverse crowd and aggregated into a single estimate for informing higher-level decision-making. Aggregation is carried out via machine learning models capable of identifying unique data features that may lead to biased forecasts, accounting for these features, and adjusting the weight of individual forecasts to produce a more reliable crowdsourced estimate.

Conceptualized in this way, ACF is a type of intelligence that plays on the relative strengths of each forecaster to achieve otherwise unobtainable outcomes [2,11,47]. Key features of this type of intelligence include humans and machines working together towards a collective goal, both agent types continually learning and improving, and the ability to achieve superior solutions than either type alone could realize [11]. A core strength of ACF is the machine models and human experts bringing unique skills to bear on their collective goal. The statistical models underpinning machine intelligence are able to accurately and efficiently identify patterns in structured data, which empowers them to make predictions that may avoid human biases. On the other hand, human experts are not reliant on structured data, which empowers them to see features in data that may go unnoticed by machine models. Together, the unique skills of machines and humans allow such an ACF to achieve superior performance.

3   Operational Collective Intelligence

Military, business, and other structured organizations rely on definable common occurrences, known as operational scenarios, to manage people, resources, and processes. Operational scenarios describe sequences of events using a set of defined agents, components, and interactions. Importantly, the agents, whether human or intelligent machines, that eventually carry out organizational processes based on operational scenarios are often privy to unique information that may bias their decision making and behavior. This feature can undermine the strengths of typical approaches to collective intelligence. Consider a military scenario in which field operators are intimately aware of situational factors that command personnel cannot observe while command personnel are privy to classified mission details that they cannot share with operators. Applying ACF, which is able to play on the strengths and weaknesses of different agents, to such operational scenarios may enable *Operational Collective Intelligence* (OCI).

3.1   Research Questions

Addressing several key, basic research questions will help us assess the viability of OCI, the main questions being whether and to what degree ACF has the potential for substantive operational impact. One of the most refined examples of an ACF is the Synergistic Anticipation of Geopolitical Events (SAGE) system [2], which was developed as part of the IARPA Hybrid Forecasting Competition [17]. SAGE is a hybrid forecasting system that gives forecasters the ability to combine their own judgments with model-based solutions. Its development emphasized making verifiable probabilistic predictions while being domain agnostic.

Importantly, empirical results show that SAGE can result in improved aggregate forecasts. One insight is that forecasters needed a base level of expertise to make the most of the inputs provided by SAGE. This observation reinforces previous findings related to crowd-based forecasts [1]. A unique feature of SAGE is its ability to facilitate qualitative (e.g., will a given candidate win a national election) and quantitative questions (e.g., what percent of the vote will each candidate receive).

Machine-aided Analytic Triage with Intelligent Crowd Sourcing (MATRICS) is also a system developed under the IARPA Hybrid Forecasting Competition [23]. Like SAGE, MATRICS combines human and machine predictions to generate a hybrid forecast. It similarly provides human forecasters guidance from a machine intelligence intended to improve their judgments before a final aggregation stage that mixes human and machine forecasts. MATRICS and SAGE differ from other machine-human hybrids in that they explicitly work to integrate wisdom-of-the-crowd models in their computation. Although neither system was explicitly developed as a solution for operational scenarios, the success of both suggests that they could be developed into relevant operational tools.

An earlier system, CrowdSynth, also sought to leverage the relative strengths of human and machine intelligence by having an AI decide how to combine multiple contributions [26]. CrowdSynth was able to optimize engagement with citizen scientists who contributed to a constellation classification task. It accomplished this by balancing expected votes from contributors with a model of what it believed would be the ultimate consensus classification. The interactive intelligence of MATRICS and SAGE differentiates them from CrowdSynth—they not only consider the wisdom of the crowd, but work directly with it to improve the crowd's performance. Although CrowdSynth was able to reduce the number of contributors needed for an accurate classification, it did not have this collective feature.

If we step away from the aggregative, interactive features of SAGE and MATRICS, there are numerous *hybrid intelligence* systems [11]. For example, Dong and coauthors developed a hybrid intelligence algorithm for E-commerce sales volume forecasting [13]. Their simulations suggest that access to the AI system is not always helpful in a purely collaborative scenario—particularly when the humans do not trust the system. Interestingly, more accurate forecasting occurred when the AI was an opponent in a competitive scenario. Another example from Wu et al. uses models of human cognition and examples from human designers, rather than actual humans, to aid an automotive design AI system [58]. They demonstrate that the system is superior to a baseline model that lacks the human model plus knowledge integration and argue that it is capable of exceptional creativity. In yet another example, Russakovsky, Li, and Fei-Fei developed a model that combined multiple algorithmic and human annotations of images to improve overall classification [49]. Although these systems have apparent utility in operational scenarios, including those that require adversarial reasoning, they are limited in that they do not aggregate and/or account for the knowledge, experience, and seniority of human staff. This core feature of ACF is what we believe will set it apart as an operational collective intelligence. However, even though experimentally validated models exist in other domains, there are still pertinent questions to raise about the viability of ACF for operational scenarios.

What Are the Determinants of ACF's Practicality for Operational Scenarios? Aggregative Crowdsourced Forecasting is a data-centric process. The limited amount of ACF research makes formal estimation of data requirements untenable, however, related research points to some guidelines. Training the core machine learning models not only requires more data than is typical for other statistical models, but the data also need to be easy to access, well-structured, and relatively errata free [3,25]. Each element needed to construct a functional ACF will have these requirements. It follows that access to high-quality, relevant training data is a key determinant of successfully deploying ACF in an operational scenario. The very nature of adversarial scenarios means that troves of valuable data are collected and maintained. For example, in a military command and control operational scenario, an effective ACF model will rely on data including features such as the opponent's plans for and perceptions of friendly forces; the opponent's doctrine, tactics, and training; environmental constraints from terrain to weather; capital resources such as ammunition, artillery, communications, personnel, etc.

Access to high-quality data is only half of the modeling task—the modeling technology needs to match the challenge as well. Modeling technology for crowd-sourced forecasting has only recently become broadly viable [21]. In geopolitical modeling, for example, robust forecasting models emerged roughly when access to big data and high-powered computing were democratized [31]. Additionally, even though combining forecasts from different sources, such as human and machine intelligence, is not new, the necessary computational power and algorithm technologies for large-scale modeling are fairly recent developments [56]. The cost of developing, maintaining, and deploying such models means that early ACF models will most likely be applied in settings where the risk of failure and cost of failure are uniquely high.

The need for extant, reliable data and established, state-of-the-art forecast modeling currently limits the operational scenarios for which ACF is a viable instrument. In the cases of SAGE [2] and MATRICS [23], the data were determined and provided by the sponsor of the competition (IARPA [17] plus they were adapted for a well-studied forecasting domain–geopolitical events. Pursuing additional work in this area would undoubtedly allow for model improvement. However, working with new data in other domains may foster faster, more reliable development [25]. One domain with well-defined, studied, and documented operational scenarios is military decision-making [54]. And even though much of military operational data is not publicly available, many military organizations allow researchers to publish appropriately cleaned data to gain access to state-of-the-art machine learning [14], meaning it may prove a viable domain for developing OCI. Other potential domains exist, such as business intelligence, but access issues commonly fetter these data too [44, 45].

What Are the Key Human Factors of a Successful OCI? The goal of operational collective intelligence is to provide ultimate decision-makers with guiding input based on the best of human and machine intelligence. An important aspect of the *how* of OCI is the human staff's response to the machine intelligence. Historically, people preferred human over algorithmic judgment (i.e., machine or artificial intelligence) [10, 12]. Whenever and wherever this tendency still exists, it may challenge OCI. Fortunately, algorithm aversion is not a foregone conclusion of human behavior—increasingly, researchers are observing instances of the opposite, that is, people seeking out algorithmic input [36]. Unfortunately, people occasionally put too much trust in algorithmic decision aids [43, 55], which may also challenge OCI. Thus, a pivotal human factor of a successful OCI is well-calibrated trust in its machine intelligence. A well-calibrated decision-maker will know when to heed and ignore an OCI's input. From a design perspective, this reality suggests a need for implementing tools to measure and predict trust in the OCI [18, 19] along with ways to calibrate that trust. The trust calibration literature is quite broad, but some obvious, simple steps include engineering the messages such that they guide users to the appropriate level of trust [55] and providing interpretable explanations of the system's output [46, 59].

Extensive evidence across a variety of domains supports the observation that a crowd can outperform experts [15, 30, 53]. Nevertheless, expertise still matters: Clever aggregation that weighs individual contributors' forecast relative to their knowledge can yield even wiser crowds [6, 7, 39, 57]. For example, in an image annotation setting where multiple annotators labeled images, modeling individual annotators as multidimensional entities with competence, expertise, and bias variables resulted in better aggregation of their opinions [57]. A similar result was observed in studies that asked participants to forecast current events and economic outcomes [6].

Situational factors, however, may undermine the effect of individual expertise. One study asked participants to estimate corporate earnings and found that having access to public information resulted in participants under-weighting their own private information [9]. This behavior resulted in individual estimates that were more accurate but crowd estimates that were less accurate—a result that underscores how important aggregation that accounts for human factors is to an OCI.

What Are the Key Machine Intelligence Factors of a Successful OCI? The machine intelligence (i.e., algorithmic) factors of a successful OCI are subject to the same limitations as machine learning more generally: they perform best on well-defined tasks [8], when the environment is simple and stable [4], and when high-quality training data are available [48]. Operational scenarios are driven by the need for predictable, defined protocols for common occurrences, meaning that the task is generally well-defined for the machine intelligence that underpins ACF systems. However, one factor that could undermine them could also make OCI invaluable: the ability to handle exceptional task cases. Thus, a critical stage in developing OCI is engineering pathways into the ACF system for handling exceptions. One solution is to empower the ACF model with a classification tool for detecting exceptions [20] and passing exceptional cases off to human staff, who are typically better at handling them [2].

Using operational scenarios is most common in stable, i.e., predictable, environments. However, stable and predictable does not necessarily mean an operational scenario is simple. Many operational scenarios exist as responses to complicated environments in which simplification can improve a given operation. Machine intelligence, at least historically, is not considered an applicable solution for tasks in complex settings, although given sufficient data and training resources, models are able to generalize their learning (e.g., [41]). Innovative modeling approaches in the space of neural-symbolic reasoning, however, may prove a solution for ACF in complex environments [16].

Access to high-quality, operation-relevant data is critical for training an ACF model. Data quality is simply the degree to which archived training data reflects the real world [22]. Moreover, a training data set's relevance is contingent on a given organization and the operational setting. For example, network intrusion detection is complicated by the fact that operational data from one network setting is rarely relevant to another, which creates a lack of training data [51]. Although network data from other operational settings could be used to train a model, it likely will not reflect "the real world" in new network security settings, meaning it is poor-quality data. The impact of poor data quality on a given model is contingent on the type of model and the task at hand [5]—if the cost of errors is low, then poor quality data may be a reasonable tool for getting a model established to facilitate collection of more relevant data [51]. In the case of ACF, data quality may be the result of how the crowd was selected [33,34]. This suggests that an OCI may benefit from tools that allow it to select which training data are used for a given operational scenario.

ACF models are subject to the same generalization challenges as other machine learning models. The models underpinning ACF typically adopt the classic statistical assumption of independent and identically distributed data (i.i.d.)—a very strong assumption that is made necessary by the intractable complexity of its absence. Out-of-Distribution (OOD) data, i.e., real-world data, can prove a significant challenge for these models. ML models for OOD data are still in their nascent phase, but improving [35], including in forecasting applications [50]. Models that are able to handle OOD data that do not abide by the i.i.d. assumption will also prove a key MI factor of successful OCI.

3.2   Potential Operational Collective Intelligence Impact(s)

Research already documents many impacts of human-machine collective intelligence. For example, one application in a healthcare setting demonstrated that significant error reduction is possible by comparing single medical diagnosticians and a CI system—the diagnosticians achieved 46% accuracy versus the system's

76% [29]. A famous, but perhaps underappreciated, example of collective intelligence is Google. It relies on judgments and decisions from people worldwide to refine its representations of content on the web and improve algorithmic recommendations [38]. The general impact of Google on individual decision-makers, collectives, and society at large is undeniable (and likely impossible to estimate). Similarly, enumerating the unique ways in which it has changed the course of human history is probably impossible.

Military, business, and other organizations define operational scenarios to improve operational outcomes. Outcome improvements result from using operational scenarios during training and simulation settings, which aids staff in learning what decision features to focus on, and using them during actual operations, which may aid staff in identifying anomalous features of an operation. We envision OCI improving organizations' decision accuracy by improving their ability to listen to the most knowledgeable staff, adapt to unpredictable scenarios by recognizing situations in which machine intelligence is underspecified, and increase decision speed by leveraging the system's ability to process new data relative to human staff alone. In an adversarial reasoning scenario, whether in military, business, or political settings, such an increase in decision time could allow an organization to gain a competitive advantage.

4   Discussion

Research documents impressive outcomes of combining human and machine intelligence, i.e., Collective Intelligence, to solve complex operational problems [52]. Significant advances in machine learning have facilitated aggregative crowdsourced forecasting, a CI capable of taking the best input from individual staff members of a crowd and intelligently guiding decisions [2,42]. Applying this technology to operational scenarios, we believe, is a way to realize Operational Collective Intelligence.

4.1   Advantages

OCI's main advantage lies in its ability to integrate human and machine intelligence while applying lessons learned from crowd wisdom quickly and accurately. Human decision-makers are simply not capable of considering troves of data or agnostically weighing input from a large number of forecasters in the same fashion. For example, a robust OCI could consider seasonal variations in the weather, such variations' impacts on operators' well-being, and the cost of delays without referring to outside resources in minutes if not seconds. It is not unreasonable for a human decision-maker to rely on a cadre of workers for each sub-prediction, which might require hours or days, and then when they integrate the various outputs, allow their own biased judgment to impact how they weigh the input from different forecasting teams.

4.2   Practicality

The key to OCI's practicality is data. The lock is well-designed machine intelligence. Without these, OCI may prove more of a hindrance than a benefit. ACF models are only as good as the data used to train them. Current state-of-the-art ACF models require more data than is typical for other statistical models, underscoring the importance of having ready access to well-structured, errata-free data [3,25]. Without such data, OCI is not practical. Additionally, although considerable effort has already gone into designing and validating ACF models, such as what is reported in [2], much work is still needed to ensure the practicality of an OCI that hinges on ACF.

The staff interacting with an OCI and their responses to it are of similar importance. Despite historical evidence of people being averse to algorithmic input [12], there is increasing evidence that people not only support but seek out algorithmic aid [36]. With this increased willingness to rely on algorithmic decision aids like OCI comes an increased need to ensure that the human staff of an operation is well-calibrated to its use [46,55].

5   Conclusion

Aggregative crowdsourced forecasting helps decision-makers overcome intractable forecasting problems, such as individual biases, by collecting many predictions and integrating the best of machine intelligence into the decision process. Operational scenarios are an obvious application of this recent advancement in collective intelligence, but translating existing ACF models for operational scenario application is not straightforward. Data, modeling, and human factors make this translation a challenge. ACF is a data-centric process in which each element requires readily available data that are well-structured and relatively errata-free. Fortunately, there are many operational applications, such as adversarial scenarios, in which troves of such data are collected. ACF also hinges on state-of-the-art forecasting models that require considerable computational resources. Beyond the data and computational requirements are the human factors of operational scenarios, from how the human staff responds to machine intelligence to their relative expertise. Addressing these challenges will enable ACF to unlock operational collective intelligence, which we believe will prove a pivotal advancement in the coordinated action of human-machine teams.

Acknowledgments. The project or effort depicted was or is sponsored by the U.S. Government under contract number W911NF-14-D-0005. The content of the information does not necessarily reflect the position or the policy of the Government, and no official endorsement should be inferred.

Disclosure of Interests. The authors have no competing interests to declare that are relevant to the content of this article.

References

1. Atanasov, P., et al.: Distilling the wisdom of crowds: prediction markets vs. prediction polls. Manag. Sci. **63**(3), 691–706 (2017)
2. Benjamin, D.M., et al.: Hybrid forecasting of geopolitical events. AI Mag. (2023)
3. Bollier, D., Firestone, C.M., et al.: The promise and peril of big data. Aspen Institute, Communications and Society Program Washington, DC (2010)
4. Brynjolfsson, E., Mitchell, T.: What can machine learning do? Workforce implications. Science **358**(6370), 1530–1534 (2017)
5. Budach, L., et al.: The effects of data quality on machine learning performance. arXiv preprint arXiv:2207.14529 (2022)
6. Budescu, D.V., Chen, E.: Identifying expertise to extract the wisdom of crowds. Manage. Sci. **61**(2), 267–280 (2015)
7. Budescu, D.V., Fiedler, K., et al.: Confidence in aggregation of opinions from multiple sources. In: Information Sampling and Adaptive Cognition, pp. 327–352 (2006)
8. Christiano, P.F., Leike, J., Brown, T., Martic, M., Legg, S., Amodei, D.: Deep reinforcement learning from human preferences. In: Advances in Neural Information Processing Systems, vol. 30 (2017)
9. Da, Z., Huang, X.: Harnessing the wisdom of crowds. Manage. Sci. **66**(5), 1847–1867 (2020)
10. Dawes, R.M., Faust, D., Meehl, P.E.: Clinical versus actuarial judgment. Science **243**(4899), 1668–1674 (1989)
11. Dellermann, D., Ebel, P., Söllner, M., Leimeister, J.M.: Hybrid intelligence. Bus. Inf. Syst. Eng. **61**, 637–643 (2019)
12. Dietvorst, B.J., Simmons, J.P., Massey, C.: Algorithm aversion: people erroneously avoid algorithms after seeing them err. J. Exp. Psychol. Gen. **144**(1), 114 (2015)
13. Dong, L., Zheng, H., Li, L., Hao, L.: Human-machine hybrid prediction market: a promising sales forecasting solution for e-commerce enterprises. Electron. Commer. Res. Appl. **56**, 101216 (2022)
14. Galán, J.J., Carrasco, R.A., LaTorre, A.: Military applications of machine learning: a bibliometric perspective. Mathematics **10**(9), 1397 (2022)
15. Galton, F.: Vox populi. Nature **75**(1949), 450–451 (1907)
16. Garcez, A.D., et al.: Neural-symbolic learning and reasoning: a survey and interpretation. In: Neuro-Symbolic Artificial Intelligence: The State of the Art, vol. 342, no. 1, p. 327 (2022)
17. Goldstein, S.: December 2015. https://www.iarpa.gov/research-programs/hfc
18. Gurney, N., Pynadath, D.V., Wang, N.: Measuring and predicting human trust in recommendations from an AI teammate. In: Degen, H., Ntoa, S. (eds.) HCII 2022. LNCS, vol. 13336, pp. 22–34. Springer, Cham (2022). https://doi.org/10.1007/978-3-031-05643-7_2
19. Gurney, N., Pynadath, D.V., Wang, N.: Comparing psychometric and behavioral predictors of compliance during human-AI interactions. In: Meschtscherjakov, A., Midden, C., Ham, J. (eds) PERSUASIVE 2023, vol. 13832, pp. 175–197. Springer, Cham (2023). https://doi.org/10.1007/978-3-031-30933-5_12
20. Haixiang, G., Yijing, L., Shang, J., Mingyun, G., Yuanyue, H., Bing, G.: Learning from class-imbalanced data: review of methods and applications. Expert Syst. Appl. **73**, 220–239 (2017)
21. Hassani, H., Silva, E.S.: Forecasting with big data: a review. Ann. Data Sci. **2**, 5–19 (2015)

22. Heinrich, B., Hristova, D., Klier, M., Schiller, A., Szubartowicz, M.: Requirements for data quality metrics. J. Data Inf. Qual. (JDIQ) **9**(2), 1–32 (2018)
23. Huber, D.J., et al.: MATRICS: a system for human-machine hybrid forecasting of geopolitical events. In: 2019 IEEE International Conference on Big Data (Big Data), pp. 2028–2032. IEEE (2019)
24. Iandoli, L., Klein, M., Zollo, G.: Enabling on-line deliberation and collective decision-making through large-scale argumentation: a new approach to the design of an internet-based mass collaboration platform. Int. J. Decis. Support Syst. Technol. (IJDSST) **1**(1), 69–92 (2009)
25. Jordan, M.I., Mitchell, T.M.: Machine learning: trends, perspectives, and prospects. Science **349**(6245), 255–260 (2015)
26. Kamar, E., Hacker, S., Horvitz, E.: Combining human and machine intelligence in large-scale crowdsourcing. In: AAMAS, vol. 12, pp. 467–474 (2012)
27. Kameda, T., Toyokawa, W., Tindale, R.S.: Information aggregation and collective intelligence beyond the wisdom of crowds. Nat. Rev. Psychol. **1**(6), 345–357 (2022)
28. Kott, A., Ownby, M.: Toward a research agenda in adversarial reasoning: computational approaches to anticipating the opponent's intent and actions. arXiv preprint arXiv:1512.07943 (2015)
29. Kurvers, R.H., Nuzzolese, A.G., Russo, A., Barabucci, G., Herzog, S.M., Trianni, V.: Automating hybrid collective intelligence in open-ended medical diagnostics. Proc. Natl. Acad. Sci. **120**(34), e2221473120 (2023)
30. Landemore, H.: Collective wisdom: old and new. In: Collective Wisdom: Principles and Mechanisms, vol. 1, pp. 1–20 (2012)
31. Leigh, A., Wolfers, J.: Competing approaches to forecasting elections: economic models, opinion polling and prediction markets. Econ. Rec. **82**(258), 325–340 (2006)
32. Levy, P., Bononno, R.: Collective Intelligence: Mankind's Emerging World in Cyberspace. Perseus Books, USA (1997)
33. Li, H., Liu, Q.: Cheaper and better: selecting good workers for crowdsourcing. In: Proceedings of the AAAI Conference on Human Computation and Crowdsourcing, vol. 3, pp. 20–21 (2015)
34. Li, H., Zhao, B., Fuxman, A.: The wisdom of minority: discovering and targeting the right group of workers for crowdsourcing. In: Proceedings of the 23rd International Conference on World Wide Web, pp. 165–176 (2014)
35. Liu, J., et al.: Towards out-of-distribution generalization: a survey. arXiv preprint arXiv:2108.13624 (2021)
36. Logg, J.M., Minson, J.A., Moore, D.A.: Algorithm appreciation: people prefer algorithmic to human judgment. Organ. Behav. Hum. Decis. Process. **151**, 90–103 (2019)
37. Lorenz, J., Rauhut, H., Schweitzer, F., Helbing, D.: How social influence can undermine the wisdom of crowd effect. Proc. Natl. Acad. Sci. **108**(22), 9020–9025 (2011)
38. Malone, T.W., Laubacher, R., Dellarocas, C.: The collective intelligence genome. MIT Sloan Manag. Rev. (2010)
39. Mannes, A.E., Soll, J.B., Larrick, R.P.: The wisdom of select crowds. J. Pers. Soc. Psychol. **107**(2), 276 (2014)
40. Mellers, B., et al.: Psychological strategies for winning a geopolitical forecasting tournament. Psychol. Sci. **25**(5), 1106–1115 (2014)
41. Mnih, V., et al.: Human-level control through deep reinforcement learning. Nature **518**(7540), 529–533 (2015)
42. Morstatter, F., et al.: SAGE: a hybrid geopolitical event forecasting system. In: IJCAI, vol. 1, pp. 6557–6559 (2019)

43. Parasuraman, R., Riley, V.: Humans and automation: use, misuse, disuse, abuse. Hum. Fact. **39**(2), 230–253 (1997)

44. Peled, A.: The politics of big data: a three-level analysis. In: European Consortium of Political Research (ECPR) General Conference, Bordeaux, France (2013)

45. Pencheva, I., Esteve, M., Mikhaylov, S.J.: Big data and AI-a transformational shift for government: so, what next for research? Public Policy Adm. **35**(1), 24–44 (2020)

46. Pynadath, D.V., Gurney, N., Wang, N.: Explainable reinforcement learning in human-robot teams: the impact of decision-tree explanations on transparency. In: 2022 31st IEEE International Conference on Robot and Human Interactive Communication (RO-MAN), pp. 749–756. IEEE (2022)

47. Rafner, J., et al.: Revisiting citizen science through the lens of hybrid intelligence. arXiv preprint arXiv:2104.14961 (2021)

48. Ratner, B.: Statistical and Machine-Learning Data Mining: Techniques for Better Predictive Modeling and Analysis of Big Data. CRC Press (2017)

49. Russakovsky, O., Li, L.J., Fei-Fei, L.: Best of both worlds: human-machine collaboration for object annotation. In: Proceedings of the IEEE Conference on Computer Vision and Pattern Recognition, pp. 2121–2131 (2015)

50. Shoeibi, A., et al.: Automated detection and forecasting of covid-19 using deep learning techniques: a review. Neurocomputing, 127317 (2024)

51. Sommer, R., Paxson, V.: Outside the closed world: on using machine learning for network intrusion detection. In: 2010 IEEE Symposium on Security and Privacy, pp. 305–316. IEEE (2010)

52. Suran, S., Pattanaik, V., Draheim, D.: Frameworks for collective intelligence: a systematic literature review. ACM Comput. Surv. (CSUR) **53**(1), 1–36 (2020)

53. Surowiecki, J.: The Wisdom of Crowds. Anchor (2005)

54. Svenmarck, P., Luotsinen, L., Nilsson, M., Schubert, J.: Possibilities and challenges for artificial intelligence in military applications. In: Proceedings of the NATO Big Data and Artificial Intelligence for Military Decision Making Specialists' Meeting, pp. 1–16 (2018)

55. Wang, N., Pynadath, D.V., Hill, S.G.: Trust calibration within a human-robot team: comparing automatically generated explanations. In: 2016 11th ACM/IEEE International Conference on Human-Robot Interaction (HRI), pp. 109–116. IEEE (2016)

56. Wang, X., Hyndman, R.J., Li, F., Kang, Y.: Forecast combinations: an over 50-year review. Int. J. Forecast. **39**(4), 1518–1547 (2023)

57. Welinder, P., Branson, S., Perona, P., Belongie, S.: The multidimensional wisdom of crowds. In: Advances in Neural Information Processing Systems, vol. 23 (2010)

58. Wu, Y., Ma, L., Yuan, X., Li, Q.: Human-machine hybrid intelligence for the generation of car frontal forms. Adv. Eng. Inform. **55**, 101906 (2023)

59. Zhang, Y., Liao, Q.V., Bellamy, R.K.: Effect of confidence and explanation on accuracy and trust calibration in AI-assisted decision making. In: Proceedings of the 2020 Conference on Fairness, Accountability, and Transparency, pp. 295–305 (2020)

ARM-COMS Motor Display System for Active Listening in Remote Communication

Teruaki Ito[✉] and Tomio Watanabe

Faculty of Computer Science and System Engineering, Okayama Prefectural University,
111 Kuboki, Soja 719-1197, Okayama, Japan
tito@ss.oka-pu.ac.jp

Abstract. Communication involves transferring information from one place, person, or group to another, typically comprising a sender, a message, and a recipient. During interactions, humans exchange various social signals and information. There are two main types of communication: verbal and nonverbal. Even when verbal communication isn't feasible, nonverbal cues like gestures and body movements can facilitate communication. Hence, nonverbal communication plays a vital role in human-robot interaction. Implementing responsive strategies enables the creation of attentive listening systems. Recent research focuses on enhancing robot interactions through attentive listening systems, aiming to establish interfaces that foster affinity and a sense of connection with robots. The authors propose ARM-COMS for remote conferences, utilizing monitors as avatars for remote participants. This interface not only detects remote participants' head movements to coordinate actions but also responds to the voices of both remote participants and speakers, physically moving the monitor to enhance interaction. This paper explores these differences and discusses the philosophy behind ARM-COMS from the perspective of attentive listening, aiming to enhance interaction with remote participants.

Keywords: Embodied communication · Augmented tele-presence robotic arm · Robot operating system · Natural involvement · Emotional projection

1 Introduction

As cutting-edge interface technologies such as AR, VR, MR, and the Metaverse continue to gain widespread acceptance, personal video communication tools have become ubiquitous. With DX technology spurred by IoT [23], Society 5.0 [38] and Industry 4.0 [23], these communication tools are expected to develop using the latest technologies such as AR, VR or Metaverse [5] tools. [21]. They're no longer solely for personal chats [4], but are also extensively utilized in business meetings, conferences, telecommuting, healthcare [24], and beyond. These interfaces are also anticipated to revolutionize the field of human-robot interactions. One promising example would be healthcare. With the number of isolated elderly individuals on the rise, facing limited opportunities for social interaction, there's a growing interest in attentive listening robots. These robots

© The Author(s), under exclusive license to Springer Nature Switzerland AG 2024
H. Mori and Y. Asahi (Eds.): HCII 2024, LNCS 14691, pp. 309–318, 2024.
https://doi.org/10.1007/978-3-031-60125-5_21

aim to provide companionship and increase the chances for elderly individuals living alone to engage in meaningful conversations. Research is ongoing to develop talking robots for addressing the situation [26].

"Active Listening" [5] refers to an approach in communication where the listener seeks to draw out the emotions of the speaker through conversation and provides support for the speaker to solve problems on their own. This method involves not just hearing the words spoken but also understanding the speaker's emotions and intentions. Active Listening aims to be sensitive to the speaker's feelings and thoughts, offering appropriate support and insights. Ultimately, it enhances communication, allowing the speaker to move towards self-directed problem-solving.

This research originated from the concept of a motion-enhanced display [47], aiming to impart a sense of presence by synchronizing the movement of a physical monitor with virtual content. For instance, the idea was born from the recognition that physically rotating a monitor to match the movement of a spinning football depicted on-screen could yield a more immersive experience than simply displaying the spinning football statically. Expanding on this concept, the study applies motion-coordinated display to a video communication system, enhancing the sense of presence by physically moving the monitor in tandem with the displayed movement of the remote party during teleconferencing. This system, known as ARM-COMS (ARm-supported eMbodied COmmunication Monitor System) [10, 15, 16], facilitates human-computer interaction via augmented telepresence systems connecting remote individuals. It was observed that the motion generated by ARM-COMS prompted reciprocal physical movements between the user and their remote communication partner. The challenge lies in crafting cyber-physical media tailored for remote communication via ARM-COMS, a task accomplished by leveraging human head motions in remote locations. These motions serve as nonverbal messages within active listening interactions.

2   Critical Role of Nonverbal Communication

Communication is basically the act of transferring information from one place, person or group to another. Every communication involves (at least) one sender, a message and a recipient. Communication is said to serve five major purposes: to inform, to express feelings, to imagine, to influence, and to meet social expectations. Each of these purposes is reflected in a form of communication. When communicating with others, humans exchange various social signals, information, others. There are two types of communication: "Verbal communication," which involves language information such as conversation, written words or printed materials, and "Nonverbal communication," which refers to communication without the use of language.

Verbal communication is the words and sounds that come out of our mouths when we're speaking, including tone of voice and things like sighs and groans. Verbal communication techniques include paraphrasing, clarifying, and reflecting feelings. Rephrasing is what the speaker has said to demonstrate understanding. Clarifying seeks further information or clarification to ensure accurate comprehension. Acknowledging and expressing understand the speaker's emotions.

Nonverbal communication is also known as non-language communication, and it includes gestures [31] such as nodding, facial expressions, eye contact, vocal pitch and tone, and gestures. Facial Expressions use facial expressions to show empathy, interest, or understanding. Eye Contact maintains appropriate and attentive eye contact to convey engagement. As for gestures, body language utilizes open and receptive body gesture to enhance communication. For example, nodding provides affirming gestures to signal attentiveness and agreement. "Non-verbal" plays a crucial role in human communication. With the increasing diversity in work styles and the promotion of remote work due to infection control measures, the use of "nonverbal" communication becomes crucial in this online era.

Communication is not only for humans but also for animals because communication is simply the act of transferring information from one place, animal or group to another. Animals do not use languages which can be understood by humans, but they use nonverbal communication methods as well as barking. For example, dogs communicate with each other using sound, scent, facial expressions and body positions [36]. Their sense of smell is their mostly highly refined ability and they use scent as their major means of communication. Dogs do not use language as humans do. However, humans can communicate with dogs via nonverbal communication, such as touching, eye-contact, gesture, etc.

"Nonverbal communication" plays an important role in human communication. With the diversification of work styles and the promotion of remote work due to infection control measures, nonverbal communication becomes increasingly important in such online times. However, fundamental problems have been pointed out, such as the inability to convey the presence of the remote person, the inability to share the atmosphere of the place, and the inability to feel the relationship with the remote person.

3   Active Listening in Nonverbal Communication

The number of isolated elderly people with few opportunities to talk to other people is currently increasing as mentioned in the introduction. There has been growing interest in active listening robots as a solution to increase opportunities for elderly individuals living alone to engage in conversation more often [38]. Research is ongoing to develop talking robots for addressing the situation.

"Active Listening" refers to an approach in communication where the listener seeks to draw out the emotions of the speaker through conversation and provides support for the speaker to solve problems on their own [41]. This method involves not just hearing the words spoken but also understanding the speaker's emotions and intentions. Active Listening aims to be sensitive to the speaker's feelings and thoughts, offering appropriate support and insights. Ultimately, it enhances communication, allowing the speaker to move towards self-directed problem-solving.

Active Listening, also known as the "listening posture," is a communication technique and refers to the listening posture advocated by Carl Rogers, an American clinical psychologist who increased awareness in client-centered therapy [31]. His central idea in the Rogerian approach is that if the practitioner is empathetic, accepts the client with unconditional positive regard, and is genuine in his or her respect for the client, positive change will occur [10]. Currently, there is a growing effort to apply this approach in business settings.

The distinctive feature of active listening is that, during a conversation, it goes beyond just attentively hearing the other person's words. Instead, it involves understanding the essential points and emotions the speaker wants to convey, actively grasping the content.

Empathy in active listening is the ability to resonate with and understand the feelings and perspectives of others [33]. The listener empathizes by putting themselves in the speaker's shoes and adopting an attitude of understanding as if it were their own experience. Nodding along and expressing empathy with phrases like "That must have been tough" or "That sounds difficult" show an understanding of the emotions the speaker is experiencing.

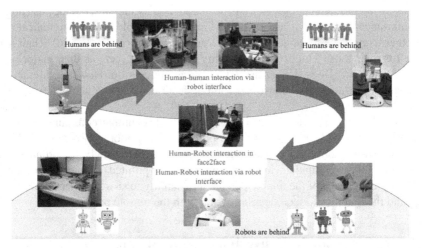

Fig. 1. Nonverbal communication as an interface for human-robot interaction

"Giving verbal nods" refers to responding to the speaker by adjusting one's responses to match their rhythm [17]. Key points include "showing interest in the conversation," "understanding the speaker's words as they are," "asking questions about unclear content," and "striving to give moderate and natural verbal nods."

In typical echoing, you simply repeat what the other person said. However, in active listening, echoing is used to identify the key points in the conversation and encourage the speaker to focus on these points, handling their words with care.

Listening dialogue refers to a state of actively listening to the other person's story. By providing appropriate reactions and empathy, it is possible to fulfill the speaker's needs. With a focus on the aging society in recent years, research has been conducted to emphasize the importance of having someone who listens to conversations regularly for the mental well-being of the elderly. The system developed by Kawahara et al. [18] demonstrates the ability to evoke a sense of having been sufficiently listened to by employing a variety of listener responses, such as acknowledgments, repetitions, empathetic responses, and in-depth questions. Sejima et al. focused on enhancing the eye-impressions of social robots to convey emotions effectively during face-to-face communication.

4 Nonverbal Communication Support System

As mentioned in the previous chapters, while the importance of nonverbal communication in communication is acknowledged, misunderstandings often arise from the insufficient understanding of nonverbal communication. Then, what does it mean to support nonverbal communication? The role of the human interface becomes crucial in facilitating this. The interface between people is embodied by robots, thus falling within the field of Human-Robot Interaction. Figure 1 illustrates the interface robot developed in the authors' research. Broadly speaking, it consists of two categories: avatar robots that facilitate communication between distant individuals, and the other one is interfaces designed to enhance affinity with robots through human-robot interaction [2]. Both human and interface robot interaction are crucial functions. However, in the former, there is a human behind the interaction, while in the latter, there is no human presence behind the interaction.

Examples of the former include telepresence robots that can be remotely operated as one's avatar, and active display systems that implement features to make communication in remote video conferences more akin to face-to-face conversations. Examples of the latter include interaction robots with force feedback, robot control interfaces that respond to hand movements, and humanoid robot interfaces that interact through voice dialogue and motion responses.

Interest in human-robot interaction is increasingly growing, with reports indicating significant improvements in affinity between humans and robots through the actions of robots. In recent years, research on robot listening systems [11] has also flourished as mentioned in the previous chapter, with efforts focused on incorporating active listening behaviors into robots. The robot Pocobee [42] for the elderly developed by Toyota Motor Corporation. The study focused on enhancing the eye-impressions of social robots to convey emotions effectively during face-to-face communication. a speech-driven pupil response system synchronized pupil dilation with speech, further enhancing emotional expression. Ishiguro et al. proposes a dialogue strategy called Agreebot Introduction Dialogue [38] to enhance the acceptability of robot statements related to actions that robots are incapable of performing.

Technology aimed at assisting in caregiving, including caregiving robots, is being developed one after another. Initiatives utilizing technologies such as AI are also beginning to emerge in the prevention and care of dementia. In these robots, interaction with robots is indeed enhanced, and there is a recognized effect where it seems as if the robot is actively listening, creating an illusion of empathy. One of the challenges faced by elderly individuals living alone is the reduced opportunity for social interaction. Social isolation is a contributing factor to frailty, a precursor to requiring care, and it also increases the risk of developing dementia [12]. Communication robots serving as companions for elderly individuals or acting as substitutes for pets have been shown to alleviate feelings of loneliness among the elderly, as evidenced by various empirical studies.

However, while it's possible to interact with emotionally and intellectually responsive pets, communicating with a robot, which inherently lacks emotions and understanding, can be seen as merely utilizing a convenient interface for exchanging commands. This doesn't imply that listening robots are not useful; rather, it's important to consider them as tools facilitating communication for mutual understanding between humans. When there's a human presence behind the listening robot, facilitating communication for mutual understanding, the significance of listening robots becomes substantial. Therefore, the Communication Support Robot (ARM-COMS) that the authors are researching is based on this perspective, aiming to be a communication aid robot aligned with these principles.

5 System Configuration to Control ARM-COMS

Concentrating on head movements as nonverbal cues crucial in face-to-face communication, the authors have introduced the concept of a motion-enhanced display. This innovative display aims to evoke a sense of presence by synchronizing the movement of a physical monitor with the virtual content displayed on the screen. To bring this idea to life, the authors developed a prototype system called ARM-COMS for remote conferencing. This system seamlessly integrates a tablet terminal with a robotic arm, enabling physical movement of the tablet. ARM-COMS comprises a tablet PC and a desktop robotic arm. The tablet PC, a common ICT device, serves as the interface, while the desktop robot arm acts as a manipulator for the tablet. Its position and movements are autonomously controlled based on the motions of a remote user engaging via ARM-COMS.

The autonomous operation of ARM-COMS relies on head movements detected by a standard USB camera using the FaceNET [36] concept. These movements are processed using the OpenCV [26] image processing library and the OpenFace [2, 28] face detection tool, which utilizes a Constrained Local Network Field (CLNF) for precise detection. Facial analysis is further enhanced by the Haar Cascade face detector, which identifies brightness differences using rectangles of various sizes. Subsequently, 68 landmarks are defined using the dlib library [7], enabling estimation of the subject's head orientation by the OpenFace tool. This dynamic attitude data is then utilized to control ARM-COMS.

Furthermore, ARM-COMS is a highly responsive system by responding to the voice of the local and remote subjects. Synchronizing head movements to increase accuracy can create a sense of presence, and the introduction of remote and local voice control has improved the responsiveness of reactions. Thanks to the introduction of control mechanism based on audio signals, ARM-COMS showed appropriate response by voice signals during a call even if there is no significant head movement when the remote subject responds.

The system configuration of ARM-COMS and the control procedure are depicted in Fig. 2. The ARM-COMS manipulator comprises 6 pairs of servo motors and motor controllers, a single board computer running Ubuntu [12, 41] as the operating system, with ROS [9, 25, 31, 44] as middleware, along with a speaker, microphone, and camera. ARM-COMS replicates the head movements of remote communication partners during video conversations, which enables active listening during remote communication.

In order to generate lifelike movements and to create empathetic spatial arrangements, ARM-COMS employs a deep generative model that integrates visual information from network cameras, direct training data instructing movement by human actions, and characteristic movements obtained from interactions with users. In other words, it serves as a module for robots to understand their environment and generate natural movements aimed at specific purposes, leveraging various multimodal information available to the robot.

Implementing a face-to-face interaction feature for autonomous control of ARM-COMS involves integrating control data derived from voice and camera images used in the system's basic configuration with control signals generated by AI modules.

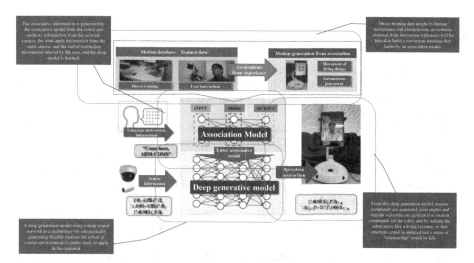

Fig. 2. System concept of ARM-COMS

6   Concluding Remarks

When there's a human presence behind the listening robot, facilitating communication for mutual understanding, the significance of listening robots becomes substantial. Therefore, the Communication Support Robot (ARM-COMS) that we are researching is based on this perspective, aiming to be a communication aid robot aligned with these principles. Focusing on head movements and audio information, such intonation, segmentation of speech, speech response, as non-verbal information in face-to-face communication, the authors have reported a method for realizing the relationship with a remote person by linking the movements with a motion-enhanced display.

Expectations for listening systems are increasingly growing, and today, research and product development tailored to meet these expectations are thriving. It is believed that the listening function plays a crucial role in realizing user-friendly interfaces for humans. By understanding human intentions and responding accordingly, computers can achieve better Human-Computer Interaction (HCI). However, no matter how clever the response may be, it is still the satisfaction of humans rather than computers understanding humans. This is fundamentally different from animals understanding humans. In this study, the importance of the listening function is discussed, and the concept of ARM-COMS for supporting human understanding through the listening function is elaborated.

Acknowledgement. This work was partly supported by JSPS KAKENHI Grant Numbers JP22K12131, Science and Technology Award 2022 of Okayama Foundation for Science and Technology, Original Research Grant 2023 of Okayama Prefectural University. The author would like to acknowledge Assoc. Prof. Takashi OYAMA, Mitsutoshi ABE and all members of Kansei Information Engineering Labs at Okayama Prefectural University for their cooperation to conduct the experiments.

References

1. Anotation. https://atonaton.com/. Accessed 12 Feb 2023
2. Anzabi, N., Umemuro, H.: Effect of different listening behaviors of social robots on perceived trust in human-robot interactions. Int. J. Soc. Robotics **15**, 931–951 (2023). https://doi.org/10.1007/s12369-023-01008-x
3. Baltrušaitis, T., Robinson, P., Morency, L.P.: OpenFace: an open source facial behavior analysis toolkit. In: 2016 IEEE Winter Conference on Applications of Computer Vision (WACV), Lake Placid, NY, USA, pp. 1–10 (2016). https://doi.org/10.1109/WACV.2016.7477553
4. Bertrand, C., Bourdeau, L.: Research interviews by Skype: a new data collection method. In: Esteves, J. (ed.) Proceedings from the 9th European Conference on Research Methods, pp. 70–79. IE Business School, Spain (2010)
5. Boston University: Active Listening Handout. Office of the Ombuds, Boston University (N.d.). https://www.bumc.bu.edu/facdev-medicine/files/2016/10/Active-Listening-Handout.pdf. Accessed July 2023
6. Dionisio, J.D.N., Burns III, W.G., Gilbert, R.: 3D Virtual worlds and the metaverse: current status and future possibilities. ACM Comput. Surv. **45**(3), 1–38 (2013). https://doi.org/10.1145/2480741.2480751. Article No. 34
7. Dlib c++ libraty. http://dlib.net/. Accessed 12 Feb 2023
8. Ekman, P., Friesen, W.V.: The repertoire or nonverbal behavior: categories, origins, usage, and coding. Semiotica **1**, 49–98 (1969)
9. Gerkey B., Smart, W., Quigley, M.: Programming Robots with ROS, O'Reilly Media, Sebastopol (2015)
10. Greene, R.R.: Carl Rogers and the person-centered approach. In: Human Behavior Theory & Social Work Practice, pp. 113–132 (2017)
11. González, A.L., Geiskkovitch, D.Y., Young, J.E.: Say what you want, I'm not listening!: a conversational self-reflection robot that does not parse user speech. i-com **22**(1), 19–32 (2023). https://doi.org/10.1515/icom-2022-0047
12. Helmke, M., Elizabech, J., Rey, J.A.: Official Ubuntu Book, 9th edn. Pearson, Berkeley (2016)
13. Hemingway, A., Jack, E.: Reducing social isolation and promoting well being in older people. Qual. Ageing Older Adults **14**(1), 25–35 (2013). https://doi.org/10.1108/14717791311311085
14. Ito, T., Watanabe, T.: Motion control algorithm of ARM-COMS for entrainment enhancement. In: Yamamoto, S. (ed.) HIMI 2016. LNCS, vol. 9734, pp. 339–346. Springer, Cham (2016). https://doi.org/10.1007/978-3-319-40349-6_32
15. Ito, T., Kimachi, H., Watanabe, T.: Combination of local interaction with remote interaction in ARM-COMS communication. In: Yamamoto, Sakae, Mori, Hirohiko (eds.) HCII 2019. LNCS, vol. 11570, pp. 347–356. Springer, Cham (2019). https://doi.org/10.1007/978-3-030-22649-7_28
16. Ito, T., Oyama, T., Watanabe, T.: Smart speaker interaction through ARM-COMS for health monitoring platform. In: Yamamoto, S., Mori, H. (eds.) HCII 2021. LNCS, vol. 12766, pp. 396–405. Springer, Cham (2021). https://doi.org/10.1007/978-3-030-78361-7_30

17. Johanson, D., Ahn, H.S., Goswami, R., Saegusa, K., Broadbent, E.: The effects of healthcare robot empathy statements and head nodding on trust and satisfaction: a video study. J. Hum.-Robot Interact. **12**(1) (2023). https://doi.org/10.1145/3549534
18. Kawarara, T., Inoue, K., Lala, D.: Intelligent conversational android ERICA applied to attentive listening and job interview. CoRR abs/2105.00403 (2021)
19. Kimachi, H., Ito, T.: Introduction of local interaction to head-motion based robot. In: The Proceedings of Design & Systems Conference. https://doi.org/10.1299/jsmedsd.2018.28.2204
20. Kubi. https://www.kubiconnect.com/. Accessed 18 Feb 2023
21. Kumar, A., Haider, Y., Kumar, M., et al.: Using WhatsApp as a quick-access personal logbook for maintaining clinical records and follow-up of orthopedic patients. Cureus **13**(1), e12900 (2021). https://doi.org/10.7759/cureus.12900
22. Lee, A., Kawahara, T.: Recent development of open-source speech recognition engine Julius. In: Asia-Pacific Signal and Information Processing Association Annual Summit and Conference (APSIPA ASC) (2009)
23. Lokshina, I., Lanting, C.: A qualitative evaluation of IoT-driven eHealth: knowledge management, business models and opportunities, deployment and evolution. In: Kryvinska, N., Greguš, M. (eds.) Data-Centric Business and Applications. LNDECT, vol. 20, pp. 23–52. Springer, Cham (2019). https://doi.org/10.1007/978-3-319-94117-2_2
24. Medical Alert Advice. www.medicalalertadvice.com. Accessed 12 Feb 2023
25. Mitsuno, S., Yoshikawa, Y., Ban, M., Ishiguro, H.: Agreebot introduction dialogue in human–robot interaction: improving the acceptability of robot statements on incapable robotic experiences. Adv. Robot. (2024). https://doi.org/10.1080/01691864.2023.2301425
26. Nishio, T., Yoshikawa, Y., Iio, T., et al.: Actively listening twin robots for long-duration conversation with the elderly. Robomech. J. **8**, 18 (2021). https://doi.org/10.1186/s40648-021-00205-5
27. OpenCV. http://opencv.org/. Accessed 18 Feb 2023
28. OpenFace API Documentation. http://cmusatyalab.github.io/openface/. Accessed 18 Feb 2023
29. Osawa, T., Matsuda, Y., Ohmura, R., Imai, M.: Embodiment of an agent by anthropomorphization of a common object. Web Intell. Agent Syst. Int. J. **10**, 345–358 (2012)
30. oVice. https://www.ovice.com/. Accessed 12 Feb 2023
31. Quigley, M., Gerkey, B., Smart, W.D.: Programming Robots with ROS: A Practical Introduction to the Robot Operating System. O'Reilly Media, Sebastopol (2015)
32. Rifinski, D., Erel, H., Feiner, A., Hoffman, G., Zuckerman, O.: Human-human-robot interaction: robotic object's responsive gestures improve interpersonal evaluation in human interaction. Hum.-Comput. Interact. **36**(4), 333–359 (2021). https://doi.org/10.1080/07370024.2020.1719839
33. Riswanda, A.F., Ferdiana, R., Adji, T.B.: The effect of anthropomorphic design cues on increasing chatbot empathy. In: 2022 1st International Conference on Information System and Information Technology (ICISIT), pp. 370–375 (2022). https://doi.org/10.1109/ICISIT54091.2022.9873008
34. Rogers, C.R.: A theory of therapy, personality, and interpersonal relationships: as developed in the client-centered framework. In: Koch, S. (ed.) Psychology: A Study of a Science. Formulations of the Person and the Social Context, vol. 3, pp. 184–256. McGraw Hill, New York (1959)
35. Rviz. https://carla.readthedocs.io/projects/ros-bridge/en/latest/rviz_plugin/. Accessed 18 Feb 2023
36. Samejima, K.: Studies on human animal interaction. J. Soc. Biomech. **43**(3), 173–178 (2019). https://doi.org/10.3951/sobim.43.3_173. (in Japanese)

37. Schoff, F., Kalenichenko, D., Philbin, J.: FaceNet: a unified embedding for face recognition and clustering. In: IEEE Conference on CVPR 2015, pp. 815–823 (2015)

38. Sejima, Y., Kawamoto, H., Sato, Y., Watanabe, T.: A speech-driven pupil response system with affective highlight by virtual lighting. J. Adv. Mech. Des. Syst. Manuf. **16**(5), JAMDSM0058 (2024)

39. Shitaoka, K., Tokuhisa, R., Yoshimura, T., Hoshino, H., Watanabe, N.: Active listening system for a conversation robot. J. Nat. Lang. Process. **24**(1), 3–47 (2017). Released on J-STAGE May 15

40. Society 5.0. https://www.japan.go.jp/abenomics/_userdata/abenomics/pdf/society_5.0.pdf. Accessed 12 Feb 2023

41. Thompson, S.: Active Listening Skills, Examples, and Exercises. Virtual Speech (2017). https://virtualspeech.com/blog/active-listening-skills-examples-and-exercises.   Accessed July 2023

42. Toyota   Pocobee.   https://www.toyota-global.com/innovation/partner_robot/robot/file/Poc obee_EN_0208.pdf. Accessed 21 Feb 2024

43. Ubuntu. https://www.ubuntu.com/. Accessed 18 Feb 2023

44. urdf/XML/Transmission. http://wiki.ros.org/urdf/XML/Transmission. Accessed 12 Feb 2023

45. Watanabe, T.: Human-entrained embodied interaction and communication technology. In: Fukuda, S. (ed.) Emotional Engineering, pp. 161–177. Springer, London (2011). https://doi.org/10.1007/978-1-84996-423-4_9

46. Wongphati, M., Matsuda, Y., Osawa, H., Imai, M.: Where do you want to use a robotic arm? And what do you want from the robot? In: International Symposium on Robot and Human Interactive Communication, pp. 322–327 (2012)

47. Yakuyama, H., Tsumaki, Y.: A motion-enhanced display. In: Proceedings of the Virtual Reality Society of Japan Annual Conference, vol. 17, pp. 574–577 (2012)

Managing Information on Goals and Benefits During Development Initiatives

Sander Krøglid[1] and Jo E. Hannay[2]([⊠]) [iD]

[1] Department of Informatics, University of Oslo, Pb. 1080 Blindern,
0316 Oslo, Norway
sandek@ifi.uio.no

[2] Simula Metropolitan Center for Digital Engineering, Center for Effective
Digitalization of the Public Sector, OsloMet, Pb. 4 St. Olavs plass, 0130 Oslo, Norway
johannay@simula.no

Abstract. The main reason for initiating a software development initiative is to produce value for stakeholders. However, software projects vary in their degrees of success in delivering the intended value. Since software projects can consume a significant amount of resources, a lack of focus on delivering value can result in bad investments. Research suggests that the absence of frameworks and techniques to support organizations in benefits management activities may be the reason for the lack of focus on value creation in daily development life. To increase the motivation for, and the focus on, benefits management, we implemented a generalized version of a set of published benefit estimation and tracking techniques so that they are accessible in an extensively used development management platform (Jira). The techniques are for declaring goals and goal structures and for expressing estimates of the system's contribution to the goals. The usability of the system was tested with IT professionals, the preliminary results are promising for further development on the present functionality and for other pieces of benefits management functionality in the future.

Keywords: Goal Structures · Benefits Management · Software Development · Project Management · Jira

1 Motivation

Development initiatives are often complex. When the public sector or a private enterprise develops portfolios of services for citizens or customers, a host of concerns must be taken into consideration regarding the design of the services, their integration with existing services, the cost of development, deployment and maintenance, the timespan and the benefits of the services and which goals are to be met by the service portfolio. If digitalization comes into the picture, as it inevitably does—not only in pure information systems, but also in systems

© The Author(s), under exclusive license to Springer Nature Switzerland AG 2024
H. Mori and Y. Asahi (Eds.): HCII 2024, LNCS 14691, pp. 319–337, 2024.
https://doi.org/10.1007/978-3-031-60125-5_22

with physical infrastructure such as roads and other constructions, further concerns regarding digital inclusion, universal accessibility and automated service provision come into play.

Managing development initiatives to success has proven hard; especially for large information-technological systems. Even under the auspices of agile development and management which explicitly put value for the customer in the high seat, there is a strong focus on the traditional control metrics of time, cost and scope to the detriment of a focus on the system's benefits toward fulfilling goals [1]. One of the basic ideas in improving on this situation is that benefit should be estimated, tracked and measured with the same rigor as one routinely does with cost. Several techniques and methods have been presented for associating benefit estimates to the product elements of development initiatives [2–4]; specifically, *Large Scale Scrum* (LeSS) [5], *Scaled Agile Framework* (SAFe) [6,7] and *Benefit Points* [8–12]—an analogy to story points for cost estimates.

It is essential, however, that professionals are able to use these techniques readily in daily work life. In project management tools there is usually functionality for recording and tracking cost estimates, but not so for benefit estimates for tracking progress toward goals. To overcome this shortcoming, an endeavor was initiated with the aim to integrate *benefit estimation and tracking* functionality in commonly used development management tools. Although the basic ideas of benefit estimation and tracking are simple, their more advanced use in calculations of benefit/cost ratios and in prioritizing which product elements to develop first, can quickly become intractable in practice in the midst of the complexity of development work—a plight shared by benefits management in general [13]. The postulate of the endeavor is that this is, to a substantial degree, *a human interface problem*, due to the lack of integrative tools that keep the simplicity of the concepts intact and hide complex calculations from users.

2 Benefit Estimation and Goal Management

Here, we describe the design and development of a particular part of benefit estimation and tracking that concerns what we will call *Benefit Estimation and Goal Management* (BEGM). For full details, see [14]. The techniques in BEGM are generalizations of a core set of techniques for *Benefit/Cost-Driven Agile Development* (BCDAS) in [10], which is a compilation of ideas put forth in [8,9,12]. The BEGM functionality was implemented as an extension to Jira, a widely-used project management and issue tracking tool.[1]

Benefit estimation is more complex than cost estimation, in that benefit is assessed as the system under development's potential to achieve a set of specified goals. Moreover, goals can be organized in tiered structures; examples being *Objectives and Key Results* (OKR) [15], *Lean Value Tree* (LVT) [16] and also more traditional project goal hierarchies.

Figure 1 illustrates the BEGM goal structure in the Jira extension (J-BEGM), together with Epics (which are represented in Jira proper). The Epics (green)

---

[1] https://www.atlassian.com/software/jira.

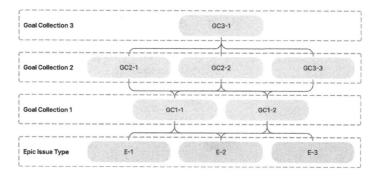

Fig. 1. Product elements (epics) and goal structure of BEGM as implemented in the Jira extension (Color figure online)

are high-level user stories specifying integral pieces of system functionality (*minimum marketable features* [17] or *minimum viable products* [18]). Above the epics are goals in collections on various tiers. The curved lines represent possible relationships for benefit assessments. Thus, the epics are assessed by assigning benefit points for their potential effects on each goal in Goal Collection 1 (which could be project objectives or effect goals expressing the desired effects of the system on the stakeholders' business and life processes). The goals in Goal Collection 1 can, in turn, affect the higher-tier goals in Goal Collection 2 (which could be organizational goals), and these can, in turn, affect higher-tier goals still (for example, societal goals). The effects that goals have on higher-tier goals are also expressed giving benefits points. One can have as many tiers as one wants, but one must have at least one goal tier for evaluating the benefit of epics.

The lines in the figure shows all possible benefit relations; for example, all goals in Goal Collection 1 can be given benefit points according to their relative contribution to every goal in Goal Collection 2. However, some goal structures might be hierarchical (such as OKR), and elements (epics or goals) on a tier would relate to a single goal on the next tier, rather than to many. In any case, the total benefit of a goal or an epic is the result of a weighted sum of the benefit points assigned to that goal or epic. The goal collection at the uppermost tier must be given benefit assessments directly, since they are not given benefit points via their contribution to higher-tiered goals.

Benefit points are relative money-agnostic estimates designed to express relative contributions, rather than absolute calculations of monetary value. Monetary value can, however be assigned to goals if desired.

Figure 2 shows an example of how this looks like in J-BEGM, where three goals EFFE-1, EFFE-2 and EFFE-3 have been declared in an uppermost goal tier. The left-hand screen shows benefit points (weights) assigned, while the right-hand screen shows the choice to assign monetary values.

Goals can be expressed in nominal, ordinal, interval and ratio terms. Examples are, respectively, *Receive media attention as the enterprise most successful in digital transformation* (nominal), *Increase customer satisfaction by one*

Fig. 2. Setting benefit for the uppermost goal tier: weights (left), monetary value (right) (Color figure online)

median point (ordinal), *Increase drop-out age for user proficiency in senior category (60yrs–90yrs) by 10 years* (interval), and *Reduce current average case processing time of 150 h by 30%* (ratio). With benefit points, also achievement on qualitative (non-financial) goals can be measured. Qualitative goals are often the main reason for initiating development initiatives—especially in the public sector—even though it is the financial goals that are often used, together with the investment cost, to justify an initiative. Financial goals tend to be efficiency goals. It is therefore important to include qualitative goals explicitly for benefit assessment in order to balance the abundance of efficiency goals off with "true" goals; e.g., public well-fare goals [19,20].

Figure 2 (leftmost table) then shows three epics BN-1, BN-2 and BN-3, which have been assigned benefit points for each of the three objectives. The monetary values of the three objectives are shown in the leftmost (purple) tags under each objective; here, monetary values of 25, 40 and 55 million, respectively, which gives weights $25/120 = 0.21$, $40/120 = 0.33$ and $55/120 = 0.46$, respectively.

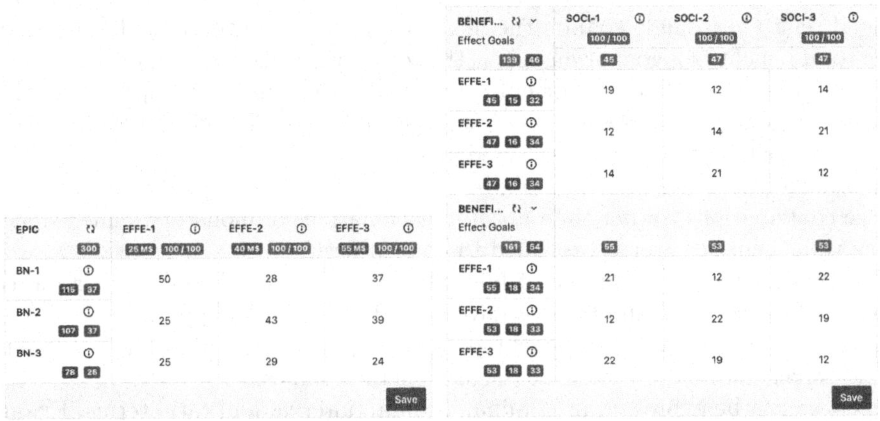

Fig. 3. Assigning benefit points to epics: Project (left), portfolio of two projects (right)

The leftmost (blue) tags for each epic show the total number of benefit points assigned to that epic (115, 107 and 78, respectively), while the rightmost (purple) tags show the weighted sum of benefit points for the epic; e.g., $50 * 0.21 + 28 * 0.33 + 37 * 0.46 \approx 37$ for BN-1. Figure 2 (rightmost table) shows two projects in a portfolio with shared goals (Fig. 3).

3 Design Approach

The endeavor of developing tool support for benefit estimation and tracking follows the following design principles:

Concreteness: The techniques should be designed for performing concrete tasks; a lack thereof will leave professionals in the dark as to what to do, even if they grasp the general idea of benefit estimation and tracking.

Noninvasiveness: The techniques should be designed to be used in the existing process flow. If methods are too complex or too invasive in day-to-day work, they will not be employed.

Satisficing: The techniques should be designed to be *good enough* for the tasks at hand and in line with *satisficing* [21], rather than optimizing.

Support for cognitive processes: The techniques should be designed to suit the nature of the cognitive processes involved in assessment [22,23].

Recognizability: The techniques should be reminiscent of existing techniques of state of practice to facilitate adoption.

The central tenet in observing these design principles is that the practitioners should concentrate on assessing one benefit relation at a time, in a relative manner. For example, one should give benefit points to each epic for its relative contribution compared to the other epics, to one goal at a time in Goal Collection 1 and then move on to the next goal. The same procedure should be used for the relations between Goal Collection i and Goal Collection $i + 1$. Note that the relations between different tiers may be the domains of different stakeholders. The relations can be assessed disjointedly, and at different times, and updated when new information is available. All the weighted sums will be automatically recalculated with any change. Thus, each task is simple and the tool should enforce this simplicity. The totality, however, is complex, and the tool should automatically calculate and recalculate the benefit points of each element according to whatever the individual assessments are. In the end, each epic receives a single benefit points value adjusted for all the goal assessments, which can be used in calculations of benefit/cost ratios and in Earned Business Value Management [9] and benefits uncertainty assessments [12].

4 Evaluation

The objective for the type of tools discussed in this article is that they will aid practitioners in performing benefits management activities; in particular, benefit estimation and tracking activities. To evaluate the degree to which such tools meet this objective, we pose the following two propositions:

Proposition 1: *Support for benefit estimation and tracking activities can be implemented in project management tools.*

Proposition 2: *The support for benefit estimation and tracking activities as implemented in project management tools are useful in practice.*

The present Jira extension (J-BEGM) is a first minimal marketable feature MMF [24].[2] Several other MMFs are planned which will extend the functionality in the present MMF. The two propositions above will be applied to all of them.

5   Study

For the the evaluation of the present Jira extension, we operationalized the propositions above as follows:

Proposition 1 Operationalization:

- *J-BEGM faithfully implements BCDAS techniques for managing goal structures*
- *J-BEGM faithfully implements BCDAS techniques of benefit estimation*
- *The terminology used in J-BEGM is consistent with that of BCDAS*

Proposition 2 Operationalization:

- *Product elements and goal structures used in development initiatives can be expressed in Jira*
- *The terminology is comprehensible*
- *The added functionality in Jira will motivate benefit estimation and tracking*
- *The added functionality in Jira will assist in benefits management*

5.1   Method

The tool is designed to be used throughout the lifecycle of a software system under development, and the best approach would be to evaluate J-BEGM in a natural setting. However, this would require a production-ready version of J-BEGM and a fully prepared development project, which was not feasible due to time constraints. Therefore, an artificial controlled setting was chosen for this evaluation.

Usability testing [25] was selected as the method for evaluation. The testing concerns how the application is experienced and understood during use and was facilitated by the first author. The specific method used was expert/task-based usability testing. The usability test has two parts, one for each proposition. In the first part, IT professionals are asked to perform a set of defined tasks in

---

[2] In incremental development, a MMF is arguably a more suitable formulation of a small integral part of value-adding functionality than a Minimum Viable Product (MVP).

J-BEGM that involve using J-BEGM's most important techniques and features. In the second part, IT professionals are asked to test a goal structure that they are using or have used in a project recently. To assess the application's usability during the usability testing, participants are observed, and potential miss-steps and struggles are noted.

5.2   Participants

The evaluation on Proposition 1 requires participants who have knowledge and experience in benefits management and, optimally, experience with BEGM. Since BEGM is a part of the current development (a generalization of BCDAS), no persons had experience with BEGM, but we asked two of the authors behind BCDAS, as well as a person involved in early stages of the development, to assess how faithful J-BEGM implements the techniques and terminology of BCDAS.

The evaluation on Proposition 2 requires participants who are familiar with Jira and who have used goal structures in their work, but preferably with no knowledge of BCDAS or BEGM (or J-BEGM). For this evaluation it was not possible to gather participants with these qualities, and we had to use the same persons to evaluate on both propositions.

Thus, three experienced IT professionals were obtained as participants for the evaluation. All the participants were picked because of their experience with the original framework, benefits management, and their experience in using Jira.

5.3   Materials

To conduct the usability testing, it was important to have an application at a sufficiently high level of maturity in which the user could perform a set of tasks. Tasks were designed so the participants could utilize all the techniques implemented from the BEGM framework as experiences through the most important features of J-BEGM. The set of tasks (translated from Norwegian) for Proposition 1 is given in Fig. 4. For Proposition 2, oral instructions were given to declare a user-defined goal structure in J-BEGM, without further detailed instructions.

In a real-life scenario, estimating the benefit in terms of distributing benefit points between epics and goals and between goals in different goal tiers can be time-consuming, and it also requires knowledge about the different goals to assess. Since the first part of the usability test (for Proposition 1) aimed at evaluating how well techniques of BCDAS were implemented, and not how well the techniques fit in a real-life scenario, a set of data was given for the tasks (Fig. 4), which the user could insert. The data was derived from the examples in [10] with some adjustments. Further, because projects and epics are managed in Jira proper (not in the J-BEGM extension), Jira projects and epics were predeclared for the tasks. One of the tasks involved connecting three projects to a portfolio, and two projects were pre-declared for this task to save time.

The usability test was observed by the facilitator (the first author), and notes were taken when the participant struggled; e.g., if a participant struggled to perform a task, or if the participant asked to find a specific use case. As

1. Click on Benefit Estimation under *Apps*
2. Initiate the project by selecting:
   (a) Epic as *the Product Element*, and
   (b) Todo, and In progress as *Issue Statuses*.
3. Create Objectives as a *Goal Collection* to the Benefit Calculator projects's *Goal Structure*:

Name	Description
Objectives	The system's intended effects on stakeholders' work/life-processes

4. Declare the following three objectives:

Obj1	Reduce the average case processing time by 30%
Obj2	Reduce the number of wrong case decisions by 90%
Obj3	Reduce the average client-case processor interaction time by 70%

5. Set benefit points to estimate the benefit of the seven epics for each objective:

	Obj1	Obj2	Obj3
E1	16	13	14
E2	25	35	11
E3	25	10	12
E4	10	13	7
E5	3	5	35
E6	6	11	9
E7	15	13	12

6. Create a *Portfolio* named The Benefits Management Agency.
7. Connect the current project (Benefit Calculator) and the projects dns.no and Benefits DB to The Benefits Management Agency portfolio.
8. Create Returns as a *Goal Collection* to The Benefits Management Agency's *Goal Structure*:

Name	Description
Returns	The organization's long-term goals

9. Declare the following three returns (higher-level goals):

Ret1	Reduce number of man-hours
Ret2	Reduce number of compensations
Ret3	Improved public image of the organization

10. Set benefit points to estimate the benefit of the portfolio items (objectives) for each return:

Benefit Calculator	Ret1	Ret2	Ret3
Obj1	12	13	15
Obj2	9	11	6
Obj3	35	5	3
dns.no			
Obj1	7	13	10
Obj2	12	10	25
Benefits DB			
Obj1	11	35	25
Obj2	14	13	16

11. Set monetary values for each return
12. Go back to the project to see if the benefit points have changed

Fig. 4. Evaluation Tasks for Proposition 1

none of the participants had any experience using J-BEGM, some mis-clicks and wrong navigation were expected.

In addition to the observations by the facilitator, questionnaires (Google Forms) for the two parts of the usability test were given to the participants. The questionnaires addressed the operationalizations of the propositions directly; see Fig. 5 (translated from Norwegian). Further, to gather feedback on the application's general usability, *The System Usability Scale* was used [26]; see Fig. 5 (lowermost part).

Each question marked with * was assessed on a scale from 1–5, where 1 signifies "Strongly Disagree", while 5 signifies "Strongly Agree".

Questionnaire for Usability Test under Proposition 1

1. To what degree are the techniques for goal structures reflected in the system?*
   − Please explain your answer:
2. To what degree are the techniques for benefit estimation reflected in the system?*
   − Please explain your answer
3. To what degree is the terminology in BCDAS reflected in the system?*
   − Please explain your answer
4. Which aspects of the system did you appreciate?
5. Which aspects of the system can be improved?

Questionnaire for Usability Test under Proposition 2

1. To what extent can goal structures in your line of work be expressed in the system?*
   − Please explain your answer:
2. To what extent can you perform benefits assessments that are relevant for your work in the system?*
   − Please explain your answer:
3. To what extent is the terminology in the system comprehensible*
   − Please explain your answer:
4. To what extent do you think the system can motivate the use of benefits assessments?*
   − Please explain your answer:
5. To what extent do you think the system is helpful for assisting in benefits assessments?*
   − Please explain your answer:

The System Usability Scale

1. I think that I would like to use this system frequently*
2. I found the system unnecessarily complex*
3. I thought the system was easy to use*
4. I think that I would need the support of a technical person to be able to use this system*
5. I found the various functions in this system were well integrated*
6. I thought there was too much inconsistency in this system*
7. I would imagine that most people would learn to use this system very quickly*
8. I found the system very cumbersome to use*
9. I felt very confident using the system*
10. I needed to learn a lot of things before I could get going with this system*

Fig. 5. Usability Test Questionnaires

5.4 Procedure

The usability tests were arranged separately for each individual and split in two sessions; one for Proposition 1 and another for Proposition 2 and the SUS. One participant completed the test online via Microsoft Teams. Each session was scheduled to last about 60 min and was started by informing the participant about the focus for that session. When the participant was ready, the facilitator handed out the set of tasks and initiated the J-BEGM application with the appropriate context. If the participants experienced any confusion during the test, they were allowed to ask questions, and the confusions were then discussed at the end of the session.

In the first session, the participants were first instructed to initialize a project, set a goal collection with corresponding goals, and then estimate benefit points for the epics using the goals in the goal collection. Then, they were instructed to create a portfolio and connect it with the their project and two other projects declared by the facilitator. To test the estimation module's portfolio items mode, the participants were also instructed to create a goal collection with corresponding goals for the portfolio. Then, the participants could estimate the projects (portfolio items) using the newly created goal collection's goals. At the end, to test setting monetary value, the participants were asked to set some monetary value to the goals of the portfolio's goal collection. When the tasks were done, the participants were given the first questionnaire.

Then, the second part of the usability test was initiated, where the participant could freely use the application to set up a goal structure from a current or previous project they had knowledge about and assess it. When the participant felt done, or if the goal structure could not be reflected in J-BEGM, the second set of questionnaires were handed out, including the SUS.

At the end, an open discussion was initiated by the facilitator, where the participants could openly discuss their experiences and thoughts on J-BEGM. The participants were allowed to use the application further during the discussion to point out issues and for asking questions.

6   Results

We present the result for each proposition. Feedback from the questionnaire and the open discussions, including the notes from observation, will be discussed where relevant. In addition, some observed issues that do not relate to the propositions are discussed at the end. As the evaluation was conducted in Norwegian, the responses and feedback have been translated into English.

6.1   Results for Proposition 1

- J-BEGM faithfully implements the BCDAS techniques for managing goal structures: All the participants agreed that the BCDAS goal-managing techniques were faithfully implemented in J-BEGM. The scores on Question 1 in the questionnaire for Proposition 1 (Fig. 5) given by the three participants were, respectively, 4, 5, and 5, resulting in an average score of 4.6. From the two participants who gave a rating of 5, there was no particular feedback other than "Don't see anything missing".

However, the participant who gave a rating of 4, expressed that the *Goal Tier* tab should have had a better introduction. However, once the participant got the hang of it, the flow increased for the rest of the session. The participant in question was, however, not alone in having issues with the *Goal Structure* and *Goal Tier* tabs. All participants had issues in finding where to insert the goals for the goal collection they created, although the other participants gave full scores on this question.

- *J-BEGM faithfully implements the BCDAS techniques of benefit estimation*: The participants also agreed that J-BEGM faithfully implemented BCDAS's techniques for benefit estimation, as the scores given by the participants on Question 2 were the same as for the previous question. Two participants expressed joy in using the estimation table in J-BEGM. One of the participants mentioned the estimation table as one of the best aspects of the system: "I liked the estimation process the most".

However, they had some suggestions for improvements. One of the participants suggested that the benefit estimates should be carried forward to Jira's standard epic view. In the current state of J-BEGM, the benefit points are stored as a parameter for the issues but are not visible outside J-BEGM. Another participant suggested that, in addition to the table, a bar chart view for each goal (on which the epics are assessed) would be useful. According to the participant in question, this could perhaps visualize the differences between each epic to a greater extent than numbers in a table, and it would enable the user to distribute points to one goal before the next, which is the approach suggested by BCDAS [10, p. 24]. Beyond this, the participants seemed very satisfied with J-BEGM's implementation of the techniques.

- *The terminology used in J-BEGM is consistent with that of BCDAS*: For the terminology, the participants were less satisfied; the scores given by the participants on Question 3 were 3, 4, and 5, resulting in an average score of 4. This is also reflected by the observations of completing the tasks and the participants' justification of their scores. The terms that the participants commented on were *Goal Structure*, *-Tier*, *-Collection*, and *Portfolio Item*. Since these terms arose when generalizing the goal structure in BCDAS to BEGM, these are not fully consistent with the ones used in the BCDAS techniques in [10]. To improve on the situation, one of the participants suggested implementing profiles, or templates tailored to different contexts. The terms regarding the estimation module, however, were familiar to the participants.

6.2   Results for Proposition 2

- *Product elements and goal structures used in development initiatives can be expressed in Jira*: This was only answered by two of the participants. The scores on Question 1 in the questionnaire for Proposition 2 (Fig. 5) given by the participants were 4 and 5, resulting in an average score of 4.5. One of the participants missed functionality for using non-financial goals in J-BEGM. The BCDAS framework supports setting monetary value to qualitative returns (non-financial gains) based on relative comparisons using a model for integrating soft and hard returns (MISHRI) [8][10, p. 31]. Since J-BEGM supports the setting of weights in addition to, or instead of, monetary value, combining financial and non-financial goals can be achieved using weights. Indeed, this generalizes the techniques for handling soft returns in [10], although this may not have been apparent to the participants. Other than that, both participants stated that they were able to reflect their goal structures in J-BEGM and assess on them.

- *The terminology is comprehensible*: As with the terminology statement for Proposition 1, the response on Question 3 for Proposition 2 on how the overall terminology of J-BEGM was understandable for more general use did not indicate satisfaction. The scores given by the participants were 3, 4, and 4, resulting in an average score of 3.6. Also here, the participants expressed confusion concerning the more general terminology introduced in the BEGM framework: "*Goal Tier* is a key concept and should have been given a more thorough introduction".

One of the participants stated that the terms *Goal Structure*, *-Tier*, *-Collection*, and *Portfolio Item* seemed rather too generic and that these are not usually used in real-life contexts. Another participant argued that his lack of knowledge of the newly introduced terminology, which also increased his navigation problems, was linked to the fact that there was no introduction or explanation of these terms in J-BEGM. The participant suggested that J-BEGM could introduce and explain the new terms to make the system more understandable, and also suggested to combine the *Goal Structure* and *Goal Tier* tabs to avoid confusion.

- *The added functionality in Jira will motivate benefit estimation and tracking.* The response regarding whether J-BEGM can motivate to increase the use of benefit estimation and tracking received relatively high scores. The scores given by the participants on Question 4 were 4, 5, and 5, resulting in an average score of 4.6. However, one of the participants stated that the application's current state might "require a user who is passionate about the idea".

As the participants struggled with the introduced terminology from the BEGM framework, and to some degree with the goal managing practices as implemented in J-BEGM, one participant stated that there is a certain user threshold, but once overcome, the application should provide significant utility.

- *The added functionality in Jira will assist in benefits management* The response to Question 5 received the same scores as the previous question. In addition, Question 2 is relevant here, and the participants scored 4 and 5, resulting in an average of 4.5.

One participant enjoyed that J-BEGM was integrated with Jira, which enables a familiar workspace, where the backlog can be directly integrated. The latter was also expressed by another participant, who stated that the process enabled easier assessment than traditional Excel sheets, which offer no integration with Jira.

6.3   Observed Issues

As stated previously, for some of the given tasks, all the participants struggled to navigate in J-BEGM to find where they could perform the tasks. Some of the most frequently occurring issues were declaring goals in a created goal collection, setting monetary value to the goals of a goal collection, and connecting portfolio items. The intuition of all participants was that goals might be created by clicking the action button of the *Goal Collection* in the *Goal Structure* tab. Only one of the participants was able to locate the *New Goal* button on their own. The rest of the participants needed guidance. The same intuition was at play when setting the monetary value of the goals. On this task, all participants needed guidance.

All the participants also needed guidance for connecting projects to portfolios. This involved a lot of navigation throughout the application. All participants checked the portfolio's *Goal Structure* tab, while some checked the project's *Settings* tab.

One of the participants, who conducted the usability testing through Microsoft Teams, had a low screen resolution, which resulted in a too-low browser height limit. Because of this, during the first estimation the participant had to scroll down, which hid the navigation bar making it difficult find the way back. One solution to this could be to use a fixed position on the navigation bar. The navigation bar is important for navigating through the different functionalities in the application.

6.4   The System Usability Scale

To calculate the System Usability Scale score (SUS score), an individual's ratings (scale positions) are converted into a *score contribution*. This is done as follows: For scores on an odd-numbered question (questions 1, 3, 5, 7, and 9), the score contribution is calculated by the scale position minus one. For even-numbered questions, the score contribution is calculated by five minus the score position. Then, the individual's score contributions are added and multiplied by 2.5. After doing this for each participant's answers, one can calculate the average score, which is the resulting SUS score. Figure 6 shows a spreadsheet used to calculate the SUS score of the usability test.

A score of above 68 is considered above average.[3] Our SUS score of 72.5 is slightly above average which is a positive result for the first evaluation of the application.

6.5   Results Summary

The evaluation results indicate mostly positive feedback regarding the statements in the propositions and for the usability of J-BEGM. However, the feedback provided by the participants identifies some aspects of J-BEGM that are confusing, and that can be improved in the next iteration of J-BEGM's development. Nevertheless, since this was the first application evaluation, the results indicate that J-BEGM has the potential to motivate and be a helpful assistance in benefits management.

---

[3] https://www.usability.gov/how-to-and-tools/methods/system-usability-scale.html.

Questions		Scale Position			Score Contribution		
	Participant:	A	B	C	A	B	C
I think that I would like to use this system frequently		5	3	3	4	2	2
I found the system unnecessarily complex		2	2	2	3	3	3
I thought the system was easy to use		4	4	2	3	3	3
I think that I would need the support of a technical person to be able to use this system		1	1	2	4	4	3
I found the various functions in this system were well integrated		5	4	4	4	3	3
I thought there was too much inconsistency in this system		2	2	1	3	3	4
I would imagine that most people would learn to use this system very quickly		4	2	3	3	1	2
I found the system very cumbersome to use		2	2	2	3	3	3
I felt very confident using the system		3	3	4	2	2	3
I needed to learn a lot of things before I could get going with this system		1	2	2	4	3	3
Sum of score contributions					33	27	27
Sum multiplied with 2.5					82.5	67.5	67.5
Average score							72.5

Fig. 6. SUS Results

7 Discussion

Research, e.g., [1] and anecdotal evidence suggest that practitioners think that benefits considerations do not play an important enough role in project decisions and that considerations of time, cost, and scope take up too much space in comparison. Initiatives have been, and are, under way to guide digitalization agencies and funding bodies in integrating benefits considerations to a greater extent in governmental guidelines. The BCDAS framework has been given as part of a course for IT professionals over several years, but although participants have expressed enthusiasm over guidelines and frameworks, few practitioners have adopted the techniques in daily work; a tendency also observed years ago [13].

Making benefits management techniques accessible in Jira could enable practitioners to adopt and adapt benefits management activities into their daily work routines, and hopefully make them more likely to perceive themselves as successful in delivering benefits [27]. The current development is intended to be a first step in that direction for benefit estimation and tracking activities. Overall, the usability tests suggest that the Jira extension contributes to making techniques accessible in daily work, but improvements and enhancements must be done.

As stated by one of the participants, adopting benefits management practices with the Jira extension as it is now might require users who are, at the outset, passionate about the idea of estimating and monitoring benefits. Hence, passionate benefits management practitioners might be the *early adopters* of the application, while most organizations and their potential users may take the role of the *late majority* who might not use the application "unless everyone else in the business does so". Early adopters, on the other hand, might use an application even when it is not optimized in usability or not even fully functional [28]. To enable easier adoption and to encourage the late majority to use the J-BEGM, shortcomings and issues regarding the current state of the application must be resolved.

In addition to the shortcoming already mentioned, the participants suggested further development along the following lines:

Templates and Information Views. To assist navigation and to explain the concept in the tool, templates might help; e.g., for various goal structures (OKR, LVT and more traditional structures). Information views could be available on each tab to explain the concepts and their use.

Enhanced Visualization. To help the user to distribute points for one goal at a time [10, p. 24] and to include an enhanced visualization of the differences in points distributed for each goal to be estimated, one participant suggested a view in which the estimation tables were split for each goal.

Benefit-Cost Index and Ranking of the Backlog. For now, the only way to see the benefit points is through J-BEGM, and there is no way of seeing them in the actual backlog or in Jira's standard issue view. Therefore, to fully integrate the benefit points in the Jira backlog, there is still some work to be done. Since Jira has a ranking system for issues, the estimated benefit points could be used together with the story points to calculate a benefit-cost index [10, p. 29] to prioritize backlog elements based on benefit and cost estimates.

8 Threats to Validity

We discuss threats to internal and external validity and reliability, as those most relevant for this usability study.[4]

8.1 Internal Validity

Internal validity in the context of usability testing refers to the degree to which the study design biases participants toward a certain response or behavior.

Questions. The questions in the questionnaires ask directly whether the application succeeds in fulfilling desired objectives. As the facilitator was present while some participants were filling out the forms, and because the participants knew that the facilitator would read their answers, a potential threat is that they gave a high score out of politeness (acquiescence bias, social acceptability bias, researcher bias, and interview bias). Another threat is that the first part of the usability test, along with the questionnaire, took much longer than anticipated. The questions were quite comprehensive, leading participants to investigate the application more thoroughly before providing answers. This could pose a threat to the evaluation's internal validity as the work of participants regarding the first questionnaire might be tiresome, which could result in less motivation for the second part of the usability test.

Tasks. Because the participants were first instructed to complete a set of tasks, the participants inhabited knowledge and user experience before they were asked to express a goal structure of a current or previous project of their knowledge. The first usability test might ease the participants' ability to express their goal structure compared to a study without those tasks.

---

[4] https://www.nngroup.com/articles/internal-vs-external-validity/.

8.2   External Validity

External validity refers to the extent to which results apply to relevant behaviors or situations in the target audience, different from those applied in the study.

Time. Because the evaluation was scheduled to last about 60 min, it is important to note that the participants, although experts in benefits management and therefore expected to detect any deviations, might have overlooked some features that do not faithfully implement the goal managing and estimation techniques of BCDAS. Another consideration is that one of the participants took the test after a long day at work and found it hard to concentrate after completing the first part of the test. Further, that particular test instance was conducted online through Microsoft Teams, and the participant was provided access to the Jira test site where the tasks were performed. This enabled the participant to complete the questionnaire at will in spare time. This might have made it easier for the participant to be more thorough in his investigation. Because the response from the evaluation arrived some days after the initial session, the participant might have forgotten some aspects of the tool. While this also has bearings on internal validity (above), the fact that the study was conducted with somewhat primed participants in an artificial setting compared to a daily work situation might pose a threat to external validity

Use of Goal Structures. For the second part of the study, participants were asked to evaluate the goal structure of a project they had previously worked on or were working on. However, one of the participants had no prior experience using goal structures in their work. Therefore, the second part of the usability test was skipped, and the first two questions of the second questionnaire were omitted since they required the participant to reflect on their work setting while using J-BEGM. This highlights the question as to whether J-BEGM should be used to encourage the use of goal structures in settings where an organization currently does not use goal structures, or whether J-BEGM should only be used to express goal structures already in place in organizations. The external validity of this study depends, in part, on what standpoint one takes on these questions.

Timing of the SUS. According to guidelines, the SUS should be used after the respondents have had an opportunity to use the evaluated system and before any debriefing or discussion takes place. The latter is to prevent "... the respondents from thinking about items for a long time", and most likely to avoid a facilitator influencing their answers. However, the SUS was, in fact, introduced as the last questionnaire. Because the usability test was divided into two parts, we wanted the participants to spend more time using the system, giving them more experience with the application that could be useful when filling out the SUS. However, as two questionnaires and some discussion took place in between, the results from the SUS might contain some bias, which poses a threat to external validity, but also to internal validity (above).

8.3   Threats to Reliability

Reliability concerns how well a study design produces the same results on separate occasions under the same circumstances [29].

Question Interpretations. In the first question of the questionnaire, one participant gave a lower score than the other participants because of issues related to the goal tier term and tab. However, all the participants discussed these issues giving the impression of similar perceptions. A reason for unequal scores under seemingly equal perceptions could be misinterpretations of the questions. This might suggest that the tasks and questions were not clearly enough defined, which may introduce variability in answers and poses a threat to the reliability of the evaluation. This could potentially have been avoided if the questions were broken down into smaller sub-questions that were more easily understood. However, the writing of well-written, non-biased questions can be challenging [30].

Time. As stated in the external validity section, one participant was tired after a long day of work, which resulted in more time spent to complete the evaluation. This poses a threat to the reliability of the evaluation, as the time given might have influenced the participant's answers. However, as this was the initial evaluation of J-BEGM, getting feedback was prioritized over reliability.

Number and Nature of Participants. Because the number of practitioners of BCDAS is unknown, it was difficult to get in touch with further participants for the evaluation. Because the participants used to evaluate the solution had knowledge of the BCDAS framework, the results for Proposition 1 would seem reliable. The results for Proposition 2, however, may not be reliable, specifically regarding J-BEGM's ability to reflect various goal structures used in development initiatives. As the second part of the usability test was completed only by two participants, the test only shows J-BEGM's ability to reflect two different goal structures compared to the variety of those that might exist in different organizations and development initiatives. Because of this, Proposition 2 needs more investigation.

9   Conclusion

Further research and development on the human-computer interface for benefits-management tool support is needed. Nevertheless, our preliminary findings, together with preliminary findings from prototyping related functionality [11] (also based on [10]), indicate a certain enthusiasm for the usefulness of such tool support. Benefits management involves activities that are inherently complex. The present study therefore tests the effect of designing and implementing a human interface to a complex totality, according to design principles that are geared toward helping practitioners to keep the task simple.

Future research and development should include easier navigation in the present tool along with enhanced visualization features and even deeper integration with the standard features of Jira. Further development is underway by several teams, and the hope for the future is that J-BEGM and other extensions that implement other techniques will be complete products that can be distributed on the Atlassian Marketplace to allow organizations and users to install them on their Jira site. This would enable IT professionals to visualize their project's benefits potential and to prioritize with a benefits/cost perspective. Our society depends on the successful management of development projects in terms of goals that reflect the true societal values for its citizens.

Acknowledgments. The authors are grateful for the efforts and feedback of the practitioners who participated in the usability tests. No sensitive information was gathered, and national regulations concerning consent and anonymity were adhered to.

References

1. Tanilkan, S.S., Hannay, J.E.: Benefit considerations in project decisions. In: Proceedings of the International Conference Product-Focused Software Process Improvement (PROFES 2022), pp. 217–234 (2022)
2. Biffl, S., Aurum, A., Boehm, B., Erdogmus, H., Grünbacher, P. (eds.): Value-Based Software Engineering. Springer, Heidelberg (2006). https://doi.org/10.1007/3-540-29263-2_1
3. Boehm, B., Huang, L.G.: Value-based software engineering: a case study. Computer **36**(3), 33–41 (2003)
4. Karlsson, J., Ryan, K.: A cost-value approach for prioritizing requirements. IEEE Softw. **14**(5), 67–74 (1997)
5. Larman, C., Vodde, B.: Practices for Scaling Lean & Agile Development: Large, Multisite, and Offshore Product Development with Large-Scale Scrum. Addison Wesley, Singapore (2010)
6. Leffingwell, D.: Agile Software Requirements: Lean Requirements Practices for Teams. Programs and the Enterprise. Addison Wesley, Upper Saddle River (2011)
7. Reinertsen, D.: Principles of Product Development Flow: Second Generation Lean Product Development. Celeritas Publishing, Redondo Beach (2009)
8. Hannay, J.E., Benestad, H.C., Strand, K.: Benefit points-the best part of the story. IEEE Softw. **34**(3), 73–85 (2017)
9. Hannay, J.E., Benestad, H.C., Strand, K.: Earned business value management-see that you deliver value to your customer. IEEE Softw. **34**(4), 58–70 (2017)
10. Hannay, J.E.: Benefit/Cost-Driven Software Development with Benefit Points and Size Points. Simula Springer Briefs on Computing, Springer, Cham (2021). https://doi.org/10.1007/978-3-030-74218-8
11. Haaber, M., Grøhøj, P.: Benefit points in scrum: a design science study, Department of Computer Science, Aalborg University, Technical report (2018)
12. Hannay, J.E., Benestad, H.C., Strand, K.: Agile uncertainty assessment for benefit points and story points. IEEE Softw. **36**(4), 50–62 (2019)
13. Breese, R., Jenner, S., Serra, C.E.M., Thorp, J.: Benefits management: lost or found in translation. Int. J. Project Manage. **33**(7), 1438–1451 (2015)
14. Krøglid, S.: Building and evaluating a web-based tool for software benefits estimation and management. Master thesis, University of Oslo, Department of Informatics (2023)
15. Greenwood, R.G.: Management by objectives: as developed by Peter Drucker, assisted by Harold Smiddy. Acad. Manag. Rev. **6**(2), 225–230 (1981)

16. Highsmith, J., Luu, L., Robinson, D.: EDGE: Value-Driven Digital Transformation. Addison-Wesley Professional, Boston (2019)

17. Denne, M., Cleland-Huang, J.: Software by Numbers: Low-Risk, High-Return Development. Prentice Hall, Upper Saddle River (2003)

18. Ries, E.: The Lean Startup. Board Book (2011)

19. Rydén, H.H., Hofmann, S., Verne, G.: The self-serving citizen as a co-producer in the digital public service delivery. In: Lindgren, I., et al. (eds.) Electronic Government, vol. 14130, pp. 48–63. Springer, Cham (2023). https://doi.org/10.1007/978-3-031-41138-0_4

20. Heggertveit, I., Lindgren, I., Madsen, C.Ø., Hofmann, S.: Administrative Burden in Digital Self-service: An Empirical Study About Citizens in Need of Financial Assistance. In: Krimmer, R., et al. (eds.) Electronic Participation. ePart 2022. LNCS, vol. 13392, pp. 173–187. Springer, Cham (2022). https://doi.org/10.1007/978-3-031-23213-8_11

21. Simon, H.A.: The Sciences of the Artificial, 3rd edn. MIT Press, New York (1996)

22. Gigerenzer, G., Goldstein, D.G.: Reasoning the fast and frugal way: models of bounded rationality. Psychol. Rev. **103**(4), 650–669 (1996)

23. Klein, G.: Developing expertise in decision making. Think. Reason. **3**(4), 337–352 (1997)

24. Denne, M., Cleland-Huang, J.: The incremental funding method: data-driven software development. IEEE Softw. **21**(3), 39–47 (2004)

25. Nielsen, J.: Usability Engineering. Morgan Kaufmann, San Francisco (1994)

26. Brooke, J.: SUS - a quick and dirty usability scale. In: Jordan, P.W., Thomas, B., Weerdmeester, B.A., McClelland, I.L. (eds.) Usability Evaluation in Industry. Taylor & Francis, London (1996)

27. Jørgensen, M.: A survey of the characteristics of projects with success in delivering client benefits. Inf. Softw. Technol. **78**, 83–94 (2016)

28. Rogers, E.M.: Diffusion of Innovations, 5th edn. Free Press, New York (2003)

29. Preece, J., Rogers, Y., Sharp, H.: Interaction Design: Beyond Human-Computer Interaction, 4th edn. Wiley, Chichester (2015)

30. Lazar, J.: Research Methods in Human Computer Interaction, 2nd edn. Elsevier, Amsterdam (2017)

Code-Sharing Platform in Programming Learning: A Proposal for a Strategy-Aware Code-Sharing Methodology

Shintaro Maeda[1]([✉]), Kento Koike[2], and Takahito Tomoto[3]

[1] Graduate School of Information and Computer Science, Chiba Institute of Technology, Chiba, Japan
front4.shintaro@gmail.com
[2] Academic Center for Computing and Media Studies, Kyoto University, Kyoto, Japan
[3] Faculty of Information and Computer Science, Chiba Institute of Technology, Chiba, Japan
https://shintaro.maeda.app/

Abstract. In learning programming, it is important to learn from the best of other people's code. So far, we have developed a code-sharing platform with a mechanism for sharing only the code of others who are close to the learner's level. We believe that sharing code that is close to learners' strategies is beneficial for helping them learn from others, so in this study we propose a method for evaluating the strategies of code and a method for calculating the closeness of strategies as similarity. We implemented a filtering method that displays only code with a certain level of similarity to the ranking, and conducted experiments to compare the rankings of our proposed method and the conventional method for expert programmers. The results suggest that the ranking of our method promotes better learning.

Keywords: Virtual Robot Programming · Learning from Others' Code · Strategy-Aware Code

1 Introduction

In learning programming it is important to learn from the best of other people's code [1], as doing so can lead to better refinement of one's own code. However, if there is a difference between the level of one's own code and the code of others from which one is trying to learn, then it may not lead to learning. The learning effect of providing learners with examples is widely known [2], so it is desirable that the difference in level between the learner's code and the code of others be small in order to promote effective learning. However, in a one-to-many programming course, it is difficult for the professor to evaluate each learner's code, create a slightly better code with less level difference, and share it with the learner, because it takes a lot of time to do so.

H. Mori and Y. Asahi (Eds.): HCII 2024, LNCS 14691, pp. 338–348, 2024.
https://doi.org/10.1007/978-3-031-60125-5_23

To solve this problem, the authors have developed a code-sharing platform for programming lectures [3,4]. Since programming lectures are attended by many learners with various levels of programming skills, we thought that the code they write could be used for learning purposes. The developed system evaluates the code written by each learner in real time and stores the data in a database. The system then uses the stored data to share the code with others who are close to each learner's level. Thus, by reusing a learner's code that has the same goal, we can share a slightly better code based on the learner's code without the need for teacher intervention or preparation.

Specifically, this system includes virtual robot programming that visualizes the behavior of code execution results, quality indicators to evaluate code, and a code-sharing control function by ranking that controls the sharing of code that is close to the learner's level based on the score of the quality indicator.

In this study we evaluated the developed system. The results suggest a certain learning effect within the range of the proposed quality indicator [5]. However, there is room for improvement in the method of code sharing. In particular, learner's strategies are not taken into consideration in the ranking function, in which slightly better code is shared with learners, which is the goal of this study. Therefore, when learners learn from others' code, there is a risk that they will not learn due to differences between the strategies in the code of others and their own.

In this study we propose a new ranking function that shares only code whose strategies are similar to the strategies of others' code that the learner is writing. The method determines the similarity between a learner's strategy and the strategies of others, and filters only code that exceeds a certain level of similarity.

We evaluated the validity of the proposed similarity by having programming experts compare a set of code presented by the conventional ranking function to a filtered set of code above a certain level of similarity.

2   Related Work

The learning effects of learning from others' code have been reported in many studies. For example, Tomoto et al. [1] assess the importance of reading others' code (code reading) in addition to writing code themselves, and attempt to develop a learning support system in the form of supporting learners' tracing activities. In addition, Campbell et al. [6] and Michael et al. [7] argue that having novice programmers read code written by experienced programmers in particular leads to better learning effects.

Learning from others is considered effective, but we believe that existing code-sharing methods may not lead to learning due to the difference in level between the learner's own code and the shared code. In general, providing learners with examples has been reported to produce beneficial learning effects [2]. In the area of programming learning, it has been pointed out that providing examples to learners promotes efficient learning, but the learning effect is limited [8,9].

As Chen et al. [10] attempt to adaptively determine how to present examples, it is important to devise ways to present appropriate examples. In Chen et al.'s

340 S. Maeda et al.

study, examples are created by the instructor, so the issue of cost still exists. Thus, learning from others' code is considered useful from an educational aspect, but it is important to devise appropriate methods of presentation (sharing).

For example, using the theory of nearest-neighbor areas of development [11], learners are said to learn effectively in areas between their own current programming level and the next level they could reach with the right support. Furthermore, since programming is a creative task, tinkering (trial and error) by the learner has been pointed out to be important [12, 13]. However, since tinkering requires support tailored to the learner's level of programming, it has been noted that providing examples and improvements based on them is effective.

From these perspectives, we believe that for beginning programmers, learning from slightly better code that is close to their own programming level may lead to beneficial learning activities.

3 Code-Sharing Platform

An example screen of the code-sharing platform developed so far is shown in Fig. 1. The main system screen displays the robot programming implemented in a virtual space and the scores of the quality indicators mentioned later. Additionally, a field with a robot and crops is presented, where learners are required to write code for the robot to properly navigate the field and plant seeds. The planted seeds grow over time, necessitating the writing of code for harvesting the grown crops. Harvesting crops earns scores, adding a gamified element and visualizing the behavior of the code execution through the robot and field interaction. This robot programming facilitates the learners' understanding of the code they have written [14].

When learning from others' code, a problem may arise if there is a difference in level between the learner's code and the other. In this study we attempt to solve this problem by using a ranking function. Specifically, code is ranked using the scores calculated by the quality indicators, allowing for a pseudo-assessment of the learners' levels (high scores). As learners are positioned at their level, code close to their level can be shared.

The actual system screen of the developed ranking function is as shown in Fig. 2. The ranking function allows users to view rankings for each quality indicator, as seen on the left side of the screen. By selecting an indicator (total score, for example), scores for that indicator are displayed in rank order in the center of the screen. By selecting a rank, the corresponding code is shared on the right side of the screen. Note that since the system is limited to displaying code close in level, selecting a higher rank will not share its code on the right side of the screen.

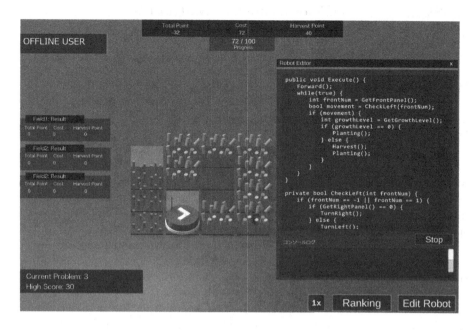

Fig. 1. Example of the code-sharing platform interface.

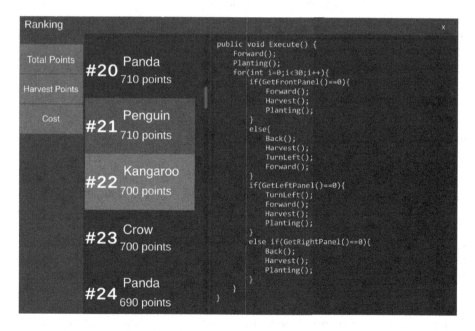

Fig. 2. Example of the interface for the ranking function.

4   Strategy-Based Code-Sharing Method

4.1   Overview

The results of previous evaluation experiments have shown that the ranking function has a certain learning effect [3,4]. However, we believe that it is also important to evaluate strategies in addition to the score-based evaluation that we have proposed, which uses quality indicators to evaluate the proximity of learners' levels.

One of the strategies used in this study is assessing the way a robot moves. This is because there are various strategies for moving the robot to the field, which is necessary to score points in this system. For example, a robot can move (A) around the edge of a field or (B) to search all the fields. When a learner who is using strategy (A) is shared the code of another person who is using strategy (B), the difference in strategy (behavior) may prevent the learner from appropriately incorporating the code into their own, which may lead to ineffective learning.

Even in general programming there are different strategies for the same objective. An example is the description of a program for sorting a one-dimensional array. Several strategies are possible for achieving this goal. The first is bubble sort, which achieves sorting by comparing adjacent values in the array and repeatedly exchanging them as needed. The second is selective sorting, which achieves sorting by finding for each position in the array the minimum value after that position and exchanging it with the element at that position.

Thus, while achieving the same sorting objective, the methods used in the process are different. In other words, sharing the code of someone who uses a selection sorting strategy with a learner who uses a bubble sorting strategy does not lead to better code writing.

Therefore, we propose a method of code sharing that takes into account the proximity of the strategies used by the learners, with the aim of facilitating better learning from the code of others.

4.2   Proposed Method

As examples of common programming strategies, the previous section listed bubble sort and selective sort. While these two types of sorting have one thing in common in that they sort arrays, their behavior when the code is executed is different. In other words, the strategies in this study correspond to algorithms that indicate the procedure for solving a problem. The learner who uses the system writes code using system-specific functions (such as the Forward function to move forward and the Planting function to plant a seed), and the strategy of the learner is the procedure of the function when the code is executed.

In order to consider strategies when sharing code, it is necessary to evaluate the strategies of the code that the learner is writing and the strategies of the code of others with whom he/she is sharing. Figure 3 illustrates how to evaluate strategies and their closeness. In the example in Fig. 3, the learner first calls the Forward function three times using a for statement to move the robot forward, then reads the Planting function to make the robot plant a seed. Thus, the learner's strategy is F?F?F?P. In the same way, we generate strategies from the code for all other learners. Then, we compare how similar their strategy is to the strategies of the others.

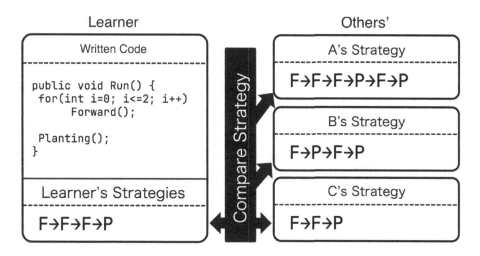

Fig. 3. Examples of comparisons of strategies between oneself and others.

We will explain how to calculate the similarity using the example of Learner A's and Learner B's strategies in Fig. 4. First, the functions (F and P) are compared one by one to determine the number of matching data points. The backtracking method is used to perform multiple searches, and the number of data points with the highest number of matches is used for the comparison. The results are then applied to the number of matches in the figure and divided by the number of data points for Learner A and Learner B. These results are then used to determine the fitness rate and the number of matched data points for Learner A and Learner B, respectively. Finally, the F value is obtained as the harmonic mean. In this study this F value is defined as the similarity of the strategies.

In the example shown in the figure, the number of matches between Learner A's and Learner B's strategies was searched and found to be 5, resulting in a 5/5 fit rate and a 5/12 reproduction rate. The F value was calculated from the fit rate and the reproducibility, and the result was 0.59. Therefore, the similarity of the strategies of Learner A and Learner B in the example shown in the figure is 0.59 (59.0)

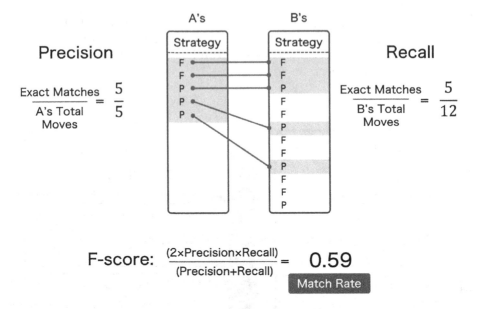

Fig. 4. Examples of similarity calculations.

4.3   Preliminary Evaluation Experiment

We implemented our method in a ranking function in this study. Specifically, as in the conventional ranking function, after sorting based on the score of the quality indicator, the similarity of our proposed method is calculated, and only code that exceeds a certain level of similarity are filtered. Figure 5 presents a set of code generated by the conventional ranking and the ranking that takes into account the strategy using our method. In this case we focused on Problem 3, in which a puddle panel is placed and a description of the process to be avoided by the robot is required. The ranking is in descending order of total score. The E code shown in the figure was chosen as the original code to generate the ranking, albeit tentatively. In addition, the strategy-aware ranking was filtered so that only code with a similarity of 0.3 or higher to the E code was presented. On the other hand, no filtering was applied to the conventional ranking.

In this study, in order to verify the validity of our method, we presented the results (code) of the conventional ranking and the ranking of our method to three proficient programmers, and investigated their impressions based on the results of a questionnaire. As part of the process, a set of code generated from each of the two rankings was presented to the experts, and they were asked to answer which ranking was more useful to the learners in terms of behavior, and to give reasons for their answers. In addition, a map showing the fields and robot locations for Problem 3 was presented, as well as an instruction manual for the system.

4.4   Experimental Results

Table 1 shows the results of the questionnaire, conducted using the 6-subject method (6: 'strongly agree' - 1: 'strongly disagree'). First, the conventional ranking was evaluated by one respondent who gave a score of 3 and two respondents who gave a score of 4, for an average of 3.67. The average rating of the ranking considering the strategy was 5.67, with 1 person selecting 5 and 2 persons selecting 6. This suggests that the latter is beneficial for code refinement activities, as it received a higher rating than the conventional ranking.

In the questionnaire participants were prompted to give reasons for their responses to the questions. The reasons given by the participants for their high evaluation of the strategy-aware ranking were as follows. "Because I thought it would be an acceptable ranking for the learners." and "In particular, the A3 code behaved similarly to the original code, but scored higher, which will help me in how to develop my own code in the future. The other code also has similar behavior, and is helpful in that it incorporates functions, repetitions, and other new behaviors." and "Because I think the code (A1-A4) that can produce good (beneficial) behavior in a fixed way is helpful. Also, the code in A3 uses the same strategy of multiple TurnLeft() as the original code, and I think it will be helpful."

Given these responses, it is suggested that the strategy-aware ranking is more acceptable to learners because they are presented with code that is similar to their own behavior. In addition, this collection of code with similar behavior suggests that learners can learn new functions by repeatedly observing the differences between their code and that of others, and that this encourages them to work on refining their code to be better.

On the other hand, one of the reasons given in the survey for the traditional ranking was as follows. "Because a lot of code is quite different from the original code, I think that learners with high ability can apply and incorporate it into their own code, but I think that learners with low ability will erase their own code and copy it in full because the code is too different." The concern is that the first-time learner will be inhibited in the form of round-copying when they try to perform refinement activities, and that the A ranking is the only code that behaves more like the learner's original code. This is a point that inhibits useful code refinement activities compared to ranking that takes strategies into account. On the other hand, some other responses were "But I don't think it's a useless ranking, since it doesn't seem to be too far from the learner's level," and "As with the A ranking, there is code (B1, B4) that can produce good behavior in a fixed way." These reasons suggest that the conventional ranking also evaluates beneficial code that promotes refinement activities in no small measure (Table 1).

4.5   Feedback

In this study we are exploring how to incorporate the strategy similarity calculation, using the previously mentioned method, into the ranking function. An example is shown in Fig. 6. In this example the similarity between the learner's

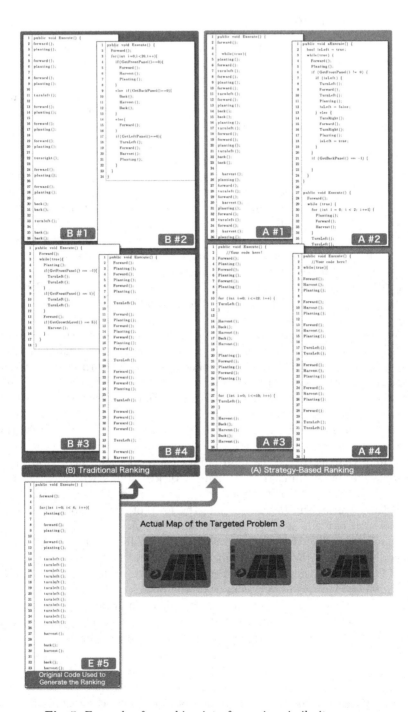

Fig. 5. Example of a ranking interface using similarity scores.

Table 1. Survey Results

No	Question Item	Average
1	Do you think the conventional ranking is useful for conducting refinement activities in terms of behavior?	3.67
2	Do you think that ranking considering strategies is useful for refinement activities in terms of behavior?	5.67

current code and others' is presented as the similarity score. Additionally, only the code with a similarity above a certain threshold is displayed in the ranking, as part of the control mechanism.

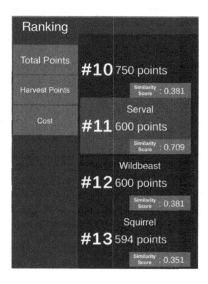

Fig. 6. Example of a ranking interface using similarity scores.

5   Conclusions

Although a code-sharing platform that encourages learning from others' code was suggested to have a learning effect based on evaluations, there was room for improvement when we focused on the ranking function that facilitates the sharing of slightly better code. In this study we have proposed a system that compares the strategies of the user and others and calculates the degree of similarity that represents the closeness of those strategies. In order to verify the effectiveness of the proposed similarity, the authors implemented it as a ranking function. In this paper we compared the code generated by the conventional ranking and the ranking by our proposed method and investigated which is more beneficial to the code refinement activity among proficient programmers. The results suggest that our proposed ranking method shares more useful code for code refinement activities than the conventional ranking method. They also suggest that there is a small number of code that is useful for code refinement activities in the conventional ranking. One of our future tasks is to actually implement and evaluate the ranking of our proposed method on a platform.

References

1. Tomoto, T., Akakura, T.: Report on practice of a learning support system for reading program code exercise. In: Yamamoto, S. (ed.) HIMI 2017. LNCS, vol. 10274, pp. 85–98. Springer, Cham (2017). https://doi.org/10.1007/978-3-319-58524-6_8
2. Sweller, J.: Cognitive load theory and educational technology. Educ. Tech. Res. Dev. **68**(1), 1–16 (2020)
3. Maeda, S., Koike, K., Tomoto, T.: A knowledge sharing platform for learning from others' code. In: Yamamoto, S., Mori, H. (eds.) Human Interface and the Management of Information: Visual and Information Design. HCII 2022. LNCS, vol. 13305. Springer, Cham (2022). https://doi.org/10.1007/978-3-031-06424-1_36
4. Maeda, S., Koike, K., Tomoto, T.: Classroom practice using a code-sharing platform to encourage refinement activities. In: Mori, H., Asahi, Y. (eds.) Human Interface and the Management of Information. HCII 2023. LNCS, vol. 14016, Springer, Cham (2023). https://doi.org/10.1007/978-3-031-35129-7_21
5. Maeda, S., Mogi, T., Koike, K., Tomoto, T.: Development and evaluation of code sharing platform using virtual robot programming (in Japanese). Trans. Jpn. Soc. Inf. Syst. Educ. (in Japanesen) **40**(3), 240–245 (2023)
6. Campbell, W., Bolker, E.: Teaching programming by immersion, reading and writing. In: 32nd Annual Frontiers in Education, vol. 1, pp. T4G–T4G. IEEE (2002)
7. Kölling, M., Rosenberg, J.: Guidelines for teaching object orientation with java. ACM SIGCSE Bull. **33**(3), 33–36 (2001)
8. Abdul-Rahman, S.-S., Boulay, B.D.: Learning programming via worked-examples: relation of learning styles to cognitive load. Comput. Hum. Behav. **30**, 286–298 (2014)
9. Zhi, R., Price, T.W., Marwan, S., Milliken, A., Barnes, T., Chi, M.: Exploring the impact of worked examples in a novice programming environment. In: Proceedings of the 50th ACM Technical Symposium on Computer Science Education, pp. 98–104 (2019)
10. Chen, X., Mitrovic, A., Mathews, M.: Learning from worked examples, erroneous examples, and problem solving: toward adaptive selection of learning activities. IEEE Trans. Learn. Technol. **13**(1), 135–149 (2019)
11. Vygotsky, L.S., Cole, M.: Mind in Society: Development of Higher Psychological Processes. Harvard University Press, Cambridge (1978)
12. Kotsopoulos, D., et al.: A pedagogical framework for computational thinking. Digital Exp. Math. Educ. **3**, 154–171 (2017)
13. Papert, S.A.: Mindstorms: Children, Computers, and Powerful Ideas. Basic Books, New York (2020)
14. Sorva, J., Karavirta, V., Malmi, L.: A review of generic program visualization systems for introductory programming education. ACM Trans. Comput. Educ. **13**(4), 1–64 (2013)

Wisdom Science of Idea and Concept Generation Integrating Diverse Worldviews

Tetsuya Maeshiro[1](✉), Yuri Ozawa[2], and Midori Maeshiro[3]

[1] Faculty of Library, Information and Media Studies, University of Tsukuba, Tsukuba 305-8550, Japan
maeshiro@slis.tsukuna.ac.jp
[2] Ozawa Clinic, Tokyo, Japan
[3] School of Music, Federal University of Rio de Janeiro, Rio de Janeiro, Brazil

Abstract. This paper discusses a model of human group creative activities using the framework of wisdom science, integrating diverse viewpoints focused by each participant, particularly in activities for new idea and concept generation. Relation of the proposed model with tacit and explicit knowledge is also discussed.

Keywords: personal background · emotion · tacit knowledge · explicit knowledge · relationality · quantitative

1 Introduction

This paper discusses a framework model to integrate diverse viewpoints generated in human creative activities, particularly new idea and concept generation in group activities. Diversity of imagination and viewpoint is one of most important aspects of creativity. Most studies on creative process, if not all, target group of humans. An aspect that is emphasized by all studies is the diverse background of people participating in the creative process such as discussions and brain storming sessions of the creative team or group. The logic is that different personal background is reflected on the different individual viewpoint or perspective or focused features of the target "problem", and finally resulting on distinct generated opinion, hopefully each participant expressing opinions and ideas different from other participants.

Although the mechanism is unknown, each participant is assumed to focus on different aspects, possibly influenced by her own background, and expresses different ideas and opinions, also influenced by her background. For background it means age, gender, personality, culture, religion, personal preferences, language, nationality, education, life style, strong and weak points, family, acquaintances, among many others. There is no explicit proof on how these features influence, not to mention that the weight or importance of each feature is completely unknown.

H. Mori and Y. Asahi (Eds.): HCII 2024, LNCS 14691, pp. 349–365, 2024.
https://doi.org/10.1007/978-3-031-60125-5_24

Very few studies treat quantitatively the idea generation and image generation that lead to innovation, besides no quantitative description model exists. Conventional studies focus on processes and mechanisms of individual act, i.e., of single person. Furthermore, even in reports analyzing multiple person discussions, a single shared viewpoint is defined without the verification of the plausibility. In most cases, however, the single viewpoint is implicitly assumed, without any discussions on the validity of this supposition. Studies on group discussions are qualitative and offer very few insights, if not valueless. Similarly, conventional models of knowledge manipulation assume manipulation based on single viewpoint, which can be reduced to an act of a single person.

This paper proposes the necessity of incorporating individual personal backgrounds and emotional aspects to model and understand the mechanism of human creative activities, particularly new idea and concept generation, extending the single person model with emotion [5]. This paper extends the single person model incorporating personal backgrounds as factors that influence idea and concept generation and decision making sequences, and extend for the group creative activities, where multiple persons of supposedly diverse backgounds participate. Description and analysis of creative processes of diverse persons become possible by assimilating personal traits represented as personal backgrounds. A model and theoretical basis to study creative activities by human beings is presented using the framework of wisdom science [4], and this paper presents a framework to analyze the influence of personal background and emotional aspects on idea, image and concept generation, and their manipulation.

Idea and concept generation is the most important and fundamental step in research and artistic activities. Two representative classes of creative activities exist. One is artistic, where the constraints that limit the freedom of creation are weak or practically non-existent. The other one is scientific discovery, where the logic and theoretical constraints of the relevant field has strong influence. Other cases lie between these two classes. Creative activity is a result of knowledge manipulation. As such, explicit knowledge corresponds to concept processing, and tacit knowledge to image processing. Another interpretation is that concept processing manipulates explicit knowledge, and image processing manipulates tacit knowledge.

We assume that human creative activities of a single person are the results of a parallel interaction between language based processing and image based processing. (*Concept Processing* and *Image Processing* in Fig. 1). The former is associated with logic, and the latter with sensibility. We denote the former as *concept processing* and the latter as *image processing*. The term "image" does not imply that the image processing is abstract or vague. On the contrary, most images are clear, although their description, usually using natural language, is difficult, but their mental manipulation is possible. Such operation would not be possible if images were vague. Creative activity is a result of knowledge manipulation. As such, explicit knowledge corresponds to concept processing, and tacit knowledge to image processing. Another interpretation is that concept processing manipulates explicit knowledge, and image processing manipulates tacit knowledge.

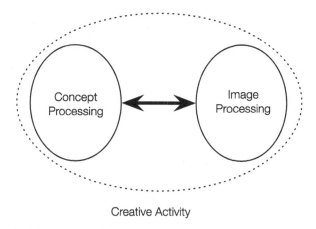

Creative Activity

Fig. 1. Parallel processes of concept processing and image processing during creative activities of a single person

The inseparability of reason and "emotion" is widely accepted [1]. However, conventional models of knowledge manipulation, for instance [6], exclude "emotive" or "non-logical" aspects. This is a flaw of conventional models. This paper treats the model of human creative activities, treating creative process as a image generation and manipulation process, not limited to concepts linked to "knowledge". Furthermore, this paper incorporates the personal background and emotional aspects, which is completely ignored in previous studies.

Wisdom science [4], upon which the present study is based, treats both explicit and tacit knowledge as two different facets of collection of knowledge elements, denoted as *knowledge ocean*. Explicit knowledge and tacit knowledge have contrasting properties, where the former can be explicitly described, is objective, can be communicated through text, shared by a group of people, and represents a consensus of a group of people. On the other hand, tacit knowledge cannot be described by text, is individual, subjective and internal, thus not shared by people, and is strongly associated with the body of each person and personal feelings.

The basic framework of wisdom science is that the elements of knowledge of a person is activated and manipulated consciously for explicit knowledge and unconsciously for tacit knowledge. Our model of tacit and explicit knowledge is fundamentally different from the conventional frameworks where tacit and explicit knowledge constitute knowledge of a person and the two types of knowledge are distinct elements of knowledge of a person (Fig. 2). Therefore, our model proposes that a given knowledge element may be activated as explicit knowledge in one instance and activated as tacit knowledge in another instance. Questioning and answering process is an example of knowledge elements being used in tacit or explicit knowledge depending on situation, represented as small circles in the bottom linked to explicit knowledge and tacit knowledge in Fig. 4. When a person is asked a question, for instance in a interview, the asked person sometimes say opinions, thoughts or ideas that the person has never said before or the person himself was not aware of. And the person himself feels surprised to recognize how the person was thinking about the asked issue. Formulating a sentence to talk involves gathering knowledge elements or concepts related to the content of the speech. In this (i) collecting process and (ii) the meaning generated by the formulated sentence, the knowledge elements that belong to tacit knowledge are activated. In conventional interpretation, this process is a tacit concept being transformed to an explicit concept. However, wisdom science models this process as a concept element that was already evoked as tacit knowledge became also evoked as explicit knowledge. As stated before, tacit knowledge and explicit knowledge are the representations of knowledge elements linked to the consciousness of the person possessing that knowledge.

Few attempts to model the simultaneous use of explicit and tacit knowledge have been reported. For instance, from the facet related to the individuality of knowledge, Nonaka treated the tacit knowledge based on the innovation process, which is a creative activity, of a group of individuals, and proposed the SECI model [6]. The SECI model connects the explicit and tacit knowledge by proposing the mechanisms involved in the endless cycle between explicit knowledge and tacit knowledge. It offers a general framework, but lacks the detailed mechanism of individual processes described in the model, particularly the mechanism of transitions among tacit and explicit knowledge.

A focus of this paper is the integrated treatment of human creative activity with influence of emotion. Activities using the knowledge, which is not limited to "intellectual" activities, is primarily an individual act. Any activity using the knowledge involves not only the explicit knowledge, but also the tacit knowledge. Conventional studies tend to treat explicit knowledge as an external layer of the tacit knowledge or explicit and tacit knowledge as two independent modules, but this paper treats the both explicit and tacit knowledge as two facets of the knowledge of a person.

Tacit knowledge is so denoted because the person cannot describe his own tacit knowledge, particularly by natural language, and is even more difficult, if not impossible, to be described by the others. However, it is often possible to describe vaguely using images or feelings. The author agrees with Polanyi's statement that the inability of description does not negate its existence. Tacit knowledge is contrasted to explicit knowledge primarily on the describability by a text. Explicit knowledge and tacit knowledge are closely related with memory skill and imagination skill, respectively. While the memorization skill is related to rationality, imagination skill is related to emotions and feelings. However, memorization of images is also linked to emotions and feelings.

Wisdom science models knowledge as a pool of knowledge elements, and the knowledge elements are recruited to represent a concept, either explicit or tacit (Fig. 4). The model assumes two distinct processing for each explicit and tacit knowledge, the concept processing and the image processing. This is the basic model. This paper proposes that the personal background and the emotion affects the manipulation of knowledge elements, which correspond to the

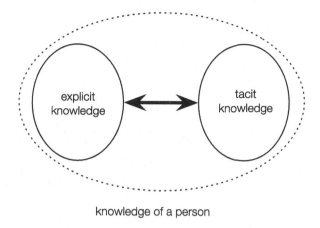

knowledge of a person

Fig. 2. Conventional interpretation of knowledge of a single person

diverse worldview of different persons. The concept and image processings are distinct, but both the personal background and the emotion affect both types of processing (Fig. 3).

2   Concept and Image Fusion

Human creative activities involve employment of personal knowledge [7]. The proposed model of creative activity focuses on the different aspect of knowledge, as the concept processing corresponds to explicit knowledge, and the image processing to tacit knowledge. From the viewpoint of describability, tacit and explicit knowledge share the same ocean that is the set of knowledge elements (bottom of Fig. 4). On the other hand, the creative activity model focuses on more dynamic aspects, and includes additional property of *describability*, which is what differentiates tacit and explicit knowledge.

Concept ocean and image ocean are represented as distinctive entities, contrary to the ocean of concept elements shared by tacit and explicit knowledge (bottom of Fig. 4). We introduced the concept of image in knowledge representation and manipulation as an element with fundamentally different properties from the concept element. The possible operations are also fundamentally distinct, as images can be fused, partially removed or gradually changed, which is impossible with concepts. Therefore, our creative activity model composed of concept and image processing offers a new facet of knowledge manipulation, describing different viewpoint from the conventional treatment of tacit and explicit knowledge

The image ocean can be interpreted as the set of knowledge elements belonging to the ocean (Fig. 6) interpreted as images. Similarly, the concept ocean consists of knowledge elements focusing on their describable aspects. Such classification based on concept and image aspect is completely different from the

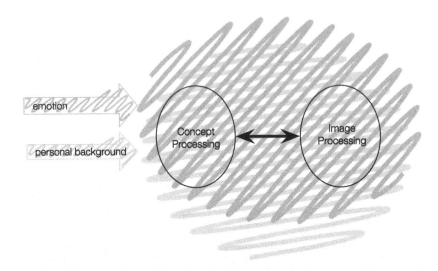

Fig. 3. Single person model of functional interactions between parallel processes of concept processing and image processing with emotion

conventional classification of tacit or explicit, which is based on the describability by the person himself.

Conventional definition that tacit knowledge is processed on unconscious level partially due to its non-describability does not apply to image processing. In this aspect, the image processing is different from tacit knowledge because image processing is executed on conscious level. Undoubtedly image processing is not executed only at conscious level, and images operated in image processing associated with tacit knowledge are manipulated at unconscious level. The basic features to define tacit knowledge are the unconscious and automatic process and inability of description. Therefore, the execution at unconscious level is an essential feature of tacit knowledge, which is not for image processing, then tacit knowledge and image processing are incompatible and are models based on different viewpoints. Consequently, image processing is distinct from tacit knowledge, and they denote different aspects of human intellectual activities. One of main similarities between image processing and tacit knowledge is the difficulty to describe manipulated elements (knowledge or image) using language. Therefore, Figs. 1, 2 and 4 are distinct models of personal knowledge, but compatible as these models share the basic elements belonging to oceans of respective models.

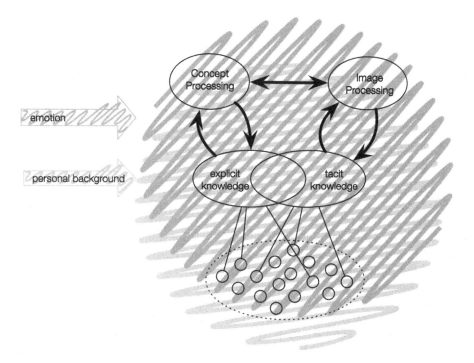

Fig. 4. Wisdom science interpretation of knowledge of a single person. Explicit knowledge and tacit knowledge as activated from the ocean of knowledge elements. Bottom dotted circle represents the core of knowledge of a person, and small circles in the bottom dotted circle denote "knowledge elements". Integrated model of functional interactions between parallel processes of concept processing and image processing with emotion

3   Sequence of Image and Concept Generation

In the sequence of images, at each instant single or multiple images are evoked. Similar is for the concepts. Not all these images and concepts are recognized by the person himself. Single or multiple, the "selection" of the next image is controlled by some mechanism, not discussed in this paper. We propose that this selection is influenced by emotion and personal background (Fig. 5). Thus the generated next image depends on the emotion and personal background, as shown in Fig. 5(B). From the image X at time $T1$, the next image is generated at time $T2$, but the generated image depends on the emotion of the person at that instant and personal background of the person. The "image Y1" is generated if the emotion is the "emotion-A", the "image Y2" if the emotion is the "emotion-B", and the "image Y3" if the emotion is the "emotion-C". The images Y1, Y2 and Y3 are not necessarily completely distinct, and they may be partially distinct. On the other hand, the personal background is assumed to be similar.

The images are probably not independent entities, i.e., there is no "collection of images" from which an image is selected. Instead, the more likely is that an

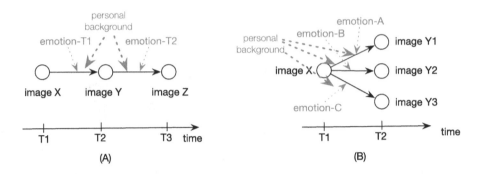

Fig. 5. Sequence of image generation with emotion and set of personal background

image is generated by composing, combining or integrating the "image elements" selected from the *image ocean* (Fig. 6). The figure illustrates that the image Y1 is generated under the emotion-A, and the image Y2 under the emotion-B.

We propose that the emotion and personal background affect on the mechanism of image generation from the image ocean (pool of image elements), similarly to the concept generation. Therefore, identical image ocean with different personal background and emotion will result in differently generated images. As previously noted, generated images are fusion of image elements, and individual image elements are not distinguishable because the images are merged and the image boundaries become blur.

Figure 6 also illustrates the detailed description of image sequence on instant $T2$, where the emotion influences the choice of "image elements" in the process of image formulation. The emotion and personal background influences the whole selection and integration process, which is the reason that the target of the arrow from "emotion" is not clearly pointed. In Fig. 6 illustrates the global influence of the emotion and personal background on the image elements evoking mechanism.

Our experiences suggest that multiple locally different emotions inside one person probably do not exist. Therefore, it is plausible to assume that the emotion is analogous to the environment or an atmosphere that involves the whole concept and image manipulation system (Figs. 6 and 7).

Figure 5 illustrates the sequence of evoked images. In each instant T_i, a subset of image elements $E_1 = (e_{11}, e_{12}, \ldots, e_{1N})$ are selected, and synthesized as a single image. Then on the next instant T_{i+1}, another subset of image elements $E_2 = (e_{21}, e_{22}, \ldots, e_{2N})$ are selected and synthesized. Basically the two subsets E_1 and E_2 are distinct, but may contain same image elements, i.e., $E_1 \cap E_2 \neq \varnothing$. Different images can be synthesized from the identical set of image elements by changing the size or relative positions among image elements in the synthesized image, but we ignore this possibility for the simplicity of the discussion. No restrictions on the number of evoked image elements exist in each time T_i and the value can be the same or not.

Figure 7 illustrates the influence of emotion and personal background on the generation of concepts, or combination of concepts to be more precise, from

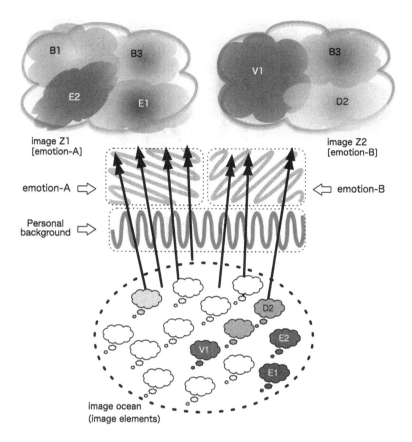

Fig. 6. Image generation affected by emotion and set of personal background. Double arrows represent selection mechanism of concept elements. Emotion-A and -B cannot coexist.

the concept ocean (pool of concept elements). The personal background affects uniformly, unless the background changes due to some reason. Such change is not rare, as a person is constantly under external influence through experiences and inter-personal interactions. On the other hand, emotional states affect more directly and differently for the same person, as the time span of variation of personal background is longer and alteration is smaller than emotion. The change of emotion, however, can be stronger and abrupt from one extreme to the other one, for instance from happy to angry in a instant. Such rapid change in personal background is ignored in this paper.

Figure 7 focuses on the consequences of different emotions' influences, and masks the changes in personal backgrounds, as we assume no multiple personal backgrounds reside in a single person, thus only one personal background is present at an instant. Furthermore, Fig. 7 does not imply the influencing order of the emotion and personal background, although the illustration might sug-

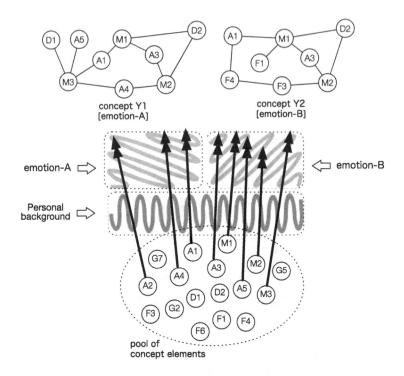

Fig. 7. Concept generation affected by emotion and set of personal background. Double arrows represent selection mechanism of concept elements. Emotion-A and -B cannot coexist.

gest that the evoking mechanism of concept elements are affected firstly by the personal background and after that impacted by the emotion. We propose that the emotion and personal background affects equally with no priority difference between them. Although this paper proposes that both emotion and personal background affect the evoking mechanism of concept elements, this paper does not discuss the detailed mechanism of influence of emotion and personal background on concept element evoking. Furthermore, we do not discuss the relative influence strength between the emotion and personal background, which one is how stronger or weaker.

The point is that different emotions and personal backgrounds result in differently generated concepts (concepts Y_1 and Y_2 in Fig. 7). Then one of these concepts Y_1 or Y_2, depending on the emotion at the moment, will be expressed by the person and subsequently exchanged with other participants of the group, after the transformation into expressed representation. We do not discuss this transformation mechanism.

When thinking about some not yet elucidated physical process, for instance, and trying to formulate a theory about the process, it is helpful to think based on images, visualizing the process as interactions among the elements that are involved in the process. More specific case examples are the airflow through the jet engine, and the airflow around a car when designing the shape of the car with the smallest drug coefficient. Although amateurs and novices cannot, experienced specialists are able to visualize mentally and imagine how the air flows on the surface of a car or a particular component of the car. The person in this situation, such as engineer or designer, is not mentally calculating the velocity of air for each region of the surface of car using mathematical formula. Instead, the person is imagining inside his brain visually, probably visualizing the air stream as thin lines with various colors, the color representing the speed, temperature or pressure. Another example is of the physicist Feynman that visualized mathematical formula of physical processes with symbols representing different variables visualized as symbols with different colors. The point is that the visualization was not descriptive using language, but is the use of images.

In music composition, image comes first and the composer places musical notes on music sheets. When musicians perform, they create images from the musical piece and translate the images to the sound by manipulating musical instruments. The idea or concept generation is not executed using language, but by generating image of the sound to be played or larger image that corresponds to the phrases or melodies. When an experienced critic listens, he is able to identify the lack of emotion, such as love, when a person plays musical instruments. It is interesting that when the playing technique is mainly pursued by the musician, the played music lacks emotional drive that influence the listeners. Moreover, happy and angry or sad emotional state of the instrument player influences the generated sound and played music.

The effects of emotion on idea and concept generation can be classified into two types: (1) affect the generation itself, generate or not the idea and concept; (2) affect the quality or type of generated idea. The former can be exemplified by scientific idea generation, as no idea emerges when the person is in deteriorating emotional state for the idea and concept generation. Note that this state is not necessarily the negative emotional state, as the emotional state that results in favorable condition is person-dependent. Examples of the latter is the music composition and musical performance. Emotion affects the image generated inside the mind of the performer, which is reflected on the sound, tempo, loudness, phrase pause, among other factors, when combined, formulate the impression of the performed music. Note that this does not apply to novices, as novices use all their effort and attention to execute exactly the notes written in music sheets.

Although no formal survey exists, from the authors' experiences and of persons around us, favorable and damaging conditions are personal, differing for each individual. However, good/accelerating and bad/damaging conditions do exist, which implies the necessity to model the influences of emotion on idea and concept generation.

Good conditions can be while in hot spring, taking shower, walking in the forest, during the wakening process from sleep, drinking tea, in sauna, listening to particular music, during the particular time of day such as early morning or evening, in quiet or loud place, light or dark place, large or small place. A good condition for one person can be a bad condition for another person.

As stated before, these conditions do not affect directly the idea and concept generation process. Instead, the influence is indirect, as these conditions evoke particular emotions that influence the idea and concept generation process.

4   Model of Group Creative Process

Figure 8 illustrates the creative activity of multiple individuals. Each individual is modeled based on the framework of wisdom science, where the concept processing and the image processing are executed in parallel under the influence of emotion and set of personal backgrounds (Figs. 4, 6, 7). Identical problem is interpreted by multiple persons, and each expresses own ideas or concepts (Fig. 9). Each person can be interpreted as an independent system with identical target problem. Individual viewpoints are represented inside individual models, where each person executes creative activity with viewpoints distinct from other people's. Furthermore, the set of image elements in the image ocean (Fig. 6) and the set of concept elements in the concept ocean (Fig. 7) are unique for each person.

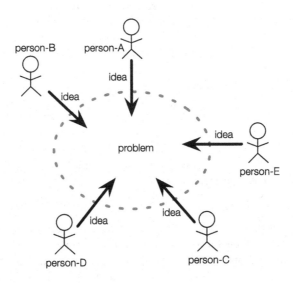

Fig. 8. Group of people in creative activity

Because the group activity necessarily requires that multiple persons are involved, the whole group activity is also modeled as as system. Therefore, the model of the whole activity (Fig. 10) has two hierarchical layers, and can be denoted as a system of systems, where the representation of individuals becomes the subsystem of the whole activity.

The multiplicity of worldviews can be modeled in two schemes. One, let us denote model-W or model-IS (identical structure), is to assume that the structure of individual viewpoint is identical, differing on the importance (weight)

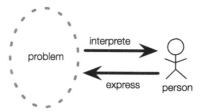

Fig. 9. Interaction of a person with the presented problem

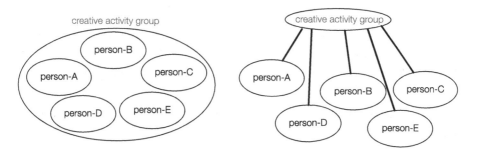

Fig. 10. Two hierarchical level descriptions of group of persons in creative activity

assigned to elements that constitute a viewpoint. The structure of viewpoint formulation corresponds to the structure of a worldview. The other one, let us denote model DS (different structure), is to assume that each viewpoint is formulated differently, thus a viewpoint of one person cannot be compared with other persons'. The mechanism to integrate distinct worldviews differs for these two assumptions. The integration for the model-W is simpler, as the description of different worldviews are similar, then each worldview can be reduced to a vector of numerical values where each number represents the weight (or the importance) of individual features that constitute a worldview. It can be represented as a bar graph or a radar chart. Then the collection of these vectors corresponds to the integration of viewpoints. The integrated representation is simple, and different worldviews can be directly compared.

Simple aggregation of separate models each representing a person, describing the outputs of persons and interactions among persons, is insufficient to model a group of persons in creative process (Fig. 11). This is typical approach of conventional studies. A framework to describe different internal mechanisms and the integrated model of individual models are necessary to analyze the details of individual mechanisms and to understand the group creative process as a whole. Most conventional systems-oriented models treat individuals as blackboxes or a model with identical mechanisms with different parameter values associated with the mechanism, and input and output symbols or information are assigned to each individual, and these intput and output are connected to other individuals' inputs and outputs.

person A

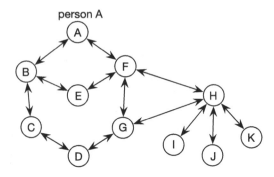

Fig. 11. Conventional model representation of group of persons in creative activity. Nodes represent persons, and bidirectional arrows represent interactions between connected persons.

A more formal model definition follows. Each person's pools of concepts and images are sets

$$P_C = \{e_{C1}, e_{C2}, \ldots e_{Cm}\} \tag{1}$$

$$P_I = \{e_{I1}, e_{I2}, \ldots e_{In}\} \tag{2}$$

where e_{Ci} denotes a concept element in the concept ocean, and e_{Ii} denotes an image element in the image ocean.

Then the concepts and images generated from respective ocean by associating them are described using the hypernetwork model [3]. Evoked images are fused images, and is not a combination of discrete elements as in the acse of evoked concepts, where the concepts and entities representing the relationships among them can be distinguished from other elements.

The generation of concepts and images influenced by emotion and personal background is modeled as a function with emotion and personal background as parameters of the functions

$$f(P_C, E, B), \text{ for concepts} \tag{3}$$

$$f(P_I, E, B), \text{ for images} \tag{4}$$

where E denotes emotion and B denotes personal background.

Since each person with different personal backgrounds presumably generates concepts and images from his own concept ocean and images distinct from other persons', we assume that the concept ocean and the image ocean are distinct from each other. Then we denote the concept ocean and image ocean of person-A as $P_{C[\text{person-A}]}$ and $P_{I[\text{person-A}]}$, respectively. By assumption, for a group of persons A, B, C,..., $P_{C[\text{person-A}]} \neq P_{C[\text{person-B}]}$, $P_{C[\text{person-A}]} \neq P_{C[\text{person-C}]}$, so on. And similarly, $P_{I[\text{person-A}]} \neq P_{I[\text{person-B}]}$, $P_{I[\text{person-A}]} \neq P_{I[\text{person-C}]}$, so on.

Furthermore, it is safe to assume that two persons share some concept elements, $P_{C[\text{person-A}]} \cap P_{C[\text{person-B}]} \neq \varnothing$. For image elements, although it is possible that two persons have completely different set of image elements, it is unlikely that no image element is shared between them. Then $P_{I[\text{person-A}]} \cap P_{I[\text{person-B}]} \neq \varnothing$. Note that this condition is not crucial.

The integrated concept ocean and image ocean of multiple persons participating into a group creative process, for instance, is simply

$$P_{C[\text{person-A}]} \cup P_{C[\text{person-B}]} \cup P_{C[\text{person-C}]} \cdots \tag{5}$$

and

$$P_{I[\text{person-A}]} \cup P_{I[\text{person-B}]} \cup P_{I[\text{person-C}]} \cdots \tag{6}$$

Figures 12 and 13 illustrates this process. The independent concept ocean and image ocean of each person (person-A, -B and -C in Fig. 12) are integrated into a ocean (Fig. 13). The ocean in Fig. 12 is the superset of oceans of person-A, -B and -C. The image ocean and the concept ocean are distinct, although only one ocean is illustrated in Fig. 12.

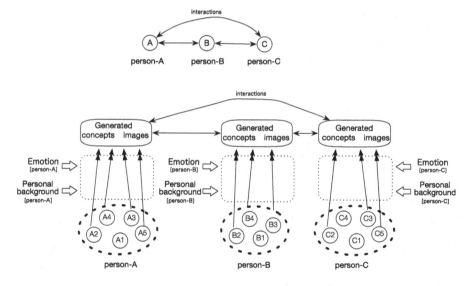

Fig. 12. Model of image and concept processings during group creative activities

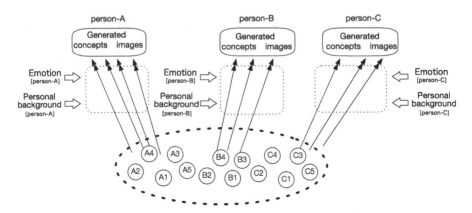

Fig. 13. Integrated model of image and concept processings during group creative activities

5   Conclusions

This paper proposes a model of creative activities of human group using the framework of wisdom science. The two main components of the model are the concept processing and image processing modules, which function side by side. Personal backgrounds are incorporated into the model, as factors that influence the concept and image processing. The hypernetwork model is used, which is capable of representing structures that cannot be described by conventional system models. The concept of system science serves as the basic framework for the modeling and analysis.

This paper is not providing detailed mechanism of the influence of emotion and personal background on the selection of concept elements and image elements. A model framework with enough description capability is necessary to describe integrated personal knowledge of tacit and explicit knowledge. Namely, the model should be able to integrate multiple facets, no prerequisite of precise structure, and no fixed boundaries. The three features are interrelated. The hypernetwork model [3] is the model framework used to describe. No other conventional model framework presents the three properties related to multiple facets. No restrictions exist on what an element represents. It can be a concept described with terms, and image, or an abstract or a fuzzy entity.

The proposed framework can be applied to model concept generation of a single person, focusing on the generation of multiple ideas and selection of a "champion" idea or concept. It is common that idea formulation by a single person is the result of considering multiple ideas, modifying, selecting and discarding ideas until converging to one or a couple of ideas or concepts. The process is related to decision making process of novices and ordinary persons [2] where a person evaluates sequentially; the ideas and concepts that come to the mind and discard or generate next idea or concept if the idea is not good. Furthermore, the proposed model can also be applied to describe how a single person can switch viewpoints, for better idea or concept generation and evaluation.

In the presented model, the interactions among individuals is deliberately omitted. Furthermore, the process of integration of individual ideas and concepts to converge to a single idea or a concept is also excluded. The modelling of these "post" production process will be discussed elsewhere.

References

1. Damasio, A.: Descartes' Error: Emotion, Reason and the Human Brain. Grosset/Putnam, New York (1994)
2. Klein, G.: A recognition primed decision (RPD) model of rapid decision making. In: Klein, G.A., Orasanu, J., Calderwood, R., Zsambok, C.E. (eds.) Decision Making in Action, chap. 6, pp. 138–147. Ablex (1993)
3. Maeshiro, T.: Framework based on relationship to describe non-hierarchical, boundaryless and multi-perspective phenomena. SICE J. Control Meas. Syst. Integrat. **11**, 381–389 (2019)
4. Maeshiro, T.: Proposal of wisdom science. In: Yamamoto, S., Mori, H. (eds.) HCII 2021. LNCS, vol. 12766, pp. 406–418. Springer, Heidelberg (2021). https://doi.org/10.1007/978-3-030-78361-7_31
5. Maeshiro, T., Ozawa, Y., Maeshiro, M.: Emotive idea and concept generation. Hum. Interface Manag. Inf. **14015**, 81–94 (2023)
6. Nonaka, I.: A dynamic theory of organizational knowledge creation. Organ. Sci. **5**, 14–37 (1994)
7. Polanyi, M.: Genius in science. Encounter **38**, 43–50 (1972)

Social Network Structure and Lurker Origins

Yurika Shiozu[1]([✉]), Soichi Arai[2], Hiromu Aso[3], Satoko Yoshida[3], Ichiro Inaba[3], and Katsunori Shimohara[3]

[1] Kyoto Sangyo University, Kamigamo Motoyama, Kita-Ku, Kyoto 603-8555, Japan
`yshiozu@cc.kyoto-su.ac.jp`
[2] Akita University, Tegata Gakuen-Cho, 1-1, Akita 010-8502, Japan
[3] Graduate School of Doshisha University, Tatara Miyakodani, Kyotanabe 610-0394, Japan

Abstract. Those who only look at information on the Web or SNS are called Lurkers. Most people are lurkers, so even if they communicate local issues on the Web, they end up only looking at the information. Nudge and incentive are considered effective in changing behavior, but it was not clear whether they are also useful when people who know each other offline communicate with each other online. This paper conducted a social experiment using an originally developed application, and the results showed that even if people know each other offline, they prefer to use functions that can only be used anonymously in online communities, even taking regional and age differences into consideration, and that the use of communication functions in online communities is promoted by both nudge and incentive. The results of the social experiment showed that even if people know each other offline, they prefer to use functions that can only be used anonymously in online communities, taking into account regional differences and age differences.

Keywords: Lurker · Nudge · Incentive

1 Introduction

Local communities face a variety of local issues, such as watching over children and ensuring public transportation. However, only a limited number of people are active in solving local issues, and even if they communicate via the Web or SNS, the majority of people only see the information. The main reason for this is the fear of using personal information online. However, the details are not yet clear, as they may provide personal information.

Nudge is a non-monetary mechanism that gives decision makers freedom of choice, but its effects may be small and its effects may not be sustainable, incentive refers to a financial mechanism, which has the disadvantages of creating cost problems and inhibiting the decision makers' goodwill in making choices. When paid volunteers are recruited with the intention of solving local issues, incentive is considered to be used to promote behavioral change. On the other hand, when recruiting free volunteers with the intention of solving local issues, nudge can be used. The previous report suggests that when people who know each other offline communicate with each other in online

© The Author(s), under exclusive license to Springer Nature Switzerland AG 2024
H. Mori and Y. Asahi (Eds.): HCII 2024, LNCS 14691, pp. 366–381, 2024.
https://doi.org/10.1007/978-3-031-60125-5_25

communities, there are no age or regional differences in the use of anonymous functions, but there are regional differences in the use of functions that can only be used non-anonymously.

Therefore, this research question was posed to determine whether a feature that allows only anonymous or named use with nudge or incentive when communicating online with those who know each other in offline communities would be a factor in Lurker behavior. Specifically, we conducted a social experiment using an application we developed to share information about local issues and visualization and verified the collected data using correlation analysis and social network analysis. The results of the analysis showed that even if people know each other offline, they prefer to use functions that can only be used anonymously in online communities, even taking into account regional and age differences, and that there is no difference in the effect of nudge and incentive on promoting the use of communication functions in online communities. In the case of promoting the use of communication functions in online communities, there was no difference in the effect of the nudge and incentive surveys, but the effect of extending the functionality from name-only to partially anonymous use was significant.

The following section describes previous studies in Sects. 2, 3 presents an overview of the data, Sect. 4 presents the verification hypothesis and then the analysis, and Sect. 5 presents conclusions and remarks.

2 Previous Studies

Local communities face a variety of issues depending on their location, such as activities to watch over children and the elderly, crime prevention patrols, and securing means of transportation due to the discontinuation of public transportation, etc. However, only a small portion of the population is active in solving local issues. Some residents are unaware of the issues, while others are aware of them but take no action or are unable to do so. Time and geographical constraints are some of the reasons for non-participation in solving local issues, and while there are attempts to utilize "online communities," they are far from sufficient. One of the reasons for the lack of utilization of "online communities" is the existence of lurkers, who only view SNS and Web services and account for 90% of the total number of lurkers and some studies suggest that they should be reevaluated (see Edelmann et al. 2017).

Why do most people become Lurkers? a study by Acquisti et al. (2016) points out that while people remain vigilant and only view web services because they do not know where and how their personal information is being used, in some situations they become unguarded.

We have also conducted research by developing their own application of gamification to help residents become aware of local issues on their own in "online communities". Gamification is the process of incorporating game elements (points, badges, rankings) into non-game matters in order to have fun and solve problems. Shiozu et al. (2022) pointed out that people avoid losing points, even if they have no monetary value, but they have developed a non-anonymous implemented a function to donate points to other participants in a non-anonymous manner and found that only a limited number of people would donate points themselves, that the utilization rate of the donation function was low in some regions, and that the function to anonymously post photos of dangerous areas with comments and to anonymously express approval of the posted photos had little bias among users and no regional or age differences. The results show that there are no regional or age differences in the use of these functions. These results suggest that the difference in function use is influenced by whether the function is anonymous or not.

There are numerous previous studies on human psychology and gamification; Hamari et al. (2013) used a causal model to find that intention to continue using online exercise support services and word-of-mouth intention are enhanced by social recognition, such as user interaction. Hamada's (2015) survey found that gamification positively influences user psychology. Regarding the majority of users becoming Lurkers online, Takahashi et al. (2003) divided Lurkers into active Lurkers and passive Lurkers, and defined those active Lurkers who convey information outside the relevant online community. Lurkers also include those who propagate information.

There are a variety of methods for understanding how Lurker uses data, depending on the subject of the study. For example, according to Honeychurch et al. (2017) and Zhu & Dawson (2023), in the online learning field, data are collected and analyzed using a combination of social network analysis, questionnaires, and observation methods. When analyzing a combination of these methods, a threshold is needed to be a Lurker, and many studies define it according to the Pareto principle.

Sun et al. (2014) also identifies four reasons why people become Lurker: environmental influences, individual preferences, individual and group relationships, and security aspects. Of these, the "economics of privacy" is an area of research related to security and individual and social welfare. Takasaki (2021) refers to Acquisti et al. (2016) and introduces that in Japan, personal information protection has been discussed mainly in terms of legislation, but economics analysis has also been conducted overseas.

3 Data

This study analyzes data obtained from a social experiment conducted for six groups over two periods in two regions by creating an "online community" using an originally developed application (hereinafter referred to as the CSD application).

3.1 Definition of Lurker in This Study

This paper focuses on active Lurker, whose significance and role have not been actively evaluated so far, based on Takahashi et al. It is shown that there are both propagators and practitioners in active Lurker. Although the behavior of others is observed through the application, it is difficult to accurately identify active lurkers as propagators, i.e., those who respond through face-to-face communication such as word of mouth. This is because it is impossible to collect data other than by relying on personal memory (e.g., recollection) or by participant observation. Therefore, in this paper, we define an active lurker as a practitioner as a lurker and analyze the role of anonymity in information diffusion behavior through applications within online communities.

3.2 Data Collection Methodology

The CSD application is intended to activate communication in the local community the CSD application introduces points, one of the elements of gamification, in order to increase continuity. The points themselves have no economic value, and are only meant as an indicator of intentionality; there are several ways to earn points in CSD, but this paper uses point-giving behavior between individuals and the ability to post photos and "like" or comment on posted photos. Those who "like" or give comments to posted photos are considered Active lurkers as practitioners, i.e., those who use the application to observe the behavior of others but respond anonymously through the application.

Point gifting behavior refers to when individual A sends a message to individual B in his/her name, either by giving his/her points to the recipient or by giving only points to the recipient in his/her name. Since the recipient is not notified when points are given, the recipient may not be aware of the point gift. However, by tapping on "Everyone's Common Point History," app users can see who has given points to whom. In other words, the message content is kept secret, but the point gift is visible to all participants. On the back end, the date and time of the point gift, the name of the sender and receiver, and the content of the message, if any, are recorded. Since the point donation action is performed under a name, the donor is considered the Poster in this paper.

The photo submission function allows users to upload their own photos on the map displayed in the application. It is also possible to display posted photos with a note attached. However, app users cannot see who posted the photo and when. Users can also post "likes" and comments on posted photos, but these are also anonymous. For other app users, the number of "likes" and the posted comments themselves are visible, but the name of the user is kept secret. In the back end, the date and time of use of these functions and the name of the user are recorded.

The typology of application functions and actions to be analyzed is shown in Fig. 1.

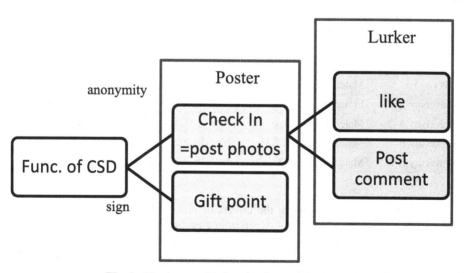

Fig. 1. Sign/anonymity function for proprietary apps

In early September 2023, during the experimental period, the point gift function was expanded to include the ability to send a gift simultaneously from Individual A to all app users, the ability to select multiple recipients, and the ability to send anonymously. This extension adds a notification function that does not require a specific reply. Therefore, point giving is not purely for supporting a specific individual, but it is now possible to give points in order to send a message to everyone. This allows for a robust check of the return nature of point gifting, as observed in the previous report.

3.3 Subjects and Duration of Social Experiments

One social experiment was conducted for each of six groups using the CSD application. The first group was NPO members, with 24 participants. The second group consisted of 9 university seniors from region A, who were also students in the same class. The fourth group consisted of 18 members of a community development NPO from Region A, who were also participants from Region A. The fifth group consisted of 11 university seniors from Region A, who were also students in the same class. The sixth group consists of 12 first-year university students from region B, who are also taking the same class. The first group was NPO1, the fourth group was NPO2, the second group was University A1, the third group was University B1, the fifth group was University A2, and the sixth group was University B2. Participants from the NPO and University A1 were given Omron activity meters for the social experiment, and participants from University A2 and University B were given smartphones with the CSD app installed, An activity meter manufactured by Omron was also distributed. A training session was held in advance for all participants to explain the operation. Before starting any of the social experiments, ethical screening was conducted at Doshisha University and Kyoto Sangyo University, and the experiments were conducted after receiving approval.

A summary of the experimental participants and the duration of the experiment is shown in Table 1.

Table 1. Overview of Social experiments

	Number of participants	period	Age
NPO	Male; 10, Female; 14	Jan. 1.2022–Mar. 31.2022	30 s–80 s
University A-1	Male; 7, Female; 2	June 2.2022–June 16.2022	20 s
University A-2	Male 11, Female; 0	June 8.2023–June23.2023	20 s
University B-1	Male; 4, Female; 7	June 30.2022–Oct. 7.2022	10 s or 20 s
University B-2	Male 9, Female; 3	June 28.2023–Aug 9.2023	10 s or 20 s

To test the difference between the effects of nudge and incentive, it was explicitly stated at the beginning of the experiment that only non-monetary points would be awarded to NPO1, NPO2, and University B1, while monetary incentives would be awarded to University A1, University A2, and University B2 for the first place in the total number of points earned during the period.

The data collected was organized using the methodology of Yamori et al. (2024).

4 Analysis

4.1 Hypothesis

The purpose of this paper is to analyze 1) whether name or anonymity is a Lurker or a factor in the communication function in online communities, and 2) whether nudge or incentive makes a difference in the use of online community applications when people know each other offline. The purpose of this study is to analyze the following questions. To this end, we test the following hypotheses.

First, for 1), we will compare the usage of each group by function. This is a comparison of the point donation function, which can only be used under a name, and the photo posting-related function, which can only be used anonymously.

Hypothesis 1: The anonymous-only feature is more widely used because Lurker is the majority in any group.

In addition, the only users of the point donation function in NPO1 were residents of Area A. Therefore, the number of users of the point donation function in NPO1 and NPO2 were the same, and the panel data were the same. This means that the number of users of the point donation function is the same for both NPO1 and NPO2, making it possible to examine whether there were any changes in the use of the function by extending the point donation function to NPO2, which only allows anonymous use of the function.

Hypothesis 2: Even if the point-giving function is extended to allow anonymous point-giving and simultaneous transmission, the basic structure of the social network of the same group remains unchanged, so point-giving is unaffected.

Next, 2) is clarified by examining the difference in the effects of nudge and incentive on the use of the CSD application to solve local problems. The following hypotheses will be examined by grouping the participants according to whether they were offered nudge or incentive.

Hypothesis 3: Nudge and incentive will differ in their use of CSD app features.

However, since the grouping in Hypothesis 3 does not take into account age and regional differences, and also includes the effects of functional expansion, it is possible to compare University B1 and University B2 in a way that takes these differences into account and is not affected by regional differences and point functional expansion. Therefore, the following hypotheses are considered.

Hypothesis 4: Nudge and incentive differ in social network structure in point-giving behavior, even after accounting for age and regional differences.

4.2 Analysis

Testing Hypothesis 1. First, we verify the hypothesis 1: The anonymous-only feature is more widely used because Lurker is the majority in any group.

The results of the histogram, scatter plot, box plot, and test of no correlation analyses of the experimental participants' use of each function are shown in Fig. 2. R. 4.2.2 was used for the analysis.

For Hypothesis 1, the histogram of the point giving function will be the first graph in the first row, first column. The histogram for the photo posting function would be the

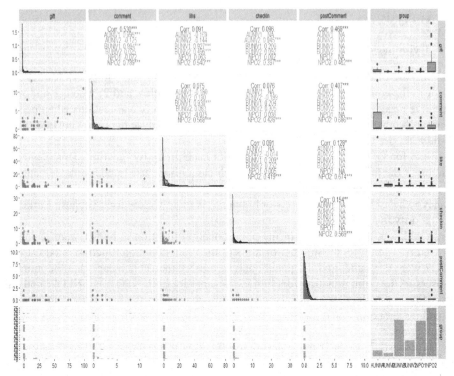

Fig. 2. Usage of each function for all participants

fourth row, fourth column (CheckIn), and the like for the photo posting would be the third row, third column (like) of the graph. Checking the vertical axis of each graph, like has the highest value, followed by photo posting, and finally point giving. This confirms that the anonymous function is used more in all groups.

To control for regional differences, we performed the same analysis as in Fig. 2 for the use of the sign/anonymous function in NPOs and University A located in the same region; Fig. 3 shows that the anonymous function is used more, as in Fig. 2. As shown in Fig. 1, those who give point gifts in the first place are Poster, so they also post photos and comment, while those who only "like" are Lurker, and we conducted these uncorrelated tests. The results showed that the correlation coefficient between point gift and "like" was 0.074, indicating that they were uncorrelated. The correlation coefficient between point gift and comment was 0.513, and that between point gift and photo posting was 0.395, rejecting the null hypothesis. But when the no-correlation test of function use by group is conducted, NPO2 results in rejection of the null hypothesis for any of the function use. This suggests that the effect of the point gift function extension or the age difference may be responsible for this result.

Testing Hypothesis 2. Next, we confirm the hypothesis 2: Even if the point-giving function is extended to allow anonymous point-giving and simultaneous transmission, the basic structure of the social network of the same group remains unchanged, so point-giving is unaffected.

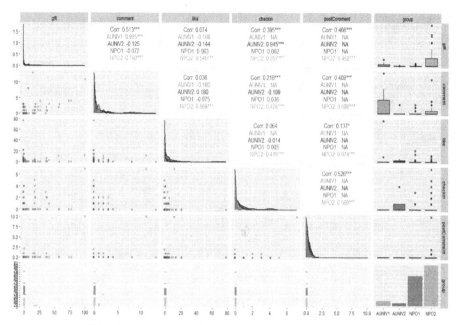

Fig. 3. Usage of each function for participants in region A

The scatter plots in Fig. 4 show that the use of the point gift function itself increased more for NPO2 after the point gift function was expanded. In addition, all the no-correlation tests between each function are rejected for NPO2. The box-and-whisker diagram indicates that NPO1 and NPO2 differ in their use of the point gift function and the comment function when giving points.

The results of Table 2 indicate that NPO1 and NPO2 differ in their use of the point donation and comment functions with a probability of significance of 0.01 or less usage of NPO1 and NPO2 differ with a significance probability of 0.01 or less.

In the CSD application, the gift function allows the donation of points from individual A to individual B either in name or anonymously on the front end. On the back end, the names of the point givers and recipients can be recorded even anonymously, allowing us to use social network analysis to show the network structure of each group's use of the gift function. To further verify the social network structure of the point gift function, we illustrate the results of the social network analysis of the average cluster coefficients for NPO1 and NPO2, the panel data. Gephi 0.10 was used in the analysis.

The average cluster coefficient C is a measure of the degree of connection between persons other than oneself in a group and can be calculated using Eq. (1). Let vi denote the degree of node i, denote the number of real edges between node i and its neighbors, and N denote the total number of nodes in the group.

$$C = \frac{1}{N} \sum_{i=1}^{N} \frac{1}{2} * \frac{e}{v_i(v_i - 1)} \tag{1}$$

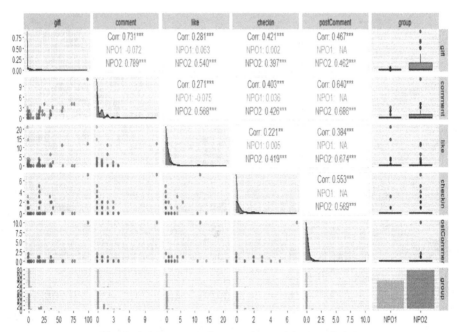

Fig. 4. Usage of each function for participants of NPO

Table 2. The difference between the population mean test for NPO1 and NPO2

	t-value	Degree of freedom	p-value	Difference between average	95% CI. Lower	95% CI upper
gift	−6.419	123.183	< 0.001	−9.987	−13.066	−6.907
comment	−2.773	185.757	0.006	−0.374	−0.641	−0.0108

Comparing Figs. 5 and 6, the number of Edges is clearly different. In Fig. 5, points are unilaterally gifted from point L to points J, U, and F. In Fig. 6, points are unilaterally gifted from point M to each point.

Table 3 is used to review the relationship between individual point giving (Out degree) and receiving (In degree) for the top seven recipients in terms of the number of times they received points.

In the case of individuals, the number of point gifts and receipts was higher for NPO2 than for NPO1. The difference between the number of gifts received minus the number of gifts given is negative in all cases for NPO2. In contrast, the difference between the number of gifts received minus the number of gifts given is negative in all cases for NPO2, while it is positive for NPO1 and zero or negative for NPO2. In other words, even in the panel data, we can say that point-giving behavior changed with the functional expansion. These findings suggest that the impact of functional expansion is significant.

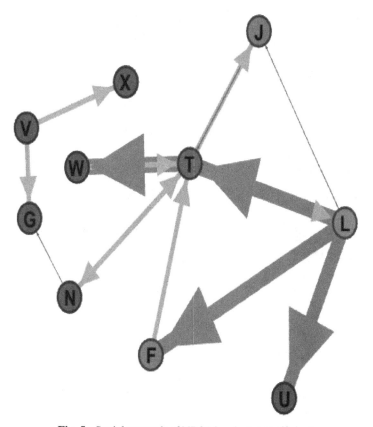

Fig. 5. Social network of NPO1 by cluster coefficient

To account for the effect of age, differences among groups of college students will be examined in a similar manner.

In Fig. 7, the box-and-whisker diagram shows that only University A1 is active in the use of the point-giving and comment functions, but that the other groups do not use these functions very much and that the correlation coefficient is significant only for the point-giving and comment functions.

Verification of Hypothesis 3. To test hypotheses 3 and 4, a social network analysis is used in the following: a summary of the networks of the NPO, University A, and University B is shown in Table 4.

Table 4 shows that the Diameter of each group ranges from 1 to 4, indicating that the individuals in the groups are connected through 1 to 4 individuals and that the size of the networks varies. However, the average degree, the average number of points given within a group, is more than once for NPO, University A1, and University B2, but less than once for University A2 and University B1. The average number of points given per gift is more than 100 for NPO, but less than 100 for both University A and University B. Density, the ratio of points actually given among the possible point-giving combinations within a group, is around 0.5 for NPO2 and UniversityA2, but less than 0.5 for other

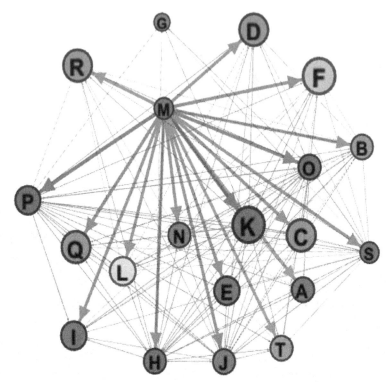

Fig. 6. Social network of NPO2 by cluster coefficient

Table 3. Ranking by In degree for each NPO members

NPO1				NPO2			
ID	In degree	Out degree	difference	ID	In degree	Out degree	difference
T	5	4	1	K	11	18	−7
J	2	1	1	P	9	19	−10
G	2	0	2	O	8	19	−11
F	1	1	0	H	8	19	−11
L	1	4	−3	S	7	19	−12
N	1	2	−1	N	8	18	−10
W	1	1	0	M	7	19	−12

groups. NPO 2 and University A are in the neighborhood of 0.5, while the rest of the groups differ between 0.1 and 0.2. The number of subgroups within a group ranges from 0 to 3. The average cluster coefficient for NPO and University A1 is above 0.2, whereas both University A2 and University B are 0.

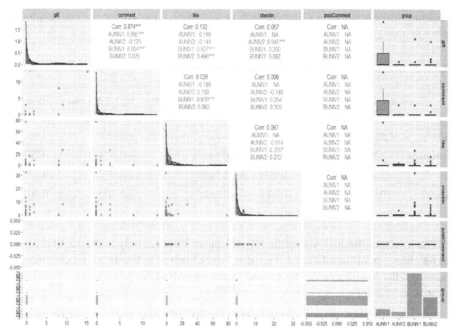

Fig. 7. Usage of each function for participants of University A and University B

Table 4. Overview of each social network structure

	NPO1	NPO2	Univ. A1	Univ. A2	Univ. B1	Univ. B2
Average degree	1.5	8.7	1.444	0.5	0.833	1.167
Average weighted degree	175	5793.3	38.444	5	55.833	99.583
Diameter	3	4	3	1	3	2
Density	0.167	0.458	0.181	0.5	0.076	0.106
Modularity class	2	0	2	0	3	0.486
Average clustering coef	0.235	0.692	0.23	0	0	0

In sum, there was no obvious difference in the network structure between the groups using nudge (NPO1, NPO2 and University B1) and those using incentive (Universities A1 and A2 and University B2).

As in Hypothesis 2, we statistically examined whether there was a difference in function use between the group using nudge and the group using incentive using a Levene test and an independent sample test. Since the significance probability of the Levene test was greater than 0.05 only for photo submission, equal-variance was assumed, and the remaining functions were examined without assuming equal-variance. The results are shown in Table 5.

Table 5. The difference between the population mean test for University A and University B

	t-value	Degree of freedom	p-value	Difference between average	95% CI. Lower	95% CI upper
gift	4.529	368.575	<0.001	3.440	1.947	4.934
comment	−1.306	68.447	0.196	−0.385	−0.974	0.203
like	−1.296	65.686	0.200	−1.589	−4.037	0.859
checkIn	−0.950	369	0.343	−0.282	−0.865	0.301

The results of the analysis verified significant differences only in the use of the point gift function, but no significant differences were observed in the use of other functions. Therefore, the hypothesis 3: Nudge and incentive will differ in their use of CSD app features, did not hold.

Testing Hypothesis 4. In order to analyze the impact of nudge and incentive on the point gift function, taking into account regional and age differences, we examine the network structure of University B1 and University B2 by means of Table 4, There is a possibility that there is some difference between University B1 and University B2 except for the Average clustering coefficient. This suggests that Hypothesis 4: Nudge and incentive differ in social network structure in point-giving behavior, even after accounting for age and regional differences, holds even when regional and age differences are taken into account.

Table 6 shows the results of the Levene test and independent sample test as in Hypothesis 2. The results indicate that there is no statistically significant difference in the use of the point gift function by nudge and incentive, and that Hypothesis 4 does not hold.

Table 6. The difference between the population mean test for University B1 and University B2

	t-value	Degree of freedom	p-value	Difference between average	95% CI. Lower	95% CI upper
gift	−1.170	132	0.224	−0.234	−0.629	0.162

5   Conclusion and Remarks

The results of the analysis showed that even if people know each other offline, they prefer to use functions that can only be used anonymously in online communities, even taking into account regional and age differences, and that there is no difference in the effect of nudge and incentive on promoting the use of communication functions in online communities. In addition, there is no difference in the effects of nudge and incentive on promoting the use of communication functions in online communities, but the effect of extending the functions from name-only to partially anonymous use is significant. The four hypotheses are discussed in detail below.

First, we examine Hypothesis 1: The majority of Lurker users, regardless of group, use the anonymous-only feature more widely than the anonymous-only feature. Hypothesis 1 is supported since the results of the analysis in 4.2.1 indicate that anonymous functions are more widely used than functions that only allow anonymous use, regardless of age and regional differences.

The results of the non-correlation test for each function also showed that there was no correlation between the use of "like" and point gift, and that there was a correlation between point gift and photo posting, suggesting that a certain number of people in any group who are Posters give both point gifts and post photos, but only give "like". As for NPO2, the correlation between point giving and liking is thought to have emerged as a result of allowing anonymous use of part of the point giving function, and it can be said that anonymous functions are preferred in online communities, even if people know each other offline.

Next, we examined Hypothesis 2: Even if the point-giving function is extended to allow anonymous point-giving and simultaneous sending, the social network of the same group would not be affected because the basic structure of the social network is unchanged. Therefore, the social network structure of NPO1 and NPO2 was illustrated by the average cluster coefficient and compared. The results revealed that the impact of some anonymous use of the point gift function was greater for NPO2 than for NPO1. In this social experiment, the groups of university students are all digital native generation. However, they are located in different areas. The University A group has known each other for nearly two years, and the University B group is a freshman class, so the relationships among the members are not as well established as in the University A group. In contrast, the NPOs have been around for a long time. In contrast, the NPOs have known each other for a long time, have been involved in local community activities, and are members of the same group, so stronger relationships have been established. However, even taking into account these differences in relationships, the results show that some anonymous use of the point-giving function had a significant impact in the online community. In other words, it is possible to interpret that, unlike offline, online community participants consider one-way delivery of the content of the message itself rather than the sender's information to be sufficient.

Regarding Hypothesis 3: There will be a difference in the use of CSD application functions between nudge and incentive, there was no obvious difference in the use of CSD application functions between the groups using nudge (NPOs 1 and 2 and University B 1) and those using incentive (Universities A1 and A2 and University B2) except for the point gift function No obvious differences were found except for the Rather, only NPO2 stood out in all indicators except Density and average cluster coefficient, suggesting the impact of extending the point gift function to allow for some anonymous use. However, since the duration of the social experiment differs between the groups and there are regional differences and differences in the age structure between NPOs and university students, we cannot immediately conclude from these results that the effect of the difference between nudge and incentive is small and that anonymous use has a greater impact on point-giving behavior.

Therefore, we examined Hypothesis 4: Whether there is a difference in the social network structure observed in point-giving behavior between nudge and incentive, even when age and regional differences are taken into account. The results of the comparison between University B1 and University B2, taking into account regional and age differences, did not support Hypothesis 4. Rather, only NPO 2 differed from the other groups in the value of each indicator of social network. Taking into account the results of Hypothesis 3, it is thought that the expansion of the point gift function to partially anonymous use has a significant impact. In combination with Hypothesis 3, this suggests that the ability to use a portion of the point function anonymously has a greater impact on promoting the use of the point function than the choice of nudge or incentive. In the comparison between NPO1 and NPO2, the point functioned only as a nudge, but the anonymous use of a part of the point function had a different effect on the use of the function. The effect of name/anonymous use is larger than that of nudge.

The analysis in this paper is preliminary and has not yet been subjected to a detailed statistical analysis. It remains to be tested whether similar results can be obtained after controlling for the sample size of each group, and whether similar results can be obtained after accounting for differences in the duration of the social experiment. Even after resolving these issues, it remains to be verified whether the name/anonymity of the communication function can be said to have a greater impact than the motivation to use the application.

Acknowledgments. The authors acknowledge and thank all participants of our social experiments for their cooperation in preparation of this paper. We received great help from Vitalify Asia Co. Ltd. in the development of the app. This study was funded by JSPS Kakenhi (Grants-in-Aid for Scientific Research by Japan Society for the Promotion of Science) No. JP21K12554 and JP23K11750.

References

Acquisti, A., et al.: The economics of privacy. J. Econ. Lit. **54**(2), 442–492 (2016)

Edelmann, N., et al.: How online lurking contributes value to e-participation: a conceptual approach to evaluating the role of lurkers in e-participation. In: 2017 Fourth International Conference on eDemocracy & eGovernment, pp. 86–93 (2017)

Hamada, T.: A literature review of empirical studies on psychological outcomes from gamification. J. Prod. Dev. Manage. **11**(2), 44–62 (2015)

Hamari, J., et al.: Social motivations to use gamification: an empirical study of gamifying exercise. In: Proceedings of the 21st European Conference on Information Systems, Utrecht, The Netherlands (2013)

Honeychurch, S., et al.: Learners on the periphery: lurkers as invisible learners. Eur. J. Open Distance e-learning **20**(1), 192–212 (2017)

Shiozu, Y., et al.: Is anonymity important in online local communities? In: Proceedings of SICE AC 2022, pp.1009–1012. Kumamoto, Japan (2022)

Sun, N., et al.: Understanding lurkers in online communities: a literature review. Comput. Hum. Behav. Hum. Behav. **38**, 110–117 (2014)

Takahashi, M., et al.: The active lurker: influence of an in-house online community on its outside environment, In: Proceedings of the 2003 International ACM SIGGROUP Conference on Supporting group Work, Sanibel Island, Florida, USA, pp. 1–10 (2003)

Takasaki, H.: Economic analysis of privacy in an emergency. J. Law Inf. Syst. **9**, 81–91 (2021)

Yamori, R., Shiozu, Y.: Proposal for effective prompt design for problem solving in program generation using Chat GPT. In: Proceedings of SICE-IS 2024, p. 6, Higashi-Osaka, Japan (2024)

Zhu, J., Dawson, K.: Lurkers versus posters: perceptions of learning in informal social media-based communities. Br. J. Edu. Technol. **54**(4), 924–942 (2023)

Making Explicit the Problem and Context to Address in Project-Based Software Engineering Courses

Tomás Vera[1,2], Anelis Pereira-Vale[1(✉)], Daniel Perovich[1],
Sergio F. Ochoa[1], and Maíra Marques[3]

[1] Computer Science Department, University of Chile, Santiago, Chile
{tvera,apereira,dperovic,sochoa}@dcc.uchile.cl
[2] Zenta Group, Santiago, Chile
[3] Computer Science Department, Boston College, Chestnut Hill, USA
marquemo@bc.edu

Abstract. In project-based software engineering courses, development teams conformed by students explore the context and problem to address in their projects, before proposing any solution. The quality of this exploration, and the resulting output, usually make a difference on how quickly the development team identifies the goal and scope of the product to be developed. This exploration activity is usually complex and time consuming, since it requires dealing with uncertainties and misunderstandings between the development team and real or fictitious stakeholders. For that reason, the early exploration of the context and problem has been identified as a major and recurrent source of problems in software projects conducted in the industry and the academia. This paper presents an interactive visual tool that helps students explore the context and problem to address in project-based software engineering courses. The tool was used and evaluated by students from four different courses in two universities. According to the participants, the perceived usability and usefulness of the tool is high, surpassing the students' previous experiences when they used requirements engineering techniques for the same purpose.

Keywords: Software project · problem and context exploration · interactive visual instrument · project-based software engineering course · visual knowledge shared space

1 Introduction

In project-based software engineering courses, students usually work in teams developing a new software product or extending an existing one. Typically, that product solves a problem or takes advantage of a business opportunity in a certain context. Experiences reported in the literature show that these courses, projects and products are diverse, and so are the approaches used to address them. However, each development team has to explore the context and the problem of the assigned project before thinking in proposing a software solution.

H. Mori and Y. Asahi (Eds.): HCII 2024, LNCS 14691, pp. 382–396, 2024.
https://doi.org/10.1007/978-3-031-60125-5_26

The output of such exploration activity is critical to understand the challenges the team has to face; formulate the project and allow the team to focus on a possible solution. According to software engineering literature, this exploration process is usually complex. It requires not only to gather and interrelate the information about the problem and context, but also to deal with typical uncertainties and misunderstandings proper from the knowledge exchange among human beings [2,5,14]. The literature recommends addressing this activity involving experts in the business and technical domains of the project [7,12,13]. However, involving experts in software engineering courses is almost impossible to achieve for many reasons, e.g., the instructors cannot ensure that the students have the required expertise, or they cannot find experts that have the time to commit to a course schedule.

On the other hand, this problem and context exploration activity is time demanding as the formal information used as input (if any) is usually scattered and its level of validity is not evident [11,15]. The time demand is also affected by the knowledge transfers from developers to (real or fictitious) stakeholders, and vice versa [2]. This exchange is also a potential source of misunderstandings since it involves structuring and transmitting knowledge from the source side, and the reception and interpretation of this information by the recipient [2].

There is a long list of challenges to address during the early exploration of a context and a problem. Therefore, this activity has been recognized as a major and recurrent source of issues in software projects conducted in both industry and academia [6]. Although the magnitude of the challenges confronted by the teams varies from project to project, in academic scenarios they tend to be high because students' background and expertise is still low.

Students teams usually have the technical knowledge and capability to develop the software solution of the assigned project. However, most of them do not know how to explore the business process and the intricacies of the context by interacting with a counterpart (e.g., a user, customer or stakeholders). Moreover, in academic settings, students have a predefined time window to perform and report their activity, which involves the specification and agreement of a complete and correct view on these two foundational components of the project.

Today, most of the project-based software engineering courses use shortcuts or bypasses to avoid dealing with these challenges. Although these approaches are valid in some project scenarios, most of industry projects will require new engineers to be able to properly address the exploration of the context and problem at the beginning of the software development phase.

This article presents an interactive visual tool designed to help students explore the context and problem to address in software projects, particularly for processes that perform information management [8]. Typically, these processes are supported by information systems; therefore, the problems that students have to address in their projects require developing, adjusting or extending one of these systems.

Next section briefly introduces the background on exploration activities in project-based software engineering courses. Section 3 illustrates the structure of the addressed process and discusses the related work. Section 4 presents the visual tool conceived to deal with the stated exploration activity. Section 5 presents the evaluation of the potential impact of the tool in academic scenarios. Finally, Sect. 6 presents the conclusions and future work.

2   Background

Today, the software industry has few alternatives to perform an exploration activity in a cost-effective way without involving experts [13,18], and these alternatives have low chances of being used in project-based software engineering courses due to the requirements and constraints to utilize them. Therefore, the exploration activity in these courses usually follows one of three basic approaches: 1) skipping the activity, 2) reducing the need to perform it, or 3) addressing it by using regular requirements engineering practices. Usually they are used in initial, intermediate and advanced courses respectively.

The first approach is frequently materialized through courses where only greenfield fictitious projects are conducted by students teams. Typically, each team proposes the context, the problem and the solution to develop. Most of these proposals are within or close to the proponents' comfort zone; therefore, the exploration activity becomes trivial. In most cases, the team can skip the activity since they already have knowledge about the context and problem required to propose a solution [16].

The second approach also involves performing greenfield fictitious projects, but in this case the team should explore the context and the problem by interacting with a counterpart (not necessarily a real stakeholder). Typically, a member of the instructional team plays the role of stakeholder. In these scenarios, the instructor usually proposes a pool of projects that are assigned to teams or the teams choose the project. Given the projects are all greenfield (i.e., there is little background to explore), not real (e.g., with a blurring scope), and the counterpart is not trying to address a real need, there is low motivation to go in-depth in the context and problem exploration. So, this activity requires to be done only superficially. Moreover, in these courses the impact of the project output is usually not evaluated, therefore, there is not much motivation among students or the instructional team to perform an in-depth exploration.

The third approach considers greenfield and brownfield projects, where there is a real counterpart and the team has to explore the context and problem (or opportunity) by interacting with stakeholders. This approach is frequently adopted in capstone courses [17], where students work in an open source project or addressing the needs of an organization. A practical capstone course is strongly recommended by ACM/IEEE [1]. In this scenario, it is mandatory to perform an appropriate context and problem exploration, because the impact of the resulting software product will be evaluated by the stakeholders at the end of the project. This is the exploration scenario that is supported by the proposed tool. In the next section we discuss the current techniques and tools to deal with this exploration activity.

3   Related Work

When software engineering project-based courses involve real projects and stake-holders (typically, advanced courses), the software process usually considers an initial stage focused on understanding the context and problem, and conceiving preliminary ideas of potential solutions. The first two components should be analyzed in-depth and validated with stakeholders. The third one should be aligned to the previous ones. Figure 1 summarizes the structure and dynamic of this exploration activity.

Typically, the activity starts when the development team receives the stake-holder's request. This request should be agreed in advance between the stake-holder and the instructor to ensure that the size, scope and complexity of the challenges are attainable for the students, and also that the different projects are equivalent in terms of knowledge and effort required to succeed. Although the project boundaries are flexible, this preliminary definition establishes an initial scenario to negotiate.

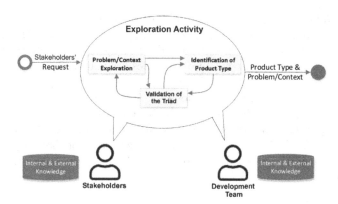

Fig. 1. Structure and dynamic of the exploration activity (based on [18].

The exploration activity has no predefined workflow, but involves three major activities that are intertwined: problem and context exploration, identification of possible solutions, and validation of that triad. It is recommended that stakehold-ers and the development team co-create and co-validate any artifact generated in this stage. For instance, the context, problem specification, and eventually the mock-ups of solution ideas. The process ends when the participants are comfort-able with the specification of the three artifacts. Making explicit the artifacts helps participants validate and reach an agreement quickly.

This exploration stage is usually materialized through a zero sprint when fol-lowing an agile development approach like Scrum [4,9]. This stage also appears as part of the conception phase of semi-structured software processes like EduPro-cess [10]. The exploration is performed in a particular time window, and has a clear output that is formally reviewed with the stakeholders and the instructional team. In this review activity, the team has to demonstrate that it has total control of the project; i.e., the context and the problem are properly identified, understood and agreed, as well as the potential solution that will be developed.

A recent systematic literature review on capstone courses shows that students are usually more interested in eliciting the requirements of the solution than understanding the problem and context they have to address [17]. Moreover, they use mainly interviews and questionnaires to gather information [13,18] and few documentation (e.g., sketches and documents) to make explicit the stakeholders needs and the team proposals [17]. The output of the exploration activity is usually poor in terms of the knowledge it provides (usually it is superficial). This result is evidenced in academic and industry projects [13,17,18], showing a clear need to improve the support for the exploration activity illustrated in Fig. 1.

4   The Interactive Visual Tool

As mentioned before, the proposed visual tool was designed to support the exploration activity when the study object is an information management process [8]. For instance, managing credits of a bank, digital records of a hospital or sales performed through a marketplace. These processes are usually supported by mobile or Web information systems, which should be frequently adjusted or extended due to changes in the market conditions, or new needs that appear in the customer organization. Therefore, the target product to explore and intervene is a business process that takes place in a particular business context. Consequently, the students will have to understand the project scenario before proposing to develop an information system (or adjust an existing one) dealing with the current situation.

4.1   The Shared Workspace

When the students (representing the development team) have to explore the information management process, in order to determine its structure, context and problem to address, they use the visual collaborative tool shown in Fig. 2. The application implements an interactive canvas, as a shared workspace, where the members of the development team and also the stakeholders can co-create, refine and evaluate the specification of the problem and context to address, and also a first idea of a potential solution. The tool also allow instructors or teaching assistants to review the status of the canvas without interfering in the exploration process.

Any particular canvas represents a project, in which the participants are enrolled as developers or stakeholders. Both profiles have the same capabilities, and they are differentiated only to make explicit the agreements between both parts. Developers and stakeholders profiles can also have one person defined as a "leader" for a particular project. The person who has the "leader" role is able to vote about the inclusion or exclusion of post-its into the canvas. The Post-it represents the classic paper sticky note that allows writing notes on it. In the context of the canvas, it enables the process of writing down the components of each section on small notes.

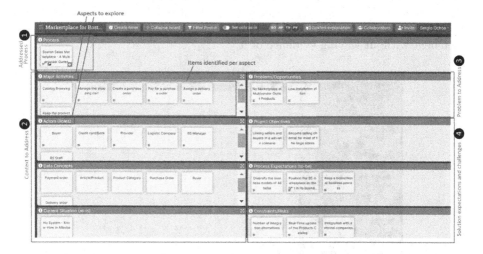

Fig. 2. Collaborative system that implements the visual instrument as a shared space.

The canvas has four major sections (highlighted in green), where their context (set of post-its) can be co-created by the development team, and validated and agreed with the stakeholders. These sections are: (1) the process to be addressed, (2) the current process description, which represents the project context, (3) the problem to address (with their own process and context), and (4) some preliminary ideas about potential solutions, including their expectations and challenges.

Each major component includes sections that characterize it and describe it in more detail. For instance, the second component (i.e., "Context to Address") should be characterized indicating the major activities of the process, the roles (actors) in charge of performing the activities, business information managed by the process (data concepts), and the type of support that the process has today (current situation), in case it is currently being performed in some way. These sections represent the items to explore by the development team, with the support of the stakeholders, in order to characterize the process, the problem and the context to address.

4.2 The Items Description

Each component to explore includes a set of post-its that represents such characterization. Figure 3 shows the detailed description of the post-it "Catalog Browsing", specified in the section "major activities" of the process described Fig. 2.

Every post-it embeds several capabilities, e.g., the possibility to be voted to determine its inclusion or exclusion of the project. Its content allows attaching multimedia resources, for instance, an audio explaining the content of the item (post-it) or a sketch that helps communicate the post-it meaning. Any modification on the content of an already voted item automatically nullifies the previous votes; therefore, a new agreement needs to be reached. This function avoids that any side (developers or stakeholders) can arbitrarily change the content of an agreement without leaving evidence of it.

Fig. 3. Description of the post-it "Catalog Browsing" specified in Fig. 2.

The items of the canvas that have been positively voted by developers and stakeholders as correct and relevant, show a badge in green in the bottom-right corner. Thus, it is easy to identify which items of the board are already agreed, and which items are still pending of being agreed by one side (shows a blue badge) or by both sides (no badge).

4.3   Services of the Tool

The application provides several services to every project (i.e., problem exploration canvas), and most of them are accessible through the toolbar (Fig. 4). The first one is the main menu that allows the users to access projects in which they are enrolled. The users can also create new projects and delete those in which they have the creator role. The main menu also provides access to a layout editor that the user can utilize to create new templates for the canvases; for instance, to explore different types of study objects, like IoT or smart systems.

Fig. 4. Services accessible through the toolbar.

After the main menu, the tool shows the public name of the project that is used as ID and also as information source to search projects by keywords. The timer (third component) allows creating a time window that is used by participants in a session to perform individual work; e.g., to co-create, review, update and vote items. The fourth component allows the users to perform zoom-in and zoom-out on the canvas or on any of its sections. The sixth and seventh components are used to filter the post-its allowing the users to see what is relevant for them according to the activity they are doing.

The coloured badges show the acronym of the participants' names who are currently connected to the project. The guided explanation is an on-demand autonomous service that delivers to the user an explanation of the canvas content. It is particularly useful for people that are just getting into the developers of stakeholders team.

The collaborators show users who are participants from every side (Fig. 5). It also indicates who are the leaders from each side, i.e., users that can vote on post-its in the canvas.

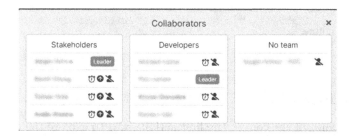

Fig. 5. Users enrolled in the current project.

The invitation service allows users to create a shared link to access the canvas, and also to send an invitation by email to a new collaborator. The last component of the toolbar shows the name of the current user, and allows the users to change the password to access the tool and their public name that is visible to other users.

5   The Evaluation Process

For the evaluation process we considered various instances of five project-based software engineering courses. Two of them were undergraduate courses delivered by the Computer Science Department of the University of Chile (CC4402 and CC5401), and other two courses were part of a software engineering professional master program offered by the same institution (CC73J and CC63H). The last course (CSCI3390) was delivered at Boston College (USA) during 2023 to undergraduate students.

All projects involved: development, adjustment or extension of a Web information system. 65% of these projects were real and involved real stakeholders. The rest of the projects were fictitious, and the members of the instructional team played the role of stakeholder. In the undergraduate courses students work in the project involved 14 weeks, and 7 weeks for graduate courses. Table 1 shows a summary of the courses and instances considered in this evaluation process.

Table 1. Summary of courses involved in the evaluation process.

Course ID	Course Name	# Students	# Projects	Stakeholders	Real Projects	Project Duration	Editions	Institution
CC4402	Project Formulation, Eval. & Mgmt	214	37	No	No	14 weeks	2022–2023	University of Chile
CC5401	Software Engineering II	363	47	Yes	Yes	14 weeks	2020–2023	University of Chile
CSCI3390	Conception of Soft. Projects and Products	20	4	No	No	14 weeks	2023	Boston Collage
CC73J*	Project Management Workshop	24	5	Yes	Yes	7 weeks	2022–2023	University of Chile
CC63H*	Requirement Engineering	40	8	Yes	Yes	7 weeks	2022–2023	University of Chile
Total		**661**	**101**					

(*) Graduate course

5.1   Evaluation Process

In every instance of the course, the first activity was to explore the context and problem (or opportunity) to address, and also to present an idea of a potential solution to develop. The output was a document specifying such information, when the team did not use the canvas; in another case, the output was the canvas. Table 2 shows the rubric used to evaluate these outputs. Moreover, the knowledge acquired by the development team about the context, problem and potential solution were evaluated through a software technical review (STR) [3], where stakeholders participated when real projects were addressed by the teams.

Every review session involved at least two people of the instructional team in charge of the course, as reviewers. The result of these reviews received a grade, which was discussed and agreed among members of the instructional

Table 2. Rubric to evaluate the output of the exploration process.

Item	Weight	Description
Context	20%	Clarity, correctness and completeness of the specification.
Problem/opportunity to address	20%	Clarity, correctness and delimitation of the problem (focus and limits).
Current situation	10%	Clarity, correctness and completeness of the specification.
Envisioned solution	10%	Clarity, correctness and completeness of the specification.
Type of users (and stakeholders)	5%	Clarity, correctness and completeness of the specification.
Expected impact	5%	Clarity, correctness and completeness of the specification.
Oral presentation	30%	Clarity of the presentation and quality of the answers to the reviewers

team playing the role of reviewer. This grading activity took place in a particular session after the STR.

Considering these grades, we compared the results of the exploration process with and without using the proposed tool. The teams that did not use the proposed tool, utilized regular requirements engineering techniques to carry out the exploration. For instance, informal and semi-structured interviews, workshops and analysis of legacy information (if any). Moreover, after finishing the problem and context exploration activity, interviews were conducted with a random sample of participants in order to gather information about the usability and usefulness perceived by them. The participation of the people in the interviews was voluntary. As reward, they received a for free and indefinite access to the tool for their organizations.

5.2 Evaluation Results

Table 3 shows a summary of the exploration activity results, with and without the support of the tool. Considering these results, and also the comments of the participants, we identified that the use of the tool had different impacts in undergraduate and graduate courses. For that reason, we present the analysis of the evaluation results considering these two perspectives.

As mentioned before, the undergraduate courses are CC4402, CC5401 (both happened in Chile) and CSCI3390 (USA). Only CC5401 (Chile) has history in performing this type of exploration activity with and without the tool. The other two courses were new, and they used the exploration tool since its first instance (in Spring 2022 and Fall 2023 respectively). In all cases where the tool was used, that was the first time the students interacted with the application (there were no previous experience using the tool).

Table 3. Results of the exploration activity with and without the tool support.

Course ID	Using the Tool					Without Using the Tool				
	Semester	# Students	# Project	Grade	Std.Dev.	Semester	# Students	# Project	Grade	Std.Dev.
CC4402	Spring 2022	46	11	6.6	0.4					
	Fall 2023	43	10	6.6	0.3					
	Spring 2023	125	16	6.3	0.5					
	Total	214	37							
	Avg	71	12	6.5	0.4					
CC5401	Fall 2022	85	8	6.5	0.1	Fall 2020	40	6	6.2	0.3
	Spring 2022	38	6	6.4	0.6	Spring 2020	39	6	6.3	0.3
	Fall 2023	26	4	6.2	0.2	Fall 2021	76	8	6.1	0.2
	Spring 2023	17	3	6.2	0.2	Spring 2021	42	6	6.2	0.4
	Total	166	21			Total	197	26		
	Avg	42	5	6.3	0.3	Avg	49	7	6.2	0.3
CSCI3390	Fall 2023	20	4	6.5	0.1					
CC73J	Fall 2023	9	2	6.8	0	Fall 2022	15	3	6.4	0.3
CC63H	Fall 2023	14	3	6.9	0.1	Fall 2022	15	3	6.1	0.2
						Fall 2021	11	2	6.3	0.2
						Total	26	5		
						Avg	13	3	6.2	0.2

Concerning the graduate courses (CC73J and CC63H, in Chile), both of them performed the exploration activity with and without the proposed application. These courses follow a professional perspective, and therefore, software engineers are enrolled in them. Similar to the undergraduate courses, the students had no previous experience using the supporting tool.

Results in Undergraduate Courses. In order to understand the impact of using the tool, let us start analyzing the results in the course CC5401. The grades in both scenarios (with and without the tool) are quite similar, showing a light improvement when the tool was used. However, the difference is not statistically significant to draw conclusions. The standard deviation between both scenarios is less than 0.1.

The results of the teams in the other two courses were consistent, and a bit better than those obtained in CC5401. Although the results are still preliminary, they seem to show a baseline in the quality of the output when the tool is being used to explore the problem and context. That quality tends to be better than when regular requirements engineering techniques are used to conduct the exploration activity.

The interviewed students provided several comments. The most frequent ones indicate that the use of the tool:

- *Reduces the effort of exploring the problem and context,* because it provides them a kind of guideline to perform the activity. Various students highlighted the fact that the information representation through a visual canvas reduces the cognitive load, particularly when they have to understand or update the canvas content.
- *Eases the discussion and allows a more in-depth understanding of the problem, context and solution.* Having the specification visible in a single page

that is shared by all participants helps relate concepts, validate them and realize how they contribute to create a big picture of the challenge to address. Although the grades obtained by the students in this activity do not necessarily reflect this aspect, it can be explained because of the "apprentice attitude" usually adopted by the students in academic activities.

- *Makes them feel more comfortable with the output of the activity.* The students feel that the canvas reflects properly both, the knowledge on the study objects, and the agreement reached with the stakeholders. According to them, this represents a better starting point to think about the solution than when the problem and context specification is based on a text document.

Results in Graduate Courses. In the case of graduate courses, the students' grades and opinions were much more conclusive, probably because they usually had experience performing this exploration activity in real projects. The results show that the outcome of the activity is considerably higher when the tool is used as support for the exploration process. The participants raised the same comments than the undergraduate students, but they also highlighted the following aspects as benefits of using the tool:

- *Low entry barrier.* The canvas structure is easy to understand and to realize the rationale behind its design. Such structure helps address the exploration process, guiding the information gathering and making that activity clear for the participants; particularly, when the provider is exploring a business domain in which it does not have much knowledge.
- *Flexible participation of providers and stakeholders.* The shared space and the collaboration services provided by the tool gives flexibility to each other's participation (the tool allows synchronous and asynchronous collaboration). Although the discussions and negotiations are usually performed in synchronous sessions, they appreciate the support for asynchronous activities, like items' creation, review and voting. Particularly, they valued having no limitations to access the problem and context specification.
- *The activity is perceived as more cost-effective.* Most graduate students think that using the tool is more cost-effective than using traditional exploration techniques for several reasons; however, they highlighted two aspects. On the one hand, the exploration can be addressed at different abstraction levels on the same canvas, e.g., first to focus on the major aspects and get an agreement on them, and then to go in-depth to agree on the details of each item. On the other hand, the agreements between providers and stakeholders are explicit; this reduces the space for uncertainties and misunderstandings.
- *The canvas acts as a compass during the project.* Although the content of the canvas is initially created and agreed at the beginning of the project, it can be then updated and re-agreed during the project execution, by adjusting mainly the scope of the problem to address and expectations on the solution. The engineers indicated that such a capability helped them be focused on the target (i.e., in the expected impact of the solution), even if it is adjusted during

the project. Moreover, they appreciated that any change in these definitions are always explicit and visible for all people involved in the project.

6   Conclusions and Future Work

This article presents an interactive visual tool, designed to help students perform the problem and context exploration activity, and to deal with several challenges that appear when regular requirements engineering techniques are used to support this exploration process. The challenges become harder when the process is performed by non-expert people, which is usual in undergraduate project-based courses.

The tool is a shared workspace that allows synchronous and asynchronous participation of stakeholders and developers enrolled in a software project. Using this application they can collaborate to explore, specify and agree the problem and context to address. The output of the activity is a canvas that embeds items. The set of items defined in the canvas characterize and describe the problem and context to address, and also the expectations stakeholders have on the solution. Based on the canvas specification, the development teams can propose solutions to deal with the problem in context.

Although the article illustrates the exploration of processes that performs information management [8], the tool embeds an editor of layouts that allows software providers to create new layouts for addressing other study objects; e.g., IoT systems or smart systems. Every new layout will be available for the users through a new canvas template.

The tool was evaluated in five project-based software engineering courses: three of them for undergraduate students (in two different institutions) and the other two for graduate students. The obtained results were positive and consistent, and the services of the tool were appreciated by both populations. However, the application had a higher impact when it was used by graduate students; in this case, experienced software engineers exploring contexts and problems in industry projects.

Although the results on the impact of this tool is still preliminary, they are highly encouraging. The next steps in this initiative is to continue evaluating the tool in new academic scenarios, and to make the tool available for use in academic institutions.

Acknowledgments. The research work of Anelis Pereira-Vale has been funded by ANID - Subdirección de Capital Humano/Doctorado Nacional/2021-21211216, Chile.

References

1. ACM/IEEE: ACM/IEEE joint task force on computing curricula: Software engineering 2014: Curriculum guidelines for undergraduate degree programs in software engineering (2014). https://ieeecs-media.computer.org/assets/pdf/se2014.pdf
2. Arduin, P.E.: On the measurement of cooperative compatibility to predict meaning variance. In: 2015 IEEE 19th International Conference on Computer Supported Cooperative Work in Design (CSCWD), pp. 42–47 (2015). https://doi.org/10.1109/CSCWD.2015.7230931
3. Barbacci, M.: The software technical review process. Technical Report CMU/SEI-88-TR-020, Carnegie Mellon University, Software Engineering Institute (1988)
4. Carlson, D., Soukop, E.: Why is sprint zero a critical activity. In: Cross Talk, pp. 35–37 (2017). https://zlmonroe.com/CSE566/Readings/3.Why_Is_Sprint_Zero_a_Critical_Activity.pdf. Accessed 12 Jan 2024
5. Fernández, D.M.: Supporting requirements-engineering research that industry needs: the napire initiative. IEEE Softw. **35**(1), 112–116 (2018). https://doi.org/10.1109/MS.2017.4541045
6. Frattini, J., et al.: An initial theory to understand and manage requirements engineering debt in practice. Info. Softw. Technol. **159**, 107201 (2023). https://doi.org/10.1016/j.infsof.2023.107201
7. Hickey, A., Davis, A.: Elicitation technique selection: how do experts do it? In: Proceedings 11th IEEE International Requirements Engineering Conference 2003, pp. 169–178 (2003). https://doi.org/10.1109/ICRE.2003.1232748
8. Jaeger, P.T., Thompson, K.M., McClure, C.R.: Information management. In: Kempf-Leonard, K. (ed.) Encyclopedia of Social Measurement, pp. 277–282. Elsevier (2005)
9. Maria, R.E., Rodrigues, L.A., Pinto, N.A.: Scrums: a model for safe agile development. In: Proceedings of the 7th International Conference on Management of Computational and Collective IntElligence in Digital EcoSystems, MEDES 2015, pp. 43-47. Association for Computing Machinery, New York (2015). https://doi.org/10.1145/2857218.2857225
10. Marques Samary, M.: A Prescriptive Software Process for Academic Scenarios. Ph.D. thesis, Universidad de Chile - Facultad de Ciencias Físicas y Matemáticas (2017). https://repositorio.uchile.cl/handle/2250/144289. Accessed 23 Jan 2024
11. Muhammad, A.P., Knauss, E., Batsaikhan, O., Haskouri, N.E., Lin, Y.C., Knauss, A.: Defining requirements strategies in agile: a design science research study. In: Product-Focused Software Process Improvement: 23rd International Conference, PROFES 2022, Jyväskylä, Finland, 21–23 November 2022, Proceedings, pp. 73-89. Springer, Berlin (2022). https://doi.org/10.1007/978-3-031-21388-5_6
12. Ochoa, S.F., Robbes, R., Marques, M., Silvestre, L., Quispe, A.: What differentiates Chilean niche software companies: business knowledge and reputation. IEEE Softw. **34**(3), 96–103 (2017). https://doi.org/10.1109/MS.2017.64
13. Pereira-Vale, A., Perovich, D., Ochoa, S.F.: Understanding the pre-contract process of small software projects. In: The 35th International Conference on Software Engineering and Knowledge Engineering, (SEKE 2023), KSIR Virtual Conference Center, USA, 1–10 July 2023, 2023, pp. 146–151. KSI Research Inc. (2023), https://www.doi.org/10.18293/SEKE2023-016

14. Quispe, A., Marques, M., Silvestre, L., Ochoa, S.F., Robbes, R.: Requirements engineering practices in very small software enterprises: A diagnostic study. In: SCCC 2010, Proceedings of the XXIX International Conference of the Chilean Computer Science Society, Antofagasta, Chile, 15-19 November 2010, pp. 81–87. IEEE Computer Society (2010). https://doi.org/10.1109/SCCC.2010.35

15. Robillard, M.P.: Turnover-induced knowledge loss in practice. In: Proceedings of the 29th ACM Joint Meeting on European Software Engineering Conference and Symposium on the Foundations of Software Engineering, ESEC/FSE 2021, pp. 1292-1302. Association for Computing Machinery, New York (2021). https://doi.org/10.1145/3468264.3473923

16. Spichkova, M.: Industry-oriented project-based learning of software engineering. In: 2019 24th International Conference on Engineering of Complex Computer Systems (ICECCS), pp. 51–60 (2019). https://doi.org/10.1109/ICECCS.2019.00013

17. Tenhunen, S., Männistö, T., Luukkainen, M., Ihantola, P.: A systematic literature review of capstone courses in software engineering. Inf. Softw. Technol. **159**, 107191 (2023). https://doi.org/10.1016/j.infsof.2023.107191

18. Vera, T., Ochoa, S.F., Perovich, D.: Requirements engineering in the pre-contract stage: exploring the processes and practices used in small and medium-sized software enterprises. In: Proceedings of the 36th Annual ACM Symposium on Applied Computing, SAC'21, pp. 1346-1353. Association for Computing Machinery, New York (2021). https://www.doi.org/10.1145/3412841.3442009

The Essential Competencies of Data Scientists: A Framework for Hiring and Training

Motahareh Zarefard$^{(\boxtimes)}$ [ID] and Nicola Marsden [ID]

Heilbronn University, Heilbronn, Germany
{motahareh.zarefard,nicola.marsden}@hs-heilbronn.de

Abstract. Data science has emerged as a critical field for organizations seeking to harness the power of big data to inform strategic decisions and gain a competitive edge. However, the demand for data scientists far exceeds the currently available pool of qualified candidates, making it a significant challenge for organizations to hire and train the right talent. The discipline of data science is inherently multi-faceted, requiring a diverse set of technical and non-technical skills that can be rare to find in individuals or teams. In response to this challenge, our study has developed a comprehensive framework, drawing insights from extensive literature, identifying and underscoring the enduring relevance of 130 distinct competencies for the future data scientist. This framework stands out for its depth and breadth, offering a more holistic perspective than existing models found in the literature. By embracing this framework, organizations can craft more effective recruitment strategies, enhance the professional growth of their data science teams, and ultimately strengthen their capacity to leverage data for making informed and strategic decisions.

Keywords: Data Science · Competency Model · Knowledge Domains · Skill Sets

1 Introduction

Data science has become an indispensable asset for organizations that leverage big data for informed decision-making and competitive advantage [1–3].

Yet, the persistent scarcity of qualified data scientists poses a significant challenge regarding recruitment and training [4,5]. A competency model that outlines the specific skills and knowledge required for various data science tasks becomes imperative to navigate this challenge effectively [6]. Such a model fosters a clear understanding of the competencies essential for specific roles within the field, thereby streamlining recruitment and training processes [7]. This paper addresses this pressing challenge by presenting a comprehensive framework drawn from the extensive literature, which identifies and emphasizes the enduring relevance of distinctive competencies essential for the future data scientist.

© The Author(s), under exclusive license to Springer Nature Switzerland AG 2024
H. Mori and Y. Asahi (Eds.): HCII 2024, LNCS 14691, pp. 397–418, 2024.
https://doi.org/10.1007/978-3-031-60125-5_27

Due to its depth and breadth, this framework provides a more comprehensive perspective than the existing models in the literature, thus addressing significant gaps. By integrating this framework, organizations can strengthen their data science teams and increase their potential to use data for strategic decision-making effectively. The competency framework introduced in this study provides consistency for assessing a wide range of behavioral characteristics among data science professionals. It sheds light on the ambiguous dimensions of human capital associated with roles within the data science domain.

2   Literature Review

2.1   Data Science and Data Scientists Roles and Skills

Provost and Fawcett (2013) outlined two reasons for the lack of clarity surrounding the concept of data science [8]. Firstly, there's a strong association and confusion between data science, Big Data, and data-driven decision-making. Secondly, data science is currently more inclined towards practical and experimental aspects than theoretical and methodological ones. In this phase of discipline development, there's a common tendency to conflate the definition of the field with the description of the roles performed by its practitioners, such as data scientists [9]. Data scientists play a significant role in organizations by utilizing their computing and analytical skills to analyze large datasets, extract actionable insights, and facilitate informed decision-making. While not all researchers require computing skills, those known as "native data scientists" have gained expertise in databases and computing through their undergraduate training and certification courses [10]. Data scientists, with skills honed from undergraduate studies and certifications, analyze datasets to support decision-making. The field's evolving terminology leads to varied job responsibilities [11,12], with data scientists often leading teams with specialized roles like data engineers and machine learning analysts. Yet, research on these roles is scant [13,14]. However, their core functions involve extracting actionable information from data, aligning questions with business goals, working with relevant data and advanced technologies, collaborating with subject matter experts, analyzing and visualizing results, and automating data processes [15,16].

Data scientists possess skills in information technology, predictive analytics, experimental design, and effective communication, enabling them to transform large datasets into meaningful insights that drive organizational goals [17,18].

The term "data scientist" describes anyone who works with data, including data management, processing, and analysis. However, the skills required for these tasks differ greatly, and as teams grow, natural specialization occurs. For instance, data science teams often have individuals who focus on analytics (data scientists) and others who focus on collecting and cleansing data (data engineers). Vertical specializations include data architects and big data engineers, and horizontal specializations include machine learning analysts. A data scientist has expertise in various disciplines and can lead a diverse team of specialists. Despite the increasing prevalence of these roles, there is a lack of published research on them. The concept of roles was not identified in a literature review of data science team processes [13, 14]. Stanton highlights the involvement and skills of data scientists in various areas, including learning the application domain, communicating with data users, understanding complex systems, data representation, transformation and analysis, visualization, and presentation, and upholding quality and ethical reasoning. Other research stresses the importance of data scientists possessing a well-rounded skill set, encompassing technical and soft skills [18–21]. The rise of AI has transformed the role of data scientists, who now integrate AI to enhance analytics and decision-making, highlighting the need for AI competencies in the field [12, 22–24].

2.2   Competencies and Competency Model for Data Scientists

The concept of competencies [25] has been extensively studied in various research fields. The discussion and development of data science competencies and the role of data scientists have been ongoing for several decades. However, in recent years, the field has gained significant attention and momentum due to the exponential growth of data and advancements in data-driven technologies.

A competency model is a descriptive framework used across an organization to identify the necessary competencies for achieving optimal performance in a particular job, industry, or organizational setting. It comprises a measurable inventory of the knowledge, skills, and characteristics exhibited through an individual's behavior, resulting in excellent job performance within a specific work environment. Each competency within the model should have a well-defined description, including measurable or observable performance indicators or standards. The evaluators will utilize These indicators or standards individuals responsible for assessing performance [2, 11, 13, 22, 26–28]. According to the guideline by [22] to establish a competency framework, we performed the following functions:

- Organized competencies and competency requirements already derived from empirical evidence or analytical methods.
- Highlighted competence requirements specific to particular groups.
- Clarified the interrelationships between different competencies.
- Revealed the factors that influence the acquisition or development of competencies.
- Identified the responsible individuals or areas of action for acquiring or promoting specific competence areas.

They employed the 'KSAVE model', a framework established by Binkley et al. (2012) to operationalize and define action competencies [29]. This perspective posits that action competencies comprise three key dimensions: knowledge, skills, attitudes, values, and ethics. Correspondingly, in HR and IT literature, the prevalent concept of competence is encapsulated in the 'KSAO model', representing Knowledge, Skills, Abilities, and Other personal characteristics essential for effective job performance, as introduced by Boyatzis [30] and further discussed by Hattingh [2]. This research, aimed at developing competency models fit for the 21st century, focused on the requisite knowledge and technical skills needed to adapt and structure the dimensions of a data scientist's competency model. Consequently, we adopted the K-S-A (Knowledge, Skills, Abilities) framework to construct the 'Data scientist' competence model. This involved amalgamating competency descriptions from our literature review into fields structured around existing and emerging competency approaches.

2.3 Related Work

The literature extensively explores the roles and competencies of data scientists across various industries [31,32]. Our research builds upon a comprehensive review of data scientist competency literature, which incorporates insights from job portal profiles [3,13,15,17,33,34] and prior studies dedicated to identifying data science skills [2,34–37]. In crafting our framework, we drew inspiration from various relevant models [2,6,22,26,27,36], particularly emphasizing the KSAO model, which encompasses Knowledge, Skills, Abilities, and Other personal characteristics [30,38–41]. Additionally, we incorporated the KSAVE model, highlighting the importance of knowledge, skills, attitudes, values, and ethics [29,39], and the KSAOs model, highlighting the knowledge, skills, abilities, and other characteristics [7], all of which are essential for effective job performance. Our approach further encompasses a holistic model [17,26,38], designed to provide a more comprehensive understanding of the competencies required for data scientists. We aim to develop a robust and adaptable competency model tailored to data science by synthesizing insights from these diverse sources.

3 Methodology

This research follows a qualitative approach [2,13,22,30,38,42], employing text mining analysis. The methodology encompassed a structured literature review facilitated by Python scripts:

1. Literature Review and Data Collection: Conducting a comprehensive literature review and collecting data spanning 2018 to 2023, extensively exploring academic databases and platforms.
2. Initial Screening: Utilizing abstract-based screening to manage the large volume of search results and identify papers with relevant insights on data science competencies, including PDF documents, for further detailed review.
3. Keyword Refinement and Source Selection: Implementing a keyword-based strategy [2,42–44], combining relevant text mining variations and competency elements to enhance precision.
4. Data Extraction: Extracting text from selected sources using the Python library pdfplumber.
5. Data Quality Assurance: Ensuring data accuracy and reliability with Python scripts, including BeautifulSoup and Scrapy libraries.
6. Data Synthesis and Categorization: Organizing and structuring the collected data into competency categories using Pandas.

7. Quantitative Analysis: Applying Python-based quantitative techniques [45] to quantify skill and knowledge frequencies in the literature.
8. Visualization and Heatmap Generation: Employing visualization tools in Python, such as Matplotlib and Seaborn, to create a heatmap.

By following this systematic process, leveraging Python scripting and relevant libraries, we provide the foundation for constructing our competency framework.

3.1 Pre-model Construction

In this phase, we combined a systematic approach with Python scripting and relevant libraries to lay the groundwork for our framework. Initially, we focused on skill analysis in data science studies using the methodology mentioned above. We have detailed the work steps as follows:

Source Selection: We targeted platforms known for their scholarly impact, like Web of Science, IEEE, Wiley Online Library, Science Direct, and Emerald. These platforms are known for their extensive coverage of scientific and technical literature across various disciplines, including data science and analytics, which is the focus of this study. The initial search focused on crafting a Data Scientist Competency Model and skills on the selected sources using Python 3.11.0. We applied the requests library to fetch web pages and BeautifulSoup pages to parse the HTML and extract information. Specialized libraries like googlesearch-python were also specifically made to simulate Google searches in Python. Our study also followed the classification of job families and skill sets in data science. Given the field's novelty and limited studies, we emphasized practical and relevant findings. Data spanned articles and journals published in English from 2018 to 2023.

Inclusion and Exclusion Criteria: We established stringent criteria to filter the literature for studies referencing data scientist competencies. In the initial sweep, we identified 118 articles, which were then narrowed down to 38 after a review for relevance based on titles and abstracts containing "data scientist" and "competency" or "skills." Additional keywords, including "data science literacy" or "data science competence," "big data," and "data analytics," were instrumental, with "data science AND competency" yielding a focused delineation of the data scientist role.

Expert Review Process: To ensure the integrity of the selection process, two subject matter experts independently reviewed the 38 shortlisted papers. The experts, equipped with an understanding of the field's requirements, employed a dual-review screening method. Each article was evaluated against the established inclusion and exclusion criteria, with discrepancies resolved through discussion to reach a consensus. This collaborative and iterative review resulted in selecting 21 articles for in-depth analysis.

Key Search Words and Extraction of Skills: The literature was combed for skills and knowledge attributions and categorized according to predefined job families through methodical content analysis. We identified four primary job families: Business Analysts, Data Scientists, Data Analysts, Developers, and System Managers [46]. Given database-specific search algorithm variations, we adapted our queries for each and meticulously documented these changes. For example, for [Database Name], we employed the search string "data scientist" AND (competency OR skills).

Inventory of Competencies List: Our analysis leveraged a text-mining approach, utilizing Python to extract pertinent skills and competencies from the selected literature. This entailed processing documents stored in a database repository to draw out keywords and relevant terms per our research objectives.

Content Analysis and Categorization Process: The subsequent phase of our research methodology entailed an in-depth content analysis to discern prevalent themes and keywords related to data scientist competencies. This process included several key steps:

Text Extraction: We utilized specific Python libraries designed for text mining, such as pdfplumber, to meticulously extract textual content from PDF documents. This library facilitates the conversion of PDF text into a manipulable format for Python, allowing for subsequent analysis.

Text Preprocessing: The preprocessing stage involves purifying the extracted text. We systematically eliminated extraneous characters, symbols, and formatting, which could potentially skew the analysis. The text was then decomposed into individual words or tokens, setting the stage for the frequency analysis.

Frequency Analysis: We implemented a computational method to enumerate the occurrences of each word within the corpus. This frequency analysis highlighted words that emerged more often, underscoring them as potential keywords and competencies of interest, as illustrated in Table 1.

Validation of Search Strategy: To bolster the reliability of our search methodology, we benefited from the expertise of a specialized systematic review researcher, incorporating inter-rater reliability metrics. Moreover, Preliminary pilot searches were an essential component of our methodology. These searches were conducted to fine-tune our strategy, confirming the relevance and precision of our queries.

Integration of Competency-Based Literature: In parallel with our empirical analysis, we consulted a breadth of competency-based literature. This review offered additional insights, enriching our understanding and supporting the development of a comprehensive competency framework.

Visualization of Competency Correlations: We visualized the relationships between the identified competencies after successfully extracting and analyzing text data. Visualization is critical to our study, translating complex data into a comprehensible and insightful graphical format. To represent the interconnectedness of competencies across the selected literature, we employed a heatmap, a powerful tool for showcasing correlation matrices [47], depicted in Fig. 1.

This heatmap graphically represented the frequency and correlation of skills and competencies identified. It offered a visual summary and deeper insights into the data trends and patterns using Python's Seaborn and Matplotlib libraries, renowned for their flexibility and aesthetic options in data visualization.

Using a color-coded matrix and a diverging color palette, the heatmap effectively depicted the correlation strengths and directions between competency pairs, with color intensities mirroring correlation coefficients for easy interpretation. It highlighted clusters of often co-occurring competencies within the research corpus, indicating key data science expertise areas and isolated skills, signifying emerging fields. This visual analysis was crucial for categorizing competencies, revealing both high-density clusters and low-density areas, aiding in developing a structured competency model for the diverse data science profession.

3.2 Adopting a Holistic Competency Approach

Our study adopts the holistic competency model by Le Deist and Winterton [48], as used by Persaud (2021) for defining big data analytics competencies [38]. This model encompasses cognitive, functional, and social dimensions aligned with the KSA framework. Cognitive competence relates to knowledge, functional competence to skills, and social competence to behavioral and attitudinal aspects. Meta-competence enhances the acquisition of these competencies. While distinct analytically, effective work requires a blend of knowledge, skills, and appropriate behavior.

We expanded this model by integrating Exploratory, Awareness, and Organization or Business Action skills [13], consistent with the hexagon model [39]. This enhancement includes additional skills vital in modern organizational contexts. In this expanded six-area competency framework, we also included transversal skills for work and life [13,49], adding layers of practical relevance to the model.

3.3 Applying Circular Competency Model

To enhance our competency model's accuracy and reflect competency's comprehensive nature, we shifted from using models like Bonesso's six-faceted framework, Hattingh's conceptual model, or Persaud's multi-dimensional approach. Recognizing the difficulty in separating cognitive, functional, and social dimensions in practical scenarios, we opted for a circular model, symbolizing the interconnectedness and overlap of these competency dimensions. Inspired by Ehler's design (2020), this circular model underscores the interdisciplinary nature and potential integration of these dimensions, offering greater flexibility in dynamic learning environments.

4 Results

Our in-depth literature analysis identified 130 distinct competencies in seven pivotal KSAEOs core and cross-functional areas of the data scientist role. Each of the 130 identified KSAEO areas was classified into seven distinct themes: Functional, Cognitive, Awareness, Social, Organizational, and Behavioral.

While Fig. 2 schematically displays the core competencies, a detailed breakdown of the sub-competencies is listed in the appendix. Core competencies in the model have been defined as follows:

Table 1. Literature Review Mapped to Research Model-test

Paper	[11]	[50]	[33]	[2]	[42]	[12]	[51]	[17]	[52]	[5]	[53]	[4]	[54]	[43]	[55]	[22]	[18]	[38]	[56]	[39]	[13]	Tot(%)
Functional Competences																						
1 Data Management	*	*	*	*	*	*	*	*	*	*	*	*	*	*	*		*		*		*	85.7
2 Data Analytics	*	*	*	*	*	*	*	*	*	*	*	*	*	*	*	*	*		*		*	90.4
3 Computational Intelligence	*	*	*	*	*	*	*	*	*	*	*	*	*	*				*		*	*	80.9
4 Digital Competence	*	*		*	*		*	*	*	*		*	*	*	*		*					61.9
5 Business Intelligence	*	*	*	*	*	*	*	*		*	*		*	*	*			*			*	71.4
6 Vocational Background	*	*		*	*	*	*	*				*	*		*		*				*	61.9
Ethical Competences																						
7 Ethical	*	*		*	*	*	*		*	*	*			*	*	*	*		*		*	71.4
8 Regulatory		*		*			*		*					*								23.8
Cognitive Competences																						
9 Analytical Thinking	*			*	*			*		*		*			*			*		*	*	47.6
10 Critical Analysis	*			*	*										*					*		23.8
11 Creative Thinking/Curiosity	*						*					*			*					*		28.5
12 Problem Solving	*			*				*				*	*	*				*			*	38.0
13 Entreprenurial Attitude					*			*		*			*	*				*		*		33.3
14 Conceptual Thinking				*	*									*						*		19.0
15 Lateral Thinking												*	*	*				*		*		23.8
16 Playfulness/Vision and Imagination										*				*						*		14.2
Awareness																						
17 Organizational Awareness								*		*	*		*	*						*	*	33.3
18 Relationship Management/Empathy												*								*		0.90
19 Social and Cultural awareness				*								*	*	*						*		19.0
20 Self-awareness										*			*							*		14.2
Social Competences																						
21 Communication and Networking		*	*	*		*		*	*	*	*	*	*	*				*		*	*	66.6
22 Collaboration and Teamwork		*	*	*		*		*		*	*	*	*	*				*		*		57.1
23 Project Management		*					*	*	*	*				*				*				33.3
24 Conflict Management																				*		4.7
25 Developing Others										*										*		0.9
26 Leadership							*	*	*			*	*	*						*	*	38
Organizational																						
27 Organizational/Managerial				*				*	*			*	*	*				*		*	*	47.6
28 Commitment towards the group										*										*	*	14.2
29 Visionary and Strategic Thinking				*				*	*			*						*		*	*	33.3
30 Organizational cultural/Integrity		*		*	*		*					*	*	*	*					*	*	42.8
Behavioral Competences																						
31 Corporate Entrepreneurship/ Intrapreneurial Behavior (IB)	*	*			*	*	*		*		*	*		*	*		*		*	*	61.9
32 Core Personal Competence/Foundational Personal Traits	*	*		*		*	*		*	*	*	*	*	*		*		*	*	71.4
Total	13	13	6	18	11	11	11	19	10	20	8	15	16	21	22	4	6	11	6	20	18	

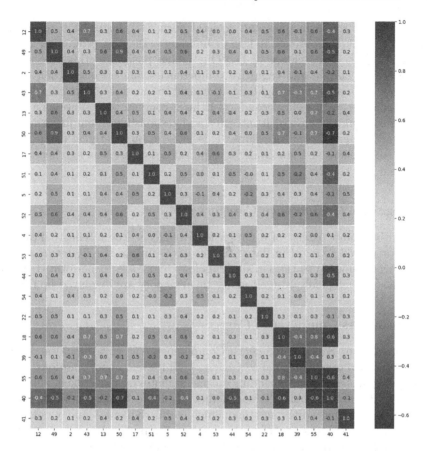

Fig. 1. Heatmap of competencies in data science papers

4.1   Functional Competence Category

The functional Competency category includes the various technical knowledge, skills, and abilities required by a data scientist. It refers to their ability to effectively perform multiple activities required in their role, leading to specific outcomes or meeting the expected standards in the field of employment. This competence necessitates possessing specific skills and utilizing them to achieve the desired result. It entails the willingness and capability to apply subject-specific knowledge and skills to execute tasks and solve problems effectively [12,38,50]. The competencies classified as the Functional Competency category are enumerated in Table 2.

4.2   Ethical Competence Category

In data science, ethics competence is essential, involving knowledge, skills, and the ability to make ethical decisions throughout the data lifecycle. It requires adherence to ethical principles and societal norms [2], fostering a responsible mindset [5]. This competence is key to building trust and promoting responsible practices in data science [9,11]. Our model positions ethical competencies between functional and cognitive competencies, underscoring their critical importance. This placement highlights the need to integrate technical skills and cognitive abilities with ethical conduct. Ethical competencies serve as a bridge for data scientists to work with integrity and responsibility, emphasizing their role in guiding actions and decisions. This integration of ethical competencies ensures a comprehensive framework for responsible data science. Further specifics are detailed in Table 2.

4.3 Cognitive Competence Category

The cognitive competencies of a data scientist refer to the intellectual abilities and skills required to excel in data science. According to the literature review, a data scientist must use the latest technology and tools to perform their role [2,38]. The competencies grouped under this category are displayed in Table 3.

4.4 Awareness Competence Category

The Awareness or Social Intelligence Competency Category includes essential skills like self and organizational awareness, vital for managing emotions, understanding others, and comprehending business contexts and stakeholder needs [39,52,57]. Positioning between social and cognitive competencies highlights their role in understanding and managing social dynamics and emotions in data science. Their integration is key to enhancing performance in data-driven projects and navigating social interactions effectively. Further details on these competencies are in Table 3.

4.5 Social Competence Category

Social competence refers to the capacity and inclination to collaborate effectively within a group, actively engage in and influence interpersonal connections, recognize and comprehend the advantages and challenges involved, and interact with others thoughtfully and responsibly [38,39]. Details on these competencies are displayed in Table 4.

4.6 Organizational Competence Category

Organizational competencies for data scientists involve the skills needed to effectively understand and engage with an organization's structure, culture, and goals [2,5,17,39]. Positioned between functional and social competencies in our model, organizational competencies bridge the gap between technical expertise and interpersonal dynamics. They enable data scientists to apply their technical skills to organizational needs and stakeholder relationships. This placement underscores the importance of organizational savvy alongside technical and social skills for achieving success in data science roles. Issues like collaboration, ethical considerations, and change management are key to this competency area, as are socio-technical aspects like data quality and technology integration. Details are provided in Appendix, Table 4.

4.7   Enhancing the Competency Mode Structure

In building upon the competency model, we have incorporated three essential elements inspired by Ehlers' (2020) studies: individual-development-related skills, individual object-related skills, and individual organization-related skills [22]. These elements are situated around 'Behavioral Skills' at the core, acknowledging that individual capabilities, object mastery, and social interaction are pivotal in shaping behavior in professional contexts. Individual development-related skills pertain to personal attributes and intrapersonal competencies, individual object-related skills refer to the handling of tools and technologies, and individual organization-related skills encompass communication and collaboration. As conceptualized by Ehlers, these domains provide a nuanced perspective on the multifaceted nature of competencies required in contemporary organizational settings.

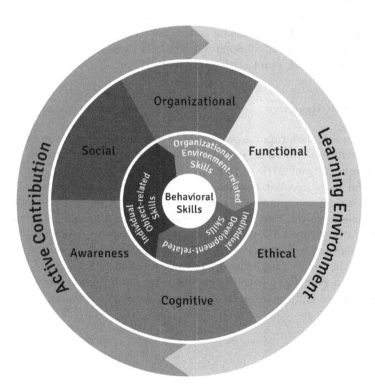

Fig. 2. The proposed data scientist competency framework

4.8 Behavioral Competence Category

Behavioral competencies are crucial for data science roles and can be categorized mainly into two areas. The first is intrapreneurial behavior, also known as corporate entrepreneurship, which is the initiative and action taken by employees within an organization to innovate and implement new ideas, processes, or products, akin to entrepreneurship but within a company's structure [58], and second, core personal competence or foundational personal traits. Incorporating Ehler's future skills model and the Big Five personality traits, we term these foundational traits as core personal competencies, underscoring their role in a data scientist's performance and approach to work. In our model, 'Behavioral Skills' are central, denoting intrinsic abilities for adaptability in professional settings [22]. Organizational environment-related skills enable effective workplace navigation, while Individual development-related skills focus on personal growth and learning agility, which are crucial for continuous professional development in a rapidly changing field. Lastly, Individual object-related skills pertain to the specific, tangible competencies required to perform tasks and achieve objectives. Simultaneously, the 'Active Contribution' dimension calls for data science professionals to employ their competencies beyond personal advancement, encouraging them to apply their skills proactively to initiate change, contribute to organizational goals, and advance industry standards. Together, these outer elements form a reciprocal loop where the learning environment feeds into the competencies developed, and professionals' active contributions enrich and evolve the learning environment itself [59,60].Table 5 details these competencies' impact on data scientists' attitudes and work approaches [4,11].

5 Discussion

Despite Data Science's rapid growth, there remains uncertainty around the specific competencies required for data scientists. Our study, conducted an extensive literature review from 2018 to 2023, addresses this by defining and categorizing essential data scientist competencies. We identified seven critical domains encompassing 130 competencies, ranging from functional and ethical to cognitive, awareness, social, organizational, and behavioral skills. This comprehensive framework informs training and career development, aligning data scientists' abilities with industry needs. It offers a practical model for evaluating and enhancing data scientist performance in various settings. For instance, balancing creativity with regulatory constraints illustrates the interplay between individual competencies and organizational needs. A data scientist's success hinges on merging technical expertise with effective communication, integration, and compliance within their organizational context. Our methodology was deliberately inclusive, aiming to comprehensively encapsulate all relevant competencies in this dynamic field. This framework lays the groundwork for tailored training and development programs, recognizing that each role within data science demands a unique combination of skills. It is imperative to acknowledge that it's impractical for a single individual to master every competency. This perspective is supported by various studies and literature in the field [8,9,11,31]. Our innovative literature review methodology also combines advanced text mining with statistical analysis, setting a precedent for future interdisciplinary research. By merging theoretical insights with practical applications, this research contributes to the academic understanding of data science competencies and serves as a valuable guide for industry practitioners. It aims to elevate data science professionals' standards and effectiveness across academic and industrial landscapes.

5.1   Limitation and Implication

While methodologically robust, our study encounters limitations that merit consideration. Firstly, it does not incorporate direct insights from the current workforce, which could provide additional real-world context to the competencies identified. Secondly, resource constraints posed challenges to the exhaustive exploration of all potential data sources, possibly limiting the breadth of our findings. Lastly, inherent biases-selection, publication, or analytical-cannot be entirely discounted and may have influenced the results. Despite these constraints, the study's design aimed to mitigate such biases through rigorous methodological checks and balances. Notwithstanding the limitations above, the implications of our study are manifold and resonate across multiple spheres. In the educational arena, our findings provide a framework that can guide curriculum development to better align with industry competencies. Professionals can leverage this insight for personal development and strategic career planning. Industries, too, stand to benefit by benchmarking organizational needs against a comprehensive competency model, thereby enhancing recruitment and training processes.

5.2 Future Work

Our research establishes a solid groundwork for future investigations, inviting more expansive and detailed analyses in the field of data science competencies. A key direction for subsequent exploration involves aligning the skills we've identified with the European Skills, Competencies, Qualifications, and Occupations (ESCO) database. This alignment would not only enhance the academic rigor of our findings but also bolster their practical applicability, especially within the European context. Additionally, integrating open data from job portals into our analysis can provide real-world validation of our competency model, further bridging the gap between academic research and industry needs.

Our pioneering approach is a potential benchmark for future research, particularly in defining essential competencies within various academic and professional fields. Its replicability and scalability are key advantages, allowing for adaptation to the evolving needs and trends in competency analysis across different industries. This adaptability ensures the continued relevance of our model, even as the demands of the data science profession and other fields undergo transformation.

6 Conclusion

Our findings indicate limited evolution in the data science field over time, affirming the consistency of our proposed framework with prior research. This framework stands out for its versatility and broad applicability, making it valuable for talent search, selection, and replacement in diverse contexts. Our contribution addresses a significant gap in the current literature, empowering employers and job seekers to identify competencies precisely. However, like any model, its effectiveness may change over time, requiring adjustments to align with evolving environmental dynamics. Continuous updates are crucial to maintain its long-term relevance and utility. Our study also pushes the envelope in methodological innovation, setting a new standard for conducting literature reviews that can yield strategic insights for academia and industry alike.

Acknowledgments. This work has been partially funded by the German Federal Institute for Vocational Education and Training (Bundesinstitut für Berufsbildung BIBB) under Grant Number 21INVI1802 as part of the project 'KI-gestütztes Matching individueller und arbeitsmarktbezogener Anforderungen für die berufliche Weiterbildung. Teilvorhaben: Nutzer*innenzentrierte Anforderungsanalyse, Konzeptualisierung und Modellierung des Lern- und Matching-Angebots unter Berücksichtigung von Gender- und Diversity-Aspekten'. The responsibility for all content supplied lies with the authors.

Appendix

Table 2. Areas and Competence Dimensions; Functional and Ethics

Domain/Category		KSAO
Functional	Data Management	Big data processing
		Programming (Python, R, SQL)
		Hadoop , SAS
		Machine Learning, Artificial Intelligence
		Natural Language Processing and Neural Networks
		Business knowledge and understanding
		Database, Data warehouse
	Data Analytics	Data modelling
		Data mining
		Statistical analysis
		Statistical/Mathematical modelling
		Data visualization
		Storytelling
		Innovation and Creativity
	Computational Intelligence	Statistics and Mathematics
		Software development, Programming/Coding
		Hardware
	Digital Competence	Information management
		Digital communication
		Digital literacy
		Digital collaboration
	Business Intelligence	Business modelling
		Business innovation
		Industry knowledge
	Vocational Background	Work experience
		Deep domain knowledge
		Professional training
		Educational background
		Qualification
Area between Functional and Cognitive; Ethical		
Ethical and Regulatory	Ethical	Proficency in managing data privacy, accuracy and intellectual property
		Social responsibility skills
	Regulatory	Knowledge of regulatory and policy issues
		Skills of effective and efficient use of data

Table 3. Areas and Competence Dimensions ; Cognitive and Awareness

Domain/Category		KSAO
Cognitive	Analytical Thinking	Analytical methods
		Statistical reasoning
		Analytical tools
	Critical Analysis	Evidence-based decision making
		Objectivity
	Creative Thinking and Curiosity	Generating multiple ideas
		Generating perspective to a problem
		Process improvement
	Problem Solving	Experiment design
		A/B testing
		Problem decomposition
		Testing methods, hypotheses
	Entrepreneurial Attitude	Knowledge of business or industry
		Business Intelligence and Business Acumen
		Opportunity identification
		Initiative
		Proactivity
	Conceptual Thinking	Pattern recognition
		Relationships within datasets
	Lateral Thinking	Creativity techniques
		Open-mindedness
		Curiosity
	Playfulness, Vision and Imagination	Imaginative mindset
		Innovative approach in data analysis
Area between Cognitive and Social; Awareness		
Awareness and Social Intelligence	Organizational Awareness	Ability to understand the political balance
		Ability to understand guiding values
		Awareness of industry and market trends
		Understanding organizational structure
	Relationship Management	Ability to understand others' feeling
		Take an active interest in their concerns
	Social and Cultural Intelligence	Cultural data proficiency
	Self-awareness	Emotional awareness
		Reflection and self-assessment

Table 4. Areas and Competence Dimensions; Social and Organizational

Domain/Category		KSAO
Social	Communication and Networking	Effective communication in team
		Oral and written skills
		Story tellling
		Communication platforms
	Collaboration and Team work	Active listening
		Interpersonal skills
		Team player mindset
		Flexibility
		Adaptability
		Both leadership and followership
	Project Management	Knowledge of project management principles
		Knowledge of methodologies
		Knowledge of project life cycle
		Resource management
	Conflict Management	Conflict resolution skills
	Developing Others	Coaching and feedback
		Mentoring and guidance, Supportive
	Leadership	Visionary problem solving
		Inspire, influence and guide others
Area between Social and Functional; Organizational		
Organizational	Organizational	Attention to details and organization
		Abilities and skills related to socio-organizational
		Abilities and skills related to socio-technical issues
		Documentation skills
		Managerial skills
	Commitment towards the group	Achievement orientation
	Visionary and Strategic Thinking	Setting roadmaps
		Engaging with stakeholders
		Strong project management skills
	Organizational Cultural	Data oriented culture
		Ability to utilize specific data
		Create inclusive work environment

Table 5. Areas and Competence Dimensions; Behavioral

Domain/Category		KSAO
Behavioral	Corporate Entrepreneurship/ Intrapreneurial Behavior	Innovative mindset
		Opportunity identification
		Intrapreneurial spirit
		Innovation and creativity
		Creativity
		Risk taking
		Resilience
		Networking
		Agile and iterative
		Entrepreneurial leadership
		Communication and influence
		Intellectual curiosity
		Willingness to new ideas
		Openness to new experiences
	Core Personal Competence/Foundational Personal Traits	Autonomy
		Self-initiative
		Self-management
		Motivation for achievement
		Personal agility
		Autonomous learning competence
		Self-efficacy
		Conscientiousness
		Tolerance for ambiguity
		Ability to reflect
		Neuroticism
		Extraversion
		Sense-making
		Future mindset
		Agreeableness

References

1. Haneke, U., Trahasch, S., Zimmer, M., Felden, C.: Data Science: Grundlagen, Architekturen und Anwendungen. dpunkt. verlag (2021)
2. Hattingh, M., Marshall, L., Holmner, M., Naidoo, R.: Data science competency in organisations: a systematic review and unified model. In: Proceedings of the South African Institute of Computer Scientists and Information Technologists 2019, pp. 1–8 (2019). https://doi.org/10.1145/3351108.3351110

3. Lovaglio, P.G., Cesarini, M., Mercorio, F., Mezzanzanica, M.: Skills in demand for ICT and statistical occupations: evidence from web-based job vacancies. Stat. Anal. Data Mining ASA Data Sci. J. **11**(2), 78–91 (2018). https://doi.org/10.1002/sam.11372

4. da Silveira, C.C., Marcolin, C.B., da Silva, M., Domingos, J.C.: What is a data scientist? analysis of core soft and technical competencies in job postings. Revista Inovação, Projetos e Tecnologias **8**(1), 25–39 (2020). https://doi.org/10.5585/iptec.v8i1.17263

5. Wu, D., Lv, S., Xu, H.: An analysis on competency of human-centered data science employment. Proc. Assoc. Inf. Sci. Technol. **57**(1), e219 (2020). https://doi.org/10.1002/pra2.219

6. Prifti, L., Knigge, M., Kienegger, H., Krcmar, H.: A competency model for Industrie 4.0 employees. In: Proceedings der 13. Internationalen Tagung Wirtschaftsinformatik (WI 2017), pp. 46–60 (2017)

7. McCartney, S., Murphy, C., Mccarthy, J.: 21st century HR: a competency model for the emerging role of HR Analysts. Pers. Rev. **50**(6), 1495–1513 (2021). https://doi.org/10.1108/PR-12-2019-0670

8. Provost, F., Fawcett, T.: Data science and its relationship to big data and data-driven decision making. Big Data **1**(1), 51–59 (2013). https://doi.org/10.1089/big.2013.1508

9. De Mauro, A., Greco, M., Grimaldi, M., Nobili, G., et al.: Beyond data scientists: a review of big data skills and job families. In: Proceedings of IFKAD, pp. 1844–1857 (2016). https://hdl.handle.net/11580/55712

10. Lyon, L.: Dealing with data: roles, rights, responsibilities, and relationships consultancy report (2007)

11. Nosarka, N.B.: Data scientist: using a competency-based approach to explore an emerging role. PhD thesis (2018). https://hdl.handle.net/10539/27155

12. Stadelmann, T., Stockinger, K., Bürki, G.H., Braschler, M.: Data scientists. In: Applied Data Science: Lessons Learned for the Data-Driven Business, pp. 31–45 (2019). https://doi.org/10.1007/978-3-030-11821-1_3

13. Smaldone, F., Ippolito, A., Lagger, J., Pellicano, M.: Employability skills: profiling data scientists in the digital labour market. Eur. Manag. J. **40**(5), 671–684 (2022). https://doi.org/10.1016/j.emj.2022.05.005

14. Saltz, J.S., Grady, N.W.: The ambiguity of data science team roles and the need for a data science workforce framework. In: 2017 IEEE International Conference on Big Data (Big Data), pp. 2355–2361. IEEE (2017). https://doi.org/10.1109/BigData.2017.8258190

15. Jerina Jean Ecleo and Adrian Galido: Surveying linkedin profiles of data scientists: the case of the Philippines. Procedia Comput. Sci. **124**, 53–60 (2017). https://doi.org/10.1016/j.procs.2017.12.129

16. Song, I.Y., Zhu, Y.: Big data and data science: what should we teach? Exp. Syst. **33**(4), 364–373 (2016). https://doi.org/10.1111/exsy.12130

17. Della Volpe, M., Esposito, F.: How universities fill the talent gap: the data scientist in the Italian case. Afr. J. Bus. Manag. **14**(2), 53–64 (2020). https://doi.org/10.5897/AJBM2019.8885

18. Schwab-McCoy, A., Baker, C.M., Gasper, R.E.: Data science in 2020: computing, curricula, and challenges for the next 10 years. J. Stat. Data Sci. Educ. **29**(sup1), S40–S50 (2021). https://doi.org/10.1080/10691898.2020.1851159

19. Stanton, W.W., Stanton, A.D.: Helping business Entry-level Requirements needed for a career in analytics: a comprehensive industry assessment of entry-level requirements. Decis. Sci. J. Innov. Educ. **18**(1), 138–165 (2020). https://doi.org/10.1111/dsji.12199

20. Kim, J.Y., Lee, C.K.: An empirical analysis of requirements for data scientists using online job postings. Int. J. Softw. Eng. Appl. **10**(4), 161–172 (2016)

21. Kim, M., Zimmermann, T., DeLine, R., Begel, A.: The emerging role of data scientists on software development teams. In: Proceedings of the 38th International Conference on Software Engineering, pp. 96–107 (2016). https://doi.org/10.1145/2884781.2884783

22. Ehlers, U.D.: Future skills: the future of learning and higher education. BoD–Books on Demand (2020). https://www.learntechlib.org/p/208249/

23. Pedro, F., Subosa, M., Rivas, A., Valverde, P.: Artificial intelligence in education: challenges and opportunities for sustainable development (2019). https://hdl.handle.net/20.500.12799/6533

24. Wang, D., et al.: Human-AI collaboration in data science: Exploring data scientists' perceptions of automated AI. In: Proceedings of the ACM on Human-Computer Interaction CSCW , vol. 3, pp. 1–24(2019). https://doi.org/10.1145/3359313

25. McClelland, D.C.: Testing for competence rather than for "intelligence". Am. Psychol. **28**(1), 1 (1973)

26. Nascimbeni, F., et al.: The Opengame competencies framework: an attempt to map open education attitudes, knowledge, and skills. In: EDEN Conference Proceedings, vol. 1, pp. 105–112 (2020)

27. Staškeviča, A., et al.: The importance of competency model development. Acta Oeconomica Pragensia **27**(2), 62–71 (2019). https://doi.org/10.18267/j.aop.622

28. Skhvediani, A., Sosnovskikh, S., Rudskaia, I., Kudryavtseva, T.: Identification and comparative analysis of the skills structure of the data analyst profession in Russia. J. Educ. Bus. **97**(5), 295–304 (2022). https://doi.org/10.1080/08832323.2021.1937018

29. Binkley, M., et al.: Defining twenty-first century skills. In: Assessment and Teaching of 21st Century Skills, pp. 17–66 (2012). https://doi.org/10.1007/978-94-007-2324-5

30. Boyatzis, R.E.: The Competent Manager: A Model for Effective Performance. John Wiley & Sons, Hoboken (1991)

31. Mike, K., Hazzan, O.: What is data science? Commun. ACM **66**(2), 12–13 (2023). https://doi.org/10.1145/3575663

32. Sanders, N.: A balanced perspective on prediction and inference for data science in industry. Harvard Data Sci. Rev. **1**(1), 1–28 (2019). https://doi.org/10.1162/99608f92.644ef4a4

33. Meyer, M.A.: Healthcare data scientist qualifications, skills, and job focus: a content analysis of job postings. J. Am. Med. Inf. Assoc. **26**(5), 383–391 (2019). https://doi.org/10.1093/jamia/ocy181

34. Shirani, A.: Identifying data science and analytics competencies based on industry demands. Issues Inf. Syst. **17**(4), 137–144 (2016). https://doi.org/10.48009/4_iis_2016_137-144

35. Ghasemaghaei, M., Ebrahimi, S., Hassanein, K.: Data analytics competency for improving firm decision making performance. J. Strat. Inf. Syst. **27**(1), 101–113 (2018). https://doi.org/10.1016/j.jsis.2017.10.001

36. Kansal, J., Singhal, S.: Development of a competency model for enhancing the organisational effectiveness in a knowledge-based organisation. Int. J. Indian Cult. Bus. Manag. **16**(3), 287–301 (2018). https://doi.org/10.1504/IJICBM.2018.090909

37. Murawski, M., Bick, M.: Digital competences of the workforce-a research topic? Bus. Process Manag. J. **23**(3), 721–734 (2017). https://doi.org/10.1108/BPMJ-06-2016-0126

38. Persaud, A.: Key competencies for big data analytics professions: a multimethod study. Inf. Technol. People **34**(1), 178–203 (2021). https://doi.org/10.1108/ITP-06-2019-0290

39. Bonesso, S., Gerli, F., Bruni, E.: The emotional and social side of analytics professionals: an exploratory study of the behavioral profile of data scientists and data analysts. Int. J. Manpower **43**(9), 19–41 (2022). https://doi.org/10.1108/IJM-07-2020-0342

40. Erpenbeck, J., Heyse, V.: Kompetenzmodelle und personalentwicklung. In: Jahrbuch Personalentwicklung, pp. 71–80 (2008)

41. Suhairom, N., Musta'amal, A.H., Amin, N.F.M., Johari, N.K.A.: The development of competency model and instrument for competency measurement: the research methods. Procedia-Soc. Behav. Sci. **152**, 1300–1308 (2014). https://doi.org/10.1016/j.sbspro.2014.09.367

42. Mina, M.A.E., Barzola, D.D.P.G.: Data scientist: a systematic review of the literature. In: International Conference on Technology Trends, pp. 476–487. Springer, Heidelberg (2018). https://doi.org/10.1007/978-3-030-05532-5_35

43. Surbakti, F.P.S., Wang, W., Indulska, M., Sadiq, S.: Factors influencing effective use of big data: a research framework. Inf. Manag. **57**(1), 103146 (2020). https://doi.org/10.1016/j.im.2019.02.001

44. Joshua, E., Zarefard, M., Marsden, N.: Investigating skill requirements and gender bias in job openings for HCI professionals across the USA, Australia, Germany, India, and South Africa. In: 2023 9th International HCI and UX Conference in Indonesia (CHIuXiD), pp. 1–6. IEEEXplore (2023). In press

45. Vijayarani, S., Janani, R.: Text mining: open source tokenization tools-an analysis. Adv. Comput. Intell. Int. J. (ACII) **3**(1), 37–47 (2016). https://doi.org/10.5121/acii.2016.3104

46. De Mauro, A., Greco, M., Grimaldi, M., Ritala, P.: Human resources for big data professions: a systematic classification of job roles and required skill sets. Inf. Process. Manag. **54**(5), 807–817 (2018). https://doi.org/10.1016/j.ipm.2017.05.004

47. Chen, T., Liu, Y.X., Huang, L.: ImageGP: an easy-to-use data visualization web server for scientific researchers. Imeta **1**(1), e5 (2022). https://doi.org/10.1002/imt2.5

48. Le Deist, F.D., Winterton, J.: What is competence? Human Res. Dev. Int. **8**(1), 27–46 (2005). https://doi.org/10.1080/1367886042000338227

49. Brown, T., De Neve, G.: Skills, training and development: an introduction to the social life of skills in the global south (2023). https://doi.org/10.1080/01436597.2023.2219615

50. Chen, C., Jiang, H.: Important skills for data scientists in china: two Delphi studies. J. Comput. Inf. Syst. (2018). https://doi.org/10.1080/08874417.2018.1472047

51. Fatih Gurcan and Nergiz Ercil Cagiltay: Big data software engineering: analysis of knowledge domains and skill sets using LDA-based topic modeling. IEEE Access **7**, 82541–82552 (2019). https://doi.org/10.1109/ACCESS.2019.2924075

52. Davies, A., Mueller, J., Moulton, G.: Core competencies for clinical informaticians: a systematic review. Int. J. Med. Inf. **141**, 104237 (2020). https://doi.org/10.1016/j.ijmedinf.2020.104237

53. Bukhari, D.: Data science curriculum: current scenario. Int. J. Data Min. Knowl. Manag. Process (IJDKP) **10** (2020). https://doi.org/10.5121/ijdkp.2020.10301

54. Sabaityte, J., Davidaviciene, V., Karpoviciute, R.: Learning skills for enhancing the use of big data. World J. Educ. Technol. Curr. Issues **12**(1), 23–36 (2020). https://doi.org/10.18844/wjet.v12i1.4438
55. Lnenicka, M., Kopackova, H., Machova, R., Komarkova, J.: Big and open linked data analytics: a study on changing roles and skills in the higher educational process. Int. J. Educ. Technol. High. Educ. **17**, 1–30 (2020). https://doi.org/10.1186/s41239-020-00208-z
56. Li, G., Yuan, C., Kamarthi, S., Moghaddam, M., Jin, X.: Data science skills and domain knowledge requirements in the manufacturing industry: a gap analysis. J. Manuf. Syst. **60**, 692–706 (2021). https://doi.org/10.1016/j.jmsy.2021.07.007
57. Dinh, L.T.N., Karmakar, G., Kamruzzaman, J.: A survey on context awareness in big data analytics for business applications. Knowl. Inf. Syst. **62**, 3387–3415 (2020)
58. Zarefard, M., Jeong, D.Y.: The Effect of Entrepreneurial Leadership Competencies in Iranian ICTs, p. 128. LAP Lambert Academic Publishing (2019). ISBN: 978-6134981484
59. Finegold, D., Notabartolo, A.S.: 21st century competencies and their impact: an interdisciplinary literature review. Transform. US Workforce Dev. Syst. **19**, 19–56 (2010)
60. Škrinjarić, B.: Competence-based approaches in organizational and individual context. Human. Soc. Sci. Commun. **9**(1), 1–12 (2022). https://doi.org/10.1057/s41599-022-01047-1

Author Index

H. Mori and Y. Asahi (Eds.): HCII 2024, LNCS 14691, pp. 419–421, 2024.
https://doi.org/10.1007/978-3-031-60125-5

Printed in the United States
by Baker & Taylor Publisher Services